DESCRIPTIVE STATISTICAL TECHNIQUES *for* LIBRARIANS

2nd Edition

ARTHUR W. HAFNER

AMERICAN LIBRARY ASSOCIATION

Chicago and London

1998

While extensive effort has gone into ensuring the reliability of information appearing in this book, the publisher makes no warranty, express or implied, on the accuracy or reliability of the information, and does not assume and hereby disclaims any liability to any person for any loss or damage caused by errors or omissions in this publication.

Project editor: Louise D. Howe

Text and cover design: Image House

Composition by Impressions Book and Journal Services, Inc. in Times Roman using Penta DeskTopPro.

Printed on 50-pound Opaque Smooth Offset, a pH-neutral stock, and bound in 10-point coated cover stock by Data Reproductions Corp.

The paper used in this publication meets the minimum requirements of American National Standard for Information Sciences—Permanence of Paper for Printed Library Materials, ANSI Z39.48-1992. ∞

Library of Congress Cataloging-in-Publication Data

Hafner, Arthur Wayne, 1943–
    Descriptive statistical techniques for librarians / Arthur W.
  Hafner. — 2nd ed., rev. and enl.
        p.   cm.
      Includes index.
      ISBN 0-8389-0692-3 (acid-free paper)
      1. Library statistics. I. Title.
    Z669.8.H33   1998
    025′.007′23—dc21   97-19098

Printed in the United States of America.

02 01 00 99 98   5 4 3 2 1

CONTENTS

PREFACE

This second edition of *Descriptive Statistical Techniques for Librarians* is a substantial revision and enlargement of the first edition. In total, it contains nearly twice as many examples, figures, practical problems, self-assessment review quizzes, and tables as in the original edition. All examples and most problems are solved in detail to allow librarians to follow the calculations one step at a time. Several new topics have been added as well, including an examination of economic and financial principles related to library applications, a discussion of benchmarking, and a consideration of continuous improvement and measurement in the library environment. There also is a new chapter that addresses survey sampling and the tallying of a survey instrument.

This book is intended to serve as both a textbook and a reference manual for practicing librarians. Its emphasis is on descriptive statistics—the basis of statistical analysis for data summary. Through application of practical statistical techniques, librarians can efficiently measure and evaluate programs and activities in the context of objectives. In brief, the objective of this text is to demonstrate some of the many uses for descriptive statistical techniques in the library environment.

To make the book accessible for those who find algebra somewhat overwhelming, concepts are explained with words in a precise and straightforward manner. Readers are not defeated by a flood of formulas, statistical notation, and jargon. The intent of the book, after all, is not to train librarians to become statisticians but, rather, to present, illustrate, and reinforce statistical principles in library scenarios. The formulas involved in these applications are introduced with extensive discussion and many illustrative examples. Although a few of the examples and problems require extensive number-crunching sessions, they effectively demonstrate the processes involved in arriving at a valid statistical measure.

It is true that the widespread use of personal computers and sophisticated calculators has changed the face of statistics. For this reason, many coding methods for handling data are no longer used, and thus are not included in this book. Grouped frequency distributions, however, are presented and illustrated because they continue to appear in the literature despite the availability of technology that makes short work of analyses of individual observations.

There is no substitute for problem solving, however, in the study of statistics. Reviewing examples and working through problems are necessary to learning statistics. Thus, the text features an appendix containing ample real-life library problems that incorporate realistic data to stimulate statistical thinking and to encourage recognition of opportunities for applying statistical analyses.

As author, I hope that librarians and other information service professionals who use this book find it useful. I encourage and welcome reader comments, suggestions for problems, and ideas for improving a future edition of the text.

INTRODUCTION TO STATISTICS

After reading this chapter, you will be able to do the following:

1. Describe the difference between descriptive statistics and inferential statistics.
2. Define the term *data* and explain its role in statistics.
3. Differentiate between a *population* and a *sample.*
4. Differentiate between a *parameter* and a *statistic.*
5. Define and list examples of a *quantitative variable* and a *qualitative variable.*
6. Define and list examples of variables whose scales of measurement are nominal, ordinal, interval, and ratio.
7. List examples of quantitative data that are discrete and that are continuous.
8. Differentiate between *reliability* and *validity.*
9. Define the term *baseline data* and provide examples of it.
10. Describe the benchmarking process and explain its application in a library setting.

Services in today's libraries are ever expanding. Much of this growth is due to affordable and accessible technology that has brought with it enlarged responsibilities and new demands for the librarian.

To meet these demands and improve continually the type and quality of services offered, librarians look for information about ways to employ technology. They read professional journals and consult with colleagues at other institutions to draw on their experiences. They attend conferences and workshops, poll clients, trustees, and administrators for preferences, and canvass consortia and network system members to "see how others do it." Librarians also seek insight from colleagues whom they know through professional associations and special interest groups.

To address everyday problems, and to develop strategic plans for improving services and collections, librarians routinely tap the rich data sources that are contained in the library's internal documents. These include the library's transaction and financial reports, circulation records, turnstile/exit counts, program attendance sheets, budget statements, overdue fee records, purchase orders, invoices, and payment vouchers. This information is at the heart of library service. Figure 1-1 identifies several of the library's most significant internal data resources.

The information gained from analyzing the library's internal reports can be applied in a variety of ways: to shape library policy, to develop short- and long-range goals as part of strategic planning, to identify the library's changing needs for existing or new services, and to help set goals and performance objectives in relation to state-of-the-art practices.

A knowledge of statistics helps librarians understand and interpret the numbers that result from gathering and analyzing data on a topic. This understanding in turn can be extended to make more effective judgments about initiating, expanding, or contracting a library initiative. It also provides librarians with a quantitative framework for allocating human and financial resources among library programs. The techniques that help librarians to manage data (e.g., organize, analyze, summarize) and eventually present it for action and implementation come out of the science of statistics.

AN OVERVIEW OF STATISTICS AND ITS LANGUAGE

Statistics refers to a body of techniques employed to analyze data. These techniques are traditionally divided into two broad classes: descriptive and inferential statistics.

Descriptive statistics is a method for summarizing, organizing, and presenting information. Its purpose is to provide librarians with a quantitative (numerical) view of how a particular characteristic is distributed among people or objects. A librarian can think of statistics as a collection of procedures or techniques that can be used to make sense out of numbers. By carefully organizing and summarizing data, librarians can use descriptive statistics to communicate trends and to spare the end user the cumbersome, and often impossible, task of looking at each piece of data individually.

For example, the National Weather Service monitors temperature continuously, but the newspapers report only the high and low temperatures of the day. These figures communicate the essence of the information and make it easier for the average person to identify warming and cooling trends. Moreover, these figures are more manageable than a long list of the succession of temperature variations during a typical day.

FIGURE 1-1 ▌ Data Sources within the Library

Business and financial files	auditor reports; budget statements; invoices; revenue from fines
Collection records	catalog or electronic lists of holdings, lost or missing items compilation; shelf list of holdings
Library reports	annual reports; minutes (trustees, departments, sections, personnel forms)
Transaction activity records	client file; collection records; gift logs; program attendance sheets; special use log (auditorium, rooms); turnstile/exit counts

In another example, suppose that a librarian wishes to study the number of people who use the library. The data for the study may be available through the library's security system if it maintains a turnstile/exit count. Alternatively, someone may have to physically gather the data by monitoring the number of persons who enter or leave the library.

To avoid the requirement of a staff member to gather the data, the librarian may decide to use an electronic counter. This is a passive device that will continuously record counts. The unit consists of a basic stamp microcontroller, an infrared door sensor, and some miscellaneous hardware. These items, costing about $150, are connected to a personal computer in a remote location. When a person passes through the continuous infrared beam to enter the library, a computer program records the time. This information can be used in a spreadsheet, arranged in user-selected increments such as 15-minute or 30-minute periods. When providing an overview of library entrance traffic, the librarian might report only the day's tally since minute-by-minute or even hour-by-hour detail might not be meaningful.

The tools used in descriptive statistics to summarize information include percents, tables, graphs, frequency distributions, measures of central tendency (averages), measures of variability (dispersion), linear regression equations, and correlation coefficients. Using these tools, librarians can prepare well-summarized and well-organized information that reveals trends, explores and highlights relationships, and suggests implications that might otherwise remain hidden. Thus, descriptive statistics ultimately help in analyzing problems and in making informed decisions. By using these techniques, a quantitative profile can be developed for improving the library's services and outputs to better satisfy client needs.

For example, in a library that charges a fee for various services, suppose a librarian notices that many of the invoices go unpaid. Deciding to summarize information about paid and unpaid invoices, the librarian performs an invoice study. The analysis reveals that statements for more than $10 are paid much less often than invoices for under $10. As a result of the analysis, it is decided that prepayment will be required for all services costing more than $10. Further, the librarian may establish deposit accounts.

The second broad class of statistics, *inferential statistics,* consists of methods that go beyond information summary. This branch aims to predict new information and to allow librarians to make broad generalizations from the results of limited studies. This book will focus exclusively on descriptive statistics or information summary.

Importance of Definitions

One of the purposes of this text is to familiarize librarians with the language of statistics. Another is to introduce librarians to various analytic techniques that they will repeatedly use and encounter in the application of descriptive statistics.

An understanding of statistics begins with learning the special terms that are employed in the field. The vocabulary of statistics is precise. Each of its terms or symbols has a standardized abbreviation for a particular idea. Because statistical terms and procedures are uniform, they can be used to communicate ideas across all fields that employ its techniques. The precision of statistics means that there are rarely disputes over terminology.

Common Statistical Terms

Descriptive statistics consists of techniques that, in effect, make sense out of numbers. The numbers are called *data*. (The singular of data is *datum*.) Measurement is the process that translates observations into data. *Raw data* have not yet been organized or summarized. Data remain "raw" until they are processed by statistical methods. An organized set of data and identification information that is commonly entered into a computer prior to analysis is known as a *data file*.

Much of the data used in statistical studies is derived from surveys. A *survey* is a controlled instrument or mechanism for collecting data about a condition or event. The U.S. census, for example, is a survey in which most Americans participate. More specifically, the census is a *statistical survey*. Its questions are carefully planned. Since participants must choose their responses from a limited list, the responses of many participants are easily tabulated, compared, and contrasted.

Statistical surveys are different from *anecdotal surveys* in which participants freely recount experiences or impressions. A diary, an astronaut's debriefing after a mission, and a grandparent's recollections of the "good old days" are examples of anecdotal surveys. The *anecdotal data* obtained through these surveys are important in explaining the nature of an event and the perceptions of the participants, even if the data do not provide measurable information.

Attribute data are data that can be described by a word, such as a word for sex (male, female), state name (Arizona, Illinois, Maine), color (red, orange, yellow), or preference (strongly agree, neutral, strongly disagree). Attribute data also can be represented by a number, but the number is for identification purposes only, such as a Social Security number, a license plate number, a library's accession number, or a library card number. Example 1-1 illustrates anecdotal data.

Example 1-1

Anecdotal Data

1. A librarian plans to make a group presentation to the Friends of the Library about the ways in which the librarian's use of technology has changed the delivery of library services. To make up for not having any statistical data, the librarian plans to feature testimonials, or *anecdotal* reports, from various librarians about the continuing transformation of library services such as acquisitions, cataloging, and interlibrary loan.
2. At a social gathering, several people share *anecdotal* reports with the librarian about how access to electronic resources has changed their individual use of the library.

Most often, librarians rely on statistical surveys. *User surveys,* for instance, are statistical surveys. They are carefully planned questionnaires or interviews designed to assess user satisfaction or dissatisfaction.

A *population* is a group of items sharing at least one common characteristic. The items may be people, objects, units, observations, or measurements. They may be inanimate, as the population of all books written in English. They may be animate, as the population of people whose age is divisible by two. A population may be defined in terms of geography, such as all academic librarians in the state of Illinois. Occupation may be used as a characteristic to define a population, as in the population consisting of personnel employed in law libraries or all students enrolled in graduate programs of library science. An attribute or experience may be used to define a population, such as the collection or *set* of all people who have a library card and who have played at least one video game. Another example is the population of all librarians who have recently obtained relief from pain after taking a medication. A *target population* is the population about which the librarian wishes to draw a conclusion. The complete enumeration of all of the population's members is called a *census.*

While all members of a population share at least one characteristic, they may vary in other characteristics. For example, librarians as a population share the common characteristic of occupation. However, librarians vary with respect to age, income, location, race, and sex, among other characteristics. A *variable* is any characteristic of a population that can vary. Examples of variables are age, color, expenditures, height, location, income, and sex.

The *value* of a variable is called a score. The *score* is the actual number that describes a particular event, object, or person. For example, if a librarian is studying the ages of children who use the library, the variable is "age." Each child's age is a score or value for the variable. Each child's sex (male or female) is a score for the variable "sex." Similarly, the child's favorite color is a variable with several possible scores, such as red, orange, yellow, green, blue, indigo, and violet. Examples of a few of the popular variables used to measure a library collection are books added, books discarded, the number of current periodical subscriptions, and the number of current microform titles. Example 1-2 illustrates several variables.

Example 1-2
Variables

1. Some variables that measure library expenditures are binding expenditures, operating expenditures, purchase of library materials (print, nonprint, digital), and expenditures such as salary, wages, and consulting fees.

2. Some variables that measure staffing are the number of nonprofessional staff (clerical, technical, and paraprofessional staff) and professional staff (librarians).

3. A few variables that measure library activity are circulation, CD-ROM searches, document delivery provided to other libraries, document delivery obtained from other institutions, interlibrary loan transactions of items borrowed or lent, reference desk transactions, and reserve circulation.

Examples of quantitative variables are income and age. These variables tell how much of a particular characteristic or attribute is contained in a member of the population. Similarly, the number of telephone calls that a library receives each hour or the number of books checked for environmental control. A population itself can serve as a backdrop for comparison. A census, for example, describes the number of people out of the total population that can be characterized as having a certain age, occupation, or income. Internal comparisons are possible as well. From the same census, the income of one person could be compared to that of another. Many such standards and comparisons are possible.

Time-population comparisons are frequently encountered in statistical analysis. For example, a time-population backdrop is used in determining the number of books published in a certain category over a time period.

Because backdrops have the power to affect perceptions of change and to set standards for comparison, they must be chosen carefully and scrutinized closely. Otherwise, statistical illusions, much like optical illusions, can be created. For example, a library manager could assert truthfully that library revenues doubled over the previous year. However, in making this statement, the manager may fail to mention that library costs quadrupled and that profits from library services actually fell. In this case, *profits* would be a more realistic backdrop for comparison and for deciding whether the added revenues justified the added costs necessary to generate them.

DATA RELIABILITY AND DATA VALIDITY

In order to be useful in decision making, data must have two qualities: reliability and validity. With regard to data, *reliability* means that each time a variable is measured using the same device (rule, procedure, instrument), the same result is obtained. That is, the data must yield results that are replicable by anyone seeking to verify the data.

An understanding of reliability can come from the use of the term in everyday conversation. If someone says, "The employee is a good worker but is not reliable," the speaker may mean that the person's work is acceptable but that his or her work attendance is poor.

Data reliability suggests consistency, dependability, stability, and predictability. For example, suppose several items are weighed on a sensitive scale and the result is recorded. Assuming that nothing changes, when the same items are again placed on the scale, the expectation is that the scale will register the same reading as before. If a different result is obtained, the process may be repeated. Different readings (data) would cause the researcher to distrust the reliability of the scale. In statistics, reliability addresses the extent to which what is observed can be obtained with each subsequent measurement for the phenomena being studied. However, not all reliable data are accurate, as illustrated in Example 1-4.

Example 1-4

Reliable but Not Accurate Data

Imagine that a person uses an oral mercury thermometer to take his or her temperature. Carefully following the manufacturer's directions, the person records the result and repeats the process several times, obtaining the same degree reading each time: {94.2, 94.2, 94.2, 94.2}. For most persons, this temperature is unusual, since healthy human beings register a body temperature of 98.6 degrees. However, since the readings are all consistent, the person might conclude that the instrument provides reliable measurements because they are repeatable, but that the instrument is not accurate.

The second quality that data must possess is validity. In effect, data *validity* is the relationship between the evidence and the argument. Validity has to do with whether the correct variable is being measured for the problem that is under study.

To illustrate the idea of validity, suppose library patrons have been complaining to staff at the circulation desk that they have to wait too long to use one of the pay telephones in the library's lobby. To test this conjecture, for several days a clerk records the approximate age of each caller who uses a lobby telephone. Regardless of how interesting the conclusions from this data may be, the result will not be valid for the problem of clientele satisfaction. The telephone user's age is not an effective variable for shedding light on the length of wait for an available telephone.

The pay phone example illustrates that validity is the degree to which a variable being examined actually sheds light on what it is supposed to be measuring. In statistics, validity is the link between the evidence (data) observed and the concept or theory that has been proposed. Validity addresses the meaning that is attributed to the observations. Clearly, if data are not reliable, then validity will be absent.

LEVELS OF MEASUREMENT AND TYPES OF MEASUREMENT SCALE

Earlier, variables were described as categorical or quantitative. In this section, the value of variables will be measured and compared to one another by the use of measurement scales.

Data come to the librarian in different qualities. Some measurements are quantitative and based on standard units such as dollars, inches, and ounces. Other measurements are expressed through labels such as "Yes" or "No." The result is that some data are better than other data, depending upon the level of measurement that has been used to quantify or categorize it.

The quality of data is determined by its *level of measurement.* There are four types of data measurement scales in statistics. These are the nominal, ordinal, interval, and ratio scales.

Nominal Scale Measurement

Nominal scale measurement permits librarians to measure a variable only by giving it a name. That is, scores are values or labels that indicate the class or category into which a particular score falls. For example, the variable *sex* has two categories or labels, Male and Female. In psychiatry, patients may be classified by descriptive labels such as depressive, neurotic, psychotic, or schizophrenic. The nominal scale shows only equality or inequality. That is, the values of two variables are either in the same category and, therefore, equal, or they are in different categories and are not equal. Example 1-5 provides more examples of nominal scale measure.

Example 1-5

Nominal Scale Measure

- book publisher {Greenwood, Mosby, Sybex}
- check number {101, A2345}
- eye color {black, blue, brown, green, hazel}

- invoice number {N98–12345, P–345}
- political party affiliation {Democratic, Libertarian, Republican}
- student residence {campus, off-campus}
- telephone extension number {2441, 3917, 4001}
- type of library {academic, medical, public, school, special}
- type of high school {parochial, private, public, vocational}

At first glance, a nominal scale measure may look like a quantitative number. In reality, however, it is only a label or a surrogate name for an object. That is, a library's accession number is a number that is used in place of an item's title. A license plate number identifies the owner of a registered vehicle for which it is issued. Similarly, a person's unique Social Security number is a coding that is used in lieu of a person's name. The numbers that comprise these labels have no other significance than for identification. Thus, it is not meaningful to perform mathematical computations on the values of nominal scale measures. That is, there is no meaning to be obtained from adding or subtracting numbers from a listing of library accession numbers or zip code numbers.

Ordinal Scale Measurement

Ordinal scale measurement is a measurement scale that places scores in rank order according to some characteristic that is to be measured. Ordinal data represent categories that have some associated order, such as lowest to highest or highest to lowest. In recording the arrangement, the concern is not how much the scores differ on the variable. Instead, the concern is only with identifying which score is first, second, or last. For example, in a marathon race the first runner to finish is called the winner because "first to finish" is the characteristic chosen to measure victory. For measuring victory, no consideration is given to whether the winner is one second or fifteen minutes ahead of the other runners. This is because the scale ranks only the variable's scores and does not make comparisons between them. Note that ordinal scale data also satisfy the definition of nominal scale measure. Example 1-6 provides more illustrations of ordinal scale data.

Example 1-6
Ordinal Scale Data

- street numbers on houses {123, 125, 126, 127, 133}
- typing speed corrected for errors {1 = fastest, 2 = second, 3 = third}
- attitude and opinion scales on a questionnaire {1 = strongly agree, 2 = agree, 3 = neutral, 4 = disagree, 5 = strongly disagree}
- the relevance of documents to queries {1 = relevant, 2 = neutral, 3 = not relevant}
- measures of social status {lower class, middle class, upper class}

Ordinal scale measurement is useful since people generally can make meaningful judgments on comparisons even when they cannot make an accurate absolute judgment. For example, a person may have difficulty identifying the rank order of five options. However, the person usually has less difficulty in identifying the best and least options. After these end points have been ranked, the person can repeat the process to rank the remaining three options from best to least. The result is that the five difficult options are placed in rank order.

A limitation of ordinal scale measurement is that it cannot be used to express distance between ranked or ordered options. For example, ordinal scale measurement is used to rank books from first to tenth on the best-seller list. However, one cannot use the rankings to determine how far ahead in actual sales the first best-seller is from the second best-seller. Similarly, the ordinal scale measurement ranks of participants in a marathon do not indicate how far ahead the first finisher was of the second, or how far ahead the second finisher was of the third. These are distinctions that require the use of interval scale measures.

Interval Scale Measurement

Interval scale measurement is the measurement scale used to rank variables that have no meaningful value of zero. For example, the degrees used in recording temperature on the Fahrenheit or Celsius scale are interval scale measures. This is because the distance between each degree is the same regardless of where it occurs on the scale. The zero on the weather temperature scale, however, is arbitrary and does not mean the complete absence of temperature. Similarly, a zero on an intelligence quotient (IQ) test probably does not mean that the person has *no* intelligence. The purpose of interval scales is to compare values, not to define the complete absence of the characteristic.

Interval measures can be added or subtracted. For instance, 39°C is 2 degrees higher than 37°C. However, since interval scale measures have no exact zero point, they cannot be multiplied or divided. That is, a temperature of 100°F is not twice as hot as a temperature of 50°F. Multiplication or division of temperatures, IQs, or other interval scale measurements yields meaningless results.

Sometimes, an ordinal scale is drawn to look like an interval scale. That is, the ordinal classes may be placed on a line or graph so that the distances between them appear to be equal. Consumers of statistics must be aware of this type of statistical deception.

Ratio Scale Measurement

Ratio scale measurement is a measure of some quantity for which an absolute zero point exists. It has equal intervals. The zero point represents the nonexistence of that which is being measured. Absolute zero points exist in scales for measuring physical units such as time, temperature (Kelvin), weight, area, and volume. The absolute zero point for weight is the total absence of weight. For time, the zero point is the instant before which time is measured. Numbers on a ratio scale can be divided by others on the scale, compared, and analyzed to obtain a useful result. A ratio scale allows accurate comparisons, such as "twice as much," "half as long," or "three times as fast."

Assertions often are based on ratio scales. For example, two pounds of fish are twice as much as one pound. Similarly, a shelf that is 48 inches tall is two-thirds as tall as one that is 72 inches tall. When ratio scale data are used, variables such as library floor space, collection size, collection costs, salaries, and circulation totals can be compared and expressed as ratios.

Measurement using ratio scale is the highest order of measurement. Measurement using nominal scale is the fundamental or first level of measure. Data that are expressed in terms of ratio scale measure automatically possess the characteristics of interval scale data. Like-

FIGURE 1-2 ▌ Properties of the Measurement Scales

Nominal

- quantitative units of measurement
- uses categories to show that the classifications are different
- measures without order

Ordinal

- unequal quantitative units of measurement
- indicates that the classifications are different and can be ranked
- uses rankings, grades, or equivalents
- measures with order

Internal

- equal quantitative units of measurement
- no meaningful zero point
- establishes numerically equal distances on the scale
- measures with order

Ratio

- equal quantitative units of measurement
- meaningful absolute zero point

---

wise, interval scale data have the characteristics of nominal scale data. Variables measured at a higher level can also be analyzed by lower-level techniques. However, the reverse is not true. Figure 1-2 identifies properties of the measurement scales.

DISCRETE AND CONTINUOUS MEASUREMENT

An important characteristic of measurement that influences the way quantitative observations are analyzed is whether the measurements are discrete or continuous. A discrete measurement is one that is counted rather than measured.

A *discrete variable* can assume only a whole-number value such as 0, 1, 2, or any other whole counting number. For example, the number of books on a library shelf is a discrete number, such as 25. The number of books cannot be 25.2. The variable "children in a family" is a discrete variable with a score such as 0, 1, 2, 3, 4, or some other whole counting number. The value of a discrete variable cannot be a fractional number. Example 1-7 illustrates additional examples of discrete variables.

Example 1-7 ▌
Discrete Variables

- daily attendance for a library instruction class
- number of clients passing through the turnstiles on a given day

- library staff size
- number of books donated to a library
- number of public parking spaces
- sex (male, female)

A *continuous* variable can theoretically assume any value between two values. For example, the age difference between two people can be a continuous variable because, in theory, the difference can be reduced by degrees. If a baby is born just before midnight on New Year's Eve and a second baby is born just after midnight, it can be said correctly that the first baby is a year, a month, a day, an hour, a minute, a second, or a millisecond older than the second baby, depending upon the accuracy of the measurement of time.

Weight also is a continuous variable. To illustrate, if a statue were weighed, any particular measurement would be approximate. This is because a measuring device of greater accuracy can always be imagined. If the weight is 2178 pounds, this means 2178 plus or minus one pound. If the scale is accurate to within one pound, a scale can be imagined that is accurate to within one-half, one-tenth, or one-hundredth of a pound. Thus, measurement of a continuous variable, such as weight or length, is always approximate. Other examples of continuous variables include light and noise levels and the life expectancy of a projector lamp.

Of course, most, if not all, observations are associated with some unavoidable finite error. Because measuring devices are of limited accuracy, and because practicality dictates that measurements are rounded off and grouped, most measurements in reality are probably discrete rather than continuous. This fact, however, should not deter the user from considering such variables as continuous.

Often, discrete and continuous data can be distinguished from one another by determining whether the data result from a count or from a measurement. A count will always yield discrete numerical data. A measure of a quantity will usually be continuous.

BASELINE DATA, THE PROCESS OF BENCHMARKING, AND REENGINEERING

Baseline data consists of a collection of measurements about an activity or process. These data provide a context for understanding measurements about the work process.

To illustrate, suppose that a library's turnstile/exit count records that 2000 persons entered the library on a particular day. A library trustee might logically wonder if this number is higher or lower than normal. If the librarian knows the usual number of visitors, then the turnstile count for the particular day can be placed in a meaningful context to answer the question. Hence, a 2000 count is high if the usual number of patrons is 1500. Alternatively, a day on which 2000 visits occur is not a blockbuster if the usual number of visits is 2500.

Library *benchmarking* is a methodology of observation and data collection for evaluating products, services, and work processes. It involves studying the best practices and operations of other libraries or organizations of similar size, budget, or geographic location. In some circumstances, comparisons are made between and among functions that are performed in areas within the same organization. Benchmarking affords the librarian an opportunity for pinpointing and closing performance gaps. Viewed in this way, benchmarking helps librarians learn about new approaches, identify paradigm shifts, and assess performance in the library environment. Benchmarking is a key technique for librarians who seek continuous improvement for their library programs and services.

Performance excellence in a library or any other organization is not due to a single attribute but to a group of critical success factors. Benchmarking "home" library performance against comparable libraries or other leaders in the field provides a librarian with insight into ways to set goals, plan workflow, and recruit personnel to improve library performance. A librarian, for example, may view a daily average of 2000 library visits in a different light if benchmarking reveals that comparison libraries generally experience 2700 daily visits. In this context, the benchmark becomes a performance target to induce the librarian to look for strategies to attract more patrons.

Benchmarking can be regarded in three general ways:

1. *Internal benchmarking* is a comparison of an organizational unit's performance with that of a similar department or section within the same organization. Such comparisons are possible since there are differences in performance between people and because departments or sections in the same organization perform at a range of levels.

2. *Competitive benchmarking* concerns institution-to-institution comparison of products, services, or work processes. By studying and imitating the superior work processes or the outstanding services and products (deliverables) of another institution, a librarian can identify and focus clues about issues that may be inhibiting improved performance at the home library.

3. *Functional benchmarking* compares a given function to a similar practice in an exceptional organization of another type.

Benchmarking reflects an active search for improvement. It is an ongoing process for observation, recognition, and action to implement ideas and move an organization toward excellence. It is a methodology for observing and collecting data about the clues and motif employed in best practices organizations. Librarians can use the intelligence gained from benchmarking in their home library to leverage technology, to overhaul processes, and to reshape organizational structure for increased performance.

Reengineering, when used with other terms such as baseline data, benchmarking, and continuous improvement, refers to a reexamination of work activity. In 1994, HarperBusiness published *Reengineering the Corporation: A Manifesto for Business Revolution,* by Michael Hammer and James Champy. These authors defined reengineering as "the fundamental rethinking and radical redesign of business processes to achieve dramatic improvements" for sustained change in performance. Some readers may recognize reengineering as a refurbishing and enhancement of process studies that derive from industrial engineering. After reengineering has occurred, incremental betterment through continuous improvement techniques keeps the refocused process current.

In a library, reengineering concepts might be applied to the work activities associated with providing reference service or document delivery. Or, they might be applied to processes that affect the patron's experiences in the library. This might include a strong customer-focus outcome for greater patron satisfaction with library services.

SUMMARY OF CRITICAL CONCEPTS

1. *Statistics* is a body of knowledge and techniques employed to collect and classify information. *Statistical analysis* is a scientific method of interpreting quantitative data.

2. *Descriptive statistics* is a method for the organization, presentation, and summarization of data. *Inferential statistics* produces new information by making predictions and generalizations based on samples.

3. Measurements collected by observation are *data*. *Raw data* are scores that have not been organized or summarized. *Anecdotal data* are the freeform recounting of experiences and impressions.

4. A *population* consists of all items that share a common characteristic, such as geography, occupation, or other attributes. A numerical measure of a population is called a *parameter*. (Parameter estimation is part of inferential statistics and is not the focus of this book.)

5. A *sample* is a subset or selection of the individuals, objects, or measurements that are drawn from a population. A sample is finite. A *statistic* is a numerical measure computed from a sample. Because a sample's statistic is easier to compute than a population's parameter, a sample's statistic is used to estimate a population's parameter. A *representative sample* contains a population's characteristics in the same proportion that they occur in the population. *Sampling* is the selection process of identifying the population elements that will constitute a sample.

6. A measurable characteristic of a population or sample is a *variable*. The value of a particular variable is called a *score*. Variables are quantitative or qualitative. *Quantitative variables* tell how much or how many of a particular characteristic or attribute are present in an object, event, person, or phenomenon. One example is the number of computers available for students to use on a campus. *Qualitative variables* classify an object, event, person, or phenomenon into categories with respect to the attributes by which they differ. For example, the language of publication of a given journal title may be English, French, Hebrew, or Spanish.

7. *Nominal scale variables* classify observations into distinct categories. Examples are variables such as marital status (single, married, divorced, widowed), political affiliation (Democratic, Republican, Libertarian), or blood type (A, B, O, AB). No mathematical properties such as "ranking" or "greater than" are associated with nominal scale variables.

8. *Ordinal scale variables* classify observations into distinct classes *and* into rank. They also express the relationship of the observations according to the degree to which they represent a particular characteristic. For example, human populations can be "ordered" by relations, such as being a resident of Illinois or being certified in cardiopulmonary resuscitation.

9. *Interval scale variables* classify, rank, and express the distance between classes. For example, the sales volume difference between books that are ranked (ordinal scale) and listed on the best-seller list is not known. In contrast, the distance in temperature between 70°F and 71°F (interval scale) is known and is constant.

10. *Ratio scale variables* classify, rank, distinguish distance, *and* provide a zero point. Length, weight, time, and income are examples of ratio scale variables, and when these variables equal zero, there is no length, no weight, no time, and no money.

11. *Quantitative data* can be classified as being discrete or continuous, usually depending on whether the data are being counted or measured. Examples of quantitative items are time, height, weight, and sound and light levels.

12. *Measurement reliability* means that there is consistency of data measurement. Reliability is the extent to which data are replicable, and it also refers to the consistency of conditions, methods, and results of data collection.

13. *Validity* concerns the extent to which a test measures what it purports to measure. Data analysis validity is the extent to which the results of an analysis can be generalized beyond the sample upon which the findings are based. Validity is dependent on reliable data.

14. *Baseline data* are measurements that provide a context for understanding other measurements about an activity or process. Baseline data tell whether an activity is increasing, decreasing, or static.

15. *Benchmarking* is an ongoing, systematic process of learning from the practices and operations of other organizations.

16. *Reengineering* is a work-transformation strategy to bring about dramatic performance improvements through fundamental rethinking the radical design of work processes. Using it, managers question all assumptions by asking "why," "why is," and "what should be."

KEY TERMS

Algorithm.   A set of rules or directions for obtaining a specific output from a specific input. The term usually is used in connection with numerical calculations.

Census.   An enumeration of all the members of a population.

Data.   Facts collected as a result of observation. *Datum* is the singular of *data*. Examples of datum are height, weight, telephone number, and zip code. Nonstatistical data are arbitrary items, such as order numbers in a sales catalog and telephone numbers in a directory. Data may be nonnumerical as well, such as occupation, political affiliation, or name. *Raw data* are unorganized statistical data. This information remains "raw" until it is processed by statistical methods.

Discrete data.   Data obtained by counting or simple enumeration rather than by measuring against a scale. For example, a librarian *counts* the number of books on a shelf or the number of units of shelving. The counted units are indivisible. Hence, there may be 52 books on a shelf, but not 52.3. Unlike continuous data, the measurement of discrete data *must* produce a whole number.

Interval scale measurement.   Measurement scale that groups observations in three ways: (1) by categorizing, as in nominal scale; (2) by ranking, as in ordinal scale; and (3) by illustrating, through the use of equal intervals, how much greater one observation is on a given attribute or characteristic than another. The interval scale measure lacks an absolute zero point.

Nominal scale measurement.   Measurement scale characterized by "either/or" types of observations. Items are not ordered. The data summary used for nominal scale data are percents or proportions of observations that exhibit a specific attribute.

Ordinal scale measurement.   Measurement scale that classifies items into categories. The scale is arranged in ascending or descending order according to some property. Examples are assigning people job titles, evaluating employee performance from outstanding to poor, or grouping military personnel according to rank (private through general).

Parameter.   A quantitative measure of a population.

Ratio scale measurement.   Measurement scale with an absolute zero point that groups observations in three ways: (1) by categorizing or classifying, as in nominal scale;

(2) by ranking, as in ordinal scale; and (3) by illustrating, through the use of equal intervals, how much greater one observation is on a given attribute or characteristic than another. Examples of ratio scale measure are time, height, distance, weight, and altitude.

Reliability.   Reliability of measurement is the consistency of the measurement. The reliability of data is the extent to which the measurements are replicable. *Reliability* also refers to the consistency of the conditions, methods used in the data collection and analysis, and to the results of the analysis. If data are not reliable, the conclusions of any study are not valid.

Sample.   A subset, portion, or segment of a population. A sample is used to make inferences about the population from which it is drawn.

Validity.   Concerns the degree to which an analysis measures what it is supposed to measure. It also refers to the extent that a study's findings can be generalized beyond the particular sample upon which it is based. If the data are not reliable, there is no reason to believe that the findings are valid.

Variable.   An ascertainable property in which people or objects in a sample or population differ. A *continuous variable* can assume any number of possible values between an upper and lower limit. Values for continuous variables are usually obtained through measurements. A *discrete variable* (also called a *discontinuous variable*) can assume only whole-number values, such as 0, 1, 2, or any other whole counting number. Fractions or decimal values are *not* examples of discrete variable data values. Values for discrete variables usually are obtained through counting. *Quantitative variables* classify objects into categories by how much they differ. Examples are number of books, staff size, or daily circulation. *Qualitative variables* classify objects with respect to the attribute by which they differ. Examples are product models, animal species, and colors.

SELF-ASSESSMENT QUIZ

1. *True* or *False*   Descriptive statistics is the orderly collection and summarization of data.

2. *True* or *False*   Descriptive statistics is the study of a sample that allows one to make inferences about the population from which the sample was drawn.

3. *True* or *False*   The name of a river is a quantitative variable.

4. *True* or *False*   An example of a discrete measurement is the number of books in a library collection.

5. *True* or *False*   An example of a continuous measurement is the count of reference desk questions received in a 2-hour period.

6. *True* or *False*   A variable may take on different values.

7. *True* or *False*   A population is a set of all objects that have one or more characteristics in common.

8. *True* or *False*   A parameter is a characteristic of a sample that is almost always known or that can be computed.

9. *True* or *False*   A statistic is a measure of a characteristic of a population.

10. *True* or *False*   If a library task force were made up of five men and five women, it would be representative of the library's full-time staff of 66 females and 34 males.

Answers to Self-Assessment Quiz

1. *True*   Descriptive statistics is the study and summarization of data.

2. *False*   Inferential statistical techniques allow one to make estimates or forecasts about the population from which a sample is drawn.

3. *False*   A name cannot be counted or quantified. A book's title and a river's name both are examples of a qualitative variable.

4. *True*   The number of books must be a whole number.

5. *False*   Counts yield discrete measurement. Continuous measurement examples include height, weight, temperature, and distance.

6. *True*   A variable is an idea or class, such as height, weight, age, or sex. A variable may have any of a variety of values, depending on what is being observed.

7. *True*   A population can also represent a set of measurements that characterize some phenomenon of interest.

8. *False*   A parameter is a measure (characteristic) of a population. A statistic is a characteristic of a sample.

9. *False*   A statistic is a measure of a sample. For example, the mean number of books that adults check out on Tuesday for their children is a statistic.

10. *False*   To be representative, the task force should have the same composition of men and women as found in the population (full-time staff). Hence, seven women and three men should comprise the task force. The sample percents should approximately equal the population percents.

DISCUSSION QUESTIONS AND PROBLEMS

1. Define *statistics* and differentiate between descriptive and inferential statistics.

2. Differentiate between a variable and the data or score for a variable. Illustrate an example of a variable and a score for it.

3. Describe the relationship between a population and sample. Illustrate an example of each.

4. Give an example of each of the following: variable; parameter; sample; statistic.

5. Identify the type of measurement scale used in each of the following:
   a. "four-star" rating system used by a movie reviewer;
   b. survey in which males are coded by 1 (M = 1) and females are coded by 2 (F = 2);
   c. Standard and Poor's bond rating system;
   d. ranking of sports teams in a league, conference, or division;
   e. survey question on state of residence.

6. Identify the following measures as discrete or continuous:
   a. number of visitors to view an exhibit of rare books;
   b. the age of persons who have a valid library card;
   c. humidity in an archive storage room;
   d. light intensity in a library reading room.

7. Identify each of the following as examples of attribute, discrete, or continuous variables:
   a. the hair color of librarians;
   b. whether the computer system is down;
   c. the number of parking spaces in the library's parking lot;
   d. the average duration of a telephone reference call.

8. From a shelf, a cataloger selects books that have been recently processed and records selected information about each, such as whether the spine label is correctly affixed to the book, the initials of the technician who processed the book, and the book's net cost. Identify the population. Identify the sample. Classify the responses for each of the three variables.

9. A librarian selects ten students who are enrolled in a library instruction class. Each student completes a survey that asks the following: the number of courses in which the student is enrolled; the student's total cost for instructional supplies; and the method that the student uses for paying expenses. Identify the population. Is it finite or infinite? Identify the sample. Classify each variable by the type of measurement scale.

10. Explain what is meant by *reliability*.

chapter two

BASIC METHODS FOR DATA ANALYSIS

After reading this chapter, you will be able to do the following:

1. Explain and apply the rules for rounding numbers.
2. Define *ratio, proportion,* and *percent* and calculate these statistics.
3. Explain and calculate comparison measures such as component percents, dollar and percent change, and ratio.
4. Describe the process of labeling data points.
5. Explain how Sigma notation helps simplify long equations.

This chapter introduces several important techniques of numerical description. For example, rounding, or rounding off, shortens numbers to bring them within a desired accuracy. Ratios, proportions, and percents are useful for comparing and contrasting numbers. In addition, other important concepts for data summarization include data labeling and Sigma notation. These and other techniques that are part of this chapter are helpful in interpreting various measures and understanding their practical application.

NUMERICAL DESCRIPTION

Rounding, or *rounding off,* is an important and common technique for abbreviating data. It is used in situations where an exact number is not necessary. For example, a librarian might report that the collection contains 2300 videotapes rather than reporting the exact number, such as 2349 videotapes.

The technique of rounding to the next dollar is familiar to persons who file income tax forms where $25,234.49 rounds to $25,234 and $43,675.51 rounds to $43,676. Rounding is a popularly used technique because it simplifies calculations and does not distort the data. Examples 2-1 and 2-2 illustrate the important technique of rounding numbers.

Guidelines for Rounding

1. Identify the digit place to which you wish to round.
2. Look at the next digit to the right.
3. If the digit to the right is 5 or higher, round up. If the digit to the right is less than 5, round down.

Example 2-1

Rounding Numbers

---

1. Round 2468 to the nearest ten.

   Analysis

   Identify that 6 is in the tens place. The number to the right of it is 8. Since the number to the right of 6 is greater than 5 (it is 8), round up, yielding 2470.

2. Round 8421 to the nearest thousand.

   Analysis

   Identify the 8 that is in the thousand place. The number to the right of 8 is 4. Since the number to the right of 8 is less than 5 (it is 4), round down, yielding 8000.

3. Round 9876.54321 to the nearest hundredth.

   Analysis

   Identify the 4 that is in the hundredths place (second place to the right of the decimal). The number to the right of 4 is 3 (third place to the right of the decimal). Since the number is less than 5 (it is 3), round down, yielding 9876.54.

Example 2-2

Rounding Dollar Amounts

The acquisitions librarian at a public library maintains a log of expenditures for book purchases. Round off the amounts to the nearest dollar and compare the rounded total with the exact total. By how much do the two differ?

Analysis

	Unrounded Dollar Amounts			Rounded Dollar Amounts	
	Year 2	Year 1		Year 2	Year 1
January	$ 1,658.33	$ 2,361.28	January	$ 1,658	$ 2,361
February	3,799.89	4,834.03	February	3,800	4,834
March	6,139.74	5,009.45	March	6,140	5,009
April	3,607.93	4,373.64	April	3,608	4,374
May	4,125.49	4,586.46	May	4,125	4,586
June	626.35	2,077.99	June	626	2,078
Total	$19,957.73	$23,242.85	Total	$19,957	$23,242

The decision rule for rounding to the next closest dollar is that the amount is rounded up if the decimal part of the number is fifty cents or more. In $1658.33, the decimal part of the number (.33) is less than fifty cents, so the amount is rounded down to $1658. In $3,799.89, the decimal part of the number (.89) is more than fifty cents, so the amount is rounded up to $3,800.

In Year 2, the difference between the exact amount and the rounded amount is $0.73 [$0.73 = $19,957.73 − $19,957]. In Year 1, the difference is $0.85 [$0.85 = $23,242.85 − $23,242]. Each of these amounts is very small, particularly when compared to the total of $20,000 for Year 2 and $23,200 for Year 1. The advantage to rounding is that the numbers are easier to read. Also, when other calculations are made using the rounded numbers, no distortion will result.

Numerical Description by Division: Ratio

Comparison by division is an important and frequently used method for numerical description. A *ratio* uses division. In a ratio, the *numerator* is divided by the *denominator*. That is, the ratio of 3 to 4 is written 3/4, where 3 is the ratio's numerator and 4 is the ratio's denominator. The numbers 3 and 4 are the *terms* of the ratio. They may also be written with a colon, as 3:4. Because division by zero is not possible, the denominator of a ratio must never equal zero.

A ratio expresses a relationship of size or amount between two numbers, or what fraction one number is of another. For example, if a subscription that costs $55 this year cost only $35 two years ago, the relationship between the subscription prices is 1.57 [1.57 = $55/$35]. This ratio shows that the cost of the subscription is slightly more than one and one-half times (1.57 exactly) the cost that it was two years ago. Of course, a librarian could have calculated the ratio in reverse to obtain 0.64 [0.64 = $35/$55]. This number tells librarians that the cost two years ago was about two-thirds (0.64 exactly) of what it is this year. Both ratios provide the same information, presented in a slightly different way.

$$\text{ratio} = \frac{\text{numerator}}{\text{denominator}}$$

When calculating a ratio, the result can be carried out to a large number of places, like 8/9 = .8888888888889. One might reasonably ask whether it is necessary to extend the answer to so many places. The answer is that it is not. In fact, there are several reasons a long decimal result should not be used:

- The result produces a false sense of precision.

- The result is difficult to manipulate.

- The result does not promote easy comparison.

A useful guideline in making calculations is to carry out the operation to two places beyond those in the original data. Then round off by one place. Therefore, if the original data consist of whole numbers, the calculations are carried out to hundredths, then rounded to tenths. If data are recorded to the nearest hundredth, the librarian calculates to ten-thousandths and expresses the result of the rounding in thousandths. In the ratio 8/9, both numbers are whole numbers, so the calculation would be carried out to two places (hundredths) and then rounded to tenths. Hence, 8/9 = 0.89 or 0.9. Example 2-3 illustrates ratio conversions.

Example 2-3
Ratio Conversions

---

1. In Washington, D.C., there are 36.1 lawyers for every 1000 residents. What is the ratio of lawyers to residents?

   Analysis

   The ratio 36.1:1000, which can be written as 36.1/1000, is 0.0361, rounded to .04. The interpretation of this result is that there are four lawyers for every one hundred residents [0.04 is 4% or 4 per 100], or one attorney for every twenty-five persons.

2. A library has a collection of 90,000 items. Of these, 17,000 are journals and 10,000 are nonprint materials. Determine how many books are in the collection and also write the ratio for the percentage of the collection that each classification represents.

   Analysis

   Since there are 90,000 items, the ratios for books, journals, and nonprint items are as follows:

Books:	$\frac{63,000}{90,000}$	Journals:	$\frac{17,000}{90,000}$	Nonprint:	$\frac{10,000}{90,000}$
	or 0.70		or 0.18		or 0.11
	or 0.7		or 0.2		or 0.1

   The interpretation is that 70% of the collection consists of books, 20% of journals, and 10% of nonprint materials. This means that 7 of every 10 items are books, 2 of every ten are journals, and 1 of every 10 is a nonprint item.

A ratio can be expressed as a fraction and a fraction can be expressed as a ratio. Hence, 4 to 5 can be written as 4/5 or as 4:5. All the rules that apply to fractions also apply to ratios.

Suppose that a library has an operating budget of $781,000 and that it receives $550,000 in municipal funding. The balance of its funding comes from other sources. The ratio of municipal funding to operating expenditures is 0.70, expressed as follows:

$$\frac{\text{municipal funding}}{\text{operating expenditure}} = \frac{\$550,000}{\$781,000} = 0.70.$$

Table 2-1 is useful for understanding the four ways that any ratio can be increased or decreased. This can be accomplished by increasing or decreasing the ratio's numerator or denominator.

1. The numerator can be increased while the denominator is held fixed. For example, suppose municipal funding were increased by $25,000 and operating expenses did not change. The numerator for municipal funding would be $550,000 + $25,000 or $575,000. The ratio is $575,000/$781,000 or 0.74.

2. The denominator can be decreased while the numerator is held fixed. In the example, if the trustees reduced the library's operating expenditures by $25,000, then the denominator would be $781,000 − $25,000 or $756,000. Since there is no change in municipal funding, the ratio is $550,000/$756,000 or 0.73. (It is a coincidence that the decimal value is close to the value obtained in the example above.)

3. Both the numerator and denominator can be increased, so long as the increase in the numerator is greater. In the example, if municipal funding increases by $25,000 to $575,000, and if expenditures rise by $15,000 to $796,000, the ratio is $575,000/$796,000 or 0.72.

4. Both the numerator and denominator can decrease, as long as the decrease in the denominator is greater. In the example, if municipal funding decreases by $10,000 to $540,000 and operating expenses decrease by $25,000 to $756,000, the ratio is 0.71 [0.71 = $540,000/$756,000].

The interpretation of the ratio 0.70 in column one of Table 2-1 is that 70 cents of every dollar spent on library operating expenditures come from municipal entitlement. The remaining 30 cents come from other sources. These could include library membership revenues; moneys from activities such as document delivery, sale of merchandise through a gift shop, or the rental of videotapes; funds from grants and endowments; overhead funds from contracts or grants awarded to persons in the library or other agencies of the municipality; bequests; one-time allocations; and cost recoveries.

TABLE 2-1 ▌ Municipal Funding for the Community Library (Thousands)

	Amount	Increase numerator	Increase denominator	Increase both	Decrease both
Municipal funding	$550	$575	$550	$575	$540
Operating expenses	$781	$781	$756	$796	$756
Ratio	0.70	0.74	0.73	0.72	0.71

TABLE 2-2 ▓ County Comparison of Library Acquisitions Expenditures

	County A	County B	Ratio
Audiovisuals	$628,710	$122,508	5.13
Books	10,338,933	1,438,938	7.19
Microforms	208,793	12,525	16.67
Periodicals	1,733,935	164,148	10.56
Total	$12,910,371	$1,738,119	7.43

For a ratio to be useful, it must express a relationship between like items. Table 2-2 compares the acquisition expenditures of the public libraries in two counties. The careful reader will verify each of the ratios for County A and County B expenditures. Each summarizes a relationship between County A and County B. For example, County A expended $628,710 for audiovisuals and County B expended $122,508. The ratio of County A expenditure to County B expenditure is $628,710/$122,508 or 5.13. This number tells librarians that County A spent over five times as much on audiovisuals as did County B. Of course, the numbers do not tell the reader *why* one county expended more or less than the other for a given acquisition category.

The meaning of a ratio is determined by the relationship between the compared data. Comparing unrelated numbers, such as the librarian's salary and the number of municipal parking spaces, or the number of librarians to the number of police officers, produces ratios that are meaningless. In Table 2-2, for example, a comparison of County B microform expenditures to County A book expenditures would have no meaning or application.

Indeed, an important consideration in any computation is the quality of the numbers. If the numbers used in a calculation are suspect, the ratios based on such figures also are suspect. Thus, whenever possible, the data from which ratios or other calculations have been derived should be shown and reviewed. Readers should be skeptical of ratios that cannot be verified.

Full-Time Equivalent (FTE)

Full-time equivalent (FTE) is a ratio that librarians frequently encounter in budget reports and discussions. It is used widely in higher education and in resource management. Increasingly, librarians confront it as a cost factor from vendors who base product prices and license fees on the number of student FTEs at the institution served by the library.

In higher education, the FTE ratio is used to identify how many students (undergraduate or graduate) carry the equivalent of a full course load. Many colleges and universities, for example, consider a full course load to be fifteen credit hours for an undergraduate student and twelve credit hours for a graduate student.

To illustrate how to calculate the FTE ratio, suppose that after the second week of classes, a college's registrar determines that 15,295 undergraduate students are registered for a total of 161,975 credit hours. The registrar determines the number of FTEs as follows:

$$\text{Full-Time Equivalent} = \frac{\text{total undergraduate credit hours}}{\text{full-time load}}$$

$$= \frac{161,975}{15} \text{ which is } 10,798.33.$$

The interpretation of this result is that there are 10,798.33 undergraduate FTEs registered at the college. If all colleges consider fifteen credit hours as a full course load for an undergraduate, comparing the number of registered college students at different colleges is easy.

Suppose that a university has 1295 graduate students who are registered this semester for 8025 credit hours. To determine the number of FTEs, one must first know that the base for being considered a full-time graduate student is usually twelve credit hours:

$$\text{Full-Time Equivalent} = \frac{\text{total undergraduate credit hours}}{\text{full-time load}}$$

$$= \frac{8025}{12} \text{ which is 668.75 FTE.}$$

The interpretation is that there are 668.75 graduate FTEs, which is 52% [51.6% = 668.75/1295], a percent representing slightly over half of the actual number of graduate students registered.

A librarian determines the number of full-time equivalent staff in a similar way. The key factor is how many hours constitute the employee's workweek. The most common workweeks are 35 hours (7-hour workdays), 37.5 hours (7.5-hour workdays), and 40 hours (8-hour workdays).

To illustrate how to calculate staff FTEs, suppose that a library employs 24 full-time and part-time persons. These staff members work a total of 658 hours during a regular five-day workweek of 35 hours. A librarian would determine the number of FTEs for staff as follows:

$$\text{Full-Time Equivalent} = \frac{\text{total staff hours worked}}{\text{hours in workweek}}$$

$$= \frac{658}{35} \text{ which is 18.8.}$$

The interpretation is that there are 18.8 FTE personnel in the library.

For another example, suppose that a library has a staff complement of 54. There are 12 full-time librarians and 8 part-time clerical staff. In addition, there are 34 part-time staff. The staff workday is 7.5 hours. To determine the number of FTEs based on a total of 1550 hours worked for the week, the key information is that the workday is 7.5 hours. This means that the workweek contains 37.5 hours [37.5 = 7.5 × 5]:

$$\text{Full-Time Equivalent} = \frac{\text{total staff hours worked}}{\text{hours in workweek}}$$

$$= \frac{1550}{37.5} \text{ which is 41.33.}$$

The interpretation of this number is that there are 41.33 staff FTEs who work 37.5-hour workweeks. Additional analysis reveals that there are 20 personnel who work full-time [20 staff = 12 librarians + 8 secretaries]. These persons worked 750 hours [750 = 20 × 37.5]. This means that the 34 part-time staff worked a total of 800 hours [800 = 1550 − 750]. Since there are 34 part-time staff, they worked an average of 23.5 hours per week [23.5 = 800/34]. Of course, some staff will have worked more hours than 23.5 and some will have worked fewer than 23.5 hours, but on average, the part-time staff worked 23.5 hours.

Numerical Description by Subtraction: Percent

Comparison by subtraction is a common technique used to contrast two quantities. For example, if a book costs $25 and another costs $22, the difference is determined by subtracting the lower cost from the higher cost. That is, $25 − $22 = $3. This is the absolute difference between the cost of the two books. This same technique can be used to determine the difference over time. For example, suppose that two years ago a popular magazine subscription cost $35 and this year it will cost $55. This cost increase is $20, since $55 − $35 = $20.

In Latin, *percent* means "per hundred" or "out of each hundred." Accordingly, 100% effort is maximum effort and 100% support is complete support. Percents show the relative size of two or more numbers. Like a ratio, a percent is calculated by dividing a numerator by a denominator. Unlike ratios, percents are then converted to a scale based on 100. This means that a percent is a fraction in which the denominator is always equal to 100.

An advantage of a percent is that it is a term most people understand. In addition, it is relatively easy to convert a fraction or decimal number into a percent. Example 2-4 illustrates the techniques for converting a decimal into a percent and a percent into a decimal.

Procedure

- To convert a decimal to a percent, move the decimal point 2 places to the *right* and add a percent sign.

- To convert a percent to a decimal, move the decimal point 2 places to the *left* and remove the percent sign.

Example 2-4

Conversion Techniques

Converting a decimal number into a percent

Analysis

Move the decimal point 2 places to the *right* and add a percent sign.

1.	.01 = 1%	5.	7.5 = 750%
2.	.33 = 33%	6.	.003 = 0.3%
3.	.125 = 12.5%	7.	1.15 = 115%
4.	2 = 200%	8.	11.5 = 1150%

Converting a percent to a decimal

Analysis

Move the decimal point 2 places to the *left* and remove the percent sign.

1.	3% = .03	5.	135% = 1.35
2.	17% = .17	6.	1000% = 10
3.	7½% = 7.5% or .075	7.	.1% = .001
4.	100% = 1.00	8.	½% = .5% or .005

DIFFERENCE BETWEEN PERCENTS AND RATIOS

There is an important difference between percents and ratios. It concerns the units for each measurement. That is, the numerator and denominator of a ratio can represent different categories of data. For example, if the numerator is expressed in miles traveled and the denominator is expressed in gallons, then the resulting unit is miles per gallon, a statistic familiar to persons who drive an automobile.

In determining a percentage, however, the numerator and denominator must be numbers that are expressed in the same units. That is, if the numerator is expressed in linear feet, the denominator must also be expressed in linear feet. If the numerator is a dollar figure, the denominator must be expressed in dollars as well.

COMMON TYPES OF PERCENT PROBLEMS

There are three types of percent problems that are commonly encountered. The first type involves determining what percent one number is of another, such as what percent 5 is of 8. The second type of problem requires finding a specific percent of a given number, such as 80% of 140. The third type of problem is finding a denominator when given a number that is a specified percent of that denominator, such as finding the number of which 30 is 12%.

Each of these types of problems involves three quantities: the numerator, the denominator, and the percent. In each type of problem, two of the quantities are known. Formula 2-1 shows the mathematical relationship. Example 2-5 illustrates solving these three common types of percent problems.

Formula 2-1

$$\text{percent} = \frac{\text{numerator}}{\text{denominator}} \times 100$$

Example 2-5

Three Common Types of Percent Problems

---

1. What percent is 3 of 5?

   Analysis

   The relationship is

   > (numerator $\times$ 100)/denominator = percentage
   > Calculation: (3/5) $\times$ 100 = 60%

2. What is 75% of 800?

   Analysis

   The relationship is

   > (percentage $\times$ denominator)/100 = numerator
   > Calculation: (75% $\times$ 800)/100 = 600

3. 30 is 12% of what number?

Analysis

The relationship is

(numerator $\times$ 100)/percentage = denominator
Calculation: (30 $\times$ 100)/12% = 250

Fortunately, those who are confident in their algebra skills can solve these problems in a slightly easier way. The key is to translate the problem from English into the language of algebra and then to solve the resulting equation. In doing this, the reader needs to recall the following about algebra: "is" translates to "equals"; "of" signals multiplication; "what" is the unknown number $W;$ and percent (%) translates to "times .01." Remember, too, that multiplication is indicated by placing a quantity in parentheses so that, for example, 5(2) means five times two and 8 (.01) = 0.08. Example 2-6 illustrates translating English language problem statements into algebra.

Example 2-6

Translating English Statements into Algebra

---

1. What is 42% of 12?

Analysis

First, 42% is 42(.01) or 42% = 0.42. Hence, W = 0.42(12), so W = 5.04.

2. 28 is 32% of what?

Analysis

First, 32% is 32 (.01) or 32% = 0.32. Hence, 28 = .32 (W) so that W = 28/.32 or W = 87.5.

3. 50% of what is 30?

Analysis

First, 50% is 50 (.01) or 50% = 0.50. Hence, .50 (W) = 30 so that W = 30/.50 or W = 60.

4. 10 is what percent of 25?

Analysis

10 = W(25) or W = 10/25 or W = .40 or W = 40%.

5. 25 is what percent of 175?

Analysis

25 = W(175) or W = 25/175 or W = .14 or W = 14%. (Notice that one could have written: W = .1428571 or W = 14.28571%, but such a long decimal result is unnecessary, as discussed previously.)

Suppose that you are part of a project team charged with developing a new information product. From survey results, the team knows that American consumers open and read 78% of the advertising text that they receive in the mail. Since the project team anticipates making a community-wide bulk mailing to 12,000 households to advertise the new information product, you logically ask yourself how many of the mail pieces will be opened and read.

The question really is, what is 78% of 12,000? When the question is translated into algebra, it becomes the following:

$$W = 0.78(12,000)$$
$$= 9360 \text{ pieces.}$$

Suppose, too, that the team member from marketing states that the team should expect only about a 2% reply rate. This statement provokes the question, what is 2% of 9360? When the librarian translates the question into algebra, it becomes the following:

$$X = .02\ (9360)$$
$$= 187 \text{ people.}$$

COMPARISON MEASURE ANALYSES

There are two techniques that are especially useful for establishing relationships and trends with percents. These are component percent analysis and dollar and percent change analysis.

Component Percent Analysis

Component percent analysis focuses on the percent relationship between a component part and the whole. This technique produces insights in addition to identifying changes and making comparisons. A percent analysis is useful for classification as well. Institutions, for example, often use a percent of time analysis as a performance guideline. Everyone's job, from technician to library director, is described and quantified in terms of the percent of time that the employee spends performing tasks.

To calculate component percents, the whole is used as the denominator and the part is used as the numerator:

$$\text{component percent} = \frac{\text{part}}{\text{whole}} \times 100.$$

Component percent analysis, often applied to library budgets, helps to identify the relative importance of an item or group of items. The example that follows shows component percents determined for public library acquisition expenditures introduced in Table 2-2.

For County A, audiovisual expenditures represent 4.9% of the total expenditures for the county. This amount is determined by dividing audiovisual expenditures by total expenditures, yielding 0.0487 or 4.9% [0.0487 = \$628,710/\$12,910,371]. The interpretation of the component percent data is that, for both counties, book expenditures represent the largest proportion of budgeted dollars, followed by expenditures for periodicals, audiovisual materials, and microforms. The component percent analysis, in turn, helps to focus on the relative importance of acquisition items to the overall budget. See Table 2-3.

Figure 2-1 illustrates a library's program of revenue-producing activities. Table 2-4 shows the revenue statement for the library depicted in the figure. Revenue-producing activities are classified into three broad categories: educational services, individualized services, and research services. In actuality, all of the library's activities and services fall into one of these three categories.

Table 2-4 illustrates a revenue statement of the library that is organized by product line. It also includes a component percent analysis. In the analysis, all items are expressed as a percent of revenue.

Under the heading *Operating expenses* are listed service items that are due a share of expenses. Some minor discrepancies in the sums of the percents are due to rounding to whole percents. At a glance, the component percents show the contribution of each component to the total. Again, the percents bring perspective to the dollar amounts in each column.

In analyzing the component percents, the librarian sees that gross profits (income after expenses) increased from 35% in Year 1 to 40% in Year 2. By the end of Year 3, however, the gross profits declined from 40% to 30%. This decline can be explained by successful cost-reduction measures over the three-year period.

The costs of the goods/services fell from 65% of revenue in Year 1 to 60% in Year 2. This decline influenced the library's net income (the bottom line), which increased from 8% in Year 1 to 15% in Year 2. Costs of goods/services increased, however, from Year 2 to Year 3. Even with decreasing operating expenses, net income declined from 15% in Year 2 to 10% in Year 3.

More information can be wrung out of the analysis of the dollar amounts. For example, net income improved significantly, from \$1545 in Year 1 to \$3682 in Year 2, an increase of almost 2.4 times. However, revenue increased faster in dollars than did net income. This means that the library had to earn more from its services in Year 3 for every dollar it retained as net income than it earned in Year 2. This shortcoming cannot be discerned from the component percents. It illustrates that changes in component percents can result from changes in the component, in the total, or in both. Hence, using a combination of these methods yields a more complete picture.

TABLE 2-3   Public Library Acquisitions Expenditures by Component Percents

	County A	County B
Audiovisuals	4.9	7.1
Books	80.1	82.8
Microforms	1.6	0.7
Periodicals	13.4	9.4
Total	100.0	100.0
(Dollars)	(\$12,910,371)	(\$1,738,119)

FIGURE 2-1   A Library's Product Mix and Listing of Billable Items That Generate Revenue through Fees, Registration, and Other Charges

Educational services	Individualized services	Research services
Communication access	Book delivery	Facilities rental
AV presentations	Books by mail	Locker rental
Computer networks	Bookmobile	Study carrels
Satellite networks	Homebound services	
Teleconferences	Nursing homes	Online literature
Meeting room rental	Book reserves	Reference research
Conference rooms		Genealogy
Auditorium	Circulation rentals	Information & referral
	Art, sculpture	Reference information services
Seminars/mini courses	Books	Telephone information services
Concerts for children	Discs, records	
CPR training	Toys	Selective Dissemination of Information
Financial planning	Videotapes	
How-to classes		
Parenting seminars	Fines	
Puppet construction		
Reader's advisory	Interlibrary loans	
Reading programs		
Resume preparation	Sale of discarded/gift books	
Tax classes		
Travelogue series	Usage fees	
	CD-ROM database access	
Story hour	FAX sending/receiving	
	Personal computer time	
	Photocopy exposures	

Dollar and Percent Change Analysis

Dollar and percent change analysis is another technique that is useful for establishing relationships and trends with percents. Identifying the percent of change in dollar or percent over time gives perspective and meaning to statistics. For example, a $5,000 budget increase has different significance, depending on whether the amount is an increase of 10% over last year's budget of $50,000 or an increase of 1% over a budget of $500,000.

A *percent change analysis* relates a base number to a comparison number. To calculate percent change, find the difference between the comparison and the base numbers, then divide by the base number. Of course, the quotient must be multiplied by 100 to convert it to a percent. Percent change is shown by Formula 2-2.

Formula 2-2

$$\text{percent change} = \frac{(\text{comparison number} - \text{base number})}{\text{base number}} \times 100$$

TABLE 2-4 ▎ Revenue and Component Percent Analysis*

	Dollars			Component percent		
	Year 3	**Year 2**	**Year 1**	**Year 3**	**Year 2**	**Year 1**
Revenue	$32,620	$24,545	$19,305	100%	100%	100%
Education	3,670	2,630	1,430	11	11	7
Communications	1,000	750	200	3	3	1
Meeting room rental	2,250	1,500	900	7	6	5
Mini courses	300	280	250	1	1	1
Story hour	120	100	80	0	0	0
Individualized Services	16,100	12,190	10,575	49	50	55
Book delivery services	2,650	2,200	1,800	8	9	9
Book reserves	120	90	75	0	0	0
Collection rentals	4,200	3,100	2,700	13	13	14
Fines	580	400	450	2	2	2
Interlibrary loans	4,900	3,500	3,150	15	14	16
Sales discard/books	500	300	200	2	1	1
Usage Fees	3,100	2,800	2,200	10	11	11
Research	12,850	9,725	7,300	40	39	38
Facilities rental	3,700	2,600	1,800	11	11	9
Online services	4,950	3,625	2,500	15	15	13
Reference research	4,200	3,500	3,000	13	14	16
Cost of goods/services	22,800	14,750	12,600	70	60	65
Gross profit	9,820	9,795	6,705	30	40	35
Operating expenses	6,558	6,113	5,160	20	25	27
Advertising	700	500	125	2	2	1
Depreciation	425	400	400	1	2	2
Insurance	250	225	210	1	1	1
Interest	125	210	180	0	1	1
Salaries	4,330	3,500	3,100	13	14	16
Telephone	600	540	900	2	2	5
Other	128	738	245	0	3	1
Net income	$ 3,262	$ 3,682	$ 1,545	10%	15%	8%

*Percentage sum discrepancies are due to rounding.

Table 2-5 depicts both the historical expenditure data for a small library and a corresponding percent change analysis. The dollar amount of change is the difference between the amount for the base year and for a comparison year. The percent change is computed by dividing the amount of change by the base number. For example, the difference between Year 3 and Year 2 salary and wage expenditures in the table is $(103 - 88)/88$. This is 15/88, or a 17% increase in Year 3 over Year 2.

There are also several points to notice about the way data are shown in Table 2-5. First, a common practice is to round financial data to thousands or millions of dollars, but the table must indicate that this has been done. Rounding should not be assumed. Second, a decrease or loss is shown by placing the quantity in parentheses. Third, a percent sign is placed after

TABLE 2-5 ░ Expenditures and Dollar/Percent Change Analysis*

Category	Expenditures in thousands			Increase/(Decrease)			
	Year 3	Year 2	Year 1	Year 3 over Year 2	%	Year 2 over Year 1	%
Salaries and wages	$103	$ 88	$ 81	$15	17%	$ 7	9%
Fringe benefits (19%)	20	17	15	3	18	2	13
Acquisitions	30	26	10	4	15	16	160
Books	23	21	7	2	10	14	200
Magazines	4	3	2	1	33	1	50
Media	3	2	1	1	50	1	100
Binding	1	1	1	0	0	0	0
Supplies & small equip.	2	2	2	0	0	0	0
Online services	7	6	6	1	17	0	0
Travel	2	1	2	1	100	(1)	(50)
Repair & maintenance	3	3	2	0	0	1	50
Other	3	2	2	1	50	0	0
Total	$171	$146	$121	$25	17%	$25	21%

*Percentage sum discrepancies are due to rounding.

the first numerical entry in a column of percents. Although this practice appears to be redundant since the column is labeled with the symbol %, the percent sign is a reminder that percents are being reported. Since most readers do not closely study headings or organization of a table, this important convention helps to reduce data misinterpretation. Last, a percent rounded down to zero should not be shown by a dash, which may imply noncalculated or unavailable figures.

Although the library's budgeted expenditures increased by $25,000 in both Year 2 [$146 − 121] and Year 3 [$171 − 146], the percent change differs. This is because the base year amount shifts from Year 1 to Year 2. Later years can also be compared with a previous base year. For example, Year 1 can be used as a base year for comparison with Year 2, Year 3, and Year 4.

A dollar and percent change analysis can be made on many types of data, as long as the data represent a positive quantity. If the base-year amount is negative or zero, no percent change can be computed. Example 2-7 illustrates finding percent change from a base amount.

Example 2-7 ░ **Finding the Percent of Increase or Decrease
of a Number from an Original Base Amount**

In midyear the library subscribed to 250 magazines. By the end of the year, the subscription list had grown to 290 titles. Find the percent of increase.

Analysis

The amount of increase is 40 titles [40 = 290 − 250]. The question now becomes, what percent of 250 is 40? In this problem, 250 is the base:

$$40 = P \times 250$$
$$40/250 = P.$$

Hence, $P = 0.16$, which shows that the percent increase is 16%.

In the early part of the year, a special library provided low-cost copy machines for public use adjacent to the journal area. Over the year, journal duplication dropped from 24,000 to 21,000 volumes. Find the percent of decrease.

Analysis

The amount of decrease is 3000 volumes [$3000 = 24,000 - 21,000$]. The question now becomes, what percent of 24,000 is 3000? In this problem, 24,000 is the base:

$$3000 = D \times 24,000$$
$$3000/24,000 = D.$$

Or, $D = 0.125$. Expressed in percent, 0.125 is 12.5%. This shows a decrease in journal duplication of 12.5%.

Pitfalls with Percents and Base Numbers

Although analyses involving percents can be helpful for giving perspective, users and producers of percents should be aware of several potential liabilities. First, the denominator used to compute the percents must be large enough to be meaningful. Percent change analyses, for instance, are particularly susceptible to distortions caused by small base numbers. This is because low initial values make a change seem greater than high initial values. If the denominator is small, it is better to use actual numerical values rather than percents. For example, suppose that a survey of three people reveals that 33% of those surveyed are frequent library users. To avoid deception, the librarian should clearly state that, of the three people surveyed, one is a frequent library user.

A similar distortion occurs when the base and percent are disguised or are not given. "I own a single share," someone may state, when in fact the situation may be that only two shares exist. The listener, however, makes assumptions in mentally supplying missing information and surmises that there are many shares. Thus, although accurate and precise, the statement misleads because it conceals the true ownership percent, which is equal to 50%.

Specifically, a librarian needs to pay close note to the base number when interpreting full-time equivalent results, particularly for staff. The reason is that the workweek can differ among institutions, being 35 hours, or 37.5 hours, or 40 hours.

There are many ways to express a relationship in order to support a desired result. This is an important point for all consumers of statistics to consider. Most likely, the method chosen to express the relationship will be the one that seems to best support the preferred option. It is, therefore, important to scrutinize data summaries to ensure that they accurately reflect the situation or circumstance under study. It is also important to confirm that the resulting conclusions are appropriate and reasonable.

DATA POINT LABELING AND SIGMA NOTATION

To use statistics effectively requires two important techniques that are, in effect, examples of shorthand notation. Data point labeling and Sigma notation are used to communicate ideas and operations efficiently and symbolically. These techniques simplify the writing of otherwise cumbersome equations. Familiarity with this shorthand is necessary to pursue more advanced statistics.

Data Point Labeling

The first technique, *data point labeling,* establishes a general procedure for analyzing a set of data. Labeling is simplified if the data points are considered as a set of Xs (or Ys, Ps, Qs, and so on) or a sequence of points, each of which is identified or "tagged" by a number. This principle is similar to taking a number while waiting in line. In the labeling process, the value of each data point is ignored. The first data point is labeled X_1 (read as "X sub-one"), the second is labeled X_2, the third is X_3, and so on. The X is called a dummy *variable.* Any letter may be used as a dummy variable. The small number to the right of and below the X is a *subscript.* The subscript identifies a particular variable, such as X_1 or X_2, but does not alter the value of the variable. The subscript serves merely for identification and is not used for computational purposes.

After all the observations have been labeled, the data set can be pictured in this way:

X_1 = first data point
X_2 = second data point
X_3 = third data point, and so on.

The last data point is conventionally represented by X_N (read as "X sub-N"), because the N is understood as representing the total number of data points in the set. The elements of the above set can be expressed as $\{X_1, X_2, X_3, \ldots, X_N\}$.

For example, from July through December, the library's collection of new videotapes grew by 27, 18, 32, 19, 20, and 24 videos, respectively. In using Sigma notation, the dummy variable X is used for the month.

The first number, 27, is tagged or labeled X_1, so $X_1 = 27$. The second number, 18, is labeled X_2, so $X_2 = 18$. The last number, 24, is labeled X_6, so $X_6 = 24$. Because there are 6 data points, N is equal to 6.

Sigma Notation

The basic rules of data point labeling help to understand *Sigma notation,* which is a symbolic way to represent the sum of a series of numbers. Sigma notation allows for the brief expression of long equations and will be used throughout this book to simplify the many algorithms presented.

Suppose that a librarian wishes to add the ages of all children present during a story hour. Such a sum can be useful in any number of statistical operations, described later in this text. For now, however, the task is to find a simple way to represent the addition of the children's ages.

If the children are asked in a random order for their ages, the ages reported are a series of observations or data points. These may be reported as $\{9, 9, 6, 7, 8, 6, 5, 9, 7\}$. Note that several of the ages, or data values, repeat and that there is no particular order to the listing of the ages. An equation adding the ages together would look like this:

Sum = 9 + 9 + 6 + 7 + 8 + 6 + 5 + 9 + 7
  = 66.

The first step in converting this equation to Sigma notation is to tag or label each data point. To accomplish this, the librarian can use A as the dummy variable to represent age. Then, A_1 stands for the age in the first observation, 9, so that $A_1 = 9$. Likewise, A stands for the second observation, also 9, so that $A_2 = 9$. The third observation, 6, is represented by A_3, 7 by A_4, and so on, until the final observation, 7, is represented by A_9.

After the data points have been labeled, the equation becomes:

$$\text{Sum} = A_1 + A_2 + A_3 + A_4 + A_5 + A_6 + A_7 + A_8 + A_9.$$

The only feature in this equation that changes is the subscript. It begins with 1 and increments by 1 with each observation, through the ninth observation. This pattern makes it possible to represent the equation symbolically.

If a symbol is used for the operation of addition, and a symbol is used to show a constantly increasing subscript, this equation—and others like it—can be simplified. The symbol mathematicians have selected to represent addition is a Greek letter, capital sigma, or Σ.

Lowercase i represents the subscript that is going to increment by one, beginning with $i = 1$ and continuing through $i = 9$. The lowercase i is called the *summation index*. Therefore, this equation can be written as follows:

$$\sum_{i=1}^{9} A_1 = A_1 + A_2 + A_3 + A_4 + A_5 + A_6 + A_7 + A_8 + A_9.$$

This construction is mathematical shorthand. It means: "In a series of 9 observations, for each observation beginning with A_1 and continuing consecutively through A_9, each in the series will be added together to find the sum total of all the observations."

Notice that if the summation index, i, is changed from 1 to another number, such as 4, the summation will begin with the fourth observation and continue through the ninth observation. A summation index of 7 directs the summing to begin with the seventh observation. Some examples are helpful:

$$\sum_{i=7}^{11} f_i = f_7 + f_8 + f_9 + f_{10} + f_{11}$$

$$\sum_{i=0}^{4} f_i y_i = f_0 y_0 + f_1 y_1 + f_2 y_2 + f_3 y_3 + f_4 y_4$$

An important convention in Sigma notation is that, if the summation index is not specified, its range is understood to be between 1 and N, where N is the number of data points in the set. So, the following expressions represent the same operation:

$$\sum_{i=1}^{N} A_i \text{ is the same as } \sum A_i.$$

To illustrate the use of Sigma notation, suppose that a technical services librarian keeps a record of the number of books purchased each month that are accompanied by a floppy disk or CD-ROM. The annual number will be the sum of items received in each of the twelve months. This is expressed as follows:

$$\text{Total} = \sum_{i=1}^{12} M_i, \text{ where } M \text{ represents month and } i \text{ designates the particular month.}$$

Notice that the subscript refers to the number of the month. Hence, M_1 represents January and M_7 represents July.

For another example, suppose $B_1 = 3$, $B_2 = 5$, and $B_3 = 4$. To use Sigma notation to determine the number of items received during the first quarter, that is, during the first three months of the year, the analysis is as follows:

$$\sum_{i=1}^{3} B_i = B_1 + B_2 + B_3$$
$$= 3 + 5 + 4 \text{ which is } 12.$$

Example 2-8 illustrates the use of Sigma notation for various types of relationships.

Example 2-8

Expressing Relationships That Use Sigma Notation

1. Write out the following:

$$\sum_{i=1}^{5} X_i.$$

Analysis

$$\sum_{i=1}^{5} X_i = X_1 + X_2 + X_3 + X_4 + X_5.$$

2. Write out the following:

$$\sum_{i=1}^{4} (X_i - 3).$$

Analysis

$$\sum_{i=1}^{4} (X_i - 3) = (X_1 - 3) + (X_2 - 3) + (X_3 - 3) + (X_4 - 3)$$
$$= (X_1 + X_2 + X_3 + X_4) - 12.$$

3. Use Sigma notation to represent the following:

$$mx_1 + mx_2 + mx_3 + mx_4 + mx_4.$$

Analysis

$$mx_1 + mx_2 + mx_3 + mx_4 + mx_4 = \sum_{i=1}^{4} mx_i.$$

4. Use Sigma notation to represent the following:

$$(x_1 - x) + (x_2 - x) + (x_3 - x) + (x_4 - x) + (x_5 - x).$$

Analysis

$$(x_1 - x) + (x_2 - x) + (x_3 - x) + (x_4 - x) + (x_5 - x) = \sum_{i=1}^{5} (x_i - x).$$

5. If $A = 1, X_1 = 3, X_2 = 5, X_3 = -1, X_4 = -3$, evaluate the following:

$$\sum_{i=1}^{4} (A - 2X_i).$$

Analysis

$$\sum_{i=1}^{4} (A - 2X_i) = (A - 2X_1) + (A - 2X_2) + (A - 2X_3) + (A - 2X_4)$$

$$= A - 2X_1 + A - 2X_2 + A - 2X_3 + A - 2X_4$$

$$= A + A + A + A + (-2X_1 - 2X_2 - 2X_3 - 2X_4)$$

$$= 4A - 2(X_1 + X_2 + X_3 + X_4)$$

$$= 4(1) - 2[3 + 5 + (-1) + (-3)]$$

$$= 4 - 2[4]$$

$$= 4 - 8 \text{ which is } -4.$$

In the example above, the algebra is more complicated than Sigma notation.

6. Using the values in (5) above, evaluate the following:

$$\sum_{i=1}^{4} [X_i (A - 2X_i)].$$

Analysis

$$\sum_{i=1}^{4} [X_i (A - 2X_i)] = X_1 (A - 2X_1)$$

$$+ X_2 (A - 2X_2) + X_3 (A - 2X_3) + X_4 (A - 2X_4)$$

$$= 3 (1 - 2[3]) + 5 (1 - 2[5])$$

$$+ (-1) (1 - 2[-1]) + (-3) (1 - 2[-3])$$

$$= 3 (1 - 6) + 5 (1 - 10)$$

$$+ (-1) (1 + 2) + (-3) (1 + 6)$$

$$= 3 (-5) + 5 (-9) + (-1) (3) + (-3) (7)$$

$$= -15 - 45 - 3 - 21 \text{ which is } -84.$$

SUMMARY OF CRITICAL CONCEPTS

1. *Rounding* numbers is necessary when data are to be expressed to a certain number of decimal places. Rounding is an important technique for simplifying, summarizing, and abbreviating data. It is used in summary tables where usually only three or four digits are shown, such as 2,347,218 volumes, which may be expressed as 2.347 million volumes. To minimize rounding error, some consistent method for rounding numbers must be followed. The *guidelines for rounding* are as follows: (a) identify the digit in the decimal place to which you wish to round; (b) look at the next digit to the right; (c) round up if the digit to the right is 5 or higher, and round down if the digit to the right is less than 5.

2. A *ratio* is a relationship between two numbers expressed by division. When expressed as a fraction, the top quantity is the *numerator* and the bottom quantity is the *denominator*. The denominator also is called the *base number*.

3. *Percent* is a frequently used statistic because of its wide acceptance and ease of computation. It is a fraction in which the denominator always is 100. Often, a percent is used for expressing change in measurement or frequency. The base number is the key to evaluating a ratio or percent. If the base is not representative, data distortion is possible.

4. *Data analysis* identifies significant relationships between and among quantities. Data analysis also concerns quantifying the amount and direction of change that has occurred over a period. Common techniques such as *dollar and percent change analysis* and *component percent analysis* are useful.

5. *Data point labeling* is statistical shorthand notation that is used to convey information about data in a concise manner. In this technique, data points are thought of as forming a sequence. Each point is assigned a number or tag, without regard for the value of the data point. The first data point becomes the first value in the sequence. It is labeled with a *subscript,* as in X_1 (read "X sub 1"). The second data point becomes the second value in the sequence, as in X_2 (read "X sub 2"). If there are N data points, the set is written $\{X_1, X_2, \ldots, X_N\}$. If there are 8 data points, the set is written $\{X_1, X_2, X_3, X_4, X_5, X_6, X_7, X_8\}$, and N is understood to equal 8.

6. *Sigma notation* is a technique for shortening equations. It uses both labeled data points *and* addition. If the data points are labeled into a sequence such as $X_1, X_2, \ldots, X_N$, then their sum, $X_1 + X_2 + \ldots + X_N$, can be written in Sigma notation. The Sigma notation for $X_1 + X_2 + \ldots + X_N$ is ΣX_i.

KEY TERMS

Component percent analysis.   A technique for using percents to focus on the relationships between component parts and a whole. Component percent analysis frequently is used in relation to budgeting for determining the relative importance of particular budgetary items (expenses).

Dollar and percent change analysis.   Techniques for comparing monetary values and percentages over time. The analysis compares the change in dollars or percents between two periods relative to some arbitrarily chosen base figure.

Percent.   A quantity expressed in hundredths. (*Percent* means "per hundred" or "out of each hundred.") Percents show the relative size of two or more numbers, and they usually are smaller than 100.

Ratio.   A quantitative relationship between two terms, indicated by division. When expressed as a fraction, the top term of the ratio is the numerator and the bottom term is the denominator. A ratio of 700 to 500 is expressed as 700:500, or 7:5, or as 1.4:1. The validity of a ratio depends on the validity of the numbers entering into its computation. Ratios are useful for identifying trends that are not readily apparent by review of the individual components of the ratio.

Sigma notation.   A symbolic means for representing the sum of a series of numbers. Sigma notation allows for the brief expression of long equations and is used to simplify statistical algorithms. The capital Greek letter sigma (Σ) is used in the notation.

SELF-ASSESSMENT QUIZ

1. *True* or *False*   Rounded to two decimal places, the number 27.745001 is 27.75.

2. *True* or *False*   A percent is a useful statistic because it is familiar and meaningful even to people who have little training in statistics.

3. *True* or *False*   When two or more quantities are being compared, it is better to compare actual numerical values than to compare percents, particularly if the base value of any of the percents is small.

4. *True* or *False*   A raise of 100% offsets a pay cut of 50%.

5. *True* or *False*   Last month, 60 compact discs were checked out. This month, 45 were checked out. The percent change was a decrease of 15%.

Answers

1. *True*   If the digit to the right is 5 or more, then round up.

2. *True*   A percent is a familiar expression and puts ratios and fractions into a convenient format.

3. *True*   When the bases are small, slight differences in the numerator cause radical changes in the percents.

4. *True*   If a quantity is reduced by 50% (halved), the new quantity must be increased by 100% (doubled) to get the old quantity again.

5. *False*   The percent decrease is the numerical difference divided by the original number, $(60 - 45)/60 = 25\%$, and is not the numerical difference alone, $(60 - 45 = 15)$.

DISCUSSION QUESTIONS AND PROBLEMS

1. Round 8765.4321 to the nearest
   a. one
   b. ten
   c. hundred
   d. thousand
   e. tenth
   f. hundredth
   g. thousandth
   h. ten-thousandth

2. Round each to the nearest thousandth.
   a. 3.4852
   b. 2.4857
   c. 2.3456789
   d. 3.1234000
   e. 3.2468000
   f. 3.8642

3. Solve the following percent problems.
   a. What is 27% of 85?
   b. 60% of 120 is what?
   c. What percent of 40 is 15?
   d. 80 is what percent of 160?
   e. 33 is 25% of what?
   f. 11.9% of what is 15?

4. Solve the following percent problems.
   a. What is 7% of 225?
   b. 125% of 50 is what?
   c. 15 is what percent of 75?
   d. 105 is what percent of 100?
   e. What percent of 725 is 650?
   f. What is 120% of 80?

5. A library purchased $10,000 worth of audiovisual equipment. A rule of thumb is that equipment repairs will cost 10% in the first year and 20% in the second year. How much money should the director budget for AV repair during Year 1 and Year 2?

6. Determine the percent increase or decrease.
   a. The price of a library office supply item increased from $.75 to $.80. What is the percent of increase?
   b. By changing vendors, a library's monthly cost for a service is decreased by $25 to $130. How much did the service cost from the old vendor and what is the percent of decrease?
   c. A librarian earns $3242 monthly and receives a 4% increase. What is the new monthly salary? On an annual basis, what is the librarian's new salary?
   d. A librarian uses a piece of equipment in consulting work that depreciates 30% of its original value in the first year. At the end of the first year, the equipment has a value of $8750. What was its original cost?

7. First-quarter circulation figures for a public library that serves a community of 30,000 are as follows:

	March	February	January
Biography	637	562	572
Fiction	4825	4343	4538
Mystery	1833	1626	1834
Science fiction	168	136	172

   a. For the first quarter, find the total number of circulations for each category.
   b. The total circulations for all library items for January, February, and March were 50,695, 48,346, and 52,490, respectively. Calculate the percentage for each of the categories listed in the table.

8. The annual circulation statistics for a public library show that 586,781 items were circulated. To provide insight into the collection's most popular circulating materials, the librarian identified 31 categories that circulated more than 5000 items during the year. Items marked Cap II Match are resources that were purchased with special matching funds.

100s	5,017	J Fiction	23,306
300s	10,696	J Paperback	30,194
600s	9,475	J Picture Book	71,996
700s	9,760	J Reader	24,233
800s	5,531	Audio Book	20,403
900s	7,618	610–619	7,392
Biography	6,632	650–659	5,946
Fiction	57,066	910–919	16,217
Mystery	22,461	Video	32,913
Large Print	7,710	J Video	12,335
Cap II Match	10,066	YA PB	6,921
Rental	5,159	J Board Book	7,282
J300	10,069	Compact Disc	20,494
J500	19,081	Paperback	18,934
J600	8,777		
J700	9,423		
J900	11,465		

a. Round the circulation figures for each category to the nearest one hundred. Arrange the categories in descending order from highest to lowest, based on the rounded numbers. Determine the percent difference between the exact circulation and the rounded circulation.

b. Using the rounded data, determine the percent that each category represents of the annual circulation. Are there any surprises?

c. What percent of the annual circulation is explained by the categories listed? What percent remains unexplained?

d. The categories that are identified with a "J" are circulations from the Juvenile collection. What percent of all circulation is represented by the Juvenile collection? What percent is represented by circulation of materials from other categories?

9. The library in problem 8 has a collection of international language titles. Last year, the circulation of items by language was as follows:

	Fiction		Nonfiction	
Language	**Adult**	**J**	**Adult**	**J**
Chinese	138	1	60	8
Czech	8	0	3	0
Danish	4	0	0	0
French	13	18	3	0
German	27	4	5	0
Greek	4	0	0	0
Hebrew	4	9	1	1
Hindi	1	0	0	0
Italian	2	0	4	0
Japanese	24	4	10	3
Korean	1,170	1	510	5
Polish	305	0	48	0
Russian	226	3	112	0
Spanish	33	88	6	26

(continued)

	Fiction		Nonfiction	
Language	**Adult**	**J**	**Adult**	**J**
Urdu	2	0	0	0
Vietnamese	0	1	0	0
Swahili	0	2	0	0

a. Determine the annual circulation of each material by language and show the total by inserting a column in the table.
b. Determine the annual percent circulation of each category of material.
c. What, if anything, do these circulation counts reveal about the community that the library serves?
d. If you were the librarian who was developing a plan to increase the circulation of international language materials, what three or four beginning steps would you identify?

10. Circulation data over the past 6 months are shown below for videotapes and compact discs.

Month	Videotape circulation (V_i)	Disc circulation (D_i)
1	240	29
2	252	46
3	238	41
4	244	45
5	255	40
6	225	36

a. What is the value of V_3? What is the value of D_5?
b. Express $V_1 + \ldots + V_6$ in Sigma notation. Find this value.
c. Express $D_1 + \ldots + D_6$ in Sigma notation. Find this value.
d. Express in Sigma notation and find the value of the following:

$$(V_1 + \ldots + V_6) / 6.$$

e. Express in Sigma notation and find the value of the following:

$$(D_1 + \ldots + D_6) / 6.$$

DATA
COMPARISONS
IN THE LIBRARY
ENVIRONMENT

Learning Objectives

After reading this chapter, you will be able to do the following:

1. Justify the need for a library mission statement and provide an example.

2. Describe the usefulness of comparison measures in analyzing library situations.

3. Apply ratio analysis to calculating library output measures.

4. Describe what it means for a product or service to be elastic or inelastic and illustrate with library examples.

5. Describe marginal productivity in the library environment.

6. Describe and illustrate the concept of diminishing returns in the library environment.

7. Explain the usefulness of benefit-cost ratio analysis in the library environment.

8. Perform and interpret the results of a benefit-cost analysis.

Library program evaluation is a key responsibility of the librarian. Evaluation involves the collection and assessment of data and can be categorized into two types, formative and summative.

In *formative evaluation,* data are collected and evaluated in order to strengthen, improve (continuously), and develop the activity that is under analysis. For the librarian, the focus of formative evaluation is on identifying users, developing services or products to satisfy clientele needs, and examining program processes and administration.

In *summative evaluation,* the librarian scrutinizes the outcomes and effects of the library's program. Data collection is undertaken to reveal the impact on the clientele and its ripple effects into the community, to measure the degree to which the library program's objectives were met, and to address the program's cost-effectiveness. Through evaluation, librarians seek to demonstrate that human, financial, and technological resources are concentrated appropriately and effectively on accomplishing the library's mission.

THE LIBRARY'S MISSION STATEMENT

A library's mission statement expresses the overall purpose for the library, incorporating beliefs, concepts, and values on which the library's program and activities are based and the goals toward which all staff efforts are directed. The adoption of a mission statement usually requires input from, or approval by, library trustees, regents, the city or village council, or the board of directors of a corporation of which the library is a part. The mission statement is the guiding document for all of the library's objectives, including the strategies and specific tactics that the librarian will follow to accomplish them.

The library's mission statement provides an assertion of purpose and sets a philosophy of operation for the library. By articulating a clearly stated mission, the trustees or senior managers who oversee the library relate it to its community, confident that all of its activities are in support of a common, agreed-upon purpose.

An example of a mission statement is, "The mission of the Library is to work as an agent and partner within the community to promote quality of life, individual self-development, and the enrichment of the citizenry through the provision of services for the dissemination of knowledge and the preservation of society's cultural heritage."

The successful library manager realizes that all decisions on strategy, marketing, services, priorities, and every other management choice—from recruitment and staff promotion to organization developments that affect the library—are made with the furtherance of the library's mission in mind.

A library's *program* consists of all activities that the librarians and library staff pursue over the course of the year. (In some academic libraries, the library's program is called its *academic agenda.*) It is the responsibility of the library director to implement and execute the program that the library trustees, or the organization's senior management, have approved. Further, the program itself might be given a name. For example, "Operation Library Information Technology" might be chosen during a year when the program's focus is on the development, implementation, or extension of new technology.

Once the library program's initiatives and objectives are established, a plan of action, or *strategy,* is identified to accomplish each program objective. Suppose that a program objective is to increase use of the library during the coming year. Six strategies to accomplish this might be as follows:

1. Increase library hours;

2. Strengthen collections;

3. Sponsor special library programs;

4. Strengthen technological efforts;

5. Make the library more appealing to clients;

6. Increase personnel to provide services.

Each strategy can be accomplished through one or more activities, or *tactics*. Librarians then apply statistics to measure the success of the tactics. Example 3-1 illustrates various strategies and associated tactics to accomplish an objective.

Example 3-1

Library Objectives, Strategies, and Tactics

Library trustees ask the director to propose six strategies and associated tactics to increase library use during the year.

Analysis

The objective is to increase library use during the year.

Strategy 1: Increase hours
Tactic 1: Open at 8 A.M., Monday through Saturday
Tactic 2: Open at 11 A.M., Sunday
Tactic 3: Close at 10 P.M., Sunday through Thursday
Tactic 4: Close at 6 P.M., Friday and Saturday

Strategy 2: Strengthen collections
Tactic 1: Purchase multiple copies of current best-sellers
Tactic 2: Purchase more children's picture books
Tactic 3: Purchase current nonfiction best-sellers
Tactic 4: Purchase more financial and investing resources
Tactic 5: Acquire captioned videos for the hearing impaired

Strategy 3: Sponsor special library programs
Tactic 1: Present monthly children's programs (puppets, storytelling, readings)
Tactic 2: Offer monthly adult programs (entertainment, lectures)
Tactic 3: Start an adult great books discussion group
Tactic 4: Develop a literacy program
Tactic 5: Sponsor an English-as-a-second-language program in the library

Strategy 4: Strengthen technology efforts
Tactic 1: Make electronic resources available through a LAN
Tactic 2: Provide Internet access for community use
Tactic 3: Provide computer bulletin board access
Tactic 4: Provide more adaptive technology for challenged persons
Tactic 5: Provide more terminals for online catalog access

Strategy 5: Make the library more appealing to clients
Tactic 1: Follow ADA guidelines to reduce barriers for disabled
Tactic 2: Improve lighting throughout the library

Tactic 3: Make the book security system less obtrusive
Tactic 4: Rent or buy decorative plants to provide a more friendly atmosphere
Tactic 5: Hold workshops for staff to learn American Sign Language
Tactic 6: Hold staff workshops for dealing with difficult clients
Strategy 6: Increase personnel to provide services
Tactic 1: Hire additional staff to perform paraprofessional tasks
Tactic 2: Hire additional personnel for professional tasks

A library's program may have several initiatives containing multiple objectives, dozens of strategies, and hundreds of tactics. These will vary with the financial and personnel resources available to accomplish them. Some librarians mistakenly think that a written library program is necessary only if there is a large budget. The purpose of the program statement, however, is to describe a plan that is related strategically to the library's resources. Developing the plan is not the task of the library director alone but of each manager and supervisor, since everyone's participation is needed for success. Example 3-2 illustrates an urban college's initiatives and program to strengthen the role of the library in the academic life of the college.

Example 3-2

A College Library—Initiatives and Program

An urban college serves 12,000 FTE students. The library is involved broadly in providing print and digital services, audiovisual media services, and teleconferencing as part of the college's distance learning activities. Its program is called Operation Library Success and consists of four initiatives that the librarian refers to as *ABCD*. These initiatives are as follows:

A—Access to Collections for Success

B—Building Collections for Success

C—Commitment of Librarians and Staff for Student Success

D—Development of Library Infrastructure for Success

The platform for all initiatives is founded on the library's faculty and staff commitment to provide the academic community with effective and efficient information services. These promote student retention, assist faculty in increasing knowledge, and help students to succeed in their academic pursuits.

The library's program and its progress should be discussed at every staff meeting. Frequent discussion serves to promote consensus, commitment, and participation. Library staff meetings also help each staff member to more fully understand that the library's business is to serve the information needs of users.

A major ongoing responsibility of the librarian is to conduct a performance evaluation of the library's program. These assessments usually are conducted at least annually. Without an evaluation that uses well-understood performance measures, the librarian will not know the extent to which the library's desired outcomes are being achieved. Equally unfortunate, the trustees or organization's senior managers also will be unaware of the program's status.

THE ROLE OF PERFORMANCE MEASURES IN LIBRARY PROGRAM DEVELOPMENT

Performance measures are quantitative assessment ratios that are used to demonstrate strengths, weaknesses, and areas for improvement. Performance measures are helpful in determining whether program goals are being achieved. They also provide markers that signal the need for further study, planning, and actions that are necessary for program improvement. Finally, performance measures help to maintain a results-oriented approach.

Quantity, it has been shown, is not always an effective indicator of performance, however. That is, more activity does not necessarily mean better activity. Analyses of library services based entirely on quantity are becoming less persuasive to administrators. Difficult financial choices cannot be justified on the strength of increases in absolute numbers alone. Today, public and institutional financial planners look beyond raw numbers to scrutinize the merit of activities. Thus, the librarian must work constantly to emphasize the value of the library's service to the institution or the community.

To this end, librarians can use performance measures to place numbers in a context that relates them to the *quality* of library services. The delivery of high-quality services and products is a universal objective among successful organizations, and performance measures are among a librarian's most effective tools for continuous library improvement. When *output measures* are achievable, realistic, specific, and timely, they provide a methodology to measure the gaps between the library's current and desired state. They provide the strong evidence needed to act on reengineering opportunities within the library's collections, activities, and personnel structure.

Many professional organizations have sponsored task forces and committees that have worked to develop performance indicators for libraries. The result of their work can include performance measures, outcome measures, benchmarks, best-practice indicators, and indicators of efficiency. Librarians can then apply these performance indicators to identify, measure, and monitor on an annual or more frequent basis. Of course, no single measure can be used to demonstrate that a library program is meeting all of its objectives. Indeed, two libraries with the same performance ratio may view it from completely differing perspectives.

There are many books on library performance measures, particularly in a public library context. One such book is *Research for Decision Making: Methods for Librarians* by Robert Swisher and Charles R. McClure (ALA, 1984). Another excellent work that provides guidelines and data collection suggestions is *Output Measures for Public Libraries: A Manual of Standardized Procedures* by Nancy A. Van House et al. (ALA, 1987).

Figure 3-1 lists many commonly used performance measures, grouped under several broad headings. Administrative and finance measures assess the library administrative performance. Community penetration measures assess the extent of the community's awareness and use of library services. Resource management measures provide a snapshot of the use of resources of money, materials, facilities, and staff. Lastly, user service performance measures assess the degree to which library clientele borrow library materials, ask questions, and attend programs sponsored by the library.

FIGURE 3-1 ▓ Selected Performance Measures

1. Administration and Finance Performance

   Library support per capita
   Material expenditures as a percentage of all library expenditures
   Percentage of staff participating in continuing education
   Salaries and wages as a percentage of total expenditure

2. Community Penetration Performance

   Community awareness of library services
   In-library use of materials per capita
   Library visits per capita
   Per capita circulation
   Registered borrowers per capita
   Users as a percentage of the community's population

3. Resource Management Performance

   Collection turnover rate
   Juveniles per capita
   Library holdings per capita
   Percentage of holdings intended for juveniles
   Range of hours library is open
   Square footage per capita
   Staff to circulation ratio
   Staff to population ratio

4. User Services Performance

   Adult program attendance per adult capita
   Author fill rate
   Borrower's fill rate
   Document delivery rate
   Interlibrary loan fill rate
   Juvenile percentage of circulation
   Juvenile percentage of materials budget
   Juvenile program attendance per juvenile capita
   Program attendance per capita
   Reference fill rate
   Reference questions per capita
   Subject fill rate
   Title fill rate
   Titles found
   Titles sought

Selected Library Performance Measures

Some of the following material on performance measures is loosely based on the text of authors Nancy A. Van House et al. (*Output Measures for Public Libraries: A Manual of*

Standardized Procedures, ALA, 1987) and Robert Swisher and Charles R. McClure (*Research for Decision Making: Methods for Librarians,* ALA, 1984), used with permission.

Per Capita Circulation

A ratio that yields the number of library items borrowed by each person in the jurisdiction population in a year is per capita circulation. The ratio is expressed as follows:

$$\frac{\text{annual circulation}}{\text{jurisdiction population}}.$$

It reveals the number of items borrowed per person in the community in one year. If the ratio is greater than one, then the annual circulation (numerator) exceeds the jurisdictional population (denominator). The more the numerator exceeds the denominator, the higher the per capita circulation. That is, if annual circulation is twice the size of the jurisdictional population, the per capita circulation is two. If the annual circulation is four times the size of the jurisdictional population, then the per capita circulation is four.

An example is helpful to illustrate how to calculate the ratio for per capita circulation. Suppose that a public library with a jurisdictional population of 15,000 circulated 161,975 items last year. The per capita circulation is computed as follows:

$$\text{per capita circulation} = \frac{\text{annual circulation}}{\text{jurisdiction population}}$$

$$= \frac{161,975}{15,000} \text{ which is } 10.79 \text{ or } 10.8.$$

The interpretation is that each person in the jurisdictional population checked out 10.8 items during the year.

Calculating per capita circulation is easy. The more difficult question is whether 10.8 per capita is a "good" number. In order to make such a determination, the librarian should have an idea of what the per capita circulation should be. Next, he or she will compare the statistic with the library's own baseline data for per capita circulation. For example, suppose that the librarian combines this year's result with data from the two previous years, yielding {10.5, 10.7, 10.8}. This demonstrates a slight increase over time, but does not yield information comparing performance with other libraries.

To determine that standing, librarians may benchmark data from other similar libraries, particularly those that might be emulated. For example, suppose that five similar libraries have current per capita statistics of {12.3, 11.9, 12.1, 12.7, 12.6}. These results may suggest that an increasing per capita circulation of 10.8 is developing toward the level at which similar libraries already operate.

It is important, however, to standardize the way circulation is counted. Not all librarians count circulation in the same way. For example, the policy at one library might be to count a title published in two volumes as a single circulation. At another library, the policy may be to count the circulation of each volume as a separate circulation. In fact, a six-cassette videotape should be counted as six rather than one. This makes sense, particularly if an item that is part of a series or set can be borrowed separately. This standardization in counting can be easily accomplished by giving each item its own bar code.

Collection Turnover Rate

A ratio that reveals the number of times materials in the library's collection are checked out over a specified period is the *collection turnover rate*. It is a measure of the intensity of use members of the community make of the collection. The ratio is expressed as follows:

$$\frac{\text{annual circulation}}{\text{total number of library items owned}}.$$

The library's total holdings include all materials that are owned by the library, both cataloged and noncataloged. To illustrate the calculation, suppose that a library's annual circulation is 200,000 items and that the library's holdings consist of 50,000 items. The collection turnover rate is computed as follows:

$$\text{collection turnover rate} = \frac{\text{annual circulation}}{\text{total library holdings}}$$
$$= \frac{200,000}{50,000} \text{ which is 4.0.}$$

The interpretation is that, on average, each library-owned item (both cataloged and noncataloged) circulates four times in one year.

The collection turnover rate yields some practical information about a library's holdings:

- A high turnover rate indicates a high circulation (numerator) compared to the collection size (denominator).
- The more the collection reflects the community's interest, the more the items will circulate.
- A low turnover rate may suggest that a lot of the collection is tied up in noncirculating reference materials that people cannot check out.
- A long circulation period will keep library resources out of circulation, making items unavailable for use by others.
- A low turnover rate may be related to having too few circulating copies of popular items.
- A low turnover rate may mean that the library has a lot of materials that no one wants to borrow.

In-Library Use of Materials per Capita

A ratio that reveals the number of items used in the library in one year is the *in-library use of materials per capita* ratio, expressed as follows:

$$\frac{\text{estimated annual number of materials used in the library}}{\text{jurisdictional population}}.$$

This ratio relies on an estimate for the annual total number of materials that are used in the library. A librarian estimates this total by counting the materials that are used in the library during an "average" week.

One way to obtain this count is to ask all library users not to reshelve the materials they use while in the library. During a one-week period, staff pass through the library at half-hour intervals and count the number of books, journals, and other items that have been left on tables or in book carts. Materials that people must obtain from the librarian are also counted. By multiplying the typical week's total by 52, the librarian can determine the estimated annual number of items used. This value is then divided by the jurisdictional population to arrive at the per capita in-library use of materials.

A high measure of per capita in-library use of materials may indicate that the library has a good reference collection, since people are using materials in the library. Further, it suggests that some people spend time in the library in order to use the reference materials. Alternately, a low measure suggests that people who come into the library are not making use of materials while there. This is not necessarily negative, however. Patrons may prefer to check out a circulating copy of a reference book rather than use the reserve copy. On the other hand, a low measure may suggest that the library does not have a comfortable or user-friendly atmosphere.

Library Visits per Capita

A ratio that yields the number of visits per person in the community in one year is the *library visits per capita* ratio, expressed as follows:

$$\frac{\text{annual total number of library visits}}{\text{jurisdictional population}}.$$

To gather data to determine the number of persons who enter the library for whatever purpose during an "average" week, one or more clerks can be stationed within view of the library's entrance(s) to count all persons who enter the library for any purpose. At the end of the typical week, the tally is multiplied by 52 to arrive at an annual count.

Program Attendance per Capita

A ratio that reveals how many persons of all ages in the jurisdictional community that attended programs sponsored by the library is the *program attendance per capita* ratio, expressed as follows:

$$\frac{\text{program attendance}}{\text{jurisdictional population}}.$$

Suppose that a librarian records program attendance for all activities that the library hosts, sponsors, or cosponsors. Over the year, records show that 6250 people attended book talks, lectures, classes, dramas, puppet shows, movies, travelogues, or tours. In a community of 24,000 people, the per capita attendance is calculated as follows:

$$\text{program attendance per capita} = \frac{\text{annual program attendance}}{\text{jurisdictional population}}$$

$$= \frac{6250}{24,000} \text{ which is } 0.26.$$

One interpretation of this statistic is that each member of the community, on average, attends 0.26 programs per year. In other words, about one out of every four members of the jurisdictional population attends a library program at least once each year.

Registration per Capita

A ratio that reveals the percent of the population that are registered library borrowers is the registration per capita ratio, expressed as follows:

$$\frac{\text{library registration}}{\text{jurisdictional population}}.$$

The numerator is the number of persons who are registered borrowers of the library. The denominator (size of the jurisdictional population) will always exceed the numerator. This means that the value of the ratio will always be less than 100%.

Suppose that a public library has issued library cards to 27,845 persons and that the library serves a community that has a jurisdictional population of 30,000. The per capita library registration is computed as follows:

$$\text{registration per capita} = \frac{\text{library registration}}{\text{jurisdictional population}}$$

$$= \frac{27{,}845}{30{,}000} \text{ which is 0.928 or 92.8\%.}$$

In interpreting data regarding per capita library registration, note that the measure's maximum value is 100%. Further, this measure gauges a person's intention to use the library. In reality, that person might actually visit or borrow anything from the library only rarely or perhaps never. On the other hand, a low value for the measure signals that many people in the community have not registered for library cards. The reasons for their failure to do so could be many. For example, people may not know about the library and its activities, or they may not feel that the library can meet their information needs.

Cautions and Opportunities in Using Performance Measures

A continuing discussion among librarians is how performance measures can be meaningfully applied to a library program that, by its nature, is multidimensional, interdependent, and complex. There is little disagreement that the individual elements of a library's program are difficult to separate for measurement purposes. Some librarians object to applying performance ratios that they feel are too simple, consisting of little more than tallies of transactions such as items circulated, items photocopied, and items shelved. In contrast, other performance measures are regarded as too complex, involving counts of staff interactions with clientele and bibliographies and pathfinders that are prepared.

Nonetheless, performance ratios do represent a way to gather information about the output level of specific library activities. This information, used in tandem with the baseline data and benchmarks, is both pertinent and enlightening to library trustees.

For example, suppose the librarian wishes to stimulate discussion among trustees or senior management about expansion of the library's facilities. Broadly, he or she would relate information about the current adequacy of the library's facility and the access patterns within the library. Some of the following assessment points might be included in the presentation:

1. Adequacy of library facilities

   - Americans with Disabilities Act (ADA) compliance
   - Complaints (regarding collections, equipment, facilities, services, staff)
   - Hours, including weekend service
   - Library traffic at various service points and areas
   - Program attendance per capita
   - Seating capacity
   - Square footage per capita
   - Visits per capita

2. Access patterns

   - Accessibility of library by car and public transportation
   - Parking availability
   - Range of services when library is open
   - Remote access use (BBS, dial-up, Internet, teleconferencing)
   - Telephone reference
   - Visits by hour
   - Visits at service points

BUDGETING AS AN AID TO PLANNING AND CONTROL

The library's budget is the expression in numerical terms of the library's plan. It is a planning document used to allocate resources that are required to achieve objectives within a specified period.

Few budgets, including those of libraries, are allocated without substantial discussion among senior managers or trustees. As a result, budget planning accomplishes at least two main purposes: it represents the library's objectives in monetary terms, offering a standard by which performance can be measured, and it necessitates periodic communication about the library's priorities and objectives.

Types of Budgets: Nonmonetary, Financial, and Operating Budgets

Nonmonetary Budgets

Budgets expressed in units such as physical facilities space, time, output, or some other quantifiable factor are *nonmonetary budgets*. For example, a library's *labor budget* shows the number of staff hours allocated to library service points such as the circulation desk, interlibrary loan, or reserves. A *space budget* identifies the square feet available for the circulation desk, group study or meeting rooms, stacks, or staff work areas. To track output, librarians may identify a *production budget* for cataloging, shelving and reshelving, and technical ser-

TABLE 3-1 ▌ Library Summer Student Staffing in Hours

	July	August	Total	Percent
Circulation	338	75	413	16%
Media services	630	172	802	31
Periodicals	330	305	635	25
Reserve desk	255	140	395	16
Technical services	165	135	300	12
Total	1,718	827	2,545	100%

vice activities associated with shelving print and digital materials. Likewise, a *time budget* shows a sequence of activities with associated time expectations for completion.

Table 3-1 illustrates a labor budget of hours that are available for summer staffing. Although it is not a monetary budget, since its focus is on staff hours rather than money, the librarian could easily determine dollar amounts by multiplying the wage per hour (assuming employees are paid a uniform hourly wage) times the number of budgeted hours. For example, if the wage is $8 per hour, summer staffing will cost $20,360 [$20,360 = $8 × 2545].

In developing a staff-hours budget, the librarian might list each staff member's name under the appropriate library area. A listing by name makes it easy to track the number of hours each employee has been allocated to work, whether the work hour limit for a given employee is being met, and the total work hours allocated overall for each staff member.

Their lack of financial content does not make nonmonetary budgets less useful to supervisors, section managers, and department heads. Typically, these persons do not need to know extensive details about staffing or dollar amounts in order to carry out the responsibilities of their positions.

Financial Budgets

Another category of library budget, the *financial budget*, shows the sources and uses of cash. Examples of financial budgets include the following: a balance sheet budget that shows assets and liabilities; a cash-flow budget that shows income and expenditures; and a capital expenditure budget that shows the cost of acquiring major assets.

Capital expenditures are expenditures for the construction or purchase of a building or the purchase and installation of major equipment. Determinations about when and how much to spend on capital facilities and equipment are among the most significant decisions that senior managers make. For this reason, librarians need to understand financial budgets in general and capital expenditure budgets in particular.

Not surprisingly, decisions about capital expenditures are not made quickly. Thus, a specific request for each capital equipment item will almost certainly be required, and capital expenditures for the fiscal year are, most likely, determined and budgeted far in advance.

A particular institution, for example, may define a capital expenditure as an expense for a durable item that will last for at least three years and that costs $500 or more. Hence, if the library needs a plain-paper fax machine that costs $750 and the library's capital expenditure threshold is $500, the fax machine must be regarded as a capital expenditure and therefore be purchased from the library's capital equipment budget.

Many libraries do not have a specific capital equipment budget, however, and must purchase needed equipment as part of the parent organization's capital equipment budget. In most cases, making such a purchase is an involved process.

Various examples of capital expenditures are helpful to characterize them:

- The cost of constructing or buying physical plant (buildings) and equipment, including freight, taxes, and installation charges (When secondhand or used property is acquired, the cost of any repairs that are necessary to put the purchase in good operating condition before placing it in use also is a capital expenditure. Repair costs after the equipment is in service are budgeted as a regular expense, however.)

- The cost of adding a floor or a wing to an existing building to enlarge it

- The cost of making such improvements as adding an elevator, replacing a staircase with an escalator, or replacing lighting

How, then, is an expenditure on books and journals categorized? This is a reasonable question that an interested librarian can discuss with the library's or the parent institution's accountants. Presently, there is no accounting standard or requirement that books or journals be recorded as assets on an institution's financial statement, though it could be argued that books and journals are capital assets. However, if an institution records resource materials as an asset, depreciation accounting practices are appropriate since most items such as books and journals are dated. While there is no general life expectancy that is commonly used, an accountant would probably accept a three-year to ten-year period as reasonable. This logic would not apply to a rare book collection, though, since such items likely retain or increase in value over time. In museum management, the practice is to not record a collection as a capital asset. This is also true of most libraries.

Operating Budgets

The library budget includes a third category—an *operating budget*—that shows the financial resources necessary to maintain current operations at a successful level. There are many examples of operating budgets, including a revenue budget that shows sources of library income, a sales budget that shows the sale of library services, a profit budget that shows anticipated library income from activities or services, and an expense budget that shows anticipated expenses for activities conducted over a given period such as a year.

A budget's structure and complexity depend upon the institution of which the library is a part. For example, a public library most likely will use the same budget scheme as the village or city in which it is located, while an academic library will use the same budget scheme as the college or university of which it is a part. The three general types of operating budgets considered in this text are lump sum, line item, and program planning. Each type is discussed briefly in the following paragraphs.

A *lump-sum operating budget* is an allocation of a single (lump) sum of money for operations. For example, a librarian may be allocated a lump sum of $890,000. These moneys are not divided into categories nor are they earmarked for specific purposes. It is the librarian's task in this case to decide how to divide the funds among personnel and nonpersonnel accounts. Usually, if the librarian is allocated a lump-sum budget, he or she expresses the funding in a line-item format.

In a *line-item operating budget,* moneys are allocated for a specific period, such as one year. Reviews may be held monthly or quarterly, but the moneys span one year. In a line-

TABLE 3-2 ▍ Village Library Line-Item Budget

Expenses		Month #10	Year-to-date	Annual budget
511110	Regular salaries	$24,358	$157,204	$365,656
511300	Salaries (overtime)	0	0	0
511410	Salaries (part-time reg.)	28,255	180,258	412,207
511510	Medical insurance	4,120	20,930	59,750
511520	Dental insurance	250	1,192	2,900
521110	Building maintenance	11,211	27,093	35,000
531782	Contractual services	5,625	39,463	68,300

item budget, the emphasis is on classifications of expenditure. Each classification becomes a line item in the budget, hence the name. For example, moneys might be earmarked for three line items such as human resources, collection acquisitions, and services. More generally, however, a line-item budget uses a chart of categories for identifying expenses and revenue sources and usually includes a dozen or more line items.

Table 3-2 shows a library's revenue budget for a municipality. The expense line items are drawn from the city's operating budget. Notice that all expense items begin with the digit 5. Revenue-producing categories would begin with a different digit to differentiate them from expense items. Table 3-2 shows some selected expenses from a line-item budget.

Note the "Contractual services" item in Table 3-2. Some budgets provide categories of contractual services to facilitate the monitoring of various service expenses. These can include audiovisual and equipment maintenance, cataloging, computer and database maintenance, general legal counsel, janitorial and custodial housekeeping, liability insurance, security services, special library programming, and temporary personnel, as well as other services.

Many institutions *encumber* budget moneys. This action is triggered when a purchase order is issued. For example, an *encumbrance* for a $100 purchase means that $100 of the library budget is earmarked to satisfy the purchase order. The $100 cannot be used for any other purpose until the encumbrance is satisfied. Satisfaction occurs when either payment is made on an invoice for the purchase or the purchase order is cancelled. Of course, if the invoice is for $98, then $2 would become available for spending. On the other hand, if the invoice received is for $102, an additional $2 is accounted as spent. The system does have advantages, as librarians working at institutions that do not encumber funds would attest. Many have had the unpleasant experience of receiving goods and services after the close of the fiscal year and wondering how the invoice will be paid, since few institutions allow budgeted moneys to be carried forward from one fiscal year to the next.

A *program-planning budget* places less emphasis on expenditures by category and more on the projects on which moneys will be spent. Instead of a single budget, there is a separate budget for each project that comprises the program. The program-planning budget includes all personnel and nonpersonnel categories.

Usually, a project consists of a collection of activities that are designed to accomplish a specific purpose. Institutions that use program planning also require each budget to meet a minimum dollar threshold, such as $25,000 or $50,000. It is not unusual to see a program that consists of three or more projects.

TABLE 3-3 ▊ Town Library Program Budget

Chart of accounts	Project 1	Project 2	Project 3	Total
100 Full-time staff	$28,500	$ 79,375	$130,000	$237,875
120 Fringe benefits	8,550	23,800	39,000	71,350
130 Part-time staff	16,725	7,500	47,500	71,725
200 Supplies	6,250	4,125	7,425	17,800
330 Books, magazines	17,125		225,900	243,025
338 Binding	3,500		65,000	68,500
410 Postage		2,875	1,750	4,625
710 Miscellaneous		750	975	1,725
Total	$80,650	$118,425	$517,550	$716,625

Table 3-3 illustrates a library program that includes three projects. These may be reference services, technical services, and special collections, or public services, library instruction, and acquisitions, or any number of other projects separately identified.

The librarian's total budget is $716,625. However, rather than a lump sum for the whole program, or an allocation by line-item category for the projects combined as a group, each library project has its own line-item budget allocation. Hence, Project 1 has an allocation of $80,650, Project 2 an allocation of $118,425, and Project 3 an allocation of $517,550.

Program budgeting allows the librarian to identify specific library projects and to individually itemize project expense, thus tying project objectives more closely to budget. Further, in the program-planning budgeting process, the librarian has the flexibility to strengthen, deemphasize, curtail, or eliminate a project and its activities. Of course, this also is possible in a line-item budget, but in a program-planning budget it is evident which projects have been allocated the larger budgets and which the lesser. This means that, in effect, a program-planning budget can be used to implement a strategic program change.

A new or restructured initiative that changes the direction of an organization's activities is a *strategic program change.* For example, when the electronic catalog replaced the card catalog, libraries experienced a strategic program change that was followed by increased office automation and the introduction of other high-technology equipment. Of course, a strategic program change is not possible unless specific moneys targeted for personnel, equipment, supplies, and other resources accompany it.

In addition, a program-planning budget can be beneficial in the event of a budget reduction. For example, if the librarian must accommodate a 10% budget reduction, rather than reduce each budget line item where possible by 10% (a process called *bleeding*), the librarian may make a *vertical cut* in the program. That is, the librarian may deemphasize or eliminate a specific project, activity, or group of activities. This way, all projects and associated activities do not suffer the effects of the budget reduction.

A program-planning budget affords considerable flexibility in describing a program and in crafting the budget to support activities. For the most part, trustees or senior managers are less interested in how moneys are programmed in the library's budget than in the results that are achieved. Thus, the librarian must keep the library performance-oriented and continually justify and publicize library activities. Well-defined projects and specific activities are more likely to be easily approved and funded at the expense of ongoing activities that are poorly understood or ambiguous.

Budget Performance Analysis

A key responsibility of a librarian is to continually inform the library's policy-making board (trustees) or other senior management about the library's successes and its outputs. This means providing reports that demonstrate progress in meeting the library's mission. Indeed, in today's climate of cost-reduction models, continual reporting is critical in order to avoid the budget-balancing reductions described in the media by euphemisms such as involuntary severance, realignment, recision, reduction-in-force (RIF), reengineering, repositioning, reshaping, re-trenchment, rightsizing, schedule adjustments, slowing of growth, and strengthening of effectiveness. Regardless of the label, these programs each translate to a smaller library staff.

Some librarians and trustees believe that the objective in managing a library budget is to underspend it. This is not correct, however. Instead, the purpose of a budget allocation is to provide moneys to accomplish specific purposes. If moneys allocated to the library's budget go unspent, the library's objectives may not be accomplished. Further, overspending or underspending of a library's budget generally indicates poor planning. If a librarian anticipates overspending or underspending, his or her senior manager or the trustees' finance subcommittee should be consulted so that proper planning can occur. However, unauthorized overspending is one sure way to lose credibility (and perhaps a job) within any organization. Likewise, underspending reflects poor planning because funds "stalled" in the library's budget are not available for constructive use elsewhere.

A deviation from the amount of money that was originally programmed for an activity is known as a *budget variance*. For example, if $5000 is budgeted but $7000 is spent, the budget variance for the category is $2000 [$-$2000 $=$ $5000 $-$ $7000]. The overspent amount may be written as $-$2000, or as ($2000), to indicate a negative amount. As a percentage, the budget variance, based on $5000, is 40% [40% $=$ 2000/5000].

If the dollar amounts are relatively small, a variance of this size may have little impact. However, a 40% variance for a large budget is significant. Most organizations periodically compare budget expenditures with budget allocations in a process called *budget performance analysis*. Frequently, such an analysis is made by quarters, or three-month periods, as in Example 3-3. For the calendar year, January, February, and March comprise the first quarter, April through June the second quarter, and so on.

In budget performance analysis, a side-by-side comparison of actual and budgeted data and all variances are identified and explained, particularly those that exceed a specified percentage or dollar amount. A useful guideline for budget variances is to be within a maximum variance of 8% at the end of the first quarter, 6% at mid-year, 4% by the end of the third quarter, and within a 2% budget variance by year-end.

Example 3-3

Determining Allocation and Expenditures by Quarters

A librarian has a materials budget of $435,000. These funds allow the librarian to pay for journal and serial subscriptions, to purchase books and audiovisual materials, to acquire CD-ROM database access, and to buy office supplies. The institution's fiscal year is the same as the federal fiscal year, which is October through September. The library's periodical and serial subscriptions consume one-half of the library's budget. Moneys for all other items are spent approximately equally over the fiscal year. Thus, the librarian expects to spend $217,500 on journals and serials and the remaining $217,500 in twelve equal amounts. At year-end, the librarian's budget record shows the following cumulative total amounts expended at the end of each quarter: first quarter, $240,000; second quarter, $300,000; third quarter, $394,000; and fourth quarter, $434,500.

1. Identify the quarter in which the librarian most likely authorized payment for the journal/serial subscriptions. Why was payment made during that period?
2. Determine the librarian's budget allocation by quarters.
3. Evaluate the librarian's budget management, applying the rule of being within budget by 8% at the end of the first quarter, 6% at the end of the second quarter, 4% at the end of the third quarter, and 2% at the end of the fourth quarter.

Analysis

Total expenditures	Budget allocated	Actual expended	Variance	Percent difference
First quarter	$271,875	$240,000	$31,875	− 13.3%
Second quarter	326,250	300,000	26,250	− 8.75
Third quarter	380,625	394,000	− 13,375	+ 3.5
Fourth quarter	435,000	434,500	500	− 0.1

1. Journal vendors generally require advance payment for a library's subscriptions. Since most subscriptions are on the regular calendar year of January through December, payment must be made before December 31. (Of course, payment made in December may mean that January or February issues will not be received, since the vendor requires processing time.) For a library on an October through September fiscal year, subscriptions are paid in the first quarter.

2. Since the library's fiscal year is October through September, the first quarter includes October, November, and December. The dollar amounts for the first quarter are the journal/serial subscription expenditures, plus the expenditures for other purchases made during the months of October, November, and December. The journal/serial subscriptions expenditure is $217,500 [$217,500 = $435,000/2]. The expenditure for all other items during the first quarter is $217,500. The monthly expenditure for supplies is $18,125 [$18,125 = $217,500/12]. Supply expenditure for the first quarter is thus $54,375 [$54,375 = 3 × $18,125]. Hence, the first quarter anticipated expenditures are $271,875 [$271,875 = $217,500 + $54,375].

3. As shown in the table, actual first-quarter expenditures are $240,000. However, the budget amount for the end of the first quarter is $271,875, so the budget is underspent by $31,875 [$31,875 = $271,875 − $240,000]. The reason for the underspending may be that expenses are typically slowed during the fourth quarter of the previous year and the librarian may not have had an opportunity to gear up acquisitions, or perhaps the budget was received late and the librarian did not begin spending until the budget was approved.

   Expenditures for the second quarter are supply costs for January, February, and March. This amount is $54,375 [$54,375 = 3 × $18,125]. Added to this figure are the first-quarter expenditures, for a total of $326,250 [$326,250 = $54,375 + $271,875].

   Second-quarter expenses are at a variance of 8.75 percent. The target is to have expenses within 6 percent of budget by the end of the second quarter. An explanation for the variance might be that the librarian expected an invoice to come during the second quarter but received it in the third quarter instead.

Third-quarter expenses are within the 4-percent margin. Fourth-quarter expenses are on target and within budget. Overall, the librarian managed the budget well, since it was within the 2-percent margin.

Budget management requires careful pacing of expenditures. For example, books ordered through a vendor often are offered at a discount that the librarian must estimate. For this reason, many librarians process book orders throughout the year, but they reduce or hold back orders during the last six or eight weeks of the fiscal year, or they hold a year-end invoice and process it at the beginning of the library's next fiscal year.

SPECIALIZED RATIOS

Benefit-Cost Analysis

A decision-making technique, *benefit-cost analysis* is used to develop quantitative information on how to allocate resources. Figure 3-2 illustrates examples of projects to which benefit-cost analysis could be effectively applied.

In conducting a benefit-cost analysis, activities, equipment, or projects are compared on the basis of cost outlays and on the cash value of real or perceived benefits. In making this comparison, data are gathered and analyzed, projection tables are prepared and interpreted, and the advice of consultants or other professionals may be sought. The cash costs for each project are then computed and compared, and the decision becomes obvious about how to direct resources most efficiently. The benefit-cost objective, in short, is to allocate money in such a way as to obtain the most "bang for the buck."

Benefit-cost analysis is an application of the techniques used in ratio analysis. It is a methodology for comparing the cost of initiating or continuing an activity to the economic benefits that the activity produces. The benefit-cost ratio can be expressed as follows:

$$\text{benefit-cost ratio:} \frac{\text{estimated benefits}}{\text{costs}}$$

FIGURE 3-2   Benefit-Cost Analysis Applied to Projects

- Converting library space used for one purpose to satisfy another, such as turning a staff room into a special collections space
- Contracting janitorial services with an outside agency to reduce custodial staff
- Outsourcing cataloging and other technical services to reduce or refocus current technical services personnel
- Converting the library's heating system from oil to gas
- Renovating or expanding the library
- Developing a special collection
- Purchasing rather than leasing a telephone system

In a benefit-cost analysis, benefits are the sum of the activity's tangible and intangible costs. In performing the analysis, the cash value of each is determined. Hence:

benefits = tangible benefits + intangible benefits.

The cash value of tangible benefits is easier to quantify in monetary terms than intangible benefits. A few examples of savings due to tangible benefits are as follows:

- Cost savings through purchase so that leases can be terminated
- Cost savings from expanded use of technology, saving employee work time
- Supply savings through volume purchase discounts
- Salary expense savings due to personnel reductions:
  staff reassignment
  substitute staffing using paraprofessional personnel
  substitute staffing using part-time or adjunct personnel
  staff reductions
- Cost offsets through service hour modifications

Intangible benefits, the other component in the benefits equation, are of two types. They are those that have a quantifiable economic or monetary value and those that cannot be assigned a dollar value. An example of a quantifiable intangible benefit is the copyright of materials produced by the library. Such intellectual property might include publications (pamphlets, books, published bibliographies), licenses (software produced by library personnel), and patents and trademarks that have been registered by library personnel or owned by the library through purchase or donation.

Other intangibles are not so easy to evaluate. For example, no one can easily put a price on the pleasure children receive from attending storyhour or seeing a puppet show in the children's room. Further, it would be difficult to quantify the quality of living improvement brought to a community through its library's programs in a host of areas, including adult literacy, film series, and gardening seminars. Lastly, it would be impossible to assign value to the number of lives saved as a result of library-sponsored programs on drug abuse, violence, first aid and CPR, or home safety.

Benefit-cost analysis is applied to determine the most rational allocation of resources. That is, the basic decision criterion is to accept only activities in which benefits exceed costs. For a librarian considering several worthy activities with benefits that exceed their costs, the benefit-cost framework can be employed to choose the option with the highest ranking. Figure 3-3 identifies three key observations about the benefit-cost ratio. Example 3-4 illustrates applying benefit-cost analysis to specific projects.

FIGURE 3-3 ▌ Key Observations about the Benefit-Cost Ratio

1. If the numerator is greater than the denominator, then benefits exceed costs.
2. If the denominator is greater than the numerator, then costs exceed benefits.
3. The benefit-cost ratio does not require monetary figures, though monetary units are most commonly used since they allow for a broader analysis and clearer understanding of costs for equipment, space, staff, and utilities.

Example 3-4

Benefit-Cost Ratio

1. Librarians estimate that the benefits of a project are $50,000 and the costs are $25,000. Determine the benefit-cost ratio.

Analysis

The benefit-cost ratio is $50,000/$25,000, or 2. Benefits exceed costs. The interpretation is that the librarian could accept the activity, providing there are funds for it, since the library could reasonably benefit by $2 for every $1 it expends in cost. In reality, the librarian may not be able to accept the activity, however, because there are not sufficient funds available to support it.

2. For another project, the estimated benefits are $30,000 and projected costs are $40,000. Determine the benefit-cost ratio.

Analysis

The benefit-cost ratio is $30,000/$40,000 or 0.75. Costs exceed benefits. Rationally, a librarian would not recommend this activity since, for every dollar spent, a benefit worth only seventy-five cents is returned. The allocation of resources to an activity that provides marginal benefits is inefficient and may show poor fiscal management.

Table 3-4 illustrates benefit-cost comparisons for five hypothetical library activities. In interpreting the table, note the use of the designation ($000s). This shorthand notation indicates that data values are recorded in thousands of dollars. Hence, the entry $210 represents $210,000.

An analysis of Table 3-4 reveals that, for all activities except the third, benefits exceed costs. The benefit-cost ratio of the third activity is 27,000/30,000 = 0.9. Assuming there are not compelling reasons to retain Activity 3, it should not be pursued because its costs exceed its benefits.

If the activities in Table 3-4 that have a favorable ratio are ranked from highest to lowest on the basis of benefit-cost ratio, the ranking for the projects is 2, 5, 1, and 4. That is, of all the projects, the second project has the highest benefit-to-cost ratio and the fourth project has the lowest. However, if the projects are ranked by *net benefit*—the difference between benefit and cost (B − C)—then the rank order of choice is projects 1, 2, 4, and 5.

TABLE 3-4   Benefit-Cost Ratios for Proposed Activities ($000s)

Activity	Benefit (B)	Cost (C)	Net benefit (B − C)	Benefit-cost Ratio (B/C)	Rank (B/C)	Rank (Net B)
1	$210	$147	$63	1.4	3	1
2	90	30	60	3.0	1	2
3	27	30	−3	0.9	5	5
4	3	2.5	0.5	1.2	4	3
5	0.3	0.2	0.1	1.5	2	4

In reality, librarians must select the final project(s) and allocate the necessary funds. This decision may depend considerably on the amount of available funds. If there are ample funds with which to work, a choice based either on net benefit or the benefit-cost ratio is acceptable. In cases of capital rationing, the ranking based on benefit-cost ratio is compelling since this is the direct ratio of per-dollar return from an activity. That is, an investment of $30,000 in the second activity will yield three times the benefit per dollar of cost. This is an important consideration in justifying new or existing activities, particularly in times of a budget reduction. Thus, benefit-cost analysis is a practical addition to the analytic technique toolbox.

There are some special concerns that librarians must consider, however, when applying benefit-cost analysis techniques. These are philosophical questions that make the technique less cut-and-dried than it may seem at first. For example, benefit-cost analysis can be a controversial technique because of the following:

1. A benefit-cost analysis does not necessarily consider future users. Rather, it is a static analysis of program effects that are apparent and in play at the time of the analysis.

2. Analysis of a benefit-cost study is complicated and not always impartial. Some costs may escape scrutiny.

3. In a benefit-cost analysis, benefits are generally more difficult to quantify than are the costs.

4. What constitutes a benefit and for whom it is a benefit is not always clear. For example, in an academic library, the librarian may see more benefits to the library to hire additional reference staff, while students may see more benefits to expanding the library's reserve collection.

5. Some costs may be encountered only later. These *downstream cost drivers,* which may not be anticipated in the librarian's benefit-cost study, include the costs for the purchase and inventory of critical components, equipment service contracts, scrap and rework services while new equipment is being aligned to function properly, shipping and handling for equipment and parts, staff travel to the vendor's site or other locations to learn how to operate and maintain equipment, and consultants or additional staffing by persons who can operate sophisticated new technology.

6. Benefit-cost analysis can be successfully applied in a for-profit enterprise but less so in a not-for-profit environment. The reason is that not-for-profit organizations provide activities that for-profit entities do not find profitable enough to perform. If the library offers some service that can be scaled to generate a profit, then a for-profit business might enter the market and begin to offer that service as well. Other companies, seeing profit potential in the activity, would then follow suit and commit resources to improving the service and to popularizing it. Faced with a scenario such as this, a librarian probably could not be successful at maintaining or growing a for-profit business within the library's framework. The library will always be a cost center. This does not mean, of course, that the librarian should not offer goods and services to the community and also try to recover the costs for doing so.

Finally, there are always personnel costs associated with changes in the library environment. These costs often are overlooked in a benefit-cost ratio proposal or discussion. In addition to the time required for planning and implementing a new system and training staff to use it, there may be losses in productivity due to lowered staff morale, unanticipated equipment breakdown, and the need for new system orientations for clients and staff.

Price Elasticity of Demand

A ratio from economics that is important to understand is *price elasticity of demand*. The ratio measures the extent to which the quantity of an item demanded responds to change in the item's price. The ratio can be written as follows:

$$\text{price elasticity of demand} = \frac{\text{percentage change in quantity demanded}}{\text{percentage change in price}}.$$

This ratio reveals some key information:

- If the numerator exceeds the denominator, demand is responsive to price change. This means that if a person regularly purchases an item for a certain amount, that person would be less inclined to buy the item if its price were appreciably more. In this situation, demand is *price elastic*.

- If the denominator exceeds the numerator, demand is not responsive to price change. This means that a person who wants to buy something would pay its cost despite a high price since the item is a "must-have" item. In this situation, demand is *price inelastic*.

Books and magazines for personal use are vital to the mind but price elastic to the consumer. Other price elastic products are jewelry, clothes, automobiles, and foods such as fruit and vegetables. Examples of price-inelastic products are gasoline, milk, some prescription drugs, and certain over-the-counter pharmaceuticals. For academic librarians who wish to avoid confrontation with faculty over cancelled journal subscriptions, the demand for scholarly journals represents inelastic demand. Scholarly journals, particularly science titles, have few or no substitutes and the titles are not published generally at any cost differential. In other words, librarians are not likely to cancel a scholarly journal subscription even though the publisher increases the price. Example 3-5 illustrates price elasticity of demand.

Example 3-5

Price Elasticity of Demand

1. A library subscribes to a national newspaper and its index. Despite a price increase of $500 for the index, the library orders a copy. Characterize the index's price elasticity.

   Analysis

   Librarian demand for the index is inelastic since there is no substitute for the publication and the librarian who ordered it considers the item a required purchase despite the increase in cost.

2. A small library subscribes to five popular news magazines. The publisher of one increases the price by $25. The librarian recommends cancellation. Characterize the news magazine's price elasticity.

Analysis

The library is small and the acquisitions librarian recommends that the subscription be cancelled. Demand is elastic because the librarian balks at paying the new price. Part of the librarian's reasoning may be that the remaining four news magazines provide adequate coverage.

Despite the simplicity of the price elasticity scenarios presented in Example 3-5, they introduce a unique consideration that is associated with journal subscription prices. Publishers seek to raise prices when there is inelastic demand, since price increases always result in an increase in the publisher's total revenues. Expectedly, a higher price will cause some buyers to choose not to subscribe or to cancel a subscription. Two events then occur. One is that the publisher's total revenue increases anyway because people renew their subscriptions at the higher price. The other is that the publisher's overall costs decrease because fewer copies are printed and mailed.

EFFICIENCY AND THE LAW OF DIMINISHING RETURNS

Efficiency involves achieving an objective at as low a cost as possible. An efficient activity is one in which outcomes reflect maximum use of the resources allocated. Likewise, *economic efficiency* entails using the best but least costly combination of physical, technological, and human resources to produce a product or service. To say that an activity is *cost effective* means that a specific objective is being achieved at the lowest cost possible.

In deciding to allocate resources to a given activity, a librarian is simultaneously choosing to withhold resources from other activities. The unavailability of resources for the other activities is described as an *opportunity cost*. For example, suppose a librarian purchases a CD-ROM product for $1000. The opportunity cost is $1000 because this is the amount of money that is not available to use in making some other purchase, such as a display case for the library gallery area. Similarly, if two staff members are assigned to work at a library service point, their wages are an opportunity cost since the two could have been assigned elsewhere. Owing to limited resources, every choice has an opportunity cost associated with it—one thing can be obtained only by giving up something else.

The *law of diminishing returns,* also known as the *law of diminishing marginal productivity,* is that increases in input beyond some point lead to increasingly smaller additions to output. For example, if more and more staff are added to an activity, after some point each extra person (unit of labor) increases total service (product) by less than the preceding person. Example 3-6 illustrates the law of diminishing returns.

Example 3-6

Law of Diminishing Returns in Staffing

An organization's Answer Center has a staff of librarians who answer incoming public telephone calls and letters. Table 3-5 provides data about the number of telephone and mail responses that result from various staffing levels. The number of librarians is the labor component, while the total number of responses is total product.

Table 3-5 illustrates average product and marginal product, two important concepts useful to the librarian in a position to modify a staff member's assignment. *Average product* is the total output divided by the quantity of the variable input. In Table 3-5 the average number of responses is average product. That is, if two employees produce 440 units of activity, the average output for the two of them is 220 units [220 = 440/2]. *Marginal product* is the output that results from an additional input. In the table below, the marginal number of responses is marginal product. When there are zero staff, there is no output. When there is one staff member, the output is 200 units. Hence, the marginal number of responses is 200 [200 = 200 − 0]. If the number of librarians is increased from four to five, output increases to 960 from 840, or 120 units [120 = 960 − 840]. Hence, an increase of one staff member results in a marginal increase in production of 120 units. The table shows that the marginal number of responses handled by staff decreases as the number of staff assigned to the activity increases, from a high of 240 with two staff to 120 with five staff.

TABLE 3-5 ▌ Staffing and Calls Answered

Number of librarians	Total number of responses	Marginal number of responses		Average number of responses	
0	0				
1	200	200	(200 − 0 = 200)	200	(200/1 = 200)
2	440	240	(440 − 200 = 240)	220	(440/2 = 220)
3	660	220	(660 − 440 = 220)	220	(660/3 = 220)
4	840	180	(840 − 660 = 180)	210	(840/4 = 210)
5	960	120	(960 − 840 = 120)	192	(960/5 = 192)
6	1020	60	(1020 − 960 = 60)	170	(1020/6 = 170)
7	1050	30	(1050 − 1020 = 30)	150	(1050/7 = 150)

In reassigning or hiring a person, the key issue is determining how much additional product (work output) will result from an additional person working a particular assignment. From a dollars-and-cents perspective, it makes good sense to reassign or hire a person to produce extra work if the value of the work units exceeds the costs of producing them. This can be a compelling argument to justify a staff position.

The interested librarian may wonder why diminishing returns are not seen until the third staff member joins the team. The answers are beyond the scope of this book; however, on an intuitive level, one can imagine that two people can divide the assignment to take advantage of each person's strengths. One might answer telephone calls and the other answer letters so that, with specialization, productivity increases. As more persons are added to work on the activity, the tasks continue to be segmented, resulting in greater and greater specialization and marginal product decreases. The segmenting of work into specialized activities for increased efficiency is called *division of labor*. But an effect of specialization is that it fosters increased interdependence among staff. When a librarian specializes, other librarians tend not to maintain their ability to duplicate his or her skill. Then, when that specialized staff member leaves the library, productivity decreases.

Summary of Critical Concepts

1. A *mission statement* is a broad statement of purpose toward which a library strives. It expresses a long-term commitment of library resources. All decisions on strategy, recruitment, marketing, services, priorities, and other management choices that affect the library are made with furtherance of the library's mission in mind. It is possible for many libraries to have the same or similar mission statements but to differ in the ways programs of strategies are funded to accomplish the missions.

2. Library *output measures* or *performance measures* are quantitative terms for evaluating a library's performance. These measures identify the success with which services are provided and resources are made available. Performance measures provide librarians with objective evidence of the relationships between library activities and resource allocation. Output measures are usually compared with some standard or identified level of achievement. However, because each library has different client needs and capabilities to finance library services, externally developed standards may be of little value. Output measures help librarians to provide a better understanding for decision-making groups that can allocate additional resources.

3. A *budget* is the library's financial expression of its plan. Nonmonetary budgets express units such as amount of output, time, or physical space. Financial budgets show the sources of revenue and the expenditure of money. A library's operating income budget reflects funds that recur annually. Hence, the library budget is a recurring budget. A capital equipment budget identifies expenditures for items that meet some predetermined threshold of expense and that are durable, lasting for a minimum period.

4. *Benefit-cost ratio analysis* is a technique for deciding how moneys should be spent, based on a ratio of the cash value of benefits divided by the cash value of costs.

5. *Price elasticity of demand* is a measure of the percent change in the quantity demand of a certain item divided by the percent change in the price. It indicates the degree of sensitiveness or responsiveness of the quantity demanded that can be attributed to a change in a variable such as the price.

6. The *law of diminishing returns* describes the relationship between fixed and variable inputs. It helps librarians understand what happens when more of one input is added to a fixed amount of another input. Basically, as more of a variable input (such as capital or labor) is added to an existing fixed input, there is a point after which each additional input returns less than the unit before it.

Key Terms

Activity.   An action or task that is required to carry out a strategy or achieve an objective. Circulation, for example, is an activity that accomplishes the objective of providing the community access to the library's collection.

Bleeding.   The process of achieving a budget reduction by across-the-board cuts. In bleeding, the budget is reduced by a dollar amount or percentage without removing any specific activity from the program.

Capital expenditure.   A cost incurred to acquire a long-lived asset that will be used for a specified minimum period, such as three years, and that costs a specified minimum amount, such as $300. The time period and financial amount are set by the accounting practices of the library or parent institution. The purchase of a new building or expensive operating equipment is a capital expenditure.

Cost driver.   Any activity that causes a cost to be incurred. For example, journal subscriptions are cost drivers.

Downstream.   An action, cost, or other event that will be experienced later. For example, when equipment is purchased, a downstream cost is the equipment's repair or replacement.

Evaluation.   The collection and assessment of data about an organization's activities. *Formative evaluation* examines ways to improve activities and potential effectiveness. Program improvements that result from formative evaluation are designed to benefit the persons for whom the activities are targeted. *Summative evaluation* examines the outcomes and effects of programs and, hence, is an assessment of a developed program. Summary results are generally prepared for persons, agencies, or bodies that set policy and determine funding.

Mission statement.   A statement that expresses a long-range commitment of an organization's resources toward a stated goal.

Vertical cut.   The elimination of an activity or group of activities to achieve a budget reduction.

SELF-ASSESSMENT QUIZ

1. *True* or *False*   Formative evaluation would be helpful to a technology committee for monitoring a new activity.

2. *True* or *False*   Summary evaluation results are like a grade for a course at the end of a semester.

3. *True* or *False*   Library performance is too intangible to be gauged by output measures.

4. *True* or *False*   Benefit-cost ratio analysis is a technique for choosing activities to initiate, expand, or contract.

5. *True* or *False*   Effectiveness measures for collection development may be the number of reserves for particular books and clientele complaints.

6. *True* or *False*   Data may be summarized in different ways for different purposes.

7. *True* or *False*   If the amount of a product demanded remains almost unaffected by per unit price change, demand is inelastic.

8. *True* or *False*   The demand for necessities is less elastic than the demand for luxury goods.

9. *True* or *False*   The more choice that a person has in buying substitutes for something, the more elastic is the demand for the item.

10. *True* or *False*   Library journal subscription renewals are inelastic while personal magazine subscription renewals are elastic.

Answers

1. *True*   Formative evaluation is growth-oriented and allows the librarian the opportunity to change tactics for continuous improvement while an activity is in progress.

2. *True*   Summative evaluation is assessment that occurs at or near the end of an activity. Its purpose is to document the extent to which objectives were met. In this way, it is similar to a course grade at the end of the semester.

3. *False*   Output measures provide indicators that are useful to a librarian in determining the extent to which librarian services and library collections are being utilized by the library's clientele.

4. *True*   Benefit-cost ratio analysis is a managerial tool used to determine the most efficient allocation of resources among competing projects or activities. It is helpful to a librarian in deciding which new projects to initiate and which existing projects to expand or contract.

5. *True*   If reserves and complaints decrease, one of two situations is occurring. Either library effectiveness has increased or the library's clientele are no longer seeking the library's resources.

6. *True*   Data can be organized or presented to emphasize certain aspects.

7. *True*   Inelastic demand means that an item's price does not affect its demand, such as the cost for medicine or gasoline. Inelastic items usually are essential items.

8. *True*   Demand for necessities such as food, water, shelter, medicine, and transportation to work are less elastic than the demand for luxury items such as jewelry, cosmetics, and furs. That is, a person will spend money for essentials regardless of their cost but will search for substitutes or will delay purchasing expensive items.

9. *True*   Choice of several similar products allows the consumer to substitute items. The availability of choice allows demand to be elastic.

10. *True*   Library subscriptions are inelastic because librarians are reluctant to cancel titles and because often there is no substitute for a particular title. Personal subscriptions are price sensitive and are, therefore, elastic.

DISCUSSION QUESTIONS AND PROBLEMS

1. Identify each of the following as an example of formative evaluation or summative evaluation. Explain.
   a. Benefit-cost analysis
   b. Cost-effectiveness analysis
   c. Feasibility assessment
   d. Impact evaluation
   e. Implementation evaluation
   f. Needs assessment
   g. Output evaluation
   h. Process evaluation

2. A college has an operating budget of $46,600,000. It has 10,000 full-time equivalent students. The college categorizes its expenditures as personnel or nonpersonnel. Complete the table that follows, in which numbers represent dollar costs in thousands (-000):

| | Personnel | Nonpersonnel | Total | Percent of college budget | |
				Personnel	Nonpersonnel
Administration	$ 9,360	$4,204	$____	____%	____%
Instruction	____	504	____	____%	60.4%
Library services	1,215	____	$1,650	____%	____%
Student services	____	246	____	____%	6.5%
Total	$41,207	$____	$____	____%	11.6%

3. A library expends its nonpersonnel budget as shown in the table below.

	Year 4	Year 3	Year 2	Year 1
Books	$ 35,746	$ 29,529	$ 42,648	$ 41,275
Serials	17,201	22,223	19,659	36,494
Journals	335,467	350,164	321,627	304,103
Audiovisual	840	1,932	221	1,641
CD-ROM services	29,573	26,285	24,568	14,182
Other	6,895	6,972	7,473	2,239
Total	$425,722	$437,105	$416,196	$399,934

a. Determine what percentage each expenditure category represents of the annual budget.

b. Assume that the cost of all print, nonprint, and digital educational resource materials experience an annual change of 6%. From reading the data, what seems to be the librarian's budgetary coping strategy?

4. The acquisitions librarian at a public library compiles a monthly report of orders that are placed through book vendors. Expenditures through October are as follows:

Orders Placed Through Vendors

	Adult	Reference	Young adult	Juvenile	Total
January	$1,142	$ 245	$104	$ 870	$____
February	2,415	1,017	128	1,275	____
March	3,403	758	49	800	____
April	2,618	239	340	1,177	____
May	2,954	139	694	800	____
June	1,343	192	349	194	____
July	2,607	586	447	317	____
August	2,288	119	327	2,309	____
September	2,122	277	362	31	____
October	2,311	674	152	804	____
November					
December					
Total	$____	$____	$____	$____	$____

The librarian also compiles monthly data for orders placed directly with a publisher. Data through October are as follows:

Orders Placed with Publishers

	Adult	Reference	Young adult	Juvenile	Total
January	$ 0	$ 587	$ 0	$ 0	$____
February	504	78	0	12	____
March	65	1,586	1,819	94	____
April	37	1,951	0	157	____
May	12	226	0	763	____
June	66	624	0	34	____
July	0	200	0	46	____
August	169	1,144	0	306	____
September	23	66	0	550	____
October	52	1,716	175	34	____
November					
December					
Total	$____	$____	$____	$____	$____

a. Complete the order tables by finding row and column totals, when possible.

b. Prepare a table that shows combined expenditures for vendor and direct purchases. Determine the percent that each category represents for the month.

c. If the library receives an average discount of 27% on purchases that it places through vendors, estimate the value of the list price of items purchased January through October.

The following information should be used to solve problems 5 through 10. A recently graduated librarian accepts a 35-hour-per-week professional position for a salary of $28,000. The staff consists of the newly appointed librarian, an assistant who works 16 hours per week at the rate of $6.50 per hour with an institutionally imposed yearly maximum of 950 hours, and a volunteer who usually helps two mornings a week. The librarian reports to the assistant administrator. The journal collection consists of 175 titles, of which 75 are on display and the others are alphabetical by title. There are 4000 bound journal volumes and about 500 books. Last year, the journal subscriptions cost $17,500. In addition, $5000 was spent on books. Book and journal prices increased by 10% for the current year. Book purchases were deferred to make up for increased journal costs. There is a CD-ROM database subscription that provides rolling access to the past thirty-six months of backfile (each new month the oldest month drops off), at a cost of $1450. Media and audiovisual services are provided by separate departments, as is photocopying. The library is rectangularly shaped, measuring 30′ × 35′. In addition to the library space, there is a 4′ × 2′ room containing two large cabinets for storage. The library has a new computer and Internet access. The librarian's first priority is to acquire a plain-paper fax machine that will cost $875.

The librarian learns the following about the budgeting process:

▪ The institution imposes a charge of $20 per square foot, but always includes this tax in the budget allocation so that the fee appears to cancel itself out.

▪ Staff who are paid a wage are eligible for fringe benefits (vacation, sick leave, medical, dental) if they work 17 or more hours per week, and the fringe rate is 31%.

▪ The benefit rate for salaried personnel is 28%.

- The institution routinely assumes a 3.5% cost-of-living increase each year for all paid employees.
- Most supplies are received through general stores at $125 per month.
- Air conditioning, electricity, and heat costs are included in the space allocation cost.
- Each outside-use telephone line costs $30 per month. An in-house-only line costs $15 per month.
- Department directors can request up to $750 per year for travel to professional meetings.
- Except for some throwaways, the library binds about 325 volumes each year at $12 per volume.
- The journal vendor estimates another 10% increase because of inflation and changing dollar values on international markets.
- The institution estimates a 4% inflation increase for supplies.
- Equipment costing more than $500 must be acquired as capital equipment.
- Department directors can request up to $200 for an institutional association membership.
- There is no charge-back or assessment to the department from the institution for Internet access.

5. The current budget is shown below. Using whole dollar amounts, rounded to the nearest twenty-five dollars, develop budget projections for next year for the following categories: a. salary and fringes; b. wages and fringes; c. supplies; d. equipment; e. data processing supplies; f. books and journals; g. telephone.

Hospital Library Budget*

Current budget amount	Percent	Chart of accounts	
$28,000	39%	100	Salary
7,850	11	110	Fringes on salary
5,400	8	200	Wages
0	0	210	Fringes on wages
1,500	2	200	Supplies and materials
21,000	—	206	Space allocation
1,450	2	259	Supplies-data processing, disks
875	1	300	Equip.-inventorial (over $500)
0	0	311	Equip.-noninventorial (to $500)
3,250	4	330	Books
19,250	26	335	Subscriptions
0	0	337	Microfilm/microform
3,900	5	338	Binding
0	0	400	Contractual services
0	0	410	Postage
550	1	420	Telephone
0	0	421	Telephone—long distance
0	0	440	Local travel
750	1	450	Out-of-town travel

Current budget amount	Percent	Chart of accounts	
0	0	500	Maintenance and repair
0	0	507	Heating, air-conditioning
200	0	706	Memberships
0	0	710	Miscellaneous
$93,975	100%		Total

*Percents exclude $21,000 for category 206, Space allocation.

6. Suggest a strategy for the book/journal allocation crisis.

7. Develop a 5% and 10% contingency reduction budget.

8. If a single-faced section of 3-foot-wide shelving holds about 125 volumes when the top and bottom shelves are empty and the shelves are at about three-quarters capacity, approximate the number of sections of shelving for this library.

9. Assume that the stacks are near capacity and it is time to send out materials for binding. What are some options for shelving the bound materials? What is your assessment of the backfile strength of the collection?

10. If a single-faced shelving section (three feet wide) can accommodate 24 titles for display, how much display shelving does the library possess to display its titles?

four

PRESENTING NUMERICAL DATA IN TABLES AND CHARTS

After reading this chapter, you will be able to do the following:

1. Describe a data array and sort data numerically in ascending or descending order.

2. Illustrate a frequency distribution for ungrouped or grouped data and describe the advantages of each for displaying data descriptively and economically.

3. Create a frequency distribution, a histogram, and a frequency polygon, and illustrate the advantage of each.

4. Illustrate a scattergram by plotting data on the *XY*-coordinate plane.

5. Construct horizontal bar, vertical column, pie, and line graphs to illustrate quantitative and qualitative comparisons.

For librarians to scale services and develop programs in an environment of competitive budgeting, they must be adept at making persuasive financial arguments. These arguments require skill in data analysis and presentation. A first step in developing such skill is to learn to organize and describe data economically.

EFFECTIVELY ORGANIZING AND DISPLAYING DATA

A useful technique to organize data is to sort the scores numerically in either ascending or descending order. This sorting produces a *data array*. Data can be arranged in an array either manually or with a computer. Most word processing and spreadsheet computer software programs contain a "sort" utility that can be used for this purpose.

The following example shows the advantages of organizing data into an array. Imagine that a librarian wishes to study the publication date of books in a particular area of the library's collection. The information will be used to determine the age of the books as part of a collection development initiative.

To collect data on the copyright dates of the books, the librarian asks a clerk to inspect 100 books that are on the open stacks within a specific call number and to record the copyright data. The raw data from the tabulation of the 100 books inspected are shown in Table 4-1. The resulting set of all scores is called a *distribution* or data set. Table 4-1 is a data *enumeration* of the scores of the books as they appear on the shelves.

In studying Table 4-1, its shortcoming is immediately apparent: the data enumeration conveys no patterns or trends. The data are useful, but the table does not help in interpreting the data.

Table 4-2 contains the same scores that appear in Table 4-1, this time arranged in ascending order. Numbers arranged in an increasing or decreasing order are said to be in an *array*.

A data array provides several advantages for enhancing understanding. First, it helps a user to more easily visualize the data. For example, Table 4-2 shows that the earliest copyright year is 1966 and the latest copyright year is 1997. Second, the data can more easily be divided into sections and it can readily be determined when particular values occur more than once or twice in the array. Lastly, the distance between successive values can be analyzed by looking at the data array.

TABLE 4-1 ▓ 20th-Century Copyright Year (*n* = 100)

68	85	72	86	74	87	92	76	92	83
77	95	82	90	77	82	88	69	79	84
84	80	89	81	70	74	94	73	70	94
74	71	85	97	91	68	79	67	76	80
97	67	79	82	80	93	66	88	69	72
75	72	91	78	89	70	79	77	95	81
82	89	83	73	84	90	68	89	75	83
80	85	88	80	95	69	70	77	76	85
93	71	94	83	75	93	68	92	78	86
87	73	87	78	76	81	84	71	87	90

TABLE 4-2 ▦ Data Array of 20th-Century Copyright Year (*n* = 100)

66	67	67	68	68	68	68	69	69	69
70	70	70	70	71	71	71	72	72	72
73	73	73	74	74	74	75	75	75	76
76	76	76	77	77	77	77	78	78	78
79	79	79	79	80	80	80	80	80	81
81	81	82	82	82	82	83	83	83	83
84	84	84	84	85	85	85	85	86	86
87	87	87	87	88	88	88	89	89	89
89	90	90	90	91	91	92	92	92	93
93	93	94	94	94	95	95	95	97	97

In Table 4-2, the librarian can divide the data listing in many ways. For example, the copyright years range from 1966 to 1997, a span of 32 years. The first sixteen years are 1966–1981 and the balance of the data fall from 1982–1997. Alternately, the librarian might note that the lower first one-quarter of the observations are from 1966 through 1973. The second quarter is from 1974 through 1981, the third quarter occurs from 1982 through 1989, and the last quarter occurs from 1990 through 1997. The configuration of the data in Example 4-1 illustrates another example of data sorting within an array.

Example 4-1 ▦ **Student Library Hours Worked: Raw Data and an Ordered Array**

33	13	22	32	26	30	20	14	23	17	29	27
10	18	20	30	18	30	32	11	27	25	35	29

Analysis

The raw data of student hours can be arranged into an array by sorting them in numerical order from low to high. The data are the same, but the arrangement is different:

10	11	13	14	17	18	18	20	20	22	23	25
26	27	27	29	29	30	30	30	32	32	33	35

The year 1996 does not appear in the data array in Table 4-2, however, and the year 1966 appears only once. The years 1967, 1986, and 1991 each appear twice. The other years appear three or more times. The table shows that the years increment by 1 from 1966 through 1995.

Although the array in Table 4-2 is decidedly an improvement over a simple raw data listing, it still is cumbersome, particularly for displaying large amounts of data. Further, while a rank order enumeration of a distribution's scores might be of some interest, it does not present a particularly useful picture of the research. For this reason, it often is necessary to condense the data. This can be accomplished by creating a frequency distribution.

A *frequency distribution* is a tabular display of data showing the number of data set observations that fall into classes or intervals. It permits the economical display of a large amount of raw data by categorizing the data into classifications. This process condenses the data by eliminating the repetition of equal values, simplifying the distribution for analysis, interpretation, and presentation. A frequency distribution brings structure and order to the data.

In a frequency distribution, *frequency* refers to repeated occurrences of an observation or score. If a score occurs four times, the score has a frequency of four. The term *distribution* refers to the spread of the scores themselves.

There are two types of quantitative frequency distributions that are used with interval and ratio scale data. The first manages ungrouped data, and the second handles grouped data. Each type offers particular advantages for data display.

Ungrouped Frequency Distributions

A frequency distribution for ungrouped data shows the distribution of each data point in the set. It is constructed by listing the data set's scores in an array from lowest to highest value and making a hash mark "/" each time a score occurs.

The number of marks represents the frequency of occurrence of each score. The marks are then tallied. Table 4-3 is a frequency distribution that illustrates this construction. The data are drawn from Table 4-2. Each score from the data set is summarized in the distribution. There are 100 values that occur over the 32 separate observation levels, beginning with the year 1966 and ending with 1997. Each observation level increments by 1, which represents an increase of one year. The table identifies each increment level in the distribution—even the year 1996, which has no score occurring in it.

The ungrouped data frequency distribution shown in Table 4-3 was constructed by first choosing the classifications, one level for each year. Next, the scores in each category are counted. The resulting table is efficient and descriptive.

TABLE 4-3 ▌ 20th-Century Copyright Years ($n = 100$)

X	f	Tally	X	f	Tally
66	/	1	82	////	4
67	//	2	83	////	4
68	////	4	84	////	4
69	///	3	85	////	4
70	////	4	86	//	2
71	///	3	87	////	4
72	///	3	88	///	3
73	///	3	89	////	4
74	///	3	90	///	3
75	///	3	91	//	2
76	////	4	92	///	3
77	////	4	93	///	3
78	///	3	94	///	3
79	////	4	95	///	3
80	/////	5	96		0
81	///	3	97	//	2

Grouped Frequency Distributions

A grouped frequency distribution is obtained by assigning raw data to similar groupings or categories, called *classes*. One might think of a class as a pigeonhole for data, and data are compressed into a few classes.

Choosing the number of classes is arbitrary, but the choice should depend on the amount of data available. If working with a lot of data, then many classes are justified. If there is not much data, however, then fewer classes should be used. In general, it is better to undersummarize data (more classes) than to oversummarize (fewer classes), but the objective is to find a good balance. Table 4-4 provides guidelines for choosing the appropriate number of classes, based on the quantity of data points in the distribution.

Once the number of class intervals has been decided upon, the next step is to establish the width of each class. Class width is determined by applying Formula 4-1.

Formula 4-1

$$\text{class width} = \frac{\text{largest score} - \text{smallest score}}{\text{number of classes}}$$

For example, Table 4-2 contains 100 data points. Following the guideline in Table 4-4, at least 8 classes should be used when constructing the frequency distribution. The largest score in Table 4-2 is 97 and the smallest score is 66. Applying Formula 4-1, the appropriate class width can be determined:

$$\text{class width} = \frac{\text{largest score} - \text{smallest score}}{\text{number of classes}}$$

$$= \frac{97 - 66}{8}$$

$$= \frac{31}{8} \text{ which is 3.8 or 4.}$$

TABLE 4-4 ▌ Minimum Number of Classes for Various Size Data Sets of Continuous Scale Observations

Number of data points	Minimum number of classes
10–15	5
16–31	6
32–63	7
64–127	8
128–255	9
256–511	10
512–1023	11
1024–2047	12
2048–4095	13
4096+	14

For the data in Table 4-2, then, a class width of four refers to a span of four years for each class.

Many statisticians recommend that the class width be an odd number, when convenient. Following this convention will simplify other computations. A common practice is to use a class width of three, or one that is a multiple of five. The class width selected should not produce more than the recommended number of classes, however. Further, for accurate data presentation, classes should be of equal width. Thus, the class width and the number of classes must be chosen carefully because factors such as these affect how the data look.

Classes also have *limits,* which are the classes' upper and lower boundaries. The score limits are the highest score and the lowest score that constitute a class interval. Suppose, for example, that a librarian counts the number of persons who daily visit the library over a period of twenty-one consecutive days. The librarian then constructs class intervals for the distribution. This illustration identifies the score limits for the class intervals:

Class interval	Score limits
1–50	1, 50
51–100	51, 100
101–150	101, 150
151–200	151, 200
201–250	201, 250
251–300	251, 300

Example 4-2 illustrates how to determine the number of classes and find class width.

Example 4-2   **Determining the Number of Classes and Finding Class Width**

During the summer, a librarian conducts a study of expenditures for staff salary and wages. There are $n = 19$ data points. The largest score is \$336,947 and the lowest score is \$115,013. Determine the class width and class limits.

Analysis

Table 4-4 suggests six class intervals if there are 19 data points. The class width is determined by using Formula 4-1:

$$\text{class width} = \frac{\text{largest score} - \text{smallest score}}{\text{number of classes}}$$

$$= \frac{\$336,947 - \$115,013}{6}$$

$$= \frac{\$221,934}{6} \text{ which is } \$36,989.$$

The recommendation is to make the class width a multiple of five, which can be easily accomplished by rounding off to \$37,000, since this number is divisible by five. Therefore, the class intervals are the following:

$115,001–$152,000

$152,001–$189,000

$189,001–$226,000

$226,001–$263,000

$263,001–$300,000

$300,001–$337,000

If the scores are expressed in thousands, the class intervals would be $115–$152, $153–$190, $191–$228, $229–$266, $267–$304, $305–$342. The intervals are different from when whole numbers are used because of rounding.

The purpose of class limits is to establish a boundary between classes so that each score can be unambiguously assigned to a single class. For example, if the first two classes were 1966–69 and 1969–73, one would not be sure where to count the observations for 1969. Would they belong in the 1966–69 class or in the 1969–73 class? The purpose of the boundary is to remove the ambiguity so that each piece of data belongs to exactly one class, making the classes *mutually exclusive*. Mutual exclusivity is an essential aspect of a well-constructed frequency distribution.

Table 4-5 presents the librarian's frequency distribution when 8 classes are used. Each class width represents four years. Notice, too, that the classes are mutually exclusive because there is no overlap among them. The table also illustrates a number pattern that helps the librarian to visually check for mutual exclusivity. It is that one class ends with a whole number and the next class begins with the next consecutive integer. That is, the first class ends with 69 and the next class begins with 70. The second class ends with 73 and the third class begins with 74. This pattern makes it easy to check the intervals.

The first class is 1966–69. It spans four years. Its frequency is the sum of scores for each of the years 1966, 1967, 1968, and 1969. This turns out to be 10 [10 = 1 + 2 + 4 + 3] since there are 1, 2, 4, and 3 scores, respectively, for the year. The second class interval consists of observation frequencies for years 1970 through 1973. These frequencies are 4, 3, 3, and 3, respectively. They sum to 13 [13 = 4 + 3 + 3 + 3]. This sum, 13, is called the *class frequency*.This process is continued through the last class, which spans the years 1994 through 1997. (Normally, a frequency distribution table would show only the classes and frequencies. The tallies are presented here for instructional purposes only.)

TABLE 4-5 ▮ Twentieth-Century Copyright Dates ($n = 100$)

Classes	Frequencies	
66–69	10	(10 = 1 + 2 + 4 + 3)
70–73	13	(13 = 4 + 3 + 3 + 3)
74–77	14	(14 = 3 + 3 + 4 + 4)
78–81	15	(15 = 3 + 4 + 5 + 3)
82–85	16	(16 = 4 + 4 + 4 + 4)
86–89	13	(13 = 2 + 4 + 3 + 4)
90–93	11	(11 = 3 + 2 + 3 + 3)
94–97	8	(8 = 3 + 3 + 0 + 2)
	$n = 100$	

Table 4-6 shows Table 4-2 data and illustrates how the data look when summarized in different class widths. If the class width is 1, this means that all years are compressed into the single class for 1966–1997. In other words, all 32 years of data are covered or spanned by the single class. This is very high data compression. If the class width is 32 years, then there are 32 classes, which is the ungrouped data model. This choice really spreads the data out. The effect of using a few classes (high compression or overcondensing) is that the numerical value of each score becomes obscured.

Once data have been summarized into a grouped frequency distribution and categorized into a class interval, each individual datum (single score) is lost. That is, if the librarian knows only that class interval 1978–1981 has a frequency of 15, he or she does not know how many individual scores there are for any particular year. The only information available may be the total frequency count for the four-year interval.

In general, it is helpful to begin with a larger number of classes (undersummarization of the data) and then determine whether fewer, broader classes are desirable. A large number of classes can be combined into fewer, broader classes. However, once data are grouped, it may be impossible to reconstruct the individual values. Table 4-6 shows the effect of various numbers of class levels on copyright year data.

Guidelines for Creating Class Intervals

1. There should be between 5 and 14 classes, depending upon the number of scores in the distribution. (Table 4-4 provides a guideline.)

TABLE 4-6 ▓ Frequency Distributions Illustrating the Effect of a Varying Number of Class Intervals

Class intervals: 2 Class width: 16		Class intervals: 3 Class width: 11		Class intervals: 4 Class width: 8	
(x)	(f)	(x)	(f)	(x)	(f)
66–81	52	66–76	33	66–73	23
82–97	48	77–87	41	74–81	29
		88–98	26	82–89	29
				90–97	19

Class intervals: 5 Class width: 7		Class intervals: 6 Class width: 6		Class intervals: 7 Class width: 5	
(x)	(f)	(x)	(f)	(x)	(f)
64–70	14	64–69	10	63–67	3
71–77	23	70–75	19	68–72	17
78–84	27	76–81	23	73–77	17
85–91	22	82–87	22	78–82	19
92–98	14	88–93	18	83–87	18
		94–99	8	88–92	15
				93–97	11

(*continued*)

TABLE 4-6 ▓ Frequency Distributions (*continued*)

Class intervals: 8 Class width: 4		Class intervals: 11 Class width: 3		Class intervals: 16 Class width: 2	
(*x*)	(*f*)	(*x*)	(*f*)	(*x*)	(*f*)
66–69	10	66–68	7	66–67	3
70–73	13	69–71	10	68–69	7
74–77	14	72–74	9	70–71	7
78–81	15	75–77	11	72–73	6
82–85	16	78–80	12	74–75	6
86–89	13	81–83	11	76–77	8
90–93	11	84–86	10	78–79	7
94–97	8	87–89	11	80–81	8
		90–92	8	82–83	8
		93–95	9	84–85	8
		96–98	2	86–87	6
				88–89	7
				90–91	5
				92–93	6
				94–95	6
				96–97	2

2. Each class interval should be mutually exclusive. That is, the classes must be defined so that there is no overlap between or among classes. In this way, a data point can belong to only one class.

3. No class interval should be omitted. All possible values from the lowest to the highest score must be shown.

4. Class interval width should be an odd number to simplify statistical calculations. Many authors suggest a class interval size of 3 or a multiple of five. That is, the interval is 3 or it is some width such as 5, 10, 15, 20, or other multiple of five.

5. The class interval size for all classes should be equal to prevent data distortion.

Continuous-Scale Data: Class Limits and Class Size

The calculation of class size and class limits is slightly more complicated when the scores are continuous-scale data. The term *continuous-scale data* refers to scores for concepts such as distance, height, light intensity, noise level, time, volume, and weight. They are continuous because, theoretically, they can assume any fractional value depending upon the accuracy of the instruments used to measure their value. In practice, however, continuous scale data may be rounded off, depending upon the application for the data. Thus, for a librarian's use, for example, the value is uncertain by a factor of plus or minus one-half of the last decimal place.

This means that the *real limits* of continuous scale data are plus or minus one half unit beyond the stated limits. An example is helpful. If the interval is 12.0–17.9, its real limits are 11.95–17.95. In another example, if the interval is 94.00–96.00, its real limits are 93.995–96.005.

Class midpoint, also called the *class mark,* refers to the exact middle of the class. This value is often very important for graphing data. Formula 4-2 shows the calculations necessary to determine the class midpoint:

Formula 4-2

$$\text{class midpoint} = \frac{\text{lower class limit} + \text{upper class limit}}{2}$$

For example, in a public library that provides users with access to computer equipment, laser printers are used. In a study of library noise, the librarian finds that the noise level for the printers falls within the interval 30.0–34.9 dB. To calculate the class midpoint for this interval, use Formula 4-2:

$$\text{class midpoint} = \frac{\text{lower class limit} + \text{upper class limit}}{2}$$

$$= \frac{30.0 + 34.9}{2}$$

$$= \frac{64.9}{2} \text{ which is } 32.45.$$

As discussed next, the class midpoint often is used in graphing. Example 4-3 illustrates how to find a class midpoint.

Example 4-3

Finding the Class Midpoint

Several different frequency distributions are presented in Table 4-6 for Table 4-3 data. Use these data to find the class midpoint when there are six class intervals.

Analysis

Class interval (x)	Frequency (f)	Class midpoint
64–69	10	66.5
70–75	19	72.5
76–81	23	78.5
82–87	22	84.5
88–93	18	90.5
94–99	8	96.5

To find the class midpoint for the first class interval 64–69, use Formula 4-2:

$$\text{class midpoint} = \frac{\text{lower class limit} + \text{upper class limit}}{2}$$

$$= \frac{64 + 69}{2}$$

$$= \frac{133}{2} \text{ which is } 66.5.$$

The other class midpoints are found by using Formula 4-2 in the same way. For example, the second class limit is 72.5; 72.5 = [(70 + 75)/2 or 145/2].

TABLE 4-7 ▌ Raw Data		TABLE 4-8 ▌ Percentages	
Question: How do you rate the convenience and ease of checking out library materials?		*Question:* How do you rate the convenience and ease of checking out library materials?	
Excellent	17	Excellent	31%
Very good	14	Very good	25
Average	13	Average	24
Poor	9	Poor	16
Not sure	2	Not sure	4

Qualitative Frequency Distributions

Constructing a qualitative frequency distribution is similar to the technique used for constructing a frequency distribution for ungrouped data. Data used to construct a qualitative frequency distribution must be either nominal or ordinal scale.

Often, the difficult part of building the frequency distribution is selecting the class intervals. For the librarian preparing a qualitative frequency distribution to describe data, however, the categories to classify the data and the data values can be helpful. For example, if the data refer to gender, the categories will be Male and Female. If the librarian is asking undergraduate students questions about the library, the categories may be freshmen, sophomores, juniors, and seniors.

To illustrate, suppose that a librarian conducts an attitude survey over a two-hour period in which 55 persons are asked for their opinions on the ease of checking out library materials. The answers to the multiple-choice question were brief—Not sure, Poor, Average, Very good, and Excellent. Table 4-7 presents the raw data results. Notice that the actual number of responses are listed for each of the categories.

Table 4-8 shows the same data as in Table 4-7, except that the data that result in Table 4-8 are reported as percents. The percents are readily understood. A finding of 31% [31% = 17/55] for the category Excellent is based on 17 responses out of a total of 55 responses, which is 0.309, or 31%.

FREQUENCY DISTRIBUTION GRAPHS

A *graph* is the visual representation of statistical data. It is a picture of points that shows the relationship between numbers. A well-constructed graph distills data into trends that illustrate the variables' rise or fall. At first glance, a well-prepared graph conveys clearly the relationships that exist between and among the variables. It communicates concepts without cumbersome details and thus commands attention. Because graphs appeal directly to people's visual sense and to the user's intellect, they help to stimulate imaginative analyses.

Graphs present data in a grid pattern of columns and rows. The columns and rows are established by two number lines that are perpendicular to one another, as shown in Figure

4-1. The horizontal number line is the *X-axis*. The vertical number line is the *Y-axis*. Except for being at right angles, or perpendicular to each other, the X-axis and Y-axis are identical. Each is a number line that extends endlessly in opposite directions from zero. Each contains a continuous set of *coordinates*. The coordinates are a pair of numbers, one from the X-axis and one from the Y-axis, that define the *coordinate plane*.

The point of intersection of the two axes is the *origin*. The origin can be thought of as the beginning of the graph. The numbers that are to the right of the origin on the X-axis (horizontal axis) are positive and are recorded in positive numbers. Measurement to the left of the origin on the X-axis is negative and is recorded as a negative value. Similarly, positive measures and positive numbers on the Y-axis (vertical axis) occur above the origin; negative measures and negative numbers on the Y-axis occur below the origin.

Those unfamiliar with algebra sometimes are mystified by negative numbers. An example of a negative number is a temperature reading such as -5 degrees. This number means that the recorded temperature is 5 units less than the zero point on the temperature scale. On the horizontal or X-axis, this reading is located 5 units to the left of the origin. On the vertical scale or Y-axis, it lies 5 units below the origin.

Negative numbers often are encountered when discussing variables such as temperatures, checkbook overdrafts, and yard penalties in football. In a library, the number of books removed from the shelves by collection weeding is reported as a negative value.

As shown in Figure 4-2, the perpendicular intersection of the XY axes separates the coordinate plane into four distinct regions, or quadrants. The axes themselves, however, are not considered to be contained in any quadrant.

The quadrants are numbered from one through four in a counterclockwise rotation. The upper right quadrant is the first quadrant. Thus, moving counterclockwise, the upper left quadrant is the second quadrant, the lower left quadrant is the third quadrant, and the lower right quadrant is the fourth quadrant. Most statistical charts use only the upper right quadrant. (Quadrant I) because studies usually generate positive numbers.

FIGURE 4-1

The Rectangular Coordinate Plane

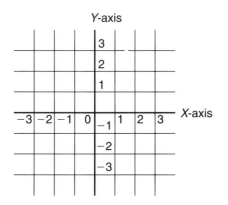

FIGURE 4-2

Coordinate Plane Showing Quadrants

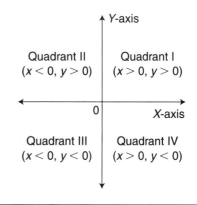

To graph a point, *P*, on the coordinate plane, a librarian uses an *ordered pair* of coordinates (*x, y*). The term *ordered* means that the *x*-axis location always is stated first, followed by the *y*-axis location. The first number of the ordered pair, *x*, refers to the location of the point with respect to the *X*-axis. The second number, *y*, refers to the location of

the point with respect to the *Y*-axis. Thus, the point (4,3) is located on the plane 4 units to the right of the *Y*-axis and 3 units above the *X*-axis. The point is in the first quadrant. Note that the origin, too, has coordinates represented by the ordered pair (0,0). Figure 4-3 illustrates the location of the point (4,3) on the coordinate plane.

FIGURE 4-3

The Coordinate Pair, *P* (4,3)

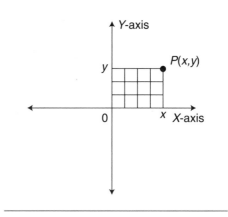

When data points are plotted on a graph, the values of the characteristic or variable being measured are conventionally shown on the horizontal axis (*X*-axis). The variable may be age, distance, income, library collections, time, population, or any other variable that is under study. On the *Y*-axis, the frequencies, relative frequency percents, or index numbers associated with the variable's classes are shown. For example, year of publication may be graphed on the *X*-axis, with the number of books published in that year (frequency) on the *Y*-axis.

Histogram

It often is useful to present graphically the information contained in a data distribution. A *histogram* is a graph composed of a series of rectangles with their bases on the horizontal axis (*X*-axis). The centers are at the class marks or class midpoints. The rectangles' widths are equal to the class interval sizes.

A histogram provides considerable information about a data set—insight that could not be learned easily from casual inspection of the frequency distribution. Figure 4-4, for example, is a histogram of the copyright dates of books from Table 4-5. Notice the clustering and possible symmetry of books published about some central value near 1983 or 1984. The graph also conveys the frequency of the intervals in relation to one another. In addition, this histogram provides a sense of the concentration of items between periods, such as 1967 and 1974 or 1982 and 1993. Notice also that the histogram in Figure 4-4 has a discontinuous or broken *X*-axis. This is designated by ─\/─ because none of the copyright data collected in this study precedes 1966. Rather than have a very wide graph with no bars between 0 and 1966, the *X*-axis is shown as "broken."

In a histogram, each rectangle or bar represents the exact number of frequencies for a class interval. The *areas* of the rectangles represent the class frequencies. If all the classes have equal widths, all the rectangles of the histogram will have equal widths. This means that *height* alone for each class interval in a histogram can represent the class frequencies. When the class widths are equal, the common practice is to set the heights numerically equal to the class frequencies.

FIGURE 4-4  Twentieth-Century Copyright Dates (*n* = 100)

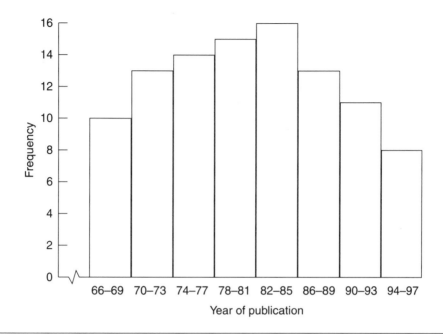

An *open-ended interval* is a class that allows either the upper or lower end of a quantitative classification to be limitless. For example, in a frequency distribution of book costs, an open class interval might be "Under $10" or "Over $100." Distributions that contain open-ended intervals require special handling. A practical guideline in library research is that open-ended intervals should be avoided whenever possible. Such intervals impose calculation limitations and present problems in graphing.

Table 4-9 illustrates an open-ended interval. The frequency distribution represents the age of library clientele of a hypothetical community with a population of 40,000. Figure 4-5 illustrates the histogram. There are seven class intervals. The first six classes are limited to certain ages. The last interval is an open-ended interval. In this interval, all the community's citizens who are aged 60 years and over are grouped together, thus a high frequency count in this interval is not surprising. This imprecision, however, is a serious limitation of open-ended intervals. The citizens in the last category all are persons aged 60 years or more.

TABLE 4-9

Age of Community's Library Clientele (Base = 40,000)

Age	Frequency
0–9	8,000
10–19	7,200
20–29	6,800
30–39	4,400
40–49	3,900
50–59	3,800
60 +	5,900

FIGURE 4-5 Age of Clientele, from Table 4-9

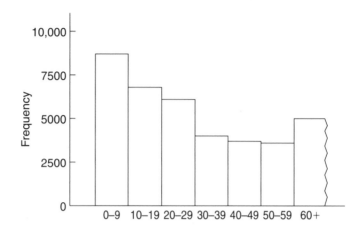

Guidelines for Constructing a Histogram

To ensure uniformity:

1. Classes are plotted on the horizontal axis (*X*-axis) with centers at the class marks. Frequencies are plotted on the vertical axis (*Y*-axis).

2. The areas of the rectangles represent class frequencies.

3. The class widths should all be of equal size.

4. The rectangles or bars of a histogram should touch each other; that is, they should be contiguous. When the chart is constructed, the practice is to leave a space between the origin and the first bar.

5. Frequencies always start at zero on the vertical scale (*Y*-axis). However, they do not necessarily start at zero on the horizontal axis (*X*-axis). The vertical axis should not be broken, because a false impression of the data almost always results.

6. In plotting the frequencies, the height of the point representing the score with the highest frequency should be approximately equal to three-fourths the length of the horizontal axis. The point of highest frequency also is known as the *mode* and will be discussed in detail in a later chapter as one of the measures of central tendency.

7. The histogram requires a title that identifies the population.

8. The frequency for the various classes is identified on the vertical scale (*Y*-axis). The axis should be clearly labeled.

9. The variable is plotted and labeled on the horizontal scale (*X*-axis). The librarian should select the class boundaries, class limits, or class marks to label along the axis.

Example 4-4 | **Qualitative Data**

The librarian determines the operating expenditures of five libraries that serve similar size communities. Prepare a histogram. Prepare a second histogram in which the amounts are rounded to thousands and the vertical axis (*Y*-axis) begins at $2,600 (in thousands). Interpret the analysis.

Analysis

Library	Operating expenditures
A	$2,865,975
B	3,113,040
C	3,206,015
D	3,237,240
E	3,061,984

Library	Operating expenditures (thousands)
A	$2,866
B	3,113
C	3,206
D	3,237
E	3,062

A visual comparison of the histograms in Figure 4-6 and Figure 4-7 reveals that, though they show the same data, the data look very different. The reason is that the vertical axis (*Y*-axis) begins at $0 for Figure 4-6 and at $2,600 for Figure 4-7. This illustrates data distortion. Such distortion through compression can be avoided by following the fifth guideline, listed previously, which requires that the vertical scale always start at zero.

FIGURE 4-6 | Library Operating Expenditures

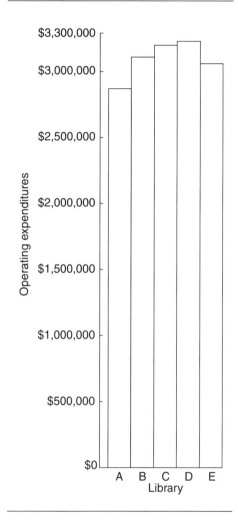

FIGURE 4-7 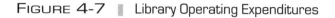 Library Operating Expenditures

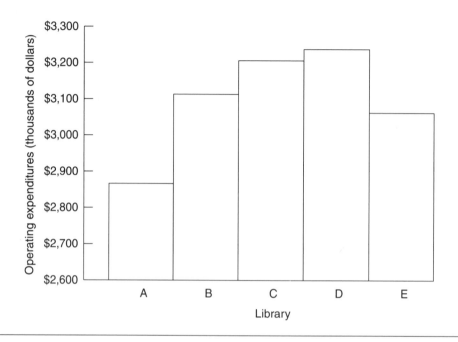

The librarian, as a consumer of statistics, needs to be aware of the importance of the fifth and sixth statements in the guidelines. They promote uniformity in the scaling of data to minimize data distortion. Graphs are suspect if part of the vertical scale is omitted or if scale units are not appropriate.

Example 4-5

Constructing a Histogram

In observing an activity, a librarian collects 19 scores and places the data in an ordered array. The resulting distribution is {3, 4, 4, 4, 4, 5, 5, 6, 6, 6, 7, 7, 7, 7, 8, 8, 8, 8, 8}.

1. Construct a histogram using the ungrouped raw data.
2. Construct a histogram by grouping the data. Use a class width of 2.

Analysis

The ungrouped frequency distribution is as follows:

Class number	Score (x)	Frequency (f)
1	3	1
2	4	4
3	5	2

Class number	Score (x)	Frequency (f)
4	6	3
5	7	4
6	8	5
		19

Figure 4-8 is a histogram that shows the ungrouped data. The grouped frequency distribution is as follows:

Class limits	Frequency (f)	Class mark (x)
2–3	1	2.5
4–5	6	4.5
6–7	7	6.5
8–9	5	8.5

Figure 4-9 is a histogram that shows the grouped data for Example 4-5.

FIGURE 4-8 Histogram for Ungrouped Data

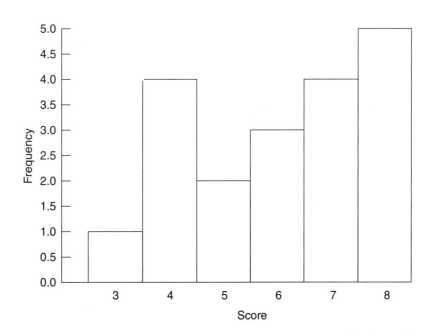

FIGURE 4-9 ▍ Histogram for Grouped Data

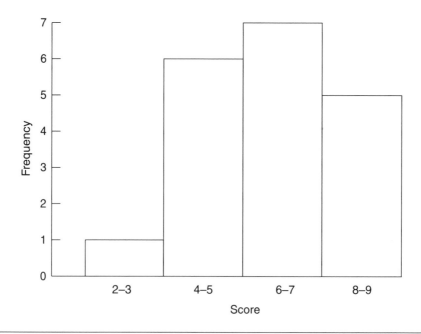

Example 4-6 ▍ **Constructing and Analyzing a Histogram**

A librarian collects and groups data, summarizes the data into a frequency distribution, and constructs a histogram.

Analysis

Class number	Class limits	Frequency (*f*)	Class mark (*x*)
1	6–10	1	8
2	11–15	0	13
3	16–20	2	18
4	21–25	5	23
5	26–30	9	28
6	31–35	11	33
7	36–40	7	38
		35	

There are several key observations from this analysis:

- There are seven class intervals. This is the number of intervals suggested by Table 4-4.

- The width of the class intervals is a multiple of 5, as suggested in the guidelines. Too few classes lead to oversummarization. Too many classes can result in insufficient data summarization. A class width of 3 would have resulted in 12 classes, which would be undersummarization for the data.

- All of the class intervals are the same width.
- The class mark is the class midpoint. Since the width was an odd number (5), the midpoint was easy to determine.
- Class limits employ a number pattern so that classes do not overlap. The pattern is 11, 16, 21, 26, 31, and 36 for the lower class limit and 10, 15, 20, 25, 30, 35, and 40 for the upper class limit.
- There is no data score for the second class interval, 11–15, but it still is shown and identified as having zero frequency.

Frequency Polygon

A *frequency polygon* is a closed-figure graph of class frequency plotted against class midpoints. It may be used in place of a histogram to illustrate a frequency distribution pictorially.

In a frequency polygon, the midpoints of class intervals are shown on the horizontal axis (*X*-axis). The frequencies are shown on the vertical axis (*Y*-axis). The frequency associated with each class interval is shown by a point that is connected to adjacent midpoints by a line. After connecting the midpoints of the classes, a closed polygon is formed by drawing a line from the next lower class midpoint to the midpoint of the first class, and then drawing another line from the last class midpoint to the next higher class midpoint. Since both of these latter class midpoints have a frequency of zero, the connecting lines will touch the horizontal axis, allowing the polygon to be closed.

A frequency polygon includes the same information as a histogram, but appears more streamlined. Figure 4-10 illustrates the difference between a frequency polygon and a histogram. In the frequency polygon, the number of observations in each interval is assumed to be concentrated at the midpoint of the interval. In the histogram, the observations are assumed to be distributed uniformly within each interval.

RELATIVE AND CUMULATIVE DISTRIBUTIONS

Most of the tabular summaries presented thus far have been of frequency distributions, showing only the frequency for the individual classes. In addition to this information, it is useful to know the fraction or percent of the total number of observations that fall into each of the classes. Formula 4-3 gives the ratio used to compute this statistic. *Relative frequency* is the number of observations occurring in each class interval, divided by the total number of observations in the data set:

Formula 4-3

$$\text{relative frequency} = \frac{\text{frequency of a single class}}{\text{sum of all class frequencies}}$$

Table 4-10 illustrates relative frequency computation. The relative frequency of the interval 6–10 is calculated by dividing the number of observations that occur in the interval, 1, by the total number of observations in the data set, 35. Hence, the relative frequency for the first interval is the fraction 1/35 or .028. Rounded off and expressed as a percent, this is 3%.

FIGURE 4-10  A Frequency Polygon

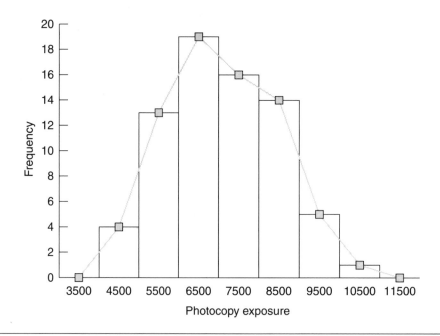

Photocopy exposure

TABLE 4-10  Relative Frequency Distribution

Class limits	Frequency (f)	Computation	Relative frequency (percent)
6–10	1	1/35 = .028	3%
11–15	0	0/35 = .000	0
16–20	2	2/35 = .057	6
21–25	5	5/35 = .143	14
26–30	9	9/35 = .257	26
31–35	11	11/35 = .314	31
36–40	7	7/35 = .200	20
	n = 35		100%

If the relative frequencies are expressed as percents, they must sum to a total of 100%. If they are expressed as decimals, they must sum to 1.00. (Note: Small errors may occur due to rounding of either percents or decimals.) If the percents do not sum to 100% or the decimals to 1.00, the total should have a footnote such as "Percentage sum discrepancies due to rounding." It is not necessary to show all calculations, however, such as 1/35 = 0.028. It is sufficient to show only the relative frequency percents.

Relative Frequency Distribution

A *relative frequency distribution* is a frequency distribution that includes relative frequency information. The relative frequencies usually are presented as percents, but they may be shown as fractions or decimals.

A graph of a relative frequency distribution can be obtained from a histogram or frequency polygon by changing the vertical scale (Y-axis) from frequency to relative frequency. The resulting graphs are called *relative frequency histograms* or *percent histograms*. The polygons are called *relative frequency polygons* or *percent polygons*.

Table 4-11 provides a numerical summary for creating a relative frequency histogram. The "Computation" column is included only to show the mathematical operations that are based on the total of 100 scores.

Notice that the copyright dates in Table 4-11 would be shown on the X-axis, while the relative frequency percent would be graphed on the Y-axis. Relative frequency graphs provide a comparison of the part to its whole. The part/whole relationship can help to express the relative importance of different data.

TABLE 4-11   Twentieth-Century Copyright Dates ($n = 100$)

Classes	Frequencies	Class mark (x)	Computation	Relative frequency (percent)
66–69	10	68	10/100 = .10	10%
70–73	13	72	13/100 = .13	13
74–77	14	76	14/100 = .14	14
78–81	15	80	15/100 = .15	15
82–85	16	84	16/100 = .16	16
86–89	13	88	13/100 = .13	13
90–93	11	92	11/100 = .11	11
94–97	8	96	8/100 = .08	8
	$n = 100$			100%

Cumulative Frequency Distribution

A *cumulative frequency distribution* is a distribution constructed by adding the distribution frequencies of successive classes together. Arranging distribution data cumulatively allows the analysis of data that lie above or below certain target levels of interest.

A "less-than" cumulative frequency distribution provides the total of all distribution frequencies that are less than or equal to a stated value. This technique would be helpful to a librarian for answering planning questions, such as, How many books were purchased last year that cost less than $25.00? or, What proportion of libraries serve a population less than 25,000? or, What percent of library books circulated for less than ten days?

A "more-than" cumulative frequency distribution provides the total of all distribution frequencies that are greater than a stated value. A "more-than" cumulative frequency distribution helps to answer strategy development questions such as, How many users borrowed more than five items at one time? or, What proportion of the collection's journal titles is included by more than five major abstracting and indexing services?

Table 4-12 illustrates construction of a "less-than" cumulative frequency distribution. This frequency distribution describes the contributions made by the Friends of the Library for developing special collections. The "less-than" distribution is built by accumulating the frequencies, beginning with the lowest class. Thus the cumulative frequency for each class reflects the number of observations that fall below the lower limit of the succeeding class.

In this example, each class interval represents an increment of $50. Since there are 24 occurrences in the interval "Up to $50," there is a cumulative total of 24 observations before the interval "$50.01–$100." Since there are 17 observations in the interval "$50.01–$100," there is a cumulative total of 41 [41 = 24 + 17] occurrences before the interval "$100.01–$150." In constructing the "less than" frequency distribution, it is not necessary to show all of the calculations.

The "less-than" cumulative distribution graph is formed by plotting the cumulative frequencies on the vertical axis (Y-axis) against the upper limits of the corresponding class interval values on the horizontal axis (X-axis). The points are then joined by straight lines to form a *cumulative frequency polygon,* as illustrated in Figure 4-11.

In this figure, cumulative frequency can also be translated into a cumulative percent, as shown on the right-hand column of the graph. Hence, the curve can be read in a glance in terms of frequencies or percents. Also, the number of cases either above or below a specified point can be seen by inspecting the curve, regardless of the sizes of the class intervals.

The "more-than" cumulative frequency distribution, illustrated in Table 4-12, is constructed by beginning with the highest class and summing the frequencies to the lowest class. The graph is constructed by plotting the lower class interval limits opposite their corresponding frequencies and then joining the points by straight lines. Figure 4-11 also illustrates the "more-than" cumulative frequency distribution.

TABLE 4-12 ▌ Cumulative Frequency Distributions (n = 200)

Class ($)	Frequency	"Less than" cumulative frequency	"More than" cumulative frequency
$0	0	0	200
Up to $50	24	(0 + 24) = 24	(200 − 24) = 176
$ 50.01–$100	17	(24 + 17) = 41	(176 − 17) = 159
$100.01–$150	20	(41 + 20) = 61	(159 − 20) = 139
$150.01–$200	25	(61 + 25) = 86	(139 − 25) = 114
$200.01–$250	28	(86 + 28) = 114	(114 − 28) = 86
$250.01–$300	26	(114 + 26) = 140	(86 − 26) = 60
$300.01–$350	23	(140 + 23) = 163	(60 − 23) = 37
$350.01–$400	18	(163 + 18) = 181	(37 − 18) = 19
$400.01–$450	14	(181 + 14) = 195	(19 − 14) = 5
$450.01–$500	5	(195 + 5) = 200	(5 − 0) = 0
Total	200		

FIGURE 4-11 ░ Friends of the Library Contributions (n = 200), from Table 4-12

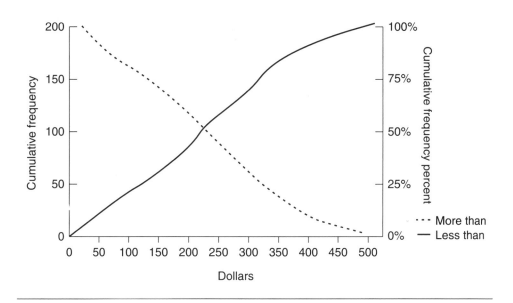

COMMON TYPES OF GRAPHS

A variety of types of graphs can be used to illustrate quantitative and qualitative comparisons, among them horizontal bar, vertical column, pie, and line graphs. These are illustrated in Figure 4-12. The types of graphs used most frequently by librarians include the following:

- bar graphs, composed of horizontal bars or vertical columns
- pie graphs, also called *circle graphs,* formed by representing parts of a whole by wedge-shaped sectors of a circle
- line graphs, formed by using straight lines to connect a series of graphed points
- diagrams, such as organizational charts, pedigrees, and genealogical trees
- combinations of the above types of graphs

In selecting a graph to portray data, keep in mind that not all illustrations are equally successful in conveying information. The first step in selecting an appropriate graph is to identify clearly the aspects of the data that are most important to illustrate. A good way to ensure that the purpose of the graph is clear is to title it before constructing it. Once the graph has a title, the next step is to determine which type of graph best illustrates the data. Figure 4-13 lists some types of graphs that are particularly suited for communicating specific kinds of information.

FIGURE 4-12 ▌ Common Types of Graphs

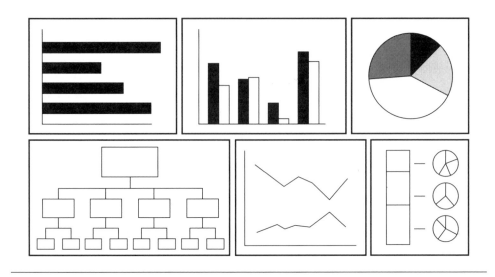

FIGURE 4-13 ▌ Types of Graphs

Type of graph	Usual uses	Examples
Horizontal bar	Comparisons between related items	Budgets of public libraries by state
Vertical bar	Change of 1 item across 1–5 time periods	Dow Jones index, Monday–Friday
Pie	Component percents	Percent-of-time analyses
Line	Change of 1 item across 5 or more time periods	Library's budget from 1980–1990

Horizontal Bar Graph

The horizontal bar graph effectively compares related items. The data in the graph may be classified by either quantitative or qualitative variables. Figure 4-14 shows average weekly circulation comparisons of different groups of books categorized by Dewey classification.

In a horizontal bar graph, the bars originate from a common baseline such as the vertical axis (Y-axis). The bar graph has one scale that extends horizontally along the X-axis length of the bars. Grid lines may run from the top to the bottom of the graph, but they do not intersect the bars. The length of each bar is determined by the value it represents and is measured by the horizontal scale. This scale may be written at the top or the bottom of the graph, or both. The width of the bars and intervening spaces provide balance and make the graph readable. Spacing between the bars is one-half the width of a bar.

FIGURE 4-14 ▌ Average Weekly Circulation

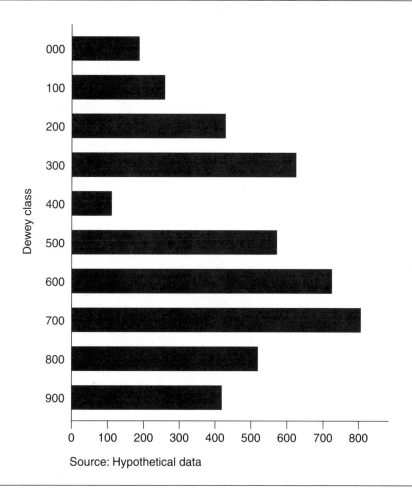

Source: Hypothetical data

An advantage of the bar graph is that one graph can accommodate many bars, which can be arranged in several ways. For example, bar graphs can be arranged chronologically or to reflect geographic regions. Or, bar graphs can be arranged in an order of decreasing length from the top to the bottom, qualitatively or numerically. When using a bar graph, the key is to keep the order of the graph's bars logical.

The bars in the graphs usually are shown solid or shaded in black or some color, or with cross-hatching. Avoid using any patterns in a graph that could distract, and thus decrease the impact of the graph. When shading variations are used in a horizontal bar graph, the progression in shade depth should be from bottom to top, with the darkest shading appearing at the bottom of the graph. Further, the bars should be continuous—not broken. An exception is when the length of the longest bar is not essential to the graph. The numeral that shows the value of the category is then placed in the broken portion, even if a scale is not shown.

FIGURE 4-15 ▓ Variations of Horizontal Bar Graphs

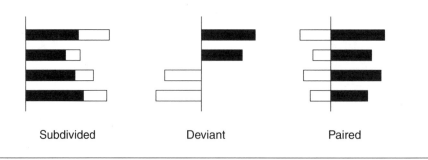

Subdivided   Deviant   Paired

FIGURE 4-16 ▓ Additional Examples of Horizontal Bar Graphs

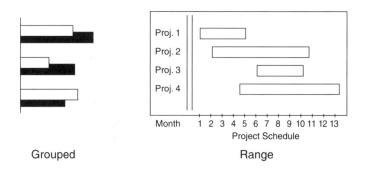

Grouped   Range

Figure 4-15 illustrates three common variations of the horizontal bar graph. The left panel is a subdivided bar graph. It shows the components that make up the total, such as volumes on hand and titles on hand. The center panel is a deviant bar chart. It shows differences, such as percent change in circulation by type of medium. The panel on the right is a paired bar chart. It shows two information elements about a component, such as expenditure for books by classification and their circulation, or project costs and project revenue.

Figure 4-16 shows two additional types of bar charts. The graph on the left is a grouped bar chart. It compares various aspects of the same item, such as the number of titles available and the number of times titles are borrowed. The second panel is a range bar chart. It shows the spread of values, such as differences between amounts, status, or phases of projects or activities.

Vertical Column Graph

The *vertical column graph* effectively compares a single variable over five or fewer time periods. This is a good graph to use to show annual circulation over a period, as shown in Figure 4-17. It also is an appropriate means to illustrate total dollar amounts, such as revenues or expenditures over periods of months or years. In addition, column graphs can dramatically portray size comparisons or large changes from one period to the next.

FIGURE 4-17 ▌ Annual Library Circulation over Four Periods

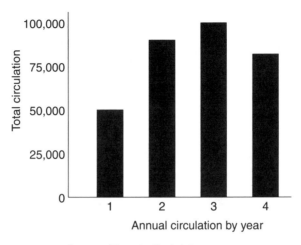

Annual circulation by year

Source: Hypothetical data

The column graph has two scales, one measuring horizontally across the graph and one measuring vertically. The horizontal scale usually represents time and the vertical scale usually represents quantity. Columns start from a baseline, drawn horizontally, and the height of the column represents its value. As in the horizontal bar graph, spacing between the columns is one-half the width of a column. The columns, which emphasize individual amounts, are effective for illustrating data that are confined to a specific period.

As with horizontal bar graphs, the practice is not to break a column—except when the bar illustrates an erratic point. The column may then be broken at the top, with the amount that is represented shown directly over it. Figure 4-18 illustrates four common variations of the vertical bar graph.

FIGURE 4-18 ▌ Common Vertical Bar Graphs

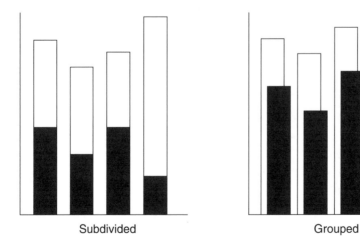

Subdivided   Grouped

(Continued)

FIGURE 4-18 ▌ Common Vertical Bar Graphs (*continued*)

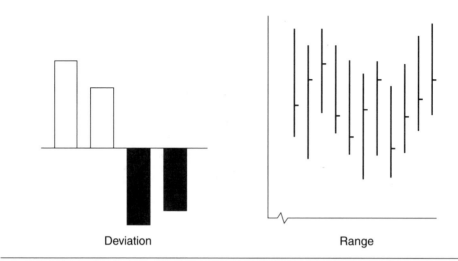

Deviation   Range

The top left-hand panel in Figure 4-18 is a subdivided column graph. It shows component parts. The top right-hand panel is a grouped column graph. It compares two items or shows relationships between them. The lower left-hand panel is a deviation column graph. It shows differences. The final panel is a range column chart and shows spread.

Pie or Circle Graph

A *pie graph,* or *circle graph,* shows components of a whole, such as budgets, assets, liabilities, or time distributions. In the pie graph, the total, or 100%, is represented by the entire circle. Each portion of the whole is conveyed by a wedge-shaped part of the circle. That is, each wedge or slice of the pie represents a specific percent of the whole. A pie graph is appropriate for graphing the distribution of a librarian's time, for example (see Table 4-13 and Figure 4-19).

In developing the pie graph, the first thing to determine is the percent allotted to each activity performed by the librarian. Table 4-13 shows that 15 hours of the librarian's 37.5 hour week are spent in general reference service. The component percent is thus 15/37.5 or 0.40, which is 40%. The component percent for online reference services is 7/37.5 or 0.19, which is 19%.

TABLE 4-13 ▌ Distribution of Librarian's Time

Activity	Hours per week	Percent of time	Degrees (rounded)
General reference service	15.0	40%	40 × 3.6 = 144
Online reference service	7.0	19	19 × 3.6 = 68
Bibliographic instruction	6.0	16	16 × 3.6 = 58
Collection development	4.5	12	12 × 3.6 = 43
Other	5.0	13	13 × 3.6 = 47
	37.5	100%	360

FIGURE 4-19   Pie or Circle Graph of Librarian's Time Distribution
by Activity

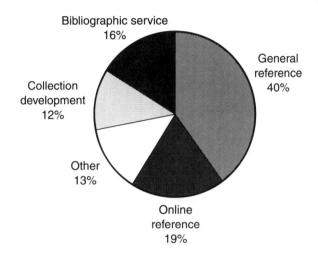

Bibliographic service
16%

General
reference
40%

Collection
development
12%

Other
13%

Online
reference
19%

After all the component percents are designated, then determine the number of degrees in each wedge of the circle. Since a circle has 360 degrees, one percent of the total can be represented by a wedge of 3.6 degrees [3.6 degrees = .01 × 360]. To determine the number of degrees a component should occupy, multiply 360 degrees by the component percent. For example, a 40 percent wedge is 144 degrees [144 = 0.40 × 360] and a 19 percent wedge is 68 degrees [68 = 0.19 × 360].

The third step is to draw a circle. Circles may be of any convenient diameter, although a diameter of 2 inches or more is suggested. A compass, protractor, and straightedge are needed to plot the angle required for each wedge. Sectors usually are plotted in a clockwise direction, beginning at the top of the circle. The left-hand portion of Figure 4-20 illustrates the finished project.

The final step is to identify each sector with a label positioned inside or adjacent to the sector. If a sector is small, the label should be placed adjacent to the graph, with an arrow pointing directly toward the sector. This helps the reader avoid confusion, as does coloring or cross-hatching to emphasize the individual sectors.

It is not unusual for a distribution to contain more categories than a pie graph. In general, pie graphs should not include more than five sectors. The reason for this restriction is that more sectors make a graph difficult to construct and tend to confuse readers. As a result, a catchall category, such as Other, Miscellaneous, or Unclassified can be introduced to consolidate multiple, smaller components of the whole.

For the librarian in the example, the category Other comprises the following activities:

Specialized filing	1.0 hour
Client callbacks	0.3 hour
Current awareness	0.2 hour
Unclassifiable	3.5 hours
Total	5.0 hours

FIGURE 4-20 | Elaboration of Librarian's Time Distribution

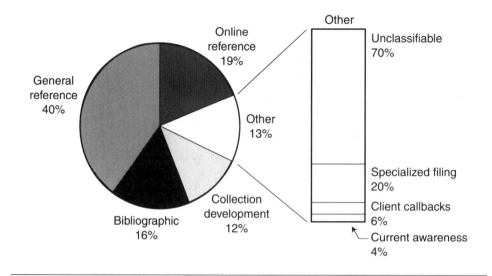

The librarian's complete time distribution can be shown by using the pie graph in combination with a vertical column graph, illustrated in Figure 4-20 with the graph of the librarian's time slightly rearranged. The lines in the Other sector show that the column graph more accurately describes that particular sector. This combination of graphing methods effectively conveys more information than does the pie graph alone.

A combination of graphing methods must be carefully planned, however. For example, when using a column graph with a pie graph, take care not to obscure the pie graph with the column graph. A column that is too large will convey a false impression of the size or importance of the category.

For example, in Figure 4-20, consider the category Unclassifiable (70%), which includes time expenditures such as telephone interruptions, drop-in visitors, and meetings. In the vertical column, this very small component of the librarian's total weekly time occupies a disproportionate amount of page space. It must be made clear that the 100% in the column graph refers to 100% of the Other sector only. This category, in turn, makes up only 13% of the total weekly time, as shown in the pie graph.

Figure 4-21, an "exploded" pie graph, emphasizes a particular segment of the time distribution shown in the preceding figure. This example illustrates the percent of time the librarian spends performing online reference services, such as a literature search. The emphasis is accomplished by shading and setting that segment off from the remainder of the pie. This technique highlights the comparison between one segment and the total activities. Because the graph's emphasis is exclusively on online searching, every activity not in this category becomes a part of the category entitled Other activities.

A pie graph is an excellent visual medium for illustrating comparisons. These graphs are relatively easy to read, being most effective when the type of relationship portrayed is uncomplicated, such as percent-of-time distribution or how the budget dollar is segmented.

FIGURE 4-21   Exploded Pie Graph to Emphasize a Segment

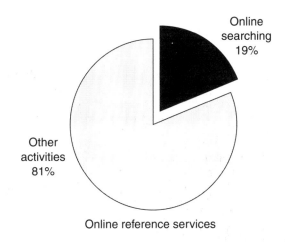

Despite its strengths, use of a pie graph to convey data may be avoided by some. Indeed, constructing a pie graph can be difficult. One of the challenges is performing the various computations that are necessary for dividing the circle into correct proportions. Also, some readers are unfamiliar with the tools used to make a pie graph, such as a compass and a protractor. Some experience difficulty when they need to estimate sector percents accurately in unmarked graphs. These barriers are overcome through practice and attention to detail in construction, however. Further, many computer packages offer sophisticated graphics software that greatly simplifies the process of constructing pie graphs. These systems yield the benefits of pie graphs with less toil.

Line Graph

A *line graph* is an effective way to show the general tendency of a variable to rise or fall. In reading a line graph, it is evident almost at first glance whether the variable is increasing, decreasing, fluctuating, or remaining generally constant.

The line graph is preferable for presenting data that extend over five or more periods. The superiority of a line graph, as compared to a bar graph, is illustrated in Figures 4-22 and 4-23. In Figure 4-22, although the rising and falling vertical bars attract and engage the viewer's attention, the graph is busy and crowded. The viewer must concentrate with effort to grasp the information that the bar graph conveys. Figure 4-23 is a line graph presenting the same data. In contrast, it allows the viewer to immediately grasp the trend conveyed by the data. It shows the generally decreasing direction from years 11 through 17. When examining the last data point (year number 21), most people would speculate that the data for the next period will continue to fall. From the figure, the data swing between the levels of four and ten percent is readily apparent.

FIGURE 4-22 ▌ Using a Bar Chart to Show Data

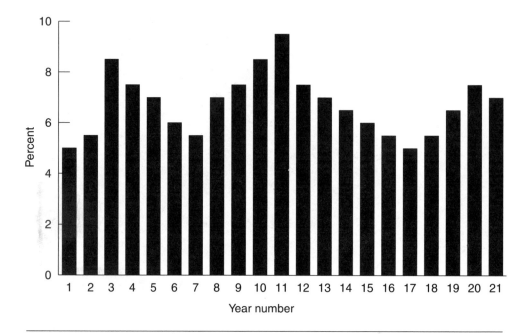

FIGURE 4-23 ▌ Using a Line Chart to Show Data

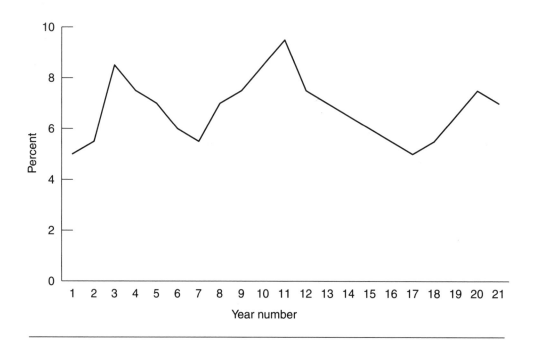

The line graph in Figure 4-24 depicts the annual circulation of medical books categorized by Dewey 610–619 classification. Figure 4-25 shows two line graphs and compares the circulation of medical and business books (Dewey classifications 610–619 and 650–659).

FIGURE 4-24 ▓ Annual Circulation of Medical Books

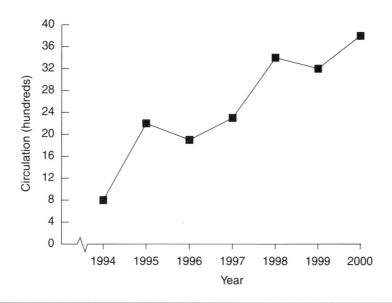

FIGURE 4-25 ▓ Medical and Business Book Circulation Comparison

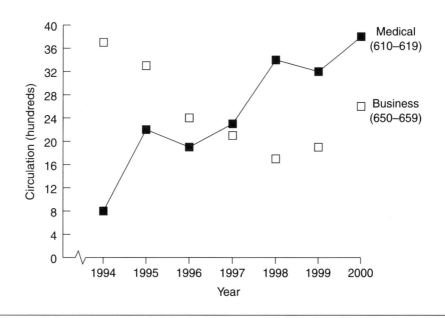

These figures represent the circulation data for a high school library. In 1996 the librarian and classroom teachers for the life sciences developed a model curriculum for college-bound students. This program was extended to business students in 1998. The line chart effectively shows the circulation results that followed.

In Figure 4-26, another example of a line graph, a library manager has compared the performance of an employee to a standard or performance expectation, both before and after a training program. Prior to the program (the left portion of the graph), the employee's performance was below the librarian's expectations. Following the training, the employee's performance was much improved, and clustered near the expectations set by the manager. This chart provides an excellent depiction of employee performance and highlights positive or negative changes in performance over time.

This method of graphical analysis is optimal when the employee's duties translate well into quantitative measurements. For example, a librarian may decide that 200 work units per week is an acceptable level of output for this position. The units may represent answering reference questions, processing invoices, reshelving books, or other similar tasks.

A *run chart* is a line graph that librarians can use to analyze a process over time. It is also called a *time plot* or *trend chart*. Figure 4-27 illustrates the daily turnstile traffic in a college library over the first four weeks of a semester.

This same type of chart can be effectively used as a *control chart*, allowing the tracking of an activity through a series of snapshots. The time between observations can be expressed in minutes or hours, or it can be conveyed in work shifts or per-some-quantity. Figure 4-28 illustrates a control chart. The upper control limit (UCL) and the lower control limit (LCL) form a corridor. The corridor is bisected by a center line, (CL). Thinking of the UCL and LCL as warning markers, the process that is being monitored is considered stable or within margin if its observations continue within the corridor. If a measurement approaches the upper or lower control limit, the process is out of control. A library application for a control chart would be humidity and temperature controls for a rare book room or storage area.

FIGURE 4-26   Line Graph of Performance Achievement

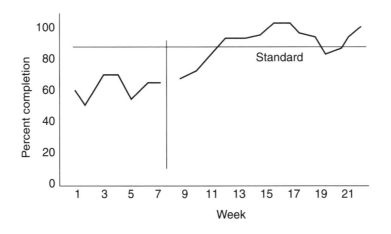

FIGURE 4-27 ▌ Library Turnstile Counts

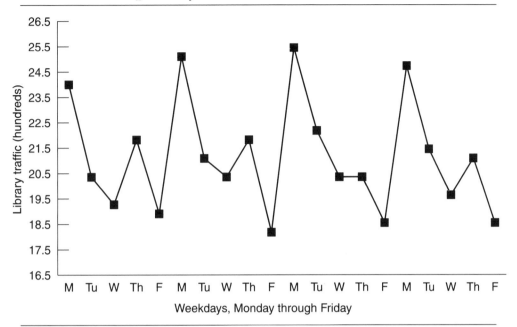

FIGURE 4-28 ▌ Control Chart

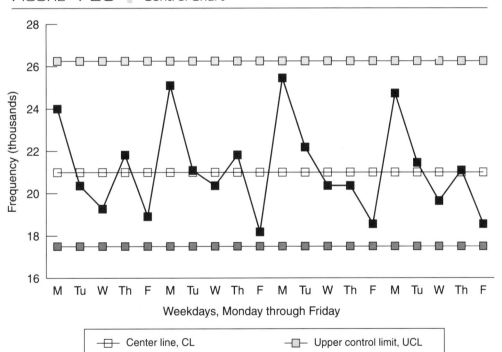

FIGURE 4-29 ▏ Line Graphs Illustrating Patterns of Rate of Change

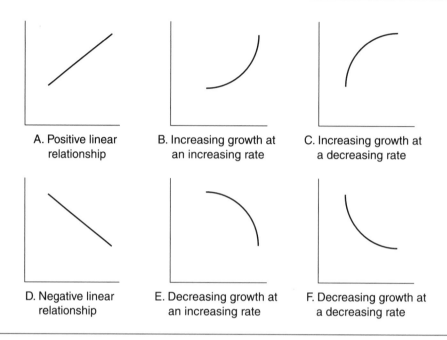

A. Positive linear relationship

B. Increasing growth at an increasing rate

C. Increasing growth at a decreasing rate

D. Negative linear relationship

E. Decreasing growth at an increasing rate

F. Decreasing growth at a decreasing rate

Line graphs also can be used to illustrate different patterns of change. Figure 4-29 contains six panels, A through F, that depict typical patterns of change. In these six panels, the value of the variable (vertical axis) is plotted against time (horizontal axis). The figure illustrates how a variable can increase and decrease. These patterns convey important information regarding trends in data.

In Figure 4-29, Panel A shows that the variable increases as it follows along the X-axis. As the x-coordinate increases, the y-coordinate also increases. When the x-coordinate numerically decreases (gets smaller), the y-coordinate also decreases. Panel B shows an increase that is occurring at an increasing rate. Panel C illustrates increasing growth, but growth that is slowing. That is, growth is occurring, but it is occurring at a slower and slower rate. This is the pattern that a librarian might expect from a journal collection or a fiction collection that is not continually refreshed with new titles. As the collection ages, fewer people look at the items and the growth is less each month. This observation might not be perceived from seeing only a total, rather than a graph of monthly data.

Panel D illustrates an inverse or negative relationship between two variables. That is, as the x-coordinate increases, the y-coordinate decreases. As the x-coordinate decreases, the y-coordinate increases. An example is the cost of a library van. If the van is one year old (age, on the horizontal axis), the van's cost (vertical axis) is high. As the van's age increases (move out on the horizontal axis), the van's cost decreases (move down on the vertical axis). Panel E illustrates decreasing growth at an increasing rate. That is, the growth is declining, and the decline is getting faster and faster. In the final panel, Panel F, the growth is declining, but at a declining rate.

Figure 4-30 illustrates declining growth that is occurring at a decreasing rate. It is an overlay of two graphs, a line graph and a vertical bar graph. Each graph presents information

FIGURE 4-30 ▌ Videocassette Rental Revenue, January–June

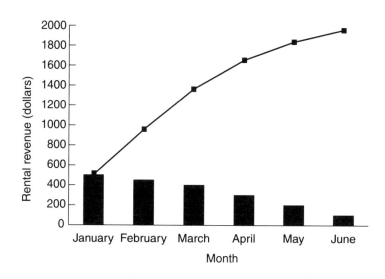

about revenue generated through videotape circulation. The line graph is a cumulative total. The bar graph shows that the growth in revenue is occurring at a slower and slower rate.

Avoiding Deception and Misuse

Once graphing styles and practices are understood, it is easy to spot misuses of data charts and displays. In interpreting data on a graph, the key is to assume that the data presented are intended to support a point of view. That is, the purpose of the graph is to convey an attitude through numbers.

Be wary of using a graph that is inappropriate to the subject. For example, if data that reveal a trend are portrayed with a bar or column graph, one should wonder why a line graph was not used instead—perhaps to obscure the trend. If a graph contains too many elements, it may be poorly designed or purposely designed to disguise unfavorable information. Similarly, if a simple pie or bar graph could illustrate data, be skeptical and carefully scrutinize a display that depends on more complicated graphic techniques.

Data distortion through the use of graphs is a problem area within data analysis. To illustrate, Figures 4-31 and 4-32 show the same data concerning the percent of anthologies in circulation by semester week. The difference is that the vertical axis is broken on Figure 4-32. In Figure 4-32, the vertical axis begins at the four percent mark and ends at the ten percent mark. In Figure 4-31, the axis numbering begins at the origin and continuously shows data through the ten percent mark. The effect of showing the axis without a break is that the data are compressed on the vertical axis. In Figure 4-32, the data are more expanded. Thus, it is imperative that the data be examined very carefully when the vertical or horizontal scales are stretched or squeezed because the origin is omitted.

FIGURE 4-31   ▌   Line Graph with an Unbroken Vertical Axis

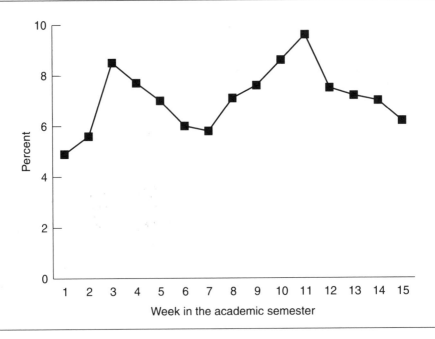

FIGURE 4-32   ▌   Line Graph with a Broken Vertical Axis

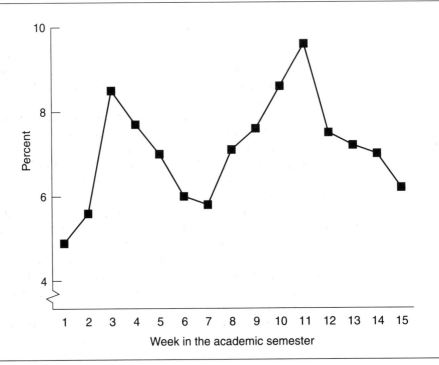

There are many sources demonstrating the effective use of graphs. These include newspapers, magazines, professional journals, reports, and other sources. Good examples should be clipped, tucked away, and referred to periodically to stimulate ideas for describing data. Live presentations are another good opportunity for employing graphs. Presentations also allow a graph to be tested upon an audience.

Guidelines for Designing Graphs

There are several important considerations in creating a graph. The following guidelines, though not exhaustive, are useful:

1. The graph's title is most effective when it is both brief and descriptive.
2. The horizontal (*X*-axis) and vertical (*Y*-axis) axes should be shown and labeled.
3. The scale should be provided for the horizontal (*X*-axis) and vertical axis (*Y*-axis).
4. Scale figures should be shown on the axis, usually supplemented with scale points or "ticks" between scale figures. Axis numbers should be large enough to read easily. If grid lines are shown, they should not be drawn to intersect columns or bars.
5. A break in the horizontal or vertical axis (*X* or *Y* axis) should be shown with a symbol such as —⋀⌐. A break in the vertical axis (*Y*-axis) should be avoided when possible, since a false impression of the data almost always results.
6. Data sources should be shown below the graph.
7. When a line graph is used to show one trend line, make the trend line bolder than the background grid lines.
8. When a line graph is used to compare the performance of two items, differentiate the lines by using a bold solid line for one and a thinner or patterned line (of short or long dashes) for the other.
9. Avoid logarithmic or ratio scale graphs unless the audience is familiar with them. In general, people are most familiar with arithmetic scales on the horizontal and vertical axes.

Through the use of personal computers and graphics software, a librarian can readily construct different types of graphs with ease. Further, computer-aided design (CAD) and graphics packages permit flexibility in the use of labels, text, legends, color, size, scale, side-by-side comparison, and other graphic manipulations.

Wringing Information from a Graph

Many people lack confidence in their ability to interpret numerical and graphical information. The objective of this section is to provide insight into how to approach a chart and recognize a trend or pattern in data. Through practice at reading graphs and increased understanding of how to interpret a chart, readers can easily "wring" information from any graph.

Figure 4-33 illustrates a bar graph that shows the number of full-time support personnel at seven libraries that are similar in size. The title of the graph is the source for this information. Since the title makes clear that the data refer to the number of full-time library personnel, the reader of the graph can assume that part-time staff are not included in the data.

FIGURE 4-33 ▌ Full-Time Support Personnel at Area Libraries

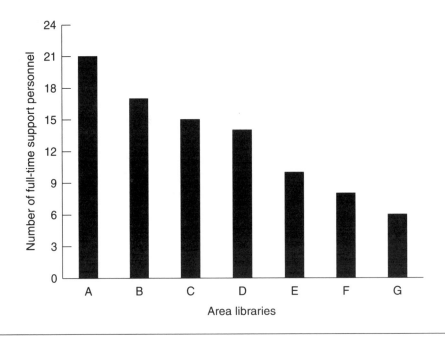

From the chart's title, the first impression may be that someone prepared the chart to show that their library does not have many full-time support staff, compared with similar libraries. Of course, the number of full-time library personnel needs to be balanced with data about the number of part-time staff. This information is important in making an informed analysis because more and more libraries favor hiring part-time personnel over full-time staff. For example, rather than support ten full-time personnel, a library may employ twenty part-timers. The reasons vary. They include the flexibility of having "on-call" personnel, of having different skill-sets available that are not needed full-time, and possible personnel savings that may be associated with hiring staff part-time.

In Figure 4-33, data are provided for seven area libraries, with the horizontal bars organized by staff size. Each bar is smaller than the one that precedes it. The first library has the largest full-time staff, with twenty-one members. The smallest staff is at the seventh library and consists of six full-time employees.

A librarian at Library E, noticing that four of the seven libraries represented have more generous staffing, may say, "We are fifth in support staff among the seven libraries with which we compare ourselves." Or, perhaps, "Our library is third from the bottom in terms of full-time support staff from among the seven libraries in our area." The figure illustrates that there are 91 persons included in the tally. The median staff size is fourteen and the mean number of staff is thirteen.

The interpretation presented so far catches most of the data's surface meaning. No trend or pattern is apparent, and there is only one data set—the numbers of which represent the staffing situation at the time that the graph was constructed.

FIGURE 4-34   Monthly Circulation of Rental Collection
(July through December)

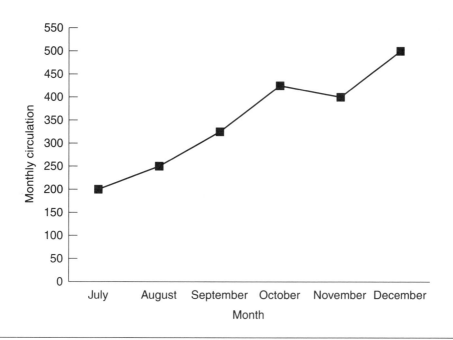

After successfully drawing the above information out of the bar chart, the work that remains is to interpret the data by forming one or more plausible interpretations and then to reflect on why these different interpretations are possible.

To begin, recognize that any reader of the chart will develop a viewpoint reflecting personal biases. For example, a librarian may analyze the chart and reason that the library employs too few full-time support staff. Another person may read the chart and wonder why the library has so many full-time personnel when others of similar size get along with fewer staff. This person will wonder whether the "excess" number of jobs could be adequately done by part-time staff. Alternately, one might consider increasing the job responsibilities of current staff in order to reduce the number of full-time staff.

For another example, imagine a public library has a collection of rental books. The purpose of the rental collection is to reduce the waiting time for people who want to read the most current best-sellers. It caters to those persons in the community who are willing to rent a library copy for a period at a certain rate, perhaps for up to seven days for one dollar. Suppose that the library began its rental collection with gift moneys and continues to use the profits to buy additional new titles. Figure 4-34 is a line graph that shows the circulation of the collection during the period of July through December.

The graph's title makes clear that the graph concerns only circulation data for the rental book collection. That is, there is no way to determine how many books are in the collection, and the graph does not reveal this information. However, the data show monthly circulation. From this, it is possible to determine the total circulation for the six-month period, which was 2100 rentals [2100 = 200 + 250 + 325 + 425 + 400 + 500].

A circulation of 2100 for July through December means that the rental collection generated $2100. This revenue will be used for buying additional books for the collection. Of course, since no information is provided for January through June circulation, the annual revenue is not known. However, it might be concluded that annual circulation potential is 4000 loans, with potential for growth as the number of popular novels grows and availability of the rental program becomes better known. If circulation drops, the librarian can simply adjust the rental fee.

If the average price of a new hardcover book is $20, the librarian can add 115 titles every six months [105 = 2100/20]. Annually, this is about 200 titles per year. If the library buys ten copies of each new best-seller, this means that twenty best-seller titles will be added to the collection each year.

From Figure 4-34, it is evident that circulation of the popular titles is generally strong. July borrowing (200 titles) is at its lowest for the six-month period, July through December. This may be because the collection is new or because people are away on vacation during the summer. If a librarian looks at the circulation count, it really is slow. This observation is based on the library being open seven days per week. Thus, a month with 30 days yields only between six and seven circulations per day. Also, there is a dip in November circulation, perhaps because of the Thanksgiving holiday. Encouragingly, the chart shows that the monthly cumulative circulation is increasing and the rate of increase is increasing.

When reading a graph, look for the following general items:

1. *The title of the graph.* The title provides a preliminary overview of the graph before it is examined for details.

2. *The names and units for the horizontal and vertical axes.* The names and units of these variables help to understand the purpose for the graph. The variable that is shown on the horizontal axis is the independent variable, or the variable over which there often is control. When the independent variable is adjusted, the effect is immediately seen on the dependent variable—the variable shown on the vertical axis.

3. *The time period.* Understand whether the graph is showing data for a specific month or year, such as July or 1999, or for a time span of a number of months, for example, such as January through June.

4. *The level of measurement represented by the data.* It is important to know whether the data are measured in nominal, ordinal, interval, or ratio scale and whether the data are discrete or continuous. This information indicates how the data most likely were collected.

5. *The type of graph.* Different types of data are best illustrated by certain types of graphs. If the best graphing vehicle for the data has not been used, be alert for possible deception or fuzzy judgment.

6. *The range or span of the data.* Identify the data's maximum and minimum values, as shown on the graph.

7. *The trend of the data.* Determine whether the data are rising, falling, or moving laterally.

8. *Data reasonableness.* Be prepared to make some calculations using the data. For example, if the graph reports activity based on a week, determine how much activity it represents per day to assess the level of activity.

SUMMARY OF CRITICAL CONCEPTS

1. An effective way to organize data is to arrange it from low to high or high to low. The resulting distribution is called a *data array.* A data array allows the librarian to recognize immediately the largest and smallest values of the data set.

2. Data can be sorted into categories and displayed in a tabular manner. The resulting *frequency distribution* shows the number of observations from the data set that fall into the various data categories. This technique classifies, condenses, and greatly simplifies data for presentation, analysis, and interpretation.

3. The categories into which frequency distribution data are sorted are called *classes.* Each class has a standard size, described as *class width.* Class width should be either three units wide or a multiple of five units wide. It is preferable that the class width for all of the classes be equal, because *intervals of equal width* make computation easier and help prevent data distortion.

4. A frequency distribution should be composed of between 6 and 15 classes. Too many classes make the information difficult to use. Too few classes overcondense the data.

5. The choice of class width and the number of classes influence the appearance of a frequency distribution. The usual practice is to compute several distributions using different class intervals and then to select the distribution that best fits the data.

6. Class intervals must be *mutually exclusive.* That is, they must be defined so that each data point can be sorted into only one class interval.

7. *Class limits* establish the lower and upper boundaries for discrete data. *Real limits* set the boundaries for continuous scale data.

8. *Graphs* are visual representations of statistical data that classify and show trends and relationships not readily apparent in tabular data. A graph is a picture of points that mark the relationship between numbers.

9. Graphs are presented in a two-dimensional picture in the *rectangular coordinate plane.* This plane is formed by the perpendicular intersection of two *real-number lines* that form the axes. The two number lines are the *horizontal (X-axis)* and the *vertical (Y-axis).*

10. A *histogram* illustrates a data set through a series of rectangles with their bases on the horizontal axis (X-axis), their centers at the class midpoints, and their widths equal to the class interval scales. The areas of the rectangles are proportional to class frequencies. Histograms are used to display absolute, relative, and cumulative frequencies.

11. A *bar graph* is one in which the length of each bar corresponds to the number of observations in a category. Bar graphs can be constructed horizontally or vertically. This chart is effective for summarizing attribute or ordinal scale data.

12. A *pie graph* or chart is a complete circle in which wedges or sectors of the circle represent the total number of measurements. The size of the wedge is proportional to the relative frequency of a particular category of data.

13. A *frequency polygon* includes much of the same information as a histogram. It is a closed-figure graph of class frequency plotted against class midpoint. This graph can be constructed easily from the histogram by connecting the midpoints of the tops of the histogram's rectangles.

14. The *horizontal bar graph* is effective for showing item comparisons. It has one scale, extending horizontally along the length of the bars.

15. The *vertical column graph* is effective for showing time and size comparisons. It has two scales. Usually, the horizontal scale represents time and the vertical scale represents quantity.

16. *Circle graphs* are effective for showing components of a whole. They work best when picturing a maximum of five items. The *line graph* is effective for illustrating whether a variable is increasing, decreasing, fluctuating, or remaining constant.

17. All illustrations are not equally successful in conveying information. Be sensitive to selecting the type of graph that best illustrates the data.

KEY TERMS

Array.   A group of numbers organized in an increasing or decreasing order. A *data array* is the arrangement of raw data in increasing or decreasing order.

Class.   A data set consisting of a group of scores. A *class interval* is a grouping of scores with a range of values. For example, the class interval 1–4 contains scores for {1, 2, 3, and 4}. In a frequency distribution, the intervals are *classes.*

Coordinate plane.   A plane formed by the perpendicular intersection of two axes. The *X-axis* is horizontal and the *Y-axis* is vertical. The point of intersection is the *origin.* A gridlike pattern of intersecting columns and rows results, forming a two-dimensional plane. Points on the plane are identified by coordinates. The convention is to identify the *X*-coordinate, then the *Y*-coordinate. The (*x, y*) coordinates of a point are called an *ordered pair.*

Cumulative frequency.   The sum of the frequencies of all values.

Frequency.   The number of times a score or group of scores (class) occurs in a sample or population. The terms *class frequency* and *interval frequency* are used interchangeably. In place of frequencies, proportions or relative frequencies often are used.

Mutually exclusive.   Separate and distinct, with no overlap. Two events are mutually exclusive if they cannot occur simultaneously. Class intervals are mutually exclusive if no overlap is permitted. The intervals 1–3 and 4–6 are mutually exclusive, but 1–3 and 3–5 are not mutually exclusive since a data value of 3 might be inconsistently counted either in the interval 1–3 or in the interval 3–5.

Open-ended interval.   A class interval that allows either the upper or lower end to be limitless, as in the interval 60 +, to indicate that all scores that are 60 or greater are included in that interval.

Relative frequency.   The frequency (*f*) of one score or group of scores divided by the total frequency of all the observations (*n*). The result is usually expressed as a percent. The relative frequencies of all classes sum to 100%.

Score.   The number assigned to a case such as people or items. A score represents the amount of some property or attribute that the case exhibits.

Trend.   A general tendency of a variable to rise, fall, or move laterally in an unchanged pattern.

SELF-ASSESSMENT QUIZ

1. *True* or *False*   In an array, data are arranged either from high to low or from low to high.

2. *True* or *False*   All classes should be of equal width.

3. *True* or *False*   Mutually exclusive classes mean that a data point can be sorted into only one class.

4. *True* or *False*   Vertical bar graphs are effective for showing change in a single variable over time.

5. *True* or *False*   Pie graphs are effective in emphasizing the size of a component relative to the total.

6. *True* or *False*   The true limits of the class interval 3–5 (for continuous data) are 2.9–5.1.

7. *True* or *False*   The width of the interval 3–5 (for continuous data) is 2.

8. *True* or *False*   An advantage of the histogram over the frequency polygon is in using it to illustrate two or more data sets on the same graph.

9. *True* or *False*   It is always possible to construct a histogram from a frequency polygon.

10. *True* or *False*   In a frequency distribution, classes need not be mutually exclusive.

Answers

1. *True*   An array is a listing of scores that is arranged in ascending or descending order. For example, {5, 11, 17, 33} is an array since the scores are arranged in ascending order. However, {17, 5, 33, 11} is not an array since the scores are not in ascending or descending order.

2. *True*   Classes of equal width help to reduce data distortion.

3. *True*   By definition, mutually exclusive classes do not allow overlap between or among them. Therefore, mutually exclusive classes help to prevent data ambiguity.

4. *True*   Vertical bar graphs are best when used to compare a variable at five or fewer time periods.

5. *True*   Pie graphs provide an excellent visual image of component percents.

6. *False*   The true limits are 2.5–5.5.

7. *False*   The true limits are 2.5–5.5, so the class width is 3.

8. *False*   Frequency polygons are superior to histograms for this purpose since multiple polygons make fewer, less confusing intersections.

9. *True*   The frequency polygon shows the midpoint and frequency for each class. The width of the classes can be inferred from the location of the midpoints. Midpoint, frequency, and width can then be used to construct a histogram.

10. *False*   Classes in a frequency distribution must be defined so that each data point is assigned to one and only one interval.

DISCUSSION QUESTIONS AND PROBLEMS

1. A librarian conducts a survey and learns the annual operating budget of sixty-two institutions. The largest budget is $1,260,798 and the smallest is $315,729. The librarian wishes to construct a bar graph.
   a. Determine the number of class intervals, based on suggestions in the text.
   b. Determine the class width for the data.
   c. Calculate the midpoint for the class intervals.

2. A library consortium canvassed its members to learn the number of days that each member's computer system was down during the previous 90 days.

Days down	0	1	2	3	4	5	6	7
Frequency	6	7	10	14	7	3	2	1

   a. Prepare an ungrouped frequency distribution.
   b. Prepare a bar graph for each frequency distribution.

3. The operating budgets of six public libraries in a certain county are listed below. Prepare a histogram and interpret the data. (Hint: Treat this data as qualitative data.)

Library	Operating budget
A	$1,105,611
B	711,561
C	830,540
D	1,163,224
E	1,323,777
F	1,162,698

4. Twenty colleges answered a questionnaire about the number of hours of public service offered by their libraries during the fall semester.

74	65	56	74	68	67	69	60	66	77
52	59	57	61	61	59	63	64	63	60

   a. Prepare a grouped frequency distribution.
   b. Prepare a bar graph.
   c. Prepare a relative frequency distribution.
   d. Prepare a cumulative frequency distribution.

5. A circulation librarian conducted a study of staffing and equipment needs at the circulation desk. Over one week, 2-hour time periods were sampled. A record was made of the time (to the nearest tenth of a minute) required for a library user to check out materials. Data for a representative 2-hour period ($n = 100$) are shown below.

2.2	2.2	1.4	0.9	1.5	1.9	1.7	0.8	2.3	2.0
2.1	1.4	2.3	0.8	1.6	1.9	1.6	2.0	1.2	1.9
2.2	1.4	1.9	2.2	1.6	1.3	1.7	1.3	2.4	1.9
1.8	0.9	2.2	1.3	1.4	0.5	1.1	1.6	1.1	2.0
2.3	1.5	2.2	0.9	2.3	1.9	1.6	1.4	1.8	1.2
1.5	2.3	0.9	1.9	0.9	1.2	1.5	1.4	1.7	1.1
1.5	1.4	1.7	1.8	1.9	0.8	1.5	1.0	1.5	1.8

2.3	1.6	1.2	1.7	1.3	1.8	2.2	1.4	2.1	1.3
2.3	2.2	2.2	1.8	1.8	1.7	1.8	2.2	2.1	1.9
1.8	0.9	1.6	1.3	0.9	0.4	1.3	1.5	1.0	1.9

a. Prepare a frequency distribution, beginning with class interval 0.4–0.6, and ending with interval 2.2–2.4.

b. Prepare a "less than" cumulative percent distribution.

c. Prepare a "more than" cumulative percent distribution.

6. A public library serving a community of 30,000 circulates videocassettes for a 3-day loan period. Revenue from the $1 fee per video is used to acquire additional videos. The following data show the number of videocassettes owned and circulated.

Month	Videocassettes owned	Videocassettes circulated
January	161	1633
February	366	2358
March	604	2521
April	864	2371
May	1162	2407
June	1503	2178
July	1844	2531

For the following questions, use the horizontal axis to show months.

a. Prepare a bar graph for the number of videocassettes owned. Discuss the rate of growth in terms of Figure 4-29.

b. Prepare a line graph and discuss the rate of growth of videocassette circulation.

7. An academic and public library microcomputer user group conducted a survey of its 100 members. Results showed that 45% used the equipment for budget and bookkeeping activities, 30% for database activities such as specialty indexes, 20% for electronic mail, 40% for graphics, 13% for invoice preparation, 75% for spreadsheet analysis, and 65% for word processing. Prepare a graph that best illustrates these data.

8. A recently promoted librarian participated in a job study of library department directors. As a part of this study, the librarian categorized job activities by the amount of time spent on the activity, expressed in percents. These activity areas were ideas, people, and things. "Idea" activities, or those associated with department planning, accounted for 20% of the staff member's time. Activities about "things," or those associated with department administration, accounted for 35%. "People" activities, or those associated with personal contact and relationships, accounted for 45% of the librarian's time. Within "People" activities were the tasks of assigning and coordinating duties (50%), monitoring outputs to established performance standards (30%), and staff development and training (20%).

a. Illustrate the three major activities of the librarian's time profile with a pie graph.

b. Illustrate the "People" component with a 100% column graph.

9. A minimum security prison recently contracted with the local public library for library services. The prison library committee asked for a leisure reading collection of approximately 1200 paperback books. After six months of operation, inmates inventoried the

collection. They also tallied the number of circulations for each item according to the circulation slip in each book. The prison library committee then forwarded the results of their data survey to the local public librarian to determine the types of materials that circulated best.

	Number of titles	Total number of circulations
Fiction		
Adventure	105	1869
Mystery	66	1958
Romance	135	5154
Science fiction/Fantasy	132	6220
Western	91	2021
Other	138	2315
Total	667	19,537
Nonfiction		
Biography	134	1392
History/Travel	255	2699
Humor	37	748
Literature	52	1247
Local interest	6	15
Self-help	35	627
Other	16	64
Total	535	6792
Grand total	1202	26,329

a. Extend the table with two columns. The first column should show the circulations per title, and the second column should show the percent that each type of book represents of the total collection of books.

b. Prepare a pie chart showing the types of books that make up the fiction books and another for the nonfiction books. Some of the categories may have to be combined, if necessary.

c. Analyze the data and determine those types of books with the highest and lowest circulation for fiction and nonfiction.

10. A college librarian tabulated survey results from 90 faculty members who responded to questions about their information-searching habits. The table below shows the librarian's findings based on responses to the question, "When you come to the library to find a specific article, how often do you find reference to the article by consulting . . . ?"

	Usually	Occasionally	Rarely
Abstracting journals	62	21	7
Bibliographies/book footnotes	46	35	9
Bibliographies/journal footnotes	15	34	41
Colleagues	11	34	45
Librarians/library staff	13	50	27
Subject bibliographies	13	17	60
Other	2	12	76

a. Construct a table showing the percent of faculty members using each source by the frequency of such use.
b. Interpret the table.

11. A media center librarian has observed that vocational items circulate differently, depending on the time of the year. At the beginning of the fall semester, the weekly circulation for the first six weeks of vocational materials is {300, 330, 350, 360, 368, 370}. Toward the last six weeks of the semester, the circulation data is {60, 75, 100, 150, 250, 450}. Discuss the curve in the context of Figure 4-29.

12. The acquisitions librarian at a medium-size college decided to review recently completed book order transactions. The review studies the success of ordering items. The study examined book orders sent directly to the book publisher and to two vendors. The first vendor maintained a large inventory of items, and the second maintained a small inventory but made extensive use of drop shipping (shipping directly from the publisher).

A review of book order cards revealed that about 125 orders had been placed with each of the sources. Using these cards, the librarian determined the number of days between when the items were ordered via electronic mail and the date of the invoice when the items were shipped.

Calendar days	Vendor I Cumulative percent	Vendor II Cumulative percent	Direct orders Cumulative percent
7	0%	0%	0%
14	33	0	35
21	66	10	72
28	70	50	84
35	72	75	87
42	74	84	90
49	75	89	94
56	80	91	99
63	85	93	100
70	90	97	
77	92	100	
84	100		

a. Draw each supplier's distribution. Discuss the general shape of each curve and determine the point where the curves peak.
b. Speculate on reasons for each distribution's shape.

13. A student group on campus conducted an attitudinal survey about the library. As part of the written report that appeared in the school newspaper, they included a horizontal bar graph to show the results of their survey. The numbers represent the number of persons who responded in each category.

Strongly agree 36	Slightly disagree 4
Agree 28	Disagree 6
Slightly agree 14	Strongly disagree 12

a. Prepare a horizontal bar graph for the data. Interpret it.

b. How many students participated in the survey?

c. Calculate the percentage of students for each category and construct a pie chart. Interpret the chart.

d. Compare and contrast the horizontal bar graph with the pie chart. Which is more effective for presenting the data and why?

14. A librarian at a public library monitored the exit counts over a six-week period and then constructed a line graph. The counts by week were {750, 1000, 1325, 1750, 1550, 1825}. These data are shown in Figure 4-35.

a. Complete the graph by giving it a name.

b. Label the independent (horizontal axis) and dependent (vertical axis) variables with proper names and units.

c. For which week was library attendance the highest?

d. What was the change in attendance between each week?

e. How much change in attendance was there between the first and last week?

FIGURE 4-35

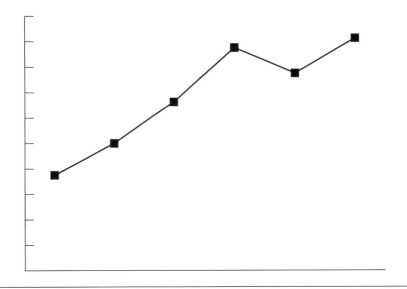

MEASURES OF CENTRAL TENDENCY

After reading this chapter, you will be able to do the following:

1. Identify the property of central tendency for ungrouped or grouped data.

2. Interpret the differences among various measures of central tendency such as the mode, median, and mean.

3. Calculate and interpret the value of the mode, median, and mean for ungrouped and grouped data.

4. Calculate and interpret the value of the weighted mean.

5. Identify distributions as symmetrical or skewed.

6. Identify and list library examples of distributions that produce J-curves, reverse J-curves, and U-curves.

7. Describe the usefulness of Pareto's 80/20 rule and interpret Pareto analysis.

S tatistical techniques, when used to analyze and present data, provide evidence for making decisions under any management method. In order to turn raw data into meaningful numbers, an understanding of statistical measures that boil down complicated data into a value that is understandable and relevant is essential. This chapter presents some of these important measures.

MEASURES OF CENTRAL TENDENCY

In the preceding chapters, raw data were organized by using data arrays, frequency distributions, and graphs. These techniques help display data in useful ways. Three key characteristics of a distribution are of particular importance in the study of statistics. The first is the spread or width of the distribution's data. The second is the distribution's middle value. The third is the distribution's general shape.

As useful as pictorial representations of data are, they have some shortcomings. Specifically, graphs do not provide quantitative statements about the data or about a distribution's three key characteristics. Another weakness is that frequency distributions or charts do not lend themselves to making easy comparisons between two or more distributions, as in evaluating several competing pieces of equipment for purchase, for example.

Measures of central tendency, or *measures of location,* are quantitative measures that allow side-by-side comparisons of distributions. The value of these *summary statistics* is that they yield a quantitative measure for the distribution's "middle." For this reason, they are often referred to as *averages.*

There are three measures of central tendency. These are the mode, the median, and the arithmetic mean. The measure that is most appropriate in any particular situation depends on the level of measurement for the data, the information that one wishes to communicate about the data, and the way data are concentrated in the data set.

The mode, median, and mean each present the data's central value. Under certain conditions, these three measures can be the same. Most often, however, they are not. Although this sounds confusing, the explanation is that each of these summary statistics has its own definition of "central" or "middle." To use these measures effectively then, one must understand the perspective that each measure presents, as well as the advantages and disadvantages associated with each measure.

Briefly, for the *mode,* the distribution's center is the data point or score that occurs most frequently in the distribution. For the *median,* the distribution's center is the value that evenly divides the distribution. That is, it is the value or score below or above which 50 percent of the observations occur. And for the third measure of central tendency, the *mean,* the distribution's center is the "balance point" of the distribution, which is based on considering the size or weight of each data point.

The Mode

The *mode* of a data set is the value (or values) occurring most often in the distribution. The mode identifies the distribution's most prevalent score or scores. For example, in the data set {1, 1, 2, 3, 4}, the mode is 1 because 1 is the value that occurs most frequently. In the data set {4, 4, 4, 5, 6, 6, 6}, there are two modes: 4 and 6. In this example, both 4 and 6 occur three times in the distribution, which is more frequently than any other value occurs. Because this data set has two modes, it is called *bimodal.*

The mode is a crude but simple measure of central tendency. It can be applied to nominal, ordinal, interval, and ratio scale data, but usually it is applied only to nominal data. In practice, the mode is not used with ordered, interval, or ratio scale data, even though it is permitted.

For *ungrouped data,* the mode is determined by observing the value in the data set that is repeated most often. For example, to determine the mode of the data set {10, 12, 20, 12, 15, 17, 25, 12}, the librarian's task is to identify the value(s) that appear most frequently. In this example, 12 occurs three times, which is more often than any other value of the set is seen. Hence, 12 is the data set's mode.

Example 5-1

Finding the Mode

Suppose 14 library staff members were asked how many different library room keys they carry, with the resulting distribution:

Number of keys	1	2	3	4	5	6	7
Number of staff	1	4	2	3	2	1	1

Analysis

The mode is 2, since more of the fourteen staff members have two keys than any other number of keys.

Table 5-1 presents hypothetical data on different types of libraries located within a particular geographical region. The data are nominal scale (categorical data) since they refer to a nonquantitative variable, type of library.

With these data, the mode is an effective measure of central tendency. From the table, the modal class is Public libraries since Public libraries occur with a frequency of 9000, which is more often than any other category appears.

When data are grouped into classes, the mode is calculated differently. First, the *modal class* must be identified. This is the class that contains the highest frequency of observations. Then the mode, a single number, is estimated from the modal class—usually the midpoint

TABLE 5-1   Type and Number of Libraries in Region A

Academic libraries	4,600
Armed forces libraries	400
Government libraries	1,600
Law libraries	400
Medical libraries	1,500
Public libraries (including branches)	9,000
Religious libraries	800
Special libraries	4,000
Total	22,300

of the modal class interval. For example, suppose a librarian groups demographic data into the following classes:

Number of children in a family	1–3	4–6	7–9
Frequency	7	6	1

In this grouping, the 1–3 class is the modal class; that is, this class has the highest frequency. The mode is estimated by using the class limits 1 and 3. The midpoint of this class, $(1 + 3)/2 = 2$, is the best estimate for the mode of the grouped frequency distribution.

Example 5-2

Finding the Modal Class with Nominal Scale Data

The children's librarian polled summer readers about their favorite mode of transportation for vacation trips. Survey results of fifty readers revealed the following replies: car, airplane, airplane, car, bus, train, airplane, bus, airplane, bicycle, train, walk, airplane, train, airplane, airplane, car, airplane, bicycle, bus, car, bicycle, train, bus, car, car, car, airplane, walk, bus, car, car, airplane, bus, train, train, car, car, airplane, car, airplane, car, bus, airplane, bicycle, train, train, walk, car, car, airplane, car, bus, car, bicycle, train, train, car, car, airplane, car, train, car.

1. Prepare a categorical frequency distribution.
2. Identify the modal response.

Analysis

1. The distribution of modes of transportation by preference is as follows:

Mode	Frequency	Mode	Frequency
Car	21	Bus	8
Airplane	15	Bicycle	5
Train	11	Walk	3

2. The modal response is Car, since Car is the preferred transportation response that occurred most frequently in the survey. The interpretation of the modal class is that, among summer readers, the favorite mode of transportation for vacation trips is the car.

As a measure of central tendency, however, the mode has some shortcomings. One is that a data set may not have a mode. For example, {2, 3, 4, 5, 6} and {2, 2, 2, 2} are data sets, yet neither has a mode since no score occurs more often than another. A second weakness, as mentioned previously, is that a data set may have more than one mode. For example, the data set {5, 7, 7, 7, 8, 9, 9, 9} has two modes. The two modes are 7 and 9, since each of these values occurs three times in the distribution. This frequency of occurrence is greater than any other in the distribution.

Some specific terms have been coined to describe the number of modes in a data set. Distributions with one mode are *unimodal;* distributions with two modes are *bimodal;* distributions with three modes are *trimodal*. Finally, distributions that have two or more modes are called *multimodal* distributions.

FIGURE 5-1   ▌ A Grouped Bimodal Distribution

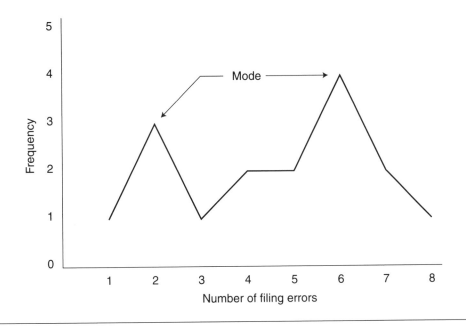

A bimodal distribution is one in which two scores occur more frequently than any other. In any multimodal distribution, the modes need not be of equal size but must stand out above the neighboring values. This leads to an important broader definition of *mode* as the value(s) around which there is the greatest clustering in a distribution. This is illustrated in Figure 5-1. It shows an example of a grouped data bimodal distribution in which the graph peaks at frequencies of 3 and 4. However, the mode is not at the frequencies, but at the corresponding readings on the *X*-axis. The distribution's modes are 2 and 6 filing errors, respectively.

A multimodal distribution suggests that dissimilar or heterogeneous data make up the data set. For example, if the income levels of hourly library wage earners were combined with the library's salaried employees, the resulting modal income classes would be so diverse as to have little meaning. More dramatically, if librarians' salaries were to be combined in a distribution with physicians' salaries, the resulting distribution would be diverse, with librarians' salaries at one end of the distribution and physicians' salaries at the other. The distribution would have two very distinct modes. Hence, to be comparable, the data used to form a distribution should be homogeneous. If distinct groups of data can be identified by using the mode, the usual practice is to try to study the groups separately and not as part of the same distribution.

The Median

The *median* of a data set is the number that divides the distribution exactly in half. That is, when a distribution's scores are arranged from smallest to largest, the median is the midpoint value of the data set. This means that one-half or 50% of the data scores are larger than the median value and one-half or 50% are smaller than the median value.

The median is an appropriate measure for ordinal, interval, and ratio scale data. It is inappropriate for nominal scale data, however, because nominal scale data cannot be ranked. The median always is expressed in the same units as the original data. Further, unlike the mode, the median always is a single value. That is, a data set cannot have more than one median.

To calculate the median for a data set, the scores are first ordered into an array. When this is completed, the resulting number of scores is either an odd number or an even number. For an odd number of scores, the median is the middle score. For an even number of scores, the median is the point between the two middle scores. Example 5-3 illustrates how to find the median.

Example 5-3

Finding the Median with an Odd Number of Scores

1. The five members of a book club were asked how many books each typically reads in a month. Responding in alphabetical order by first name, the members reported that they read 7, 9, 12, 2, and 6 books, respectively.

   Analysis

   To determine the median, the data are arranged in order from lowest to highest, {2, 6, 7, 9, 12}. Since there are five observations, the median is the middle value, or 7. This is the value that is in the third of five positions. Its interpretation is that the members of the reading club read a median "average" of seven books each month.

2. A librarian surveys 15 college libraries that are open on weekends to determine their hours of service. The number of hours is noted as each library is telephoned: {15, 15, 8, 12, 12, 14, 14, 16, 8, 17, 18, 15, 12, 10, 14}.

   Analysis

   To determine the median, the fifteen scores are arranged in ascending order, {8, 8, 10, 12, 12, 12, 14, 14, 14, 15, 15, 15, 16, 17, 18}. The middle score is the eighth in the distribution. The value of the 8th score is 14. The interpretation of the median is that the college libraries are open a median "average" of 14 hours on weekends.

3. Expressed in thousands, the annual expenditures for journals at six libraries was {$234, $229, $226, $234, $299, $250}.

   Analysis

   In rank order, the scores are {$226, $229, $234, $234, $250, $299}. The median lies between the third and fourth scores, both of which are $234. [$234 = ($234 + $234)/2, or $468/2].

4. A library received special funding to purchase books. During the first week, only a few items were received. Beginning with the second through the sixth week, the library received 26, 42, 36, 52, 39 books, respectively.

   Analysis

   The number of books received during the first week is not known. Since only a "few" books were received, one could surmise that the library received more books during each of the weeks following the first week. In rank order, the scores are {x, 26, 36, 39, 42, 52}, where x refers to the unknown number of books, initially received. The median lies between the third and fourth scores, and is 37.5. However, since the value must be a whole number (discrete value), the median is 38 [38, since 37.5 = (36 + 39)/2, or 75/2]. This example shows that the median can be found even if there is a missing data value.

Suppose there is concern about the availability of parking spaces in a lot adjacent to the library. On a particular day, the number of available parking spaces each hour over an eight-hour period are {10, 2, 4, 3, 0, 0, 3, 1}. When the librarian arranges the scores into an array, the distribution is {0, 0, 1, 2, 3, 3, 4, 10}. Since there are eight scores, the median is the number that lies between the fourth and fifth values in the data set. Thus, the median number of available parking spaces each hour is 2.5 parking spaces, which is rounded to 3 since the median value must be a discrete value [3, since 2.5 = (2 + 3)/2].

In the parking space distribution, 10 is an extreme score that does not affect the median. The interpretation of the median is *not* that there are literally 2.5 parking spaces available. Rather, the interpretation is that the number of available parking spaces clusters around 2 or 3 each hour.

The data in the previous examples have not been grouped. Finding the median for *grouped data* is done differently than for ungrouped data. The following example helps to illustrate the procedure.

Suppose a librarian wishes to determine the median time required for interlibrary loan personnel to fill requests. To begin the analysis, the librarian examines the number of requests and then prepares a frequency distribution, as shown in Table 5-2.

Each of these 156 records contains the clerk's notation of the number of days required to fill the request. (A designation of zero days means that the request was filled on the day it was received.) Since the frequency distribution does not show the raw data values for the distribution, the librarian cannot list the actual values included in the class interval that contains the median. Because of this, the librarian must determine the median through a method known as *interpolation*.

In Table 5-2, $n = 156$. So, the rank of the median lies midway between the 78th and 79th scores. The frequency distribution shows that this score is contained in the interval whose real limits are 7.5 to 11.5. The 78th item is the sixth element in the median class [6 = 78 − 72]. Thus, to arrive at the desired 78th rank, the librarian must determine the value of

---

TABLE 5-2 ▨ Summary of Days Required to Fill Interlibrary Loan Requests ($n = 156$)

Class interval	Frequency (f)	Upper class boundary	Cumulative frequency
0–3	24	3.5	24
4–7	48	7.5	72
8–11	40	11.5	112
12–15	15	15.5	127
16–19	14	19.5	141
20–23	9	23.5	150
24–27	6	27.5	156
	$n = 156$		

going six steps into the interval 7.5 to 11.5. Because the interval contains 40 steps, since $f = 40$, the median must lie 6/40 of the way between 7.5 and 11.5. The calculations are as follows:

$$\tilde{X} = 7.5 + \frac{6}{40}(11.5 - 7.5)$$

$$= 7.5 + 0.15(4.0)$$

$$= 7.5 + 0.6 \text{ which is 8.1 days.}$$

Formula 5-1 shortens the calculations needed to compute the median for grouped data. The symbol $\tilde{X}$ is read "X-tilde."

Formula 5-1

$$\tilde{X} = L + \frac{w}{f}\left(\frac{n}{2} - F\right)$$

where L = lower class boundary of the median class

n = total number of observations in the data set

F = cumulative frequency up to, but not including, the median class

f = frequency of the median class

w = size of the median class

To test the result obtained, apply Formula 5-1 to the example. In it, $L = 7.5$, $n = 156$, $F = 72$, $f = 40$, and $w = 4$.

$$\tilde{X} = 7.5 + (4/40)[0.5(156) - 72]$$

$$= 7.5 + .1(78 - 72)$$

$$= 7.5 + .1(6)$$

$$= 7.5 + 0.6 \text{ which is 8.1 days.}$$

The median is a valuable measure of central tendency for grouped data when there is an open-ended class, unless the median itself falls in the open-ended class.

Example 5-4 illustrates the technique to find the median of grouped data with an open class interval. The data for the example are found in Table 5-3.

Example 5-4 | **Finding the Median of Grouped Data with an Open-Ended Class**

Referring to Table 5-3, the median class is the class containing the 37th observation. The boundaries of the interval containing the median are 11.95 and 13.95.

Analysis

Applying Formula 5-1, where $L = 11.95$, $n = 73$, $F = 35$, $f = 16$, and $w = 2$:

$$\tilde{X} = L + \frac{w}{f}\left(\frac{n}{2} - F\right)$$

$$= 11.95 + \frac{2}{16}\left[\frac{73}{2} - 35\right]$$

$$= 11.95 + \frac{1}{8}(36.5 - 35)$$

$$= 11.95 + \frac{1}{8}(1.5)$$

$$= 11.95 + 0.1875 \text{ which is } 12.1375 \text{ or } 12.1 \text{ hours.}$$

Notice that the result is rounded to the nearest one-tenth hour because the original values were stated in tenths.

The median is an excellent measure of central tendency for ordinal data. For example, a librarian might apply it in interpreting ordinal scale questionnaire responses that measure attitudes and opinions.

Suppose that a librarian wishes to study clientele attitudes about the quality and usefulness of services provided in the library's microform room. To gather this attitudinal information, the librarian asks questions that can be answered with the following responses: Excellent, Good, Fair, Poor, or Needs improvement. After a pilot test to make sure that the questions are clearly stated, 24 persons complete the survey and the librarian begins to study the ordinal scale data.

To make tabulation of the survey easier, each of the categories is assigned a numerical score. These scores are as follows: Excellent = 5, Good = 4, Fair = 3, Poor = 2, and Needs improvement = 1. When viewing these data, the librarian must keep in mind that the

TABLE 5-3 ▓ Student Employee Hours per Week at XYZ University ($n = 73$)

Number of hours worked	Number of students	Class limits	Cumulative frequency
Less than 3	1	—	1
4.0–5.9	1	5.95	2
6.0–7.9	6	7.95	8
8.0–9.9	9	9.95	17
10.0–11.9	18	11.95	35
12.0–13.9	16	13.95	51
14.0–15.9	7	15.95	58
16.0–17.9	9	17.95	67
18.0–19.9	4	19.95	71
20.0 or more	2	—	73
	$n = 73$		

numerical designations are rankings, not exact measurements. In other words, a ranking of Good, represented by 4, is not twice as good as a ranking of Poor, represented by 2.

Table 5-4 shows a tabulation of 24 responses to Question 1. In this frequency distribution, the librarian has organized the data from low to high. It is not necessary to write the values horizontally in an array. Since there are 24 responses, the median value lies between the 12th and 13th responses. In the distribution, this point is between the categories Good and Fair.

In previous examples in which the median fell between two observations, the median was reported as an intermediate value. This was seen in the earlier example about parking spaces in a lot adjacent to the library. In the situation that was described, the median number of parking spaces was between 2 and 3, which is equal to 2.5. The number of parking spaces is a ratio scale measurement, because the intervals between observations are equal and because there is an absolute zero point.

The observations Good and Fair, however, are ordinal scale measurements. Further, the intervals between observations such as Good, Fair, and Poor, cannot be assumed to be equal. All that can be observed is that the median lies between 3 and 4, or between Good and Fair. No intermediate value can be calculated. Had there been an odd number of scores, the median could have been reliably identified as a single category, such as Good.

Determining the median of scores based on ordinal scale measurement commonly leads to confusion. The way to avoid uncertainty is to be particularly alert for occasions in which discrete ordinal classes are treated as though they were continuous. When this happens, the data have been incorrectly treated as though the ordinal rankings were exact measurements.

The median is an excellent measure of central tendency when some scores have undetermined value. For example, suppose that a librarian tabulates the number of days that five vendors require to complete an identical order. Four of the vendors ship the items within 45 days, the maximum length of time over which the librarian conducts the test. Properly, the librarian does not record a score or result for the vendor that failed to provide the order within the 45 days. It would be incorrect to record 45 days for this vendor, since the order was not received within that time period. The rationale for leaving the number of days blank is that, because in reality some vendors do not ship items—for whatever reason, the librarian is basing the analysis on real-world conditions.

The Arithmetic Mean

The arithmetic mean, popularly called the *average* or the *mean,* is a measure familiar to almost everyone. The mean for ungrouped observations is obtained by first adding all the scores in the data set and then dividing the sum by the total number of scores.

TABLE 5-4   Responses to Question 1

Category	Frequency
Excellent = 5	5
Good = 4	7
Fair = 3	6
Poor = 2	4
Needs improvement = 1	2
Total	24

The mean is an appropriate measure for interval or ratio scale data. It is not appropriate for nominal or ordinal scale measurements, however, since these types of data cannot be added together.

If each data point is represented by X, and if there are N scores, $\{x_1, x_2, x_3, \ldots, x_N\}$, the mean for the data set—called x-bar or $\bar{X}$—is provided by Formula 5-2.

Formula 5-2

$$\bar{X} = \frac{\sum_{i=1}^{N} X_i}{N}$$

$$= \frac{X_1 + X_2 + X_3 + \ldots + X_N}{N}$$

As Formula 5-2 shows, each data observation is used in determining the mean. Hence, an extreme data value will pull the mean toward it. Despite this limitation, the mean is the most widely used measure of central tendency.

To illustrate calculating the mean, imagine a library that has ten computer printers that are available for public use. The annual number of days that the individual terminals are out of service is $\{8, 9, 4, 9, 8, 4, 5, 3, 6, 4\}$. To find the mean, apply Formula 5-2. In this example, the $N = 10$ data points are as follows:

$x_1 = 8$	$x_6 = 4$
$x_2 = 9$	$x_7 = 5$
$x_3 = 4$	$x_8 = 3$
$x_4 = 9$	$x_9 = 6$
$x_5 = 8$	$x_{10} = 4$

Substituting in Formula 5-2:

$$\bar{X} = \frac{\sum_{i=1}^{10} X_i}{10}$$

$$= \frac{x_1 + x_2 + x_3 + x_4 + x_5 + x_6 + x_7 + x_8 + x_9 + x_{10}}{10}$$

$$= \frac{8 + 9 + 4 + 9 + 8 + 4 + 5 + 3 + 6 + 4}{10}$$

$$= \frac{60}{10} \text{ which is 6 days.}$$

The interpretation of the mean is that each terminal was out of service for 6 days, on average. Examined in a larger context, the interpretation is that one of the 10 terminals was out of service on 60 workdays during the year.

In another example, suppose that the salary of five public library directors from similar size cities is $57,500, $48,600, $50,800, $58,000, and $47,500. To determine the mean salary, again apply Formula 5-2. The $N = 5$ data scores are $x_1 = \$57,500$, $x_2 = \$48,600$, $x_3 = \$50,800$, $x_4 = \$58,000$, and $x_5 = \$47,500$. Substituting in Formula 5-2:

$$\overline{X} = \frac{\sum\limits_{i=1}^{5} X_i}{5}$$

$$= \frac{x_1 + x_2 + x_3 + x_4 + x_5}{5}$$

$$= \frac{\$57,500 + \$48,600 + \$50,800 + \$58,000 + \$47,500}{5}$$

$$= \frac{\$262,400}{5} \text{ which is } \$52,480.$$

The interpretation is that the mean salary of the five library directors is $52,480. When examining the data, $52,480 is a reasonable "middle" value for the data set. Some amounts are more than the mean and some are less. It was not required for the librarian to create an array to find the mean, but it is instructive to see the array, which is {$58,000, $57,500, $48,600, $50,800, $47,500}.

Example 5-5

Finding the Mean

The operating budgets of five libraries (in thousands) of similar size towns is $527, $478, $504, $72, and $495. Find the mean.

Analysis

The mean is determined using Formula 5-2. The $N = 5$ data scores are $x_1 = \$527$, $x_2 = \$478$, $x_3 = \$504$, $x_4 = \$72$, and $x_5 = \$495$. Substituting in Formula 5-2:

$$\overline{X} = \frac{\sum\limits_{i=1}^{5} X_i}{5}$$

$$= \frac{x_1 + x_2 + x_3 + x_4 + x_5}{5}$$

$$= \frac{\$527 + \$478 + \$504 + \$72 + \$495}{5}$$

$$= \frac{\$2076}{5} \text{ which is } \$415.2.$$

The interpretation of $415.2 is that the mean is $415,200, since the budgets are expressed in thousands of dollars. Yet, this measure does not represent the data very well. This becomes easy to see if the data are examined in an array: {$72, $478, $495, $504, $527}.

   The mean turns out to be smaller than any value in the data set, with the exception of the $72,000 value, which is an extreme (low) value. The value of $72,000 is an outlier. It tends to pull the mean toward it, thereby distorting the interpretation of the data set's central value.

This example demonstrates that the mean value is always sensitive to extreme scores in the distribution. If the data set has one or more extreme scores—either high or low—the mean may not represent the data set.

When a distribution contains extreme values, an option is to calculate two means, one that includes the extreme value and one that does not. In the example above, four of the values are of a similar magnitude: {$527, $478, $504, and $495}. The mean of the data set is $501 [$501 = ($527 + $478 + $504 + $495)/4]. This amount is much more representative of the other scores, which, when placed in an array, are {$478, $495, $504, $527}. Another strategy for the librarian to consider for reporting data that contain one or more extreme values is to report the mean along with the median and mode, since the median and mode are less sensitive to extreme values.

When determining the mean, usually it is not necessary to write all of the detail shown previously, however. For example, use of sigma notation is a shortcut that proves very useful:

$$\sum X_i \text{ is equivalent to } \sum_{i=1}^{N} X_i.$$

Typically, the values for x_1, x_2, and so on would not be written out. The following example will serve as an illustration.

Suppose that the members of a consortium report the annual amount that each member institution spends on document delivery services. The respective amounts for members A through G are {$17,500, $18,500, $18,250, $17,750, $18,500, $24,750, $17,750}. To find the mean, using Formula 5-2, with $N = 7$,

$$\overline{X} = \frac{\sum X_i}{7}$$

$$= \frac{X_1 + X_2 + X_3 + X_4 + X_5 + X_6 + X_7}{7}$$

$$= \frac{\$17,500 + \$18,500 + \$18,250 + \$17,750 + \$18,500 + \$24,750 + \$17,750}{7}$$

$$= \frac{\$133,000}{7} \text{ which is } \$19,000.$$

It is instructive to look at the amounts arranged in an array: {$17,500, $17,750, $17,750, $18,250, $18,500, $18,500, $24,750}. The mean value $19,000 exceeds all the scores in the data set except for $24,750, which is the amount reported by Institution F. Institution F's expenditure is an extreme value that is not representative of the other six values. If this outlier score of $24,750 were to be excluded from the calculation, the mean for the remaining six institutions would be $18,041.67 or $18,042. [$18,042 = ($17,500 + $17,750 + $17,750 + $18,250 + $18,500 + $18,500)/6, or $108,250/6]. This value, $18,042, is representative of the six scores in the data set, excluding the extreme score of $24,750.

The median score for all seven scores is $18,250. The median statistic is less sensitive to extreme values and provides a more accurate of the distribution's "center" when there are extreme scores.

When a data set's scores are negative, special care with the algebraic signs must be exercised. The negative scores must be included in the tabulation in the same way that the positive scores are included. Example 5-6 illustrates the procedure for finding the mean when negative scores are involved.

Example 5-6

Finding the Mean with Some Negative Scores

A library clerk compares the cash in the library's cash register(s) with the register's tapes at the end of each day. If no cash errors have been made, there should be no difference between the amount of cash in the drawer(s) and the final balance shown on the cash register tape(s). The differences recorded for a sample one-week period are as follows: {$0.25, $0.50, $−1.10, $0.25, $−1.25, $−0.70, $−0.75}. Find the mean.

Analysis

A value of $0.25 means the cash in the register drawer exceeds the tape balance by $0.25. The value $−1.10 means the cash drawer is short by $1.10. Using Formula 5-2, $N = 7$, yields the following:

$$\bar{X} = \frac{\sum X_i}{7}$$

$$= \frac{X_1 + X_2 + X_3 + X_4 + X_5 + X_6 + X_7}{7}$$

$$= \frac{0.25 + 0.5 + (-1.10) + 0.25 + (-1.25) + (-0.7) + (-0.75)}{7}$$

$$= \frac{0.25 + 0.5 - 1.10 + 0.25 - 1.25 - 0.7 - 0.75}{7}$$

$$= \frac{-2.80}{7} \text{ which is } \$-.40.$$

The interpretation of this result is that during the one-week period, the cash register(s) averaged a daily loss of 40 cents. If this loss is representative for the year, the annual loss to the library is $146.00 [$146 = (365 days × $0.40/day)]. Given this information, this method of reporting has some potential planning implications. For example, accuracy with using the cash register may be a performance standard to be included on the employee's annual performance evaluation.

Calculating the Mean from a Grouped Frequency Distribution

If data are organized in a grouped frequency distribution, the mean is determined by multiplying the class midpoint of each class interval by the frequency of observations in that class. These products are then totaled and divided by the number of observations in the distribution. In mathematical terms, this is expressed in Formula 5-3.

Formula 5-3

$$\bar{X} = \frac{\sum\limits_{i=1}^{k} f_i M_i}{\sum\limits_{i=1}^{k} f_i}$$

$$= \frac{f_1 M_1 + f_2 M_2 + f_3 M_3 + \ldots + f_k M_k}{f_1 + f_2 + f_3 + \ldots + f_k}$$

where f = frequency or number of observations in each class
M = class midpoint for each class interval
k = number of classes

Formula 5-3 can be illustrated using the book copyright data in Table 5-5. These data are organized in a group frequency distribution of 8 classes ($k = 8$).

TABLE 5-5 ▌ Copyright Dates ($n = 100$)

Interval	Frequency (*n*)	Midpoint (*M*)	Frequency × midpoint (*n*M*)
66–69	10	67.5	675.0
70–73	13	71.5	929.5
74–77	14	75.5	1,057.0
78–81	15	79.5	1,192.5
82–85	16	83.5	1,336.0
86–89	13	87.5	1,337.5
90–93	11	91.5	1,006.5
94–97	8	95.5	764.0
	$n = 100$		Sum = 8,298.0

From Table 5-5, the librarian sees the following values:

$f_1 =$	10	$M_1 =$	67.5
$f_2 =$	13	$M_2 =$	71.5
$f_3 =$	14	$M_3 =$	75.5
$f_4 =$	15	$M_4 =$	79.5
$f_5 =$	16	$M_5 =$	83.5
$f_6 =$	13	$M_6 =$	87.5
$f_7 =$	11	$M_7 =$	91.5
$f_8 =$	8	$M_8 =$	95.5
	100		

$$\sum f_i = f_1 + f_2 + f_3 + f_4 + f_5 + f_6 + f_7 + f_8$$

$$= 10 + 13 + 14 + 15 + 16 + 13 + 11 + 8 \text{ which is } 100.$$

Now, substituting into Formula 5-3, with $k = 8$,

$$\overline{X} = \frac{\sum\limits_{i=1}^{k} f_i M_i}{\sum\limits_{i=1}^{k} f_i}$$

$$= \frac{f_1 M_1 + f_2 M_2 + f_3 M_3 + f_4 M_4 + f_5 M_5 + f_6 M_6 + f_7 M_7 + f_8 M_8}{f_1 + f_2 + f_3 + f_4 + f_5 + f_6 + f_7 + f_8}$$

$$= \frac{10(67.5) + 13(71.5) + 14(75.5) + \ldots + 11(91.5) + 8(95.5)}{10 + 13 + 14 + 15 + 16 + 13 + 11 + 8}$$

$$= \frac{675.0 + 929.5 + 1057.0 + \ldots + 1006.5 + 764.0}{100}$$

$$= \frac{8098}{100} \text{ which is } 80.98, \text{ or } 81.$$

Since the data are discrete, the mean is rounded to 81. This statistic tells the librarian that the average copyright date of the 100 books in the study is 1981. Excluding a rare book or archive collection, this statistic confirms that the books in the study are old by today's date.

In another example, suppose a tally is made of the time required for checking out library materials in a busy library. The distribution is as follows:

Time (minutes)	Number of clients (f)	Class midpoint (M)	$f_i * M_i$
0–1.99	17	1	17
2–3.99	23	3	69
4–5.99	36	5	180
6–7.99	29	7	203
8–9.99	14	9	126
10 and over	1*	18	18
Total	120		613

*Required 18 minutes

In this example, $k = 6$ and the values for f_i and M_i are the following:

$$\begin{array}{ll}
f_1 = 17 & M_1 = 1 \\
f_2 = 23 & M_2 = 3 \\
f_3 = 36 & M_3 = 5 \\
f_4 = 29 & M_4 = 7 \\
f_5 = 14 & M_5 = 9 \\
f_6 = \underline{1} & M_6 = 18 \\
120 &
\end{array}$$

From the data, $\Sigma f_i = 120$ [$120 = 17 + 23 + 36 + 29 + 14 + 1$]. Substituting $k = 6$ into Formula 5-4 yields the following:

$$\overline{X} = \frac{\displaystyle\sum_{i=1}^{k} f_i M_i}{\displaystyle\sum_{i=1}^{k} f_i}$$

$$= \frac{f_1 M_1 + f_2 M_2 + f_3 M_3 + f_4 M_4 + f_5 M_5 + f_6 M_6}{f_1 + f_2 + f_3 + f_4 + f_5 + f_6}$$

$$= \frac{17(1) + 23(3) + 36(5) + 29(7) + 14(9) + 1(18)}{17 + 23 + 36 + 29 + 14 + 1}$$

$$= \frac{17 + 69 + 180 + 203 + 126 + 18}{17 + 23 + 36 + 29 + 14 + 1}$$

$$= \frac{613}{120} \text{ which is 5.1 minutes.}$$

The interpretation is that an average of 5.1 minutes is required for checking out materials.

The Weighted Arithmetic Mean

The *weighted arithmetic mean* is used to assign different "weights" to individual measurements. In the weighted mean, weights $\{w_1, w_2, w_3, \ldots, w_k\}$ are associated with the data points $\{X_1, X_2, X_3, \ldots, X_k\}$. The weight assigned depends on the significance or importance attached to the item of interest. The weighted mean, X_w-bar, is expressed by Formula 5-4:

Formula 5-4

$$\overline{X}_w = \frac{\displaystyle\sum_{i=1}^{k} w_i X_i}{\displaystyle\sum_{i=1}^{k} w_i}$$

$$= \frac{w_1 X_1 + w_2 X_2 + w_3 X_3 + \ldots + w_k X_k}{w_1 + w_2 + w_3 + \ldots + w_k}$$

An example of the weighted mean with which students are familiar is when an instructor assigns different weights to quizzes, tests, and other assignments in determining a student's final grade. For example, suppose an instructor assigns points and different weights to tests and assignments and a student achieves the results listed under Score, as follows:

Class activity	Points	Weight w	Score X	Product (w_iX_i)
Test 1	100 points	10%	90	9.0
Test 2	100 points	20	75	15.0
Test 3	100 points	20	78	15.6
Final test	200 points	30	77	23.1
Assignments	100 points	10	65	6.5
Participation	100 points	10	68	6.8
Total Points	700 points	100%		76.0

Analysis

The student's average is calculated using Formula 5-4. In this problem, $k = 6$, and the values for w_i and X_i are as follows:

$$
\begin{array}{ll}
w_1 = .10 & X_1 = 90 \\
w_2 = .20 & X_2 = 75 \\
w_3 = .20 & X_3 = 78 \\
w_4 = .30 & X_4 = 77 \\
w_5 = .10 & X_5 = 65 \\
w_6 = \underline{.10} & X_6 = 68 \\
 1.00 &
\end{array}
$$

Substituting in Formula 5-4:

$$
\begin{aligned}
\overline{X}_w &= \frac{\displaystyle\sum_{i=1}^{k} w_iX_i}{\displaystyle\sum_{i=1}^{k} w_i} \\[2ex]
&= \frac{w_1X_1 + w_2X_2 + w_3X_3 + w_4X_4 + w_5X_5 + w_6X_6}{W_1 + W_2 + W_3 + W_4 + W_5 + W_6} \\[2ex]
&= \frac{.10(90) + .20(75) + .20(78) + .30(77) + .10(65) + .10(68)}{.10 + .20 + .20 + .30 + .10 + .10} \\[2ex]
&= \frac{9 + 15 + 15.6 + 23.1 + 6.5 + 6.8}{1.00} \quad \text{which is 76.0.}
\end{aligned}
$$

The interpretation of the result is that the student's class average is 76%. Notice that Test 1 has a value of 100 points. Since the student's score is 90, the student received 90 of the 100 points. In contrast, the final test has a value of 200 points, and the student received a 77. This means that the student received 77% of the 200 points, or 154 points.

Example 5-7

Weighted Mean to Determine Average Cost

At different times over a 12-month period, a librarian purchased 208 shares of a mutual fund as part of an IRA annual savings program. The total spent in the 12-month period is $2000. The record of purchases is shown as follows:

Mutual fund activity	Number of shares (*w*)	Cost of shares (*X*)	Transaction cost (w_iX_i)
Purchase #1	40	$12.50	$ 500.00
Purchase #2	62	8.00	496.00
Purchase #3	50	10.00	500.00
Purchase #4	56	9.00	504.00
	208		$2,000.00

Determine the mean cost per share. Compare it with the simple mean.

Analysis

The simple mean is $9.88 [$9.88 = $12.50 + $8 + 10 + $9]. The values to substitute into Formula 5-4 are $k = 4$ and the following w_i and X_i values: $w_1 = 40$, $w_2 = 62$, $w_3 = 50$, $w_4 = 56$, $X_1 = \$12.50$, $X_2 = \$8.00$, $X_3 = \$10.00$, and $X_4 = \$9.00$:

$$
\overline{X}_w = \frac{\displaystyle\sum_{i=1}^{k} w_iX_i}{\displaystyle\sum_{i=1}^{k} w_i}
$$

$$
= \frac{w_1X_1 + w_2X_2 + w_3X_3 + w_4X_4}{W_1 + W_2 + W_3 + W_4}
$$

$$
= \frac{40(\$12.50) + 62(\$8.00) + 50(\$10.00) + 56(\$9.00)}{40 + 62 + 50 + 56}
$$

$$
= \frac{\$2000}{208} \text{ which is } \$9.615 \text{ or } \$9.62.
$$

The interpretation of this result is that the average cost per share was $9.62.

Example 5-8 is a useful example of applying the weighted mean on the business side of library administration. It concerns evaluating the bids from each of two vendors.

Example 5-8   **Determine Average Material Costs**

A village library builds a two-story addition of 20,000 gross square feet. The project requires conduit to contain fiber optic and coaxial cables to link the addition to the media center and computer facility in the old building. Six sizes of conduit, ranging from 1 inch to 4 inches in circumference, are required. These varying sizes cost between $6 and $18 per installed foot. Bids are received from two vendors. Vendor A states that, for an average price of $11 per foot, his firm will install the conduit. For an additional $2.50 per foot, his firm will pull the required cables. Vendor B submits a bid of $28,375, which *includes* the cost of running the conduit and pulling the required cables. The librarian evaluates the following data to decide which vendor, if either, will be selected:

Conduit size	Quantity required (w)	Cost per foot of conduit (X)	Product ($w_i X_i$)
A	620	$ 6.00	$ 3,720
B	475	7.00	3,325
C	500	9.00	4,500
D	350	11.00	3,850
E	225	15.00	3,375
F	200	18.00	3,600
	2,370		$22,370

Analysis

In analyzing the two bids, the librarian first computes the weighted mean for Vendor A. Using Formula 5-4, with $k = 6$, the computation is as follows:

$$\overline{X}_w = \frac{\sum\limits_{i=1}^{k} w_i X_i}{\sum\limits_{i=1}^{k} w_i}$$

$$= \frac{w_1 X_1 + w_2 X_2 + w_3 X_3 + w_4 X_4 + w_5 X_5 + w_6 X_6}{w_1 + w_2 + w_3 + w_4 + w_5 + w_6}$$

$$= \frac{620(6.00) + 475(7.00) + 500(9.00) + 350(11.00) + 225(15.00) + 200(18.00)}{620 + 475 + 500 + 350 + 225 + 200}$$

$$= \frac{3720 + 3325 + 4500 + 3850 + 3375 + 3600}{2370}$$

$$= \frac{22,370}{2370} \text{ which is 9.439 or \$9.44.}$$

The interpretation of $9.44 is that Vendor A seems to have arrived at his average by finding the mean of the cost per foot ($11.00) for the six conduits without regard to the required quantity [$11 = $6.00 + $7.00 + $9.00 + $11.00 + $15.00 + $18.00]. However, since the quantities differ, simple averaging of the costs is inaccurate.

Using the amount of $11 per foot for 2370 feet of conduit, the bid from Vendor A is $26,070 [$26,070 = $11.00 × 2370] plus the cost of wire pulling, which is an additional $5925 [$5925 = $2.50 × 2370] for a total bid of $31,995 [$31,995 = $26,070 + $5925]. Since the vendor has separated the price for pulling the wires, presumably this option can be declined and awarded to another party, if desired.

The bid from Vendor B for the complete job is $28,375, which is less than the bid of Vendor A. Even so, the bid from Vendor B may be less attractive since the library's flexibility in shopping for cable pulling is reduced. If Vendor B, like the other vendor, has factored in a cost of $2.50 per foot to pull the cables, the installation portion of the job is $22,450 [$22,450 = $28,375 − $5,925]. This amount is very close to the cost one would expect, based on using the weighted mean.

The bid from Vendor B is the better choice, all other things being equal, unless the librarian can obtain a lower bid for pulling the cables. Too, the librarian must consider factors such as the vendor's reputation for quality work, timeliness of job completion, and other similar concerns.

A DISTRIBUTION'S SHAPE AND THE APPROPRIATE AVERAGE

At the beginning of this chapter, the mode, median, and mean were identified as measures of central tendency that inform the reader about a distribution's average or "middle measure." But which of these three measures is best?

There is no easy answer to this question since the "best" measure depends on the distribution's shape and on the information that is to be communicated about the distribution.

To form a clearer appreciation of the three central tendency measures, it is nonetheless useful to analyze how each measure differs from the others in two key situations. The first situation is when the scores in the data set cluster at the center of the distribution. The second situation is when the data scores tend to cluster toward the distribution's higher values or lower values. In each case, there is an advantage to using a particular measure of central tendency.

SYMMETRIC DISTRIBUTIONS

A *symmetric distribution* is one in which the distribution's median and mean are equal. In such distributions, the data scores are fairly close together, clustered toward the center of the distribution so that few data points are at the extremes.

In symmetric distributions, the mean is the preferred measure of central tendency because it presents other advantages that are useful in applying advanced statistical techniques. In contrast, the mode is not accorded much attention because it is unstable as a measure of central tendency.

Figure 5-2 illustrates several common symmetrical distributions. The distribution depicted on the left approximates the *normal distribution*. This bell-shaped distribution is repeatedly used in inferential statistics. The distribution in the center illustrates a *rectangular distribution* in which all the scores occur with the same frequency. Lastly, the distribution shown on the right is an example of a mound-shaped *unimodal symmetrical distribution*.

To illustrate a symmetrical distribution, suppose that a library clerk collected data about the copyright date of 100 books as they arrived from the vendor over several weeks. The data are illustrated in Table 5-6. In recording the data, the clerk wrote 98–00 to represent the years 1998–2000.

FIGURE 5-2   Common Symmetrical Distributions

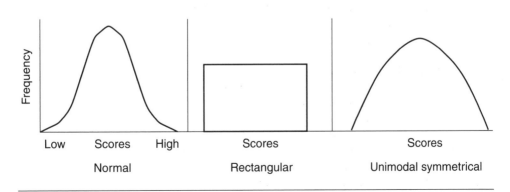

TABLE 5-6 ▌ Copyright Date of Books Received ($n = 100$)

Year of publication	Midpoint (M_i)	Frequency (f)	Product (f_iM_i)
98–00	99	1	99
95–97	96	8	768
92–94	93	22	2,046
89–91	90	36	3,240
86–88	87	24	2,088
83–85	84	6	504
80–82	81	3	243
		100	8,988

In Table 5-6, the model class is the class with the highest frequency. This is the class 89 to 91 since the frequency of this class is 36—more than for any other class. The class midpoint is 90 [90 = (91 + 89)/2].

The median for Table 5-6 data lies between the 50th and 51st scores in the distribution. These two scores are in the class interval 89–91. The midpoint for the 89–91 class is 90.

The mean for Table 5-6 data is 89.88 [89.88 = 8988/100] which rounds to 90. This result refers to the copyright year 1990.

Table 5-6 data represent a symmetric distribution since the distribution's median and mean are the same. Either of these measures, including the mode as the third choice, could be used to describe the distribution's average. Since the mean is best known, and is the preferred measure because of its advantages in more advanced statistical techniques, it is the statistic of choice for describing the distribution's center.

Figure 5-3 is a histogram of the distribution of the 100 copyright dates. The graph shows that the mode, median, and mean divide the distribution into two halves. The left and right sides of the graph are very similar since the scores are concentrated at the center of the distribution.

Skewed Distributions

A distribution is *skewed* if its median and mean are not equal. When the median and mean are not equal, the data are unevenly distributed in the distribution. It is important to be aware of this circumstance because it indicates that the data tend toward either the low or high extreme in the distribution, giving rise to a "tail" relative to the distribution's central portion.

In a skewed distribution, the median is generally preferred as the measure of central tendency. The reason concerns the extreme scores that create a skewed distribution. Extreme scores at either end of the distribution have their greatest effect on the mean, rendering the mean a less effective measure of the distribution's center. Extreme scores have less effect on the median, and they usually have no effect on the mode.

Figures 5-4 and 5-5 show two skewed distributions. Figure 5-4 depicts a distribution skewed to the right (positively). Figure 5-5 depicts a distribution skewed to the left (negatively). In a skewed distribution, the mode always occurs at the highest peak of the curve.

FIGURE 5-3 ⫿ Book Study Copyright Dates (*n* = 100)

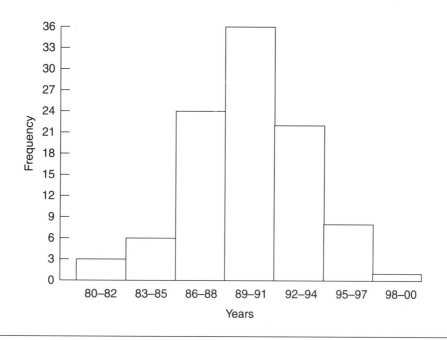

FIGURE 5-4 ⫿ A Distribution with a Positive Skew

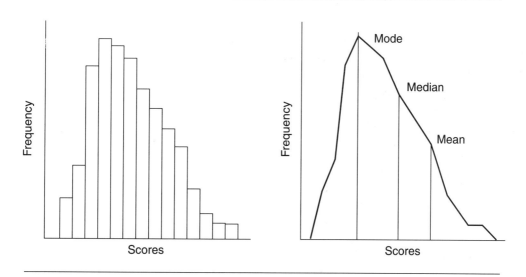

As Figure 5-4 illustrates, in a positively skewed distribution, the sequence of the three measures of central tendency, from left to right, is mode, median, and mean. In a negatively skewed distribution, the sequence of the three measures of central tendency from left to right, is mean, median, and mode. A method for remembering this information is to note that, in a negatively skewed distribution, the central tendency measures occur in alphabetical order.

FIGURE 5-5 ▓ A Distribution with a Negative Skew

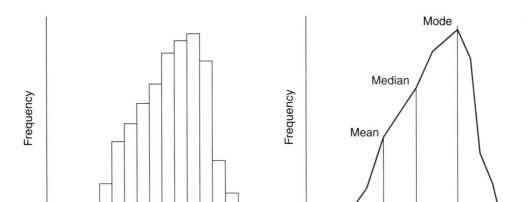

Figures 5-4 and 5-5 also show that, in a skewed distribution, the median is always closer to the mean than to the mode, just as the words *median* and *mean* are closer than the words *median* and *mode* in the dictionary. Since the mode is the highest point in the curve, the other two measures are easy to identify.

To illustrate a skewed distribution, suppose that a library clerk tallies the annual number of workdays that 98 library employees were absent due to illness. The results are presented in Table 5-7.

In Table 5-7, the modal class is the interval with the highest frequency. It is 0–2 days absence. This makes the 0–2 class the modal class. Its midpoint is 1 day, which makes one day of absence the modal class.

The median for Table 5-7 data lies between the 50th and 51st scores in the distribution. This value is between the midpoint of the 0–2 class interval and the midpoint of the 3–5 class interval. This value is calculated by finding the average of the two midpoints, which is 2.5 [2.5 = (1 + 4)/2]. The value represents a median value of 2.5 workdays of absence.

TABLE 5-7 ▓ Employee Sick Days for the Year

Days absent	Midpoint (x)	Frequency (f)	Product (f_iX_i)
0–2	1	50	50
3–5	4	30	120
6–8	7	6	42
9–11	10	5	50
12–14	13	4	52
15–17	16	2	32
18–21	19	1	19
		98	365

Applying Formula 5-3, the mean for Table 5-7 data, where $k = 7$, is determined as follows:

$$\overline{X} = \frac{\displaystyle\sum_{i=1}^{k} f_i M_i}{\displaystyle\sum_{i=1}^{k} f_i}$$

$$= \frac{f_1 M_1 + f_2 M_2 + f_3 M_3 + f_4 M_4 + f_5 M_5 + f_6 M_6 + f_7 M_7}{f_1 + f_2 + f_3 + f_4 + f_5 + f_6 + f_7}$$

$$= \frac{50(1) + 30(4) + 6(7) + 5(10) + 4(13) + 2(16) + 1(19)}{50 + 30 + 6 + 5 + 4 + 2 + 1}$$

$$= \frac{50 + 120 + 42 + 50 + 52 + 32 + 19}{100}$$

$$= \frac{365}{98} \text{ which is 3.72, or 3.7 days.}$$

The calculations and Figure 5-6 show that the median and mean are not equal. This tells the librarian that the distribution is skewed. The data reveal an early concentration about the mode and then a long tail that extends in the direction of the higher end of the scale. For this reason, the distribution is *positively skewed.*

FIGURE 5-6 ▓ Employee Sick Days ($n = 98$)

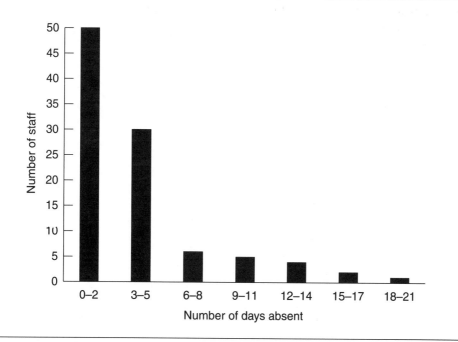

The interpretation of the data is that the typical library employee is absent a median average of 2.5 days per year. The median is used since the distribution is skewed.

It also is instructive to note that the data reveal that the 98 library employees lost a total of 365 workdays. Since there are about 260 workdays in the year for each employee, this loss of time is equivalent to 1.4 full-time employees being absent the whole workyear.

Further, the situation of the employee who was absent 18–21 days is interesting to examine. If the person suffered an illness that required a long recovery period, the employee's time report will show that the days absent were accumulated over a short period. If, however, the person is regularly absent each month, then the productivity loss is different and can be predicted. Since there are 260 workdays per year, including holidays, an annual absence of 19 days means that the person is not at work each thirteenth or fourteenth workday. This statistic may be discussed at the employee's annual performance evaluation.

J-Distributions

Highly skewed distributions are *J-distributions,* because the highest frequencies occur in the distribution's first or last category. Graphically, their curve resembles either the letter *J* or its mirror image, a *reversed-J.* Distributions of this type do not adapt well to summary descriptions. Figures 5-7 and 5-8 illustrate both of these skewed distributions.

For example, a distribution of library fund-raising contributions produces a reverse J-curve, as in Figure 5-7. This is because most contributions are small. Additional examples of reverse J-curves include the following: the distribution of library card holders, categorized by the person's age; the distribution of users of a library service, where most library card holders are infrequent users and the repeat users form the distribution's tail; and the distribution of employee absences, since most employees are not absent, but a few are absent many days. In contrast, J-distributions, as shown in Figure 5-8, are less often encountered in the library environment. Examples of J-distributions are the total number of scientific and technical journals published in the United States over the past 200 years and the growth of total library resource expenditures over the past 20 years.

FIGURE 5-7   A Reverse J-distribution

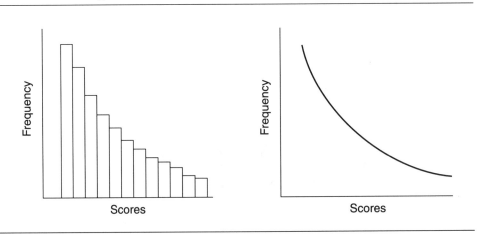

FIGURE 5-8 █ A J-distribution

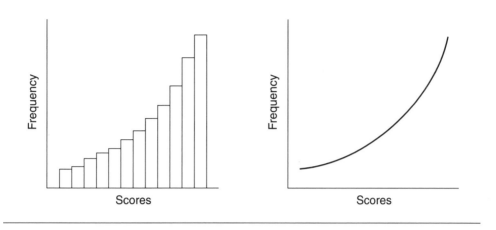

Pareto's 80/20 Rule

Distributions that produce J-curves or reverse J-curves tend to give credence to a general observation called the *80/20 rule,* which is also known as *Pareto's rule.*

Vilfredo Pareto, a nineteenth-century Italian economist, examined the distribution of wealth in Italy and discovered that 80% of it was in the ownership of 20% of the population. Subsequently, this 80/20 rule has been found to apply across a wide range of situations. Pareto's rule, or the 80/20 rule, reflects the idea of "the vital few" and "the trivial many."

In almost every business, for example, it turns out that 80% of turnover is due to about 20% of the product range. Similarly, businesses find that 80% of transactions come from about 20% of the customers. In librarianship, bibliometric studies of journals reveal that 80% of the citations refer to a core of 20% of the titles. A user study of videocassette circulation at a public library likely would reveal that 80% of the circulation is due to 20% of the users. Of course, the exact split may not be 80/20, but the principle is that a few usually are responsible for most of a situation.

Pareto's rule can be used to separate a problem's major causes from its minor ones. By graphing the distribution that produces a J-curve, the chart can effectively display the relative importance of problems in contributing to a situation. This elaboration can help in focusing and prioritizing use of resources.

To illustrate Pareto analysis, suppose that during a two-week period 500 college students were asked to complete a survey about the campus library. In tabulating the data, seven categories were used to identify reasons students do not use the library more. The categories were then arranged in rank order. The data are presented in Table 5-8.

The median for Table 5-8 data is 43 and the mean is 71.4 [71.4 = 500/7]. There is no mode. Since the median and mean are not equal, the data set is a skewed distribution. Since the median is less than the mean, the distribution is skewed to the right.

When the frequencies for each complaint category are graphed, the curve is seen to be a J-distribution. The librarian can also observe that two of the seven total categories, which represent 29% [29% since 0.286 = 2/7], account for 79% of the complaints. Thus, action taken should address situations described by those two complaint categories in particular— Pareto's vital few.

TABLE 5-8   ▌   Library Complaints

Type of complaint	Frequency	Percent	Cumulative percent
Category C	226	45%	45%
Category A	170	34	79
Category D	39	8	87
Category G	28	6	93
Category E	18	4	97
Category B	12	2	99
Category F	7	1	100
	500	100%	

The taller columns at the left of the diagram in Figure 5-9 illustrate the complaint categories that require action. Inspection of the curve shows that it increases, but at a decreasing rate. Now that the categories are clearly identified, the librarian is in a position to develop an action plan to address the concerns. When the study is repeated, the librarian would expect that the order of the complaint categories would shift and/or that the curve itself would be flatter because more categories would be required to reach 100%.

FIGURE 5-9   ▌   Category of Library Complaint

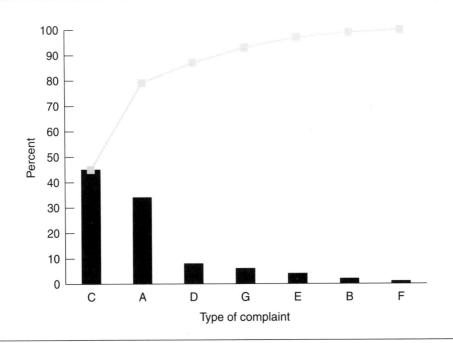

U-Distributions

Figure 5-10 depicts a *U-distribution,* in which a high number of frequencies occur in the first and last categories, with few in the middle categories. An example of a U-distribution is the ages of persons who use a public library. Children and seniors tend to use the facility more often than persons in the middle age groupings. Costs for library services, too, are U-shaped when graphed because the cost per unit depends upon how many units are produced. The more units produced, the lower the cost of each. This is because the cost (numerator) is divided by the quantity (denominator).

In determining production costs, the product's *indivisible set-up costs* must be considered. These are the costs that are incurred before a single item is produced. For a book, for example, the publisher's indivisible set-up costs include editing and typesetting. The more books that the publisher prints, the lower are the indivisible set-up costs per book. Of course, the publisher wants to print only the number of books that can be reasonably expected to sell within a well-defined period. At some point, per-unit cost for each printed book increases as a result of an increase in output. Diseconomies of scale occur as staff and physical plant grow to accommodate outputs. Costs again begin to rise more quickly than productivity.

FIGURE 5-10   A U-distribution

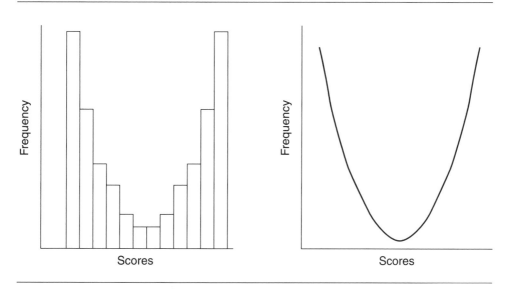

EFFICIENCY METHODOLOGIES: DIVISION OF LABOR, TECHNOLOGY, STAFF SCHEDULING

Few employees of libraries today can say that they have not seen dramatic changes in the way that libraries are organized, staffed, and equipped with sophisticated technology. All staff are being called upon to perform different kinds of jobs than they performed only a few years ago. Today's rapidly growing electronic environment for information resources requires the extensive use of computer technology that continues to bring about job changes for staff at all levels.

Increasingly, libraries are being viewed in more of a business context. Librarians and library managers, like the managers of other businesses, have narrowed employee job descriptions to specialize the professional and technical staff in the performance of job activities. An example is the reference librarian whose main focus is to conduct library instruction classes, or the librarian who specializes in answering business reference questions, or the clerk who primarily makes photocopies or shelves library materials. The technology that librarians use also is customized with specialty programs for tasks such as cataloging, circulation, word processing, statistics collection, budget analysis, invoicing, and other library tasks. Staff and equipment are tied together through a schedule so that the employee's workday is most efficiently used. Indeed, *efficiency* has taken on a new meaning and importance in the library environment. Part of the impetus for it is that costly technology has raised the library's profile, and as communities or organizations marshal their limited resources, the library becomes a larger target for realignment. Further, librarians, too, are striving to operate the library as effectively as possible for the benefit of the clientele that it serves.

At the close of the eighteenth century, economist Adam Smith wrote about the merits of staff specialization to permit a wide variety of services. He emphasized efficient job performance at a relatively low cost per unit of output. His ideas and observations have influenced business operations ever since.

Today, each library staff member's specialization increases the library's "scale of plant," resulting in more complexity in the library environment. The result is that more staff time is assigned to coordinate, assist, interface, and monitor operations for continuous quality and efficiency. The consequence of this scheduling, however, is that less aggregate staff time is available to provide customer service.

Increased "scale of plant" results in lines of communication that are less direct. The size of the staff increases, as does the number and frequency of committee meetings. Training becomes imperative for new staff, along with retraining for existing staff. Within a short period, the librarian finds that the necessity for coordinating staff increases the cost of each unit of library service. This additional cost then causes the library's total cost curve to incline upward.

The business side of library administration must be sensitive to the trends identified by U-distributions and the implications from the increased use of technology and scientific management principles. While efficiency certainly has its place, its downside is that staff at all levels within the library's organization may come to feel a sense of dehumanization and alienation. There is every reason to believe that performance pressures will continue and even increase. A possible solution, which must be reflected in the library's program objectives, is for the librarian to strategically involve all staff in a collegial, participatory environment.

Example 5-8 illustrates a statistical application that a librarian might use in a study to increase efficiency at the circulation desk.

Example 5-8

Interpreting Graphs and Understanding Data

A clerk monitors the circulation desk for a period and records how long it takes each person to complete a transaction. The clerk also records how many items each person borrows. These data are shown in Table 5-9.

1. Use Figures 5-11 and 5-12 to construct two frequency distributions. The first is for the amount of time that each library client waits at the circulation desk for service. The second is for the number of library items that each person borrows.

2. Why are there more classes for the number of items borrowed than for the time spent waiting for service?

3. How many items were borrowed?

4. How many people were observed in this study?

5. Find the class midpoints for the class intervals.

6. Identify the frequency for the class interval 91–120.

7. Identify the modal class.

8. What is the median of each distribution?

9. Interpret $X = 4$ for the number of items borrowed.

10. What was the greatest number of items borrowed at one time?

11. Find the mean for each distribution.

TABLE 5-9   Circulation Desk Service Time and Items Borrowed

Circulation desk waiting time		Number of items borrowed during a library visit	
Class (in seconds)	Frequency (f)	Items borrowed (X)	Frequency (f)
1–30	12	1	5
31–60	24	2	12
61–90	29	3	25
91–120	9	4	27
121–150	5	5	8
151–180	2	6	3
		7	1

FIGURE 5-11 ▏ Circulation Desk Service Time

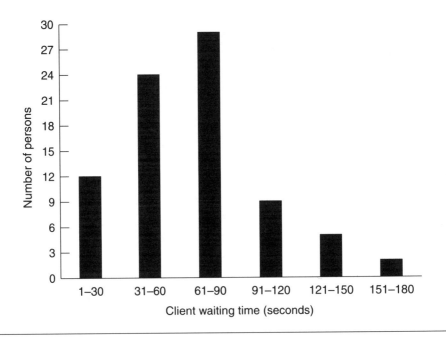

FIGURE 5-12 ▏ Number of Library Items Borrowed ($n = 81$)

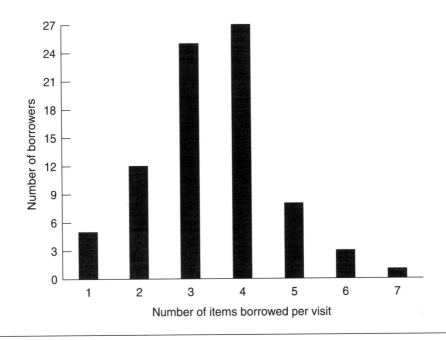

Analysis

1. Using Table 5-9 data, Figure 5-11 shows a bar graph for the frequency distribution for circulation. Figure 5-12 is a bar graph for the number of items borrowed.

2. When the librarian designed the study, six classes were selected for waiting time, perhaps because all of the observed persons completed their transaction within three minutes. For a similar reason, the librarian selected seven classes to represent the number of items borrowed, because at most seven items were borrowed during the period that the study was conducted.

3. To determine the number of items borrowed, multiply the number of items by the frequency. Hence, the number of items borrowed is 277. The calculation is as follows:

    Items borrowed = 1(5) + 2(12) + 3(25) + 4(27) + 5(8) + 6(3) + 7(1)

    = 5 + 24 + 75 + 108 + 40 + 18 + 7 which is 277.

4. The frequency of waiting time is $f = 81$ [81 = 12 + 24 + 29 + 9 + 5 + 2]. Similarly, the frequency for the number of persons borrowing items is $f = 81$ [81 = 5 + 12 + 25 + 27 + 8 + 3 + 1]. The data tell the librarian that 81 persons waited in line and that all 81 persons checked out at least one item.

5. This question refers to circulation desk service time since these data are grouped. The first class interval is 1–30. The class midpoint is 15.5 [15.5 = (30 + 1)/2]. The second class interval is 31–60. The class midpoint is 45.5 [45.5 = (60 + 31)/2]. Continuing similar calculations, the class midpoints of all the intervals are as follows: 15.5, 45.5, 75.5, 105.5, 135.5, and 165.5.

6. The class interval 91–120 has a frequency of 9. This means that there are nine observations that fall between 91 and 120. Since the class midpoint is 105.5, the librarian assumes that the observations are evenly distributed in the class interval about the midpoint. The ability to determine this information is the reason class midpoints are used in various calculations.

7. The modal class is the class that occurs most frequently. In the distribution of circulation desk service time, the modal class is 61–90 because it occurs 29 times—more often than any other class interval. In the distribution of the number of library items borrowed, the modal class is 4 since its frequency is 27, which is more than any other class.

8. The distribution for circulation desk waiting time contains $n = 81$ scores. The median is the 41st observation. It lies in the interval 61 to 90. Formula 5-1 is used to determine the median. The values to substitute in the formula are $L = 60.5, n = 81, F = 36$ [36 = 12 + 24], $f = 29$, and $w = 30$:

$$\tilde{X} = L + \frac{w}{f}\left(\frac{n}{2} - F\right)$$

$$= 60.5 + \frac{30}{29}\left(\frac{81}{2} - 36\right)$$

$$= 60.5 + \frac{30}{29}(40.5 - 36)$$

$$= 60.5 + 1.03\,(4.50)$$

$$= 60.5 + 4.7 \text{ which is } 65.2 \text{ seconds.}$$

The distribution for the number of items borrowed contains $n = 81$ scores. The median is the 41st observation, which is 3.

9. The interpretation of $X = 4$ for the number of items borrowed is that 27 people borrowed 4 items. This is the modal class, too.

10. The most items borrowed by any one person were seven items.

11. The mean for the circulation desk waiting time distribution is calculated using Formula 5-3. The key to using this formula is knowing the class interval midpoints.

Class interval (X)	Frequency (f)	Midpoint (M)	Calculation to find the midpoint
1–30	12	15.5	[15.5 = (1 + 30)/2]
31–60	24	45.5	[45.5 = (31 + 60)/2]
61–90	29	75.5	[75.5 = (61 + 90)/2]
91–120	9	105.5	[105.5 = (91 + 120)/2]
121–150	5	135.5	[135.5 = (121 + 150)/2]
151–180	2	165.5	[165.5 = (151 + 180)/2]
	81		

The mean is calculated as follows:

$$\text{Mean} = \frac{f_1M_1 + f_2M_2 + f_3M_3 + f_4M_4 + f_5M_5 + f_6M_6}{f_1 + f_2 + f_3 + f_4 + f_5 + f_6}$$

$$= \frac{12(15.5) + 24(45.5) + 29(75.5) + 9(105.5) + 5(135.5) + 2(165.5)}{12 + 24 + 29 + 9 + 5 + 2}$$

$$= \frac{186 + 1092 + 2189.5 + 949.5 + 677.5 + 331}{81}$$

$$= \frac{5425.5}{81} \text{ which is 66.98 or 67.}$$

The mean for the number of items borrowed is calculated as follows:

$$\text{Mean} = \frac{f_1X_1 + f_2X_2 + f_3X_3 + f_4X_4 + f_5X_5 + f_6X_6 + f_7X_7}{f_1 + f_2 + f_3 + f_4 + f_5 + f_6 + f_7}$$

$$= \frac{5(1) + 12(2) + 25(3) + 27(4) + 8(5) + 3(6) = 1(7)}{5 + 12 + 25 + 27 + 8 + 3 + 1}$$

$$= \frac{5 + 24 + 75 + 108 + 40 + 18 + 7}{81}$$

$$= \frac{277}{81} \text{ which is 3.42.}$$

The result of 3.42 tells librarians that a mean of 3.42 books were borrowed.

SUMMARY OF CRITICAL CONCEPTS

1. *Frequency distributions* provide a useful technique for organizing and displaying data. However, because they do not provide quantitative summary statements about the data, they are limited in their application.

2. *Measures of central tendency* are summary statements that describe the center of a distribution. These measures are the mode, median, and mean.

3. Each central tendency measure is a value that best describes the distribution "center" or "middle" from a particular viewpoint. For the mode, the center is the data point or points that occur most frequently. For the median, the center is the value that evenly divides the distribution into two parts. For the mean, it is the distribution's balance point.

4. The *mode* is the distribution's most frequently occurring score. It is easy to calculate and can be used with any scale of measurement (nominal, ordinal, interval, ratio). It is the only measure of central tendency that may have no value or may have more than one value. The mode usually is not used alone as a measure of central tendency to describe a data set.

5. The *median* of a data set is the value that is above the lower one-half and below the upper one-half of the values. The median can be thought of as the most central measure of a distribution. Every data set has a median that is unique. Even so, the median is not necessarily one of the values of the data set. The median is affected by the number of observations in the data set, but not by their values. Hence, the median is not affected by extreme scores.

6. There are four key situations in which the *median* is the preferred central tendency measure for distributions. These occur (a) when there are a few extreme scores, such as in an income distribution; (b) when there is an open-ended distribution; (c) when the data are ordinal scale; and (d) when some scores have undetermined values.

7. The *mean* is among the most popularly used statistic for summarizing data. Each data set has a mean that is unique. The mean value for a data set is not necessarily one of the values of the data set. The mean is based on all the observations in a data set. Because of this, the mean is very sensitive to extreme scores, either high or low. If a distribution has an open-ended class interval, it is not possible to compute the mean. The *mean for a series of ungrouped observations* is obtained by first adding all the scores in the data set and then by dividing this sum by the total number of scores. The mean also is known as the arithmetic average.

8. *Measures of skewness* describe a data set as symmetrical or asymmetrical about a central point.

9. In a *symmetrical distribution,* the mean equals the median. The mean is the preferred measure of central tendency.

10. A nonsymmetrical distribution is called *asymmetrical* or *skewed.*

11. In a skewed distribution, the mean does not equal its median. In a *positively skewed* distribution, the tail goes toward the right, so that the median is less than the mean. In a *negatively skewed* distribution, the tail goes toward the left, so that the mean is less than the median. In a skewed distribution, the median is the preferred measure of central tendency.

12. Highly skewed distributions sometimes are called *J-distributions* or *reverse J-distributions*. Data that produce highly skewed distributions give credence to a general observation known as the 80/20 rule or Pareto's rule. This rule states that 80% of total activity is due to 20% of those elements that cause the activity.

13. Cost curves for activities that are subject to *economies and diseconomies of scale* tend to be U-shaped. Such distributions suggest that the average "cost per unit" of a product or service decreases as the scale of operation increases to produce more output.

KEY TERMS

Central tendency.   The middle of a distribution of scores.

Data point labeling.   The use of dummy variables (*X, Y, P, Q, . . .*) to tag data points and simplify long equations. In data point labeling, the value of the individual data points is ignored.

Extreme value.   A score or value that falls outside the range of the other measurements in the data set. For example, in the data set {1, 2, 3, 3, 9}, the value 9 is extreme. Similarly, in the data set {1, 6, 6, 8, 8, 9}, the value 1 is extreme.

Pareto's rule or **80/20 rule.**   The common observation that 80 percent of turnover can be attributed to 20 percent of products or clientele.

Skew.   Lack of symmetry in a frequency distribution.

Symmetrical distribution.   A distribution in which the mean and median equal each other. In a symmetrical distribution, the graph looks balanced about its center.

SELF-ASSESSMENT QUIZ

1. *True* or *False*   In a distribution with a mode, the mode is the highest point in the distribution.

2. *True* or *False*   A multimodal distribution may show that a set is composed of dissimilar or heterogeneous data.

3. *True* or *False*   If there are 100 items in a distribution, the median is the 50th item in the array.

4. *True* or *False*   In an academic library where the workweek is 37.5 hours, a student working 20 hours per week is working more than the median number of workweek hours.

5. *True* or *False*   It is not possible to determine the data set's mean if the distribution contains an open-ended class interval.

6. *True* or *False*   If 5 were subtracted from each score in a data set of 3 items, the distribution's mean would be reduced by 5.

7. *True* or *False*   The mean is the central tendency measure most popularly used for describing an income distribution.

8. *True* or *False*   If the mean and median are equal, the distribution is probably symmetric.

9. *True* or *False*   If the median is less than the mean, the distribution is skewed to the right.

10. *True* or *False*   The weighted mean would be an appropriate statistic for determining the "average" cost of two or more types or grades of floor covering, such as carpet and tile.

Answers

1. *True*   The mode is the highest point in a distribution because it occurs with the greatest frequency.

2. *True*   An example to illustrate this is that men tend to weigh more than women. A frequency distribution of weights of men and women selected at random is bimodal. This suggests that weight data for men and women should be reported in two separate distributions, each of which would then be unimodal.

3. *False*   The median is the mean of the two middle terms of an array having an even number of scores. For an array of 100 items, the median is located midway between the 50th and 51st items.

4. *False*   Without knowing how many hours the other students work, the median cannot be determined.

5. *True*   The mean can be computed only for interval or ratio scale.

6. *True*   Convince yourself of this by working through the formula. Suppose there are three scores. These are X_1, X_2, X_3. The mean of these scores less 5 points from each is the following:

$$\text{Mean} = \frac{(x_1 - 5) + (x_2 - 5) + (x_3 - 5)}{3}$$

$$= \frac{x_1 - 5 + x_2 - 5 + x_3 - 5}{3}$$

$$= \frac{x_1 + x_2 + x_3 - 15}{3}$$

$$= \frac{x_1 + x_2 + x_3}{3} - \frac{15}{3}$$

$$= \text{Mean} - 5.$$

These calculations show that the statement is true for three scores. Of course, it is true for any size data set. Hence, subtracting any constant from, or adding any constant to, every term will decrease or increase the mean by that constant.

7. *False*   The median is the most popularly used central tendency measure for describing income distributions. This is because income distributions usually have extreme values, and medians are not affected by extreme values.

8. *True*   If the mean and median are approximately equal, the data values are consolidated toward the distribution's center. This will make the distribution generally symmetric.

9. *True*   In a skewed distribution the mean is pulled in the direction of the tail. Since the median is less than the mean, the tail must be toward the right in the distribution, or skewed to the right.

10. *True*   The weighted mean is used to determine the mean when the quantities and costs (frequencies and weights) are different.

DISCUSSION QUESTIONS AND PROBLEMS

1. A librarian conducted an informal survey to estimate the average age of library users. During a representative 2-hour period, a staff member, known to be good at guessing ages, made the following tabulation:

Age	Frequency
1 and under 10	15
10 and under 20	20
20 and under 30	26
30 and under 40	18
40 and under 50	15
50 and under 60	3
60 and under 70	2
70 and under 80	1
Total	100

Determine the mean and median of the distribution.

2. Explain the effect on the mode, median, and mean of the following:
   a. adding 5 points to all scores
   b. subtracting 5 points from all scores
   c. increasing all scores by 5%.

3. A librarian tabulated the number of times that eighteen popular novels circulated over a three-month period. Use the results presented to prepare a frequency distribution and identify the distribution's mode, if any.

Title A	7	Title G	6	Title M	5
Title B	8	Title H	7	Title N	2
Title C	3	Title I	6	Title O	4
Title D	1	Title J	5	Title P	9
Title E	8	Title K	4	Title Q	7
Title F	6	Title L	6	Title R	5

4. The librarian has asked you to estimate the number of titles in the library's collection. Over the past several years the library has operated under the assumption that collection size is about 47,500 volumes. The library has not yet converted to an online catalog system and there is no actual title count of library holdings. In estimating collection size, you will be using two methods and will then compare your results. Data are provided below on the number of shelflist cards per 1-inch section of the shelflist catalog and the number of books per section of shelving. To increase the accuracy of your estimate, the counts have been repeated several times.

Number of titles per one inch of shelflist	Books per section of shelving
94	180
106	195
99	185
96	193
102	164
103	156
97	170
104	169
98	160
101	178

a. Since the cards in the shelflist catalog measure 500 inches, what is a "best estimate" for the collection's size?

b. If the library has 376 sections of shelving, and if 75% of them are full, estimate the size of the collection.

c. Using the answer from (a) as the base, determine the percent difference in estimates derived from the two methods.

d. Estimate the number of new titles that can be accommodated on the 25% of shelving that is now unoccupied.

5. The director of technical services for a public library that serves a community of 30,000 is preparing a report requiring the calculation of certain ratios between adult and juvenile materials added to the collection. The data source for this report will be materials cataloged by area of Dewey classification over the previous two years.

Dewey Class		Adult Year 2	Juvenile Year 2	Adult Year 1	Juvenile Year 1
000–099	General Works	53	15	45	29
100–199	Philosophy	39	15	44	14
200–299	Religion	41	2	60	11
300–399	Social Sciences	448	76	338	68
400–499	Language	3	7	6	1
500–599	Pure Sciences	63	75	54	52
600–699	Technology	470	49	378	67
700–799	The Arts	343	54	293	47
800–899	Literature	169	38	113	29
900–999	Geography & History	290	77	262	46
Fiction		933	524	849	207
Biography		90	79	85	61

a. Calculate the percent change in the number of books in each category that are cataloged by Dewey classification for both adult and juvenile materials between Year 1 and Year 2.

b. Find the mean percent change for both adult and juvenile materials cataloged.

   c. For each Dewey classification, calculate the ratio of juvenile to adult materials cataloged in each year.

   d. Calculate the mean ratio of juvenile to adult materials cataloged.

   e. If any of the ratios differs widely from the mean, speculate on reasons.

6. The technical services director wishes to check the time lag between when a book order is received and when it is ready to be entered into the collection. In conducting this study, your data source will be the book order cards that are kept in the permanent order files. When an order card is received, a staff member stamps it with that day's date. After the item has been verified (checked that it is not already owned by the requesting unit and that the item is in print), the item is ordered, and again the card is dated. Upon receiving the invoice from the vendor, the date is again recorded. Then, after the book has been cataloged and is ready to be entered into the collection, the date is recorded on the card for a final time.

   To study the various lag times in the acquisitions and technical services process, a clerk collects data from completed transactions as recorded on cards in the permanent order file. For each card, the clerk computes and records the number of elapsed calendar days. Although there are 775 order records in the file, only 440 cards have all four dates and can be used in the study.

Number of days	Days before ordering	Days for vendor to fill order	Days to process item
1–7	16.4	0.2	8.0
8–14	44.8	0.4	17.8
15–21	73.7	0.6	30.3
22–28	89.8	19.2	59.8
29–35	98.7	38.3	75.9
36–42	99.8	86.0	87.3
43–49	100.0	91.0	93.9
50–56	100.0	94.9	95.9
57–63	100.0	98.3	97.5
64–70	100.0	99.4	98.6
71–77	100.0	100.0	99.5
78–84	100.0	100.0	100.0

   a. Next to each column in the chart, determine percents.

   b. Graph the cumulative frequency distribution for each of the three columns of data. Interpret your findings.

   c. Determine the mean number of days required for a book to be ordered, for the vendor to fill the order, and for the item to be processed.

   d. Speculate on ways that the technical services director might reduce the lag time evidenced in each of the data columns.

7. Acquisitions librarians from a consortium of ten corporate libraries tabulated their collection size and yearly acquisitions as follows:

Library	Collection size	Acquisitions
1	42,000	2150
2	15,000	2025
3	11,000	554
4	8000	500
5	7350	46
6	6500	500
7	5150	303
8	975	63
9	812	53
10	630	42

   a. Using the above data, calculate the ratio of acquisitions to collection size for each library and express your answers as percents.
   b. Find the mean percent for the ratio of acquisitions to collection size.
   c. Provide a reasonable explanation for the value observed for Library 2. (Hint: Library 2 has been in operation for only 3 months.)
   d. Provide a reasonable explanation for the value observed for Library 5. (Hint: The librarian has not weeded the collection for several years but will begin this activity next month.)

8. A librarian collects data that have a mean of 27 and a median of 32. Is it more likely that the distribution is symmetrical, negatively skewed, or positively skewed?

9. As part of a furniture needs analysis, the librarian records the number of persons who use carrels. The data show that 5.5 persons use the furniture during the specific period. The computed median is 15.5 for the time period. Are there an even or odd number of scores in the data set?

10. Examine each of two data sets, A and B. Data set A contains ten scores and data set B contains fifteen scores:

   A: {3, 4, 4, 4, 4, 4, 6, 6, 6, 7}
   B: {1, 1, 1, 1, 2, 4, 4, 4, 4, 4, 6, 7, 10, 10, 13}.
   a. What can be said about the two data sets?
   b. Identify the mode, median, and mean.
   c. Describe the shape of the distribution.

11. The local chapters of two library associations jointly share meeting and exhibit space. The meeting sessions of each association are separate, but registered conference members are permitted to attend and participate in any meetings that are held. To determine which conference was more interesting, twenty attendees are asked to submit reports of how many sessions they attended of each association.

a. Determine the mode, median, and mean for attendance at each association's meeting sessions.

b. Which association offered a more interesting meeting, based on session attendance of the 20 persons?

Association A Sessions attended						Association B Sessions attended				
7	8	8	9	7		5	3	2	7	4
4	6	3	2	4		5	4	4	2	5
4	9	6	9	8		2	7	4	6	6
8	9	7	10	10		6	5	7	5	4

MEASURES OF VARIABILITY

After reading this chapter, you will be able to do the following:

1. Describe and list the advantages of measures of variability, such as the range, percentile, percentile range, interquartile range, and standard deviation.

2. Calculate the value of the range, percentile range, interquartile range, and standard deviation.

3. Explain and illustrate how the measures of variability augment measures of central tendency.

4. Describe the usefulness of Chebyshev's theorem as a rule of thumb for describing a distribution.

5. Calculate the coefficient of variation and explain its function in analyzing the variation in two data sets.

In Chapter 5, the central tendency measures of mode, median, and mean were explained and illustrated. These three measures are effective for identifying the center of a distribution. As the text discussed, these measures are not used interchangeably, however. Each central tendency measure has a different focus in its measure of the distribution's average or center.

To completely understand distributions, however, it is necessary to visualize and measure how data points are grouped or clustered about the center of the distribution. For example, two sets of data may have identical means or medians, but the data may differ considerably in spread or distribution about its mean. These concerns are addressed by measures of dispersion, also called measures of variability.

ANALYZING DATA DISPERSION

Summary statistics, like the measures of central tendency or the measures of dispersion, can obscure or hide erratic data performance. For example, suppose that a cataloger is expected to catalog 15 books per day. To confirm the cataloger's performance, entries from the cataloger's log for the past month are inspected. The data are listed in Table 6-1.

In calculating the mean for the data in Table 6-1, the librarian discovers that the cataloger cataloged an average of 15 books each day [15 = 300/20]. However, this statistic does not accurately reflect daily performance, which fluctuated widely. On two days, over 30 books were cataloged; on two other days, no books were cataloged. These fluctuations may be caused by irregular book shipments, the cataloger's absence due to illness or attendance at a professional meeting or seminar, or even an unresolved question about the particular call number to assign certain titles. Whatever the cause, this data fluctuation suggests that there may be a problem that the summary statistic alone tends to obscure.

To describe a specific data set accurately, measures of central tendency (mode, median, mean) need to be augmented by *measures of variability,* also known as *measures of dispersion.* These statistics describe how data are scattered or spread about a distribution's mean.

Figure 6-1 illustrates variability. The figure presents three distributions, each of which has a mean value equal to the others. Similarly, the area under each of the three curves is the same. The data that form Distribution A, however, have less spread than do the data of Distributions B or C. Also, Distribution B has less variability or dispersion from its center point, which is the mean, than does Distribution C.

Of the three distributions, the mean of Distribution C is the least representative of the data as a whole because the data are the most widely spread or dispersed of the three distri-

TABLE 6-1   Daily Log of Books Cataloged

Date	Books cataloged	Date	Books cataloged	Date	Books cataloged	Date	Books cataloged
3	1	10	13	17	16	24	17
4	15	11	15	18	15	25	29
5	24	12	0	19	28	26	6
6	2	13	10	20	14	27	14
7	0	14	34	21	15	28	32

FIGURE 6-1 ▌ Variability of Distributions with the Same Mean

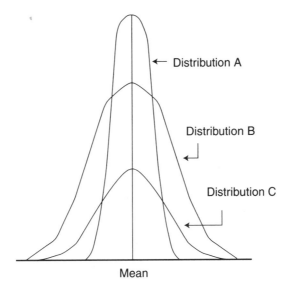

butions. Distribution A's mean value is the most representative of its data points. In other words, Distribution A's data tend to concentrate toward the center of the distribution, showing that the data are more homogeneous than those of the other two distributions.

Measures of variability are important. They allow the *reliability* of central tendency measures to be judged. Measures of variability are used to identify distributions that are composed of widely dispersed data. To adequately describe a distribution, its variability must be characterized. In general, be wary of data deception if measures of variability are not presented along with mean or median measures.

Measures of variability serve another purpose. They help develop a sense of how a distribution's graph looks. By knowing a distribution's dispersion, one can predict certain distribution characteristics.

Range

The simplest measure of variability is the *range*. For ungrouped data, the range is the difference between the two extreme values of a data set. A distribution's range is obtained by subtracting the smallest measurement (X_L) from the largest (X_H) in a data set. Range is calculated by Formula 6-1:

Formula 6-1

$$\text{range} = \text{highest score} - \text{lowest score}$$
$$= X_H - X_L$$

For example, the number of full-time staff at five public libraries is given by the data set {61, 75, 72, 73, 30}. Using Formula 6-1, the highest value of the data set is $X_H = 75$ and the lowest value is $X_L = 30$.

$$\text{range} = X_H - X_L$$
$$= 75 - 30 \text{ which is } 45.$$

Example 6-1

Finding the Range of a Data Set

Each day, the library receives deliveries of books. For the past ten days, the number of books delivered form the data set {16, 5, 1, 9, 3, 12, 8, 4, 20, 2}. Find the range.

Analysis

Using Formula 6-1, where the highest score in the data set is $X_H = 20$, and the lowest value is $X_L = 1$, the following calculation yields:

$$\text{Range} = X_H - X_L$$
$$= 20 - 1 \text{ which is } 19.$$

For *grouped data,* the range is the difference between the value of the upper class limit of the highest class and the value of the lower class limit of the lowest class. Thus, if the highest class is 700–750 and the lowest class is 300–350, the range is 451 [451 = 750.5 − 299.5]. In this example, the upper class limit is 750.5 and the lower class limit is 299.5.

The range has three shortcomings, however, as a measure of variability. The first is that it cannot be calculated if either the lowest and highest classes are open. For example, if the lowest class of a distribution is "less than 3 hours" or the highest class is "20 hours or more," the range cannot be computed. The reason is that some scores are higher than 20, and some scores are less than 3.

The second shortcoming is that the range considers only the highest and lowest values of a distribution; it is not sensitive to the dispersion of data between the extreme values. This drawback is illustrated by the following three distributions, each of which has a range of 10.

Distribution 1: {12, 13, 14, 15, 16, 17, 18, 19, 20, 21, 22}

Distribution 2: {12, 13, 14, 14, 14, 14, 16, 16, 18, 19, 22}

Distribution 3: {12, 12, 12, 12, 12, 13, 14, 16, 17, 17, 22}

Visual inspection of these distributions reveals that there are substantial differences in the dispersion among the three data sets. However, the range of $R = 10$ [10 = 22 − 12] offers no hint of this difference in the data's dispersion.

The range's third shortcoming is that it tends to increase as the number of observations in the distribution increases. This is because more observations make it increasingly likely that it will include extreme values from both ends of the distribution. This lack of stability decreases the range's usefulness.

Despite these disadvantages, the range does have merit as a simple measure of variability, as in discussing "the data range between 68 and 96." But like its mode, a data set's range should not be used alone to describe the dispersion of data.

Percentiles

Percentiles are numbers that divide a set of ranked data into 100 equal parts. The most widely used statistical measure of relative position in a distribution, percentiles are almost always used to describe a large data set. In any distribution, the percentiles are abbreviated by P_1, P_2, P_3, . . . , P_{99}. Most librarians are familiar with percentiles from large data sets such as standardized tests (ACT, GMAT, GRE, LSAT, MCAT, SAT, TOEFL, and others). Having taken many such tests, most students know that the interpretation of a test result depends upon two related but different outcomes. The first is how well the person performed on the test (test score expressed in percent of the number of total possible points). The second is the relative position of the person's test result in the distribution of the test results of others who took the test (percentile). The position is revealed by the person's percentile score. For example, a student's score of 90% correct on a test generally is good. This score, however, may lose favor if the relative position of a 90% correct score places the individual in the 20th percentile of the distribution of persons who took the test. The interpretation of a 20th percentile score is that 20% of the scores fell below a score of 90%. Stated another way, 80% of the scores were greater than 90%.

To illustrate the idea of a percentile, suppose a librarian has a set of scores that are listed in rank order. Since these data points could represent anything, they can be listed and labeled as follows: $\{x_1, x_2, x_3, \ldots, x_n\}$. The *P-th percentile* is a value *X,* such that *P* percent of the data is less than or equal to *X*. Similarly, $(1 - P)$ percent of the data is greater than or equal to *X*. The procedure to determine the *j*-th percentile, P_j, of ungrouped data is as follows:

1. Place the data in an array, arranged in ascending order.

2. The location of the percentile in the array is identified by small letter "l." The formula is $l = jn/100$, where *n* is the number of scores in the distribution and *j* is the desired percentile.

3. (a) If l is an odd number, round it up to the next integer. That integer represents the position (location) of the desired percentile in the distribution. That is, if $l = 3.4$, rounded up to the next integer, $l = 4$. This means that the desired percentile is the fourth score in the array. (b) If l is a whole number, then average the numbers that are in the l-th and $(l + 1)$-th positions. That is, if $l = 12$, then the desired percentile is the mean of the numbers that are in the 12th and 13th positions in the distribution. The *l* value indicates the location of the percentile in the distribution when it is ordered into an array.

To illustrate how to calculate a percentile from ungrouped data, suppose that a library science instructor administers a test to three sections of undergraduate students ($n = 111$) who are taking an introductory course in library instruction. The scores, when ranked, are as follows:

02	02	05	06	06	10	10	11	12	19	20	20	22	23
25	25	25	26	26	32	35	35	36	36	38	39	39	39
40	41	42	44	46	48	48	50	50	50	50	50	51	52
60	61	61	61	61	63	65	65	66	66	69	69	70	70
71	71	73	73	74	74	76	76	77	77	77	77	78	78
78	80	80	84	84	87	87	88	88	88	88	89	89	89
89	90	90	90	90	90	90	90	90	94	94	94	94	94
94	94	94	94	94	95	95	97	97	98	98	98	98	

To find the 10th percentile, P_{10}, the librarian follows the procedure by first calculating the location "l" value for $j = 10$:

$$l = jn/100$$
$$= (10) (111)/100 \text{ which is } 11.1.$$

Since this value is not a whole number, the procedure is to round the value up to the next whole number, which is 12. Hence, the 10th percentile is the 12th number in the distribution, which is 20. This score is identified by counting twelve scores up from the beginning score in the array. Hence, $P_{10} = 20$. The 10th percentile is the point in the distribution where 10% of the scores are less than 20. It also is the point where 90% of the distribution's scores are great than 20. Continuing the example above, to find P_{90}, the procedure is similar, with $j = 90$, $n = 111$:

$$l = jn/100$$
$$= (90) (111)/100 \text{ which is } 99.9.$$

Since this value is not a whole number, it must be rounded up to the next whole number, which is 100. Hence, the 90th percentile for this distribution is the score that is in the 100th place. This score turns out to be 94. Count 100 scores, beginning with the bottom score in the distribution, to find the score. The 90th percentile refers to the place in the distribution where 90% of the distribution's scores are below the value of 100. The 90th percentile also marks the point in the distribution where 10% of the distribution's scores are above the value of 100.

This example shows that it is not necessary to perform many calculations to determine a percentile. Although this example featured 111 data points, librarians can determine percentile with many fewer scores. For example, if there are six data points {0, 1, 2, 3, 4, 5}, the value of P_{60} is calculated in the same way as before, with $j = 60$, $n = 6$. That is, $l = (60) (6)/100$ or $l = 3.6$. When l is rounded up to the next whole number, it tells that the 60th percentile is the 4th score in the distribution. The fourth score corresponds to 3.

Suppose that one has a raw score and wishes to determine its percentile in a distribution. The percentile of a score x is provided by the following:

$$\text{Percentile of } x = \frac{100 \text{ (number of data values } \leq x)}{\text{total number of data values}}.$$

The notation "$\leq$" is read as "less than or equal to."

To illustrate how to determine the percentile of a score relative to a distribution, suppose a student took a test after the others in the class and received a score of 60%. To determine this score's percentile in the distribution, the first step is to count the number of scores in the distribution that are less than or equal to 60. Counting from the lowest score, there are 43 scores that meet this criteria. Hence, percentile of $60 = 100(43)/111$, which is 39. This tells that a student's score of 60% places the student in the 39th percentile of the distribution of 111 students, or $P_{39} = 60$. The interpretation of the percentile is that 39 percent of the scores in the distribution are less (or lower) than the student's score of 60%. It also means that 61% of the distribution's scores are greater than 60. If the student had scored 70% instead of 60%, a change of ten percent [$10\% = 70\% - 60\%$] the new percentile would be 50, which is the median for the distribution.

Formula 6-2 is used to determine the percentile in grouped distributions:

Formula 6-2

$$P_j = L + \frac{w}{f}\left(\frac{jn}{100} - F\right)$$

where j = the desired percentile

L = lower class boundary (real limit) of the percentile class

w = class interval of the desired percentile class

n = total number of observations in the data set

F = cumulative frequency less than the desired percentile class

f = frequency of the interval containing the percentile class.

Table 6-2 presents a sample frequency distribution of the examination scores of 200 students who are enrolled in a library instruction class. To locate the 90th percentile, P_{90}, the librarian first locates the 90th percentile class by computing $(jn)/100$. This is 180 [$180 = (90)(200)/100$]. Hence, the 90th percentile class lies in the class interval that contains the 180th item.

TABLE 6-2   Frequency Distribution of Student Test Scores ($n = 200$)

Scores	Class midpoint (M)	Number of students less than upper class limits	Cumulative frequency
300 and under 350	325	2	2
350 and under 400	375	8	10
400 and under 450	425	22	32
450 and under 500	475	37	69
500 and under 550	525	65	134
550 and under 600	575	47	181
600 and under 650	625	12	193
650 and under 700	675	6	199
700 and under 750	725	1	200
Total		200	

The 180th item lies in the class interval "550 and under 600." Therefore, in Formula 6-2, where $j = 90$, $L = 550$, $w = 50$, $n = 200$, $F = 134$, and $f = 47$, calculations are as follows:

$$P_{90} = 550 + \frac{50}{47}(180 - 134)$$

$$= 550 + \frac{50}{47}(46)$$

$$= 550 + 48.9 \text{ which is } 598.9.$$

The interpretation of P_{90} is that 90 percent of the students taking this examination achieved scores that are less than or equal to a score of 598.9.

Percentiles also can be estimated by graphing techniques. The data in Table 6-2 can be graphed as a less-than-cumulative percent polygon. Figure 6-2, constructed from the data in Table 6-2, shows that the median score, P_{50}, is 523.8. Other percentiles could be estimated from this graph in a similar way.

The formula for percentile, Formula 6-2, is similar to the formula for the median, presented in the previous chapter. This is not coincidental. The reason is that the median is the 50th percentile, P_{50}. That is, the median divides a distribution into two equal parts; percentiles divide a distribution into 100 equal parts.

Related measures include the three *quartiles* (Q_1, Q_2, Q_3), which divide a distribution into 4 parts, and *deciles* (D_1, D_2, . . . , D_9), which divide it into 10 parts. (The *quartiles* are discussed in greater detail below.) All these measures may be determined from Formula 6-2 by using the appropriate value for P_j.

FIGURE 6-2 ▌ Determining Percentiles for Student Examinations

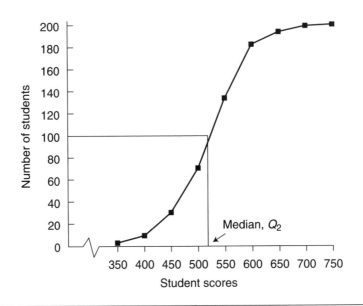

Quartile measures may be used in many applications. For example, they may assist young readers in locating words in the dictionary. In attempting to locate a word, it is helpful to know in which quartile of the dictionary the word will be found. Using the mnemonic device AEMS conjures up an effective mental image: Aunt Eleanor Makes Soup or Angry Elephants Mash Spiders.

The first letters of each of the above words approximately separate the four quartiles of words in the dictionary.

A to D   the first 25% of the words

E to L   the second 25% of the words

M to R   the third 25% of the words

S to Z   the fourth 25% of the words.

Thus, in trying to look up the word *book,* the reader should target the first quartile of the dictionary. Similarly, the reader will find the word *manuscript* in the third quartile and the word *whippersnapper* in the fourth quartile of the dictionary.

Percentile Ranges

Percentiles can be combined with ranges to yield *percentile ranges.* For instance, the *10-to-90th percentile range* is the distance between the 10th and the 90th percentiles. This measure is useful to estimate the range because it excludes high and low extreme scores.

To calculate the 10-to-90th percentile range, first determine the 10th and 90th percentiles, and then calculate the difference of $P_{90} - P_{10}$. For example, $P_{90} = 598.9$ for the data in Table 6-2. To determine P_{10}, keep in mind that j refers to the desired percentile and n refers to the total number of observations in the data set:

$$\frac{jn}{100} = \frac{10(200)}{100} \text{ which is } 20.$$

This means that the 10th percentile lies in the class containing the 20th item. Table 6-2 shows that this is the class in which $L = 400$, $w = 50$, $F = 10$, and $f = 22$.

$$P_j = L + \frac{w}{f}\left(\frac{jn}{100} - F\right)$$

$$P_{10} = 400 + \left(\frac{50}{22}\right)(20 - 10)$$

$$= 400 + \frac{50(10)}{22}$$

$$= 400 + 22.7 \text{ which is } 422.7:$$

Since $P_{90} = 598.9$ and $P_{10} = 422.7$, the 10-to-90th percentile range for the data in Table 6-1 is as follows:

$$P_{90} - P_{10} = 598.9 - 422.7 \text{ which is } 176.2.$$

The interpretation of this measure is that the middle 80 percent of the test scores lie between the test scores 422.7 and 598.9. The remaining 20 percent of the scores lie either below 422.7 or above 598.9.

The percentile range is a sophisticated and useful measurement of deviation, superior to the simple range. This is because the percentile range excludes extreme values that form the tails of the distribution at either end of the array.

Interquartile Range

A variation on percentile range is the interquartile range. Like the 10-to-90th percentile range, the interquartile range minimizes the influence of extreme observations. This is accomplished by excluding a specific proportion of data on each end of the distribution. The *interquartile range* is the distance between the first and the third quartile, Q_1 and Q_3. Formula 6-3 expresses this relationship.

Formula 6-3

$$\text{Interquartile range} = Q_3 - Q_1.$$

As the prefix *quar-* implies, quartiles divide a distribution into four equal parts. Accordingly, $Q_1 = P_{25}$, $Q_2 = P_{50}$, $Q_3 = P_{75}$, and $Q_4 = P_{99}$. Note that Q_2 is the median. In a grouped frequency distribution, quartiles Q_1 and Q_3 can be determined by using Formula 6-2, where $j = 25$ and $j = 75$:

$$P_{25} = L + \frac{w}{f}\left(\frac{25n}{100} - F\right)$$

$$P_{75} = L + \frac{w}{f}\left(\frac{75n}{100} - F\right).$$

In Figure 6-3, the interquartile range refers to the observations that lie in the middle portion of the distribution between the first quartile, Q_1, and the third, Q_3. The middle one-half of distribution observations are included in this range. Because the interquartile range deals with the middle 50% of the observations, it is more stable than the simple range since extreme scores are excluded.

Quartiles and quartile ranges also can be calculated for ungrouped data. The rank of the quartile is equal to the number of items in the data set, (N), times the percent of the data that will fall below the desired quartile. For Q_1, for example, that would be 25%.

Because the rank of quartiles in a distribution can be calculated in a variety of ways, it is possible to find different formulas in different books for determining a quartile's rank. Formula 6-4 presents a method for calculating either Q_1 or Q_3:

Formula 6-4

Rank of $Q_1 = 0.25N$

Rank of $Q_3 = 0.75N$

FIGURE 6-3 | A Distribution's Quartiles and Interquartile Range

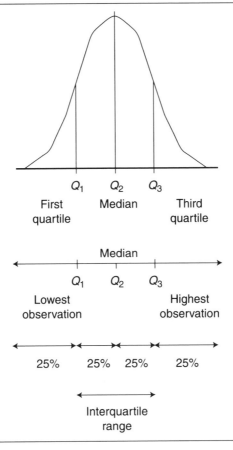

If a distribution has 100 scores, the 25th score marks the first quartile, Q_1. To determine the actual value, array the scores in ascending order and then count to the 25th score. The value of that score marks Q_1. Then, applying Formula 6-4 in this same distribution, $N = 100$, the calculation yields 25 [25 = 0.25(100)].

The advantage of using Formula 6-4 for calculating the rank of quartiles is more apparent when the distribution has a size for which calculations are less obvious than 100. For example, if the data set has 30 scores, then the rank of Q_1 in the distribution is 7.5 [7.5 = 0.25(30)]. This means that the value of the first quartile lies midway between the seventh and eighth values in the data array, arranged in ascending order.

Example 6-2 |

Using Quartile Ranges to Set Work Objectives

The circulation librarian at a college library employs students to shelve books and journal volumes. Items for reshelving are initially staged and later retrieved from the circulation desk and from tables and study carrels. These items are then sorted, placed on carts, sorted in a second staging area, and then reshelved.

The librarian has noticed that some days the clerks pick up books from tables and carrels but overlook those that are staged at the book reshelving area. Other days, the clerks neglect to collect items from the tables and carrels.

In an effort to establish quantitative work standards and to minimize day-to-day variation in the number of materials shelved, the librarian decides to use the interquartile range to form work goals.

To accomplish this task, over a 16-day period the librarian counts the number of materials picked up from each area. The data are then ranked from low to high. For example, the fewest books collected from all library tables on a specified day was 3 and the most was 83. These data are shown in Table 6-3.

The quartiles can be determined easily since there are 16 scores. The first quartile, Q_1, occurs at rank 4 [0.25 = 4/16]. The second quartile, Q_2, which is the median, occurs at rank 8 [0.50 = 8/16]. Similarly, Q_3 occurs at rank 12 [0.75 = 12/16].

With this information, the librarian can establish work objectives for the student employees. The standards, although crude, might be that between 12 and 58 items must be cleared from the tables and carrels, and between 34 and 71 items must be cleared from the book reshelving staging area. Once the students become accustomed to these new work objectives, the evaluation process can be refined.

TABLE 6-3 | Overlooked Library Items

| | Rank order | |
Rank	On tables/carrels	In staging area
1	3	1
2	6	7
3	7	20
4	8	33
5	12	34
6	13	35
7	16	36
8	17	43
9	26	52
10	39	64
11	47	69
12	58	71
13	61	75
14	71	76
15	76	80
16	83	82

MEAN DEVIATION MEASURES

Unlike the various measures of variability that have been presented thus far, there are two popular dispersion measures that include the value of each observation in the set. These are the *standard deviation* and the *variance* for a distribution.

Each of these measures is based on the mean of the distribution, and shows the absolute difference, or *deviation,* between each score in the distribution and the mean. If the data set's observations are clustered close to the distribution's mean, the mean deviation measures will be small. If, however, the scores show considerable dispersion from the mean, the mean deviation measures will be large.

Standard Deviation

The standard deviation probably is the most important measure used in dispersion analysis. It is a powerful and versatile statistic with uses and implications that are far reaching. Once the standard deviation for a distribution is calculated, many important facts can be inferred about a distribution.

Briefly, *standard deviation* tells how far the typical data point in a distribution strays from the mean of the distribution. A significant clue to the meaning of this measure is present in the familiar meanings of the words *standard* and *deviation:*

1. *Standard* reflects that the measurement is a kind of uniform guideline to the nature of the distribution. The measure is standard because it applies uniformly to all data points in the distribution.

2. *Deviation* reflects that the measure relates to the differences in placement of data points associated with some norm.

When used in association with a sample, standard deviation commonly is symbolized by the lowercase letter *s*. For a population, standard deviation is symbolized by the lowercase Greek letter sigma, σ. Note that in the study of statistics, the lowercase Greek letter sigma, σ, differs in significance from the capital Greek letter sigma, Σ, that is used in summation notation.

To understand the significance of the standard deviation, it is worthwhile to understand how the measure is constructed. Beginning with a set of *n*-data points, each of the points is labeled as follows: $\{X_1, X_2, \ldots, X_n\}$. For this data set, assume that the mean is $\overline{X}$.

In developing an equation for the standard deviation, first it must be determined how far each data point is from the data set's mean. For example, the first data point, X_1, is $(X_1 - \overline{X})$ distance from the mean. This distance or deviation is represented by d_1.

The deviation of each data point from the data set's mean is determined as follows:

$$d_1 = X_1 - \overline{X} \text{ (first data point's deviation from the mean)}$$
$$d_2 = X_2 - \overline{X} \text{ (second data point's deviation from the mean)}$$
$$d_3 = X_3 - \overline{X} \text{ (third data point's deviation from the mean)}$$
$$\cdots$$
$$d_n = X_n - \overline{X} \text{ (deviation of the } n\text{th data point from the mean).}$$

When the individual deviations are squared, the results are added. The resulting sum is known as the *sum of squared deviations* from the mean, or, simply, the *sum of squares*. The standard deviation for the distribution is then calculated by first dividing the sum of squares by $(n - 1)$, and then calculating the square root of this quotient. Formula 6-5 expresses the relationship:

Formula 6-5

$$s = \sqrt{\frac{\sum_{i=1}^{n} (X_i - \bar{X})^2}{n - 1}}$$

$$= \sqrt{\frac{(X_1 - \bar{X})^2 + (X_2 - \bar{X})^2 + \cdots + (X_n - \bar{X})^2}{n - 1}}$$

Example 6-3

Guessing about Data Dispersion

Examine the two distributions below and speculate on which has a larger standard deviation:

A: $\{1, 5, 13, 17, 25, 29\}$, $n = 6$
B: $\{1, 1, 1, 2, 2, 3, 3, 3\}$, $n = 8$.

Analysis

Standard deviation refers to the spread of data away from the distribution's mean. On inspection, Distribution A data are spread out more than are the data in Distribution B. That is, the data are less concentrated about the mean of Distribution A. Based on this realization, one can determine that the standard deviation of Distribution A will be larger than that of Distribution B.

To determine standard deviation, either construct a table or apply Formula 6-5. Although not required, it is common to add columns to the table to facilitate computations. Anyone who is new to calculating a standard deviation may find it instructive to study the calculations in the table below and then follow them carefully through Formula 6-5. The expanded table and the formulas are illustrated in Example 6-4.

Example 6-4

Calculating Standard Deviation

Find the standard deviation of the following distribution: {1, 5, 13, 17, 25, 29}.

Analysis

The distribution's mean is 15 [15 = 90/6]. To calculate the standard deviation requires the following calculations:

Score (X)	Score − Mean ($X - \bar{X}$)	(Score − Mean)^2 (Deviation)^2
1	−14 [−14 = 1 − 15]	196 [196 = $(-14)^2$]
5	−10 [−10 = 5 − 15]	100 [100 = $(-10)^2$]
13	−2 [−2 = 13 − 15]	4 [4 = $(-2)^2$]
17	2 [2 = 17 − 15]	4 [4 = $(2)^2$]
25	10 [10 = 25 − 15]	100 [100 = $(10)^2$]
29	14 [14 = 29 − 15]	196 [196 = $(14)^2$]
90 Sum		600 Sum

Using Formula 6-5, with $n = 6$,

$$s = \sqrt{\frac{\sum_{i=1}^{n} (X_i - \bar{X})^2}{n - 1}}$$

$$= \sqrt{\frac{(X_1 - \bar{X})^2 + (X_2 - \bar{X})^2 + \cdots + (X_6 - \bar{X})^2}{n - 1}}$$

$$= \sqrt{\frac{(1 - 15)^2 + (5 - 15)^2 + (13 - 15)^2 + (17 - 15)^2 + (25 - 15)^2 + (29 - 15)^2}{6 - 1}}$$

$$= \sqrt{\frac{(-14)^2 + (-10)^2 + (-2) + (2)^2 + (10)^2 + (14)^2}{5}}$$

$$= \sqrt{\frac{(196) + (100) + (4) + (4) + (100) + (196)}{5}}$$

$$= \sqrt{\frac{600}{5}}$$

$$= \sqrt{120} \text{ which is } 10.954.$$

In another example, suppose that a librarian is asked to report about the number of days that each one of the library's ten terminals was out of service last year. After consulting repair records the librarian determines the following:

Terminal number	1	2	3	4	5	6	7	8	9	10
Out-of-service days	8	9	4	9	8	4	5	3	6	4

In preparing to write the report, the librarian first verifies that the mean is 6 days [6 = 60/10] for the data. To calculate the standard deviation, the librarian builds Table 6-4 as follows:

Using Formula 6-5, with $n = 10$,

$$s = \sqrt{\frac{\sum_{i=1}^{n} (X_i - \bar{X})^2}{n - 1}}$$

$$= \sqrt{\frac{(X_1 - \bar{X})^2 + (X_2 - \bar{X})^2 + \cdots + (X_n - \bar{X})^2}{n - 1}}$$

$$= \sqrt{\frac{\begin{array}{c}(8 - 6)^2 + (9 - 6)^2 + (4 - 6)^2 + (9 - 6)^2 + (8 - 6)^2 \\ + (4 - 6)^2 + (5 - 6)^2 + (3 - 6)^2 + (6 - 6)^2 + (4 - 6)^2\end{array}}{10 - 1}}$$

$$= \sqrt{\frac{\begin{array}{c}(2)^2 + (3)^2 + (-2)^2 + (3)^3 + (2)^2 \\ + (-2)^2 + (-1)^2 + (-3)^2 + (0)^2 + (-2)^2\end{array}}{9}}$$

$$= \sqrt{\frac{(4) + (9) + (4) + (9) + (4) + (4) + (1) + (9) + (0) + (4)}{9}}$$

$$= \sqrt{\frac{48}{9}}$$

$$= \sqrt{5.333} \text{ which is } 2.309, \text{ or } 2.31 \text{ days.}$$

Seeking more specific information for the report, the librarian calculates the hours of terminal downtime. The results are shown in Table 6-5.

Standard deviation is sensitive to the units of measurement. In Table 6-4, computer terminal downtime for each of the library's computer terminals is measured in days. If the time had been measured in hours, as in Table 6-5, the calculations for standard deviation would have been different.

TABLE 6-4 ▓ Out-of-Service Days per Terminal for 1997

Terminal number	Score (X)	Score-Mean ($X - \bar{X}$)	(Deviation)^2
1	8	2 [2 = 8 − 6]	4 [4 = (2)^2]
2	9	3 [3 = 9 − 6]	9 [9 = (3)^2]
3	4	−2 [−2 = 4 − 6]	4 [4 = (−2)^2]
4	9	3 [3 = 9 − 6]	9 [9 = (3)^2]
5	8	2 [2 = 8 − 6]	4 [4 = (2)^2]
6	4	−2 [−2 = 4 − 6]	4 [4 = (−2)^2]
7	5	−1 [−1 = 5 − 6]	1 [1 = (−1)^2]
8	3	−3 [−3 = 3 − 6]	9 [9 = (−3)^2]
9	6	0 [0 = 6 − 6]	0 [0 = (0)^2]
10	4	−2 [−2 = 4 − 6]	4 [4 = (−2)^2]
	60 Sum		48 Sum

TABLE 6-5 ▌ Hours of Terminal Downtime

Terminal number	Observation X (hours)	Deviation $(X - \overline{X})$	Squared deviation $(X - \overline{X})^2$
1	192	48	2,304
2	216	72	5,184
3	96	−48	2,304
4	216	72	5,184
5	192	48	2,304
6	96	−48	2,304
7	120	−24	576
8	72	−72	5,184
9	144	0	0
10	96	−48	2,304
	1,440 Sum	0	27,648

To illustrate this, Table 6-5 shows the number of hours of downtime per computer terminal. The mean is 144 [144 = 1440/10]. When Formula 6-5 is applied with $n = 10$, the following is determined:

$$s = \sqrt{\frac{\sum_{i=1}^{n} (X_i - \overline{X})^2}{n - 1}}$$

$$= \sqrt{\frac{(X_1 - \overline{X})^2 + (X_2 - \overline{X})^2 + \cdots + (X_n - \overline{X})^2}{n - 1}}$$

$$= \sqrt{\frac{\begin{array}{l}(192 - 144)^2 + (216 - 144)^2 + (96 - 144)^2 + (216 - 144)^2 + (192 - 144)^2 \\ + (96 - 144)^2 + (120 - 144)^2 + (72 - 144)^2 + (144 - 144)^2 + (96 - 144)^2\end{array}}{10 - 1}}$$

$$= \sqrt{\frac{\begin{array}{l}(2304) + (5184) + (2304) + (5184) + (2304) \\ + (2304) + (576) + (5184) + (0) + (2304)\end{array}}{9}}$$

$$= \sqrt{\frac{27,648}{9}}$$

$$= \sqrt{3072} \text{ which is a standard deviation of 55.4 hours.}$$

In examining the result, the librarian sees that the standard deviation for downtime in hours ($s = 55.4$ hours) is 24 times larger than the standard deviation for downtime in days ($s = 2.31$ days). When every element of a data set is multiplied by a constant, the standard deviation also is multiplied by the same constant. When Table 6-4 data were converted from days to hours, each score was multiplied by a factor of 24.

There are several factors that affect the standard deviation of a data set. Tables 6-4 and 6-5 present the same data, for example, except that the units are different. The data have the same variability because the data are identical. Yet the measure of variability, reported by the standard deviation, for each data set is different.

In descriptive statistics, there are two key factors that affect the measure of variability. The first factor is the occurrence of extreme scores. As the range of a data set increases, its standard deviation increases. This means that it is important to exercise care when evaluating the standard deviation of a data set that has one or two extreme values. For example, if the difference between a score and the mean is 10, then the square of the deviation contributes 100 to the sum of squares $[100 = (10)^2]$.

The second factor affecting the measure of variability concerns the number of scores that form the data set. Additional scores tend to increase the range within a data set. This occurrence serves to bring the first factor—extreme scores—into play.

Calculating Standard Deviation for Grouped Data

If the data are grouped, the standard deviation still can be calculated. In this case, the midpoint of each interval is represented by $M_1, M_2, M_3, \ldots, M_k$ and each respective frequency is $f_1, f_2, f_3, \ldots, f_k$. Then, the standard deviation is calculated by Formula 6-6:

Formula 6-6

$$s = \sqrt{\frac{\sum_{i=1}^{n} (M_i - \overline{X})^2 f_i}{n - 1}}$$

$$= \sqrt{\frac{(M_1 - \overline{X})^2 f_1 + (M_2 - \overline{X})^2 f_2 + \cdots + (M_n - \overline{X})^2 f_n}{(f_1 + f_2 + f_3 + \cdots + f_n) - 1}}$$

The standard deviation of Table 6-6 data is determined by first calculating the mean, which is 69.66 or 69.7. Then, after performing the calculations for the various columns in Table 6-6, the sum, 6066.72, is divided by 92 $[92 = 93 - 1]$. The result is 65.943 $[65.943 = 6066.72/92]$. The square root of 65.943 is 8.12 years. This result is the standard deviation.

It also is instructive to study the calculations that are presented below. Notice the numbers from the columns in Table 6-6, with $n = 93$.

TABLE 6-6   Grouped Data on Book Publication Dates ($n = 93$)

Class	Frequency (f_i)	Midpoint (M_i)	Deviation ($M_i - \overline{X}$)	Product ($M_i - \overline{X})^2 f_i$	
55–58	8	56.5	− 13.2	1393.92	$[= (-13.2)^2 \cdot 8]$
59–62	13	60.5	− 9.2	1100.32	$[= (-9.2)^2 \cdot 13]$
63–66	14	64.5	− 5.2	378.56	$[= (-5.2)^2 \cdot 14]$
67–70	16	68.5	− 1.2	23.04	$[= (-1.2)^2 \cdot 16]$
71–74	16	72.5	2.8	125.44	$[= (2.8)^2 \cdot 16]$
75–78	10	76.5	6.8	462.40	$[= (6.8)^2 \cdot 10]$
79–82	9	80.5	10.8	1049.76	$[= (10.8)^2 \cdot 9]$
83–86	7	84.5	14.8	1533.28	$[= (14.8)^2 \cdot 7]$
	93 Sum			6066.72 Sum	

$$s = \sqrt{\frac{\sum\limits_{i=1}^{n}(M_i - \overline{X})^2 f_i}{n - 1}}$$

$$= \sqrt{\frac{(M_1 - \overline{X})^2 f_1 + (M_2 - \overline{X})^2 f_2 + \cdots + (M_n - \overline{X})^2 f_n}{(f_1 + f_2 + f_3 + \cdots + f_n) - 1}}$$

$$= \sqrt{\frac{\begin{array}{c}(56.5 - 69.7)^2(8) + (60.5 - 69.7)^2(13) + (64.5 - 69.7)^2(14) \\ + (68.5 - 69.7)^2(16) + (72.5 - 69.7)^2(16) + (76.5 - 69.7)^2(10) \\ + (80.5 - 69.7)^2(9) + (84.5 - 69.7)^2(7)\end{array}}{(8 + 13 + 14 + 16 + 16 + 10 + 9 + 7) - 1}}$$

$$= \sqrt{\frac{\begin{array}{c}(-13.2)^2(8) + (-9.2)^2(13) + (-5.2)^2(14) + (-1.2)^2(16) \\ + (2.8)^2(16) + (6.8)^2(10) + (10.8)^2(9) + (14.8)^2(7)\end{array}}{(93) - 1}}$$

$$= \sqrt{\frac{\begin{array}{c}(174.24)(8) + (84.64)(13) + (27.04)(14) + (1.44)(16) \\ + (7.84)(16) + (46.24)(10) + (116.64)(9) + (219.04)(7)\end{array}}{92}}$$

$$= \sqrt{\frac{\begin{array}{c}(1393.92) + (1100.32) + (378.56) + (23.04) \\ + (125.44) + (462.40) + (1049.76) + (1533.28)\end{array}}{92}}$$

$$= \sqrt{\frac{6066.72}{92}}$$

$$= \sqrt{65.94} \text{ which is 8.12 years.}$$

Those who are familiar with the standard deviation probably have seen formulas similar to Formulas 6-5 and 6-6, but with the divisor n rather than $(n - 1)$. The difference in division results from the difference between calculating the standard deviation for a sample and calculating the standard deviation for a population.

The reason for dividing by $(n - 1)$ or n is not important in the practical use of the standard deviation, however. It is enough to know that the divisor $(n - 1)$ is used in finding the standard deviation of a sample.

Further, those with some experience with statistics also may have encountered the term *variance* in conjunction with standard deviations. *Variance* is the square of the standard deviation, or s^2. This measure of dispersion is important in inferential statistics and other advanced applications. In this text, however, the focus is on the standard deviation for a distribution.

Using Standard Deviation to Describe Data

The standard deviation of a distribution has a very definite relationship to the shape of a distribution's curve. This relationship was first described by the Russian mathematician P. L. Chebyshev. He expressed this relationship in a theorem that carries his name. *Chebyshev's theorem* states that for any set of data, and for any selected number of standard deviations, k, the equation $1/k^2$ equals the proportion of data beyond k standard deviations of the mean. A corollary to this is the equation $1 - (1/k^2)$, which tells the minimum proportion of the data that lie within k standard deviations of the mean. These relationships are true for distributions of both populations and samples.

For example, within 1.5 standard deviations from the mean lies 55.6% of the data [.556 = 1 − 1/(1.5^2)]. Therefore, in *any* distribution, at least 55.6% of the data lie within 1.5 standard deviations on either side of the mean. Thus, if k = 2, 75% [0.75 = 1 − 1/(2^2)] of the data in any distribution is within 2 standard deviations of the mean. Equally important is that not more than 44.4% of the data in the first example [44.4% = 100% − 55.6%] and 25% in the second example [25% = 100% − 75%] lie beyond 1.5 and 2 standard deviations, respectively.

Chebyshev's theorem yields the *minimum* proportion of data within k standard deviations from the mean. For many distributions, the value returned by 1 − (1/k^2) falls on the conservative side because the theorem is designed to work with *any* set of data. It even applies to data that have very erratic or irregular curves. In more regular mound-shaped distributions, such as those in Figure 6-1, estimates of proportions can be made with great accuracy and confidence. Distributions such as those in Figure 6-1 are called *normal distributions*. In normal distribution, the interval within 1 standard deviation on either side of the mean invariably contains 68% of all data points. Within 1.5 standard deviations, 86.6% of all data points can be found. Within 2 standard deviations, 95% of all data points can be found. Finally, 99.7%— or virtually all of the data points—can be found within 3 standard deviations of the mean.

Often, statistical reports provide only numerical values for means and standard deviations. The value of Chebyshev's theorem and the normal distribution is that the statistical consumer can use the reported standard deviation and mean to build a mental picture of the frequency distribution.

Estimating a Distribution's Standard Deviation

The standard deviation for a mound-shaped distribution can be estimated easily and accurately. This is because virtually all the data in a mound-shaped distribution are within 3 standard deviations of the mean. The rule of thumb is that the range of a set of data is approximately 4 to 6 times the standard deviation. The multiple of 4 provides a good estimate for a data set containing a small number of observations, while 6 is an appropriate multiple for a larger number of observations.

Assume, for example, that members of a library consortium report a mound-shaped distribution of collection sizes from a low score of 4700 volumes to a high of 153,000 volumes. When reading these data, a librarian knows that 99.7% of the data will be contained within 3 standard deviations of the mean, or, mathematically, within the interval expressed by $\overline{X}$ − 3s to $\overline{X}$ + 3s. The total span of this interval is 6s. Hence,

$$6s = 153,000 - 4700$$
$$6s = 148,300, \text{ so } s = 24,717 \text{ volumes } [24,717 = 148,300/6].$$

This estimate of the standard deviation reveals that considerable data are dispersed. Therefore, the arithmetic mean would not be a particularly useful measure in describing these data. This suggests that the median would be a better measure of central tendency for the data.

COEFFICIENT OF VARIATION

Sometimes it is useful to compare how two distributions vary. For example, a librarian may want to know how library operating expenses vary compared to the variation in similar libraries. A librarian may first form this ratio:

$$\frac{s \text{ (operating expense Library A)}}{s \text{ (operating expense Library B)}}.$$

However, a simple ratio of standard deviations is not meaningful because the simple ratio can be inflated or deflated by changing the units (thousands of dollars, dollars, cents) in which operating expenses are measured. This inflation was illustrated earlier in data from Tables 6-4 and 6-5.

One calculates the *coefficient of variation, V,* to make sure that a comparison of standard deviations is not biased by differences in the magnitude of the values in the two data sets. The *coefficient of variation* is the ratio of a distribution's standard deviation to its mean multiplied by 100. This relationship is expressed in Formula 6-7:

Formula 6-7

$$CV = \frac{100s}{X}$$

To illustrate Formula 6-7, refer again to the data drawn from Tables 6-4 and 6-5:

$$\frac{V \text{ (downtime in hours)}}{V \text{ (downtime in days)}} = \frac{100 \left(\frac{55.4}{144} \right)}{100 \left(\frac{2.31}{6} \right)} = \frac{38.5\%}{38.5\%} \text{ which is 1.}$$

The ratio of coefficients of variation equals 1. This is because the distribution has the same variability whether it is measured in hours or in days.

The coefficient of variation requires only that both data sets be measured in ratio scale. That is, both distributions must be measured with scales that have absolute zero points. Thus, the coefficient of variation cannot be used to compare distributions of intelligence or achievement scores, because educational and psychological scales have no absolute zero point.

The coefficient of variation is used to adjust for size differentials and to prevent incorrect assumptions that may arise from focusing on the standard deviation alone. Suppose, for example, that the standard deviation in the budget for a multibranch library has been increasing over the past three years:

Year	Mean budget of all branches	Standard deviation	Coefficient of variation
Year 3	$1,000,000	$90,000	9.0%
Year 2	893,000	85,759	9.6
Year 1	850,000	87,500	10.3

To follow the calculation for each year, where CV_1, CV_2, and CV_3 represent the coefficient of variation for Year 1, Year 2, and Year 3, respectively:

$$CV_1 = \frac{100\,(87,500)}{850,000} \qquad CV_2 = \frac{100\,(85,759)}{893,000} \qquad CV_3 = \frac{100\,(90,000)}{1,000,000}$$

$$= \frac{8,750,000}{850,000} \qquad\qquad = \frac{8,575,900}{893,000} \qquad\qquad = \frac{9,000,000}{1,000,000}$$

$$= 10.3\% \qquad\qquad\quad = 9.6\% \qquad\qquad\qquad = 9.0\%.$$

While the standard deviation shows that the disparity among the branches has grown, the coefficient of variation correctly shows that any inequity has decreased over the period. The coefficient of variation adjusts for the increase in standard deviation due to the growth in the overall mean budget for all the branches.

In the above example, the coefficient of variation can be used to measure the percent of change in variation from Year 1 through Year 3. The rate of decrease in budgetary inequity, as expressed by the coefficient of variation for Year 1 to Year 2, is $(10.3\% - 9.6\%)/10.3\%$ $= 0.068$, or about 7%. Inequity decrease from Year 2 to Year 3 is $(9.6\% - 9.0\%)/9.6\% =$ .062, or slightly over 6%.

The librarian will encounter the coefficient of variation in many areas. For example, in financial analysis of the librarian's IRA or 401k plan, standard deviation of return on a stock is used to calculate a measurement of the stock's risk. Also, in performance assessment, the standard deviation can be used to compare the production consistency of machines or people. Example 6-5 illustrates an application of the coefficient of variation.

Example 6-5

Variability

The incomes of the librarians at Institution X have a mean of $45,000, with a standard deviation of $10,000. The librarians at Institution Y have a mean income of $35,000, with a standard deviation of $5000. Which institution shows more variability in income for its librarians?

Analysis

	Mean salary	Standard deviation	Coefficient of variation
Institution X	$45,000	$10,000	22.2%
Institution Y	$35,000	5,000	14.3

Applying Formula 6-7:

$$\text{For Institution X, } CV = \frac{100(10,000)}{45,000}$$

$$= 22.2$$

$$\text{For Institution Y, } CV = \frac{100(5,000)}{35,000} \text{ which is } 14.3.$$

The interpretation is that Institution X shows more variability in its income for librarians than does Institution Y.

For another example, suppose that Librarian A and Librarian B each perform mediated online literature searches. Each month, for six months, the number of searches that each completes is recorded. The mean and standard deviations for these data are as follows:

Librarian	Mean number of searches per month	Standard deviation	Coefficient of variation
A	26	4.70	18.1% [18.1 = 100 (4.70)/26]
B	91	11.75	12.9% [12.9 = 100(11.75)/91]

Librarian B's standard deviation shows greater absolute variation in output than does Librarian A's standard deviation, at 11.75 searches as compared to 4.70 searches. However, Librarian B performs substantially more searches than does Librarian A.

This output disparity makes the standard deviation an unreliable measure for interpreting Librarian B's output variation compared to that of Librarian A. The coefficient of variation overcomes this disparity and shows that Librarian B exhibits less relative variation than does Librarian A, at 12.9% as compared to 18.1%. Another illustration of this concept is found in Example 6-6.

Example 6-6

Understanding Data

A clerk monitors the circulation desk for a period and records how long it takes for persons to complete their transactions.

Distribution A Circulation desk waiting time		Distribution B Number of items borrowed during a library visit	
Class (seconds)	Frequency (*f*)	Items borrowed (*X*)	Frequency (*f*)
1–30	12	1	5
31–60	24	2	12
61–90	29	3	25
91–120	9	4	27
121–150	5	5	8
151–180	2	6	3
		7	1

1. In each distribution, are the data discrete or continuous?

2. For Distribution A, find the class midpoints.

3. Find the frequency for each distribution.

4. Identify the frequency for class interval 91–120.

5. In Distribution A, identify the modal class, if any.

6. Identify the range for both distributions.

7. Interpret $f = 24$ in Distribution A and interpret 6 in Distribution B.

8. Find the mean for each distribution.

9. Find the standard deviation for each distribution.

10. For Distribution A, estimate Q_1, Q_2, Q_3, P_{10}, P_{90}.

11. For Distribution A, find the interquartile range, $Q_3 - Q_1$.

Analysis

1. The variable is time, which is continuous.

2. The first class interval is 1–30. Since the data are continuous, the real class limits for the interval are 0.5–30.5. Formula 4-2 yields the class midpoint. For the first class interval 1–30, the midpoint is 15.5 [15.5 = (0.5 + 30.5)/2]. The class midpoint for the second class is 45.5 [45.5 = (30.5 + 61.5)/2], and so on.

Several columns have been added to the table to facilitate various computations. For Distribution A:

Class interval	Frequency (f_i)	Midpoint (M_i)	Product (f_iM_i)	Deviation $(M_i - \bar{x})$	(Deviation)^2 $(M_i - \bar{x})^2$
1–30	12	15.5	186.0	−51.5	2652.25
31–60	24	45.5	1092.0	−21.5	461.39
61–90	29	75.5	2189.5	8.5	72.59
91–120	9	105.5	949.5	38.5	1482.25
121–150	5	135.5	677.5	68.5	4692.25
151–180	2	165.5	331.0	98.5	9702.25
	81		5425.5		19,062.98

The mean is 67 [67 = 5425.5/81].

$$\text{Now, } s = \sqrt{\frac{19{,}062.98}{(81 - 1)}}$$
$$= \sqrt{238.29} \text{ which is } 15.44.$$

For Distribution B:

Score (X)	Frequency (f)	Product (f_iX_i)	Deviation $(X - \bar{X})$	(Deviation)^2 (f_i) $(X - \bar{X})^2 (f_i)$
1	5	5	−2.4	28.80
2	12	24	−1.4	23.52
3	25	75	−0.4	4.00
4	27	108	0.6	9.72
5	8	40	1.6	20.48
6	3	18	2.6	20.28
7	1	7	3.6	12.96
	81	277	4.2	119.76

The mean is 3.4 [3.4 = 277/81].

Now, $s = \sqrt{\dfrac{119.76}{(81-1)}}$

$= \sqrt{1.5}$ which is 1.22.

3. Distribution A: The total frequency is the sum of the individual frequencies, which is 81 [81 = 12 + 24 + 29 + 9 + 5 + 2]. Distribution B: The frequency is 81 [81 = 5 + 12 + 25 + 27 + 8 + 3 + 1].

4. The class interval 91–120 has a frequency of 9. This means that nine observations of transactions required between 91 seconds and 120 seconds to complete.

5. The modal class is the class that has the highest frequency. Class interval 61–90 has a frequency that is greater than the frequency of any other class.

6. For Distribution A, the range of the distribution is 180 [180 = 180.5 − 0.5]. For Distribution B, the range of the distribution is 6 [6 = 7 − 1].

7. In Distribution A, the interpretation of $f = 24$ is that there were 24 transactions that required between 31 and 60 seconds. In Distribution B, the interpretation of 6 is that this number tells the librarian how many items were borrowed by a person. It turns out that three persons borrowed six items.

8. In Distribution A, the mean is 66.98 or 67 [67 = 5425.5/81]. In Distribution B, the mean is 3.4 [3.4 = 277/81].

9. In Distribution A: The columns in the table allow easy calculation of most of the values required for the standard deviation. The table's columns show the deviation of each midpoint from the mean. For the class interval 1–30, the deviation of the midpoint from the mean is −51.5 [−51.5 = 15.5 − 67]. For the second class interval, 31–60, the deviation of the midpoint from the mean is −21.5 [−21.5 = 45.5 − 67]. The other deviations are calculated in a similar way. The deviations are then squared. For example, the first deviation, −51.5, when squared is 2652.25 [2652.25 = (−51.5)^2]. To complete the calculations, the librarian now must divide the sum of the squared deviations by $(n − 1)$, where $n = 81$. This yields 238.29 [238.29 = 19,062.98/80]. Finally, the librarian finds the square root of this result to yield the standard deviation: 15.44 [15.44 = $\sqrt{238.29}$].

   In Distribution B: The columns in the table allow the librarian to calculate most of the values required.

10. First Quartile Q_1: Using Formula 6-4, the rank of the first quartile is identified as the value of the 20.25 score [20.25 = 0.25(81)]. This means that it lies in the second class interval, 31–60, since the first interval has a frequency of 12 and the second interval has a frequency of 24, for a cumulative frequency of 36. Formula 6-2 yields the following, with $j = 25$, $L = 30.5$ (continuous data, so use the real limits), $w = 30$, $n = 81$, $F = 12$, $f = 24$:

$$P_{25} = 30.5 + \frac{30}{24}\left[\frac{25(81)}{100} - 12\right]$$

$$= 30.5 + \frac{30}{24}[20.25 - 12]$$

$$= 30.5 + \frac{30}{24}[8.25]$$

$$= 30.5 + 10.31, \text{ which is } 40.81.$$

The processes for finding Q_2, Q_3, P_{10}, and P_{90} are similar and use the same formula, Formula 6-2. The following values hold for each of the calculations:

For Q_2, the rank of the value is 40.5 [40.5 = 0.50(81)]. The values for Formula 6-2: $j = 50$, $L = 60.5$, $w = 30$, $n = 81$, $F = 36$, $f = 29$. $Q_2 = 65.2$.

For Q_3, the rank of the value is 60.75 [60.75 = 0.75(81)]. The values for Formula 6-2: $j = 75$, $L = 60.5$, $w = 30$, $n = 81$, $F = 36$, $f = 29$. $Q_3 = 86.1$.

For P_{10}, the rank of the value is 8.1 [8.1 = 0.10(81)]. The values for Formula 6-2: $j = 10$, $L = 0.5$, $w = 30$, $n = 81$, $F = 0$, $f = 12$. $P_{10} = 20.75$.

For P_{90}, the rank of the value is 72.9 [72.9 = 0.90(81)]. The values for Formula 6-2: $j = 90$, $L = 90.5$, $w = 30$, $n = 81$, $F = 65$, $f = 9$. $P_{90} = 116.83$.

11. The interquartile range is $Q_3 - Q_1$, which is 45.3 [45.3 = 86.1 − 40.8].

SUMMARY OF CRITICAL CONCEPTS

1. Measures of dispersion or *measures of variability* describe the dispersion, or spread, of data about a central point.

2. The most common *measures of dispersion* are the *range* and *standard deviation*.

3. *Range* is the difference between the largest and smallest values in a data set. Range is sensitive to extreme scores. The range is determined by the high and low observations in the data set and is unaffected by the total number of observations.

4. A deviation is the distance between any measurement in a set of data and the mean of the set. It is represented mathematically by $(X - \overline{X})$. *Standard deviation* is an average of the size or magnitude of all squared deviations for a set of data. Standard deviation is a measure of the spread or dispersion of scores in a data set from its center, as measured by the mean. Standard deviation reveals the shape of distributions. The larger the value of the group's standard deviation, the more spread out the observations.

5. The range of homogeneous data is small because homogeneous data tend to be concentrated. This means that the data's range, interquartile range, and standard deviation will be small. An extreme case of concentrated data occurs when all of the values are the same. That is, all of the observations are the same, there is no data variation. This means that the range, interquartile range, and standard deviation are zero.

6. The greater the range of data, the more spread out or dispersed it is. Widely dispersed data will have a large range, interquartile range, and standard deviation.

KEY TERMS

Coefficient of variation. A relative measure of dispersion that expresses the standard deviation as a percent of the mean. It is useful for comparing the variability of two or more data sets or for comparing two data sets of widely varying magnitudes. This measure is applicable only in variables that are measured in ratio interval scale.

Dispersion (variability). The amount of variation in a data set. Dispersion measures are range, interquartile range, standard deviation, and variance.

Interquartile range. Measure of dispersion or variability. It is the difference between the third quartile and the first quartile. Stated mathematically, the interquartile range is $Q_3 - Q_1$.

Quartile. One of four data points, each representing an increment of 25% of the scores in a data set.

Variance. The square of standard deviation. It is an indicator of the spread of scores in a distribution. The larger the dispersion of data in a distribution, the larger the variance.

SELF-ASSESSMENT QUIZ

1. *True* or *False* A dispersion measure such as the standard deviation identifies how well central tendency measures describe a data set.

2. *True* or *False* It is not possible to determine a distribution's range if the distribution contains an open interval.

3. *True* or *False* In a symmetrical distribution, the mean and median are equal.

4. *True* or *False* In the data {15, 4, 26, 13, 3}, the range is 26.

5. *True* or *False* Percentiles divide a data set into 10 equal parts.

6. *True* or *False* The standard deviation is a measure that describes how far a specific observation in a data set lies from the mean.

7. *True* or *False* It is possible to calculate the standard deviation of a data set if it has an open-ended interval.

8. *True* or *False* A distribution's standard deviation considers the value of each data point.

9. *True* or *False* An advantage of the quartile deviation is that it is not sensitive to extreme scores.

10. *True* or *False* The standard deviation of {101, 102, 103} is greater than that of {1, 2, 3}.

11. *True* or *False* The data set {1, 5, 9} shows more variability than does the data set {101, 106, 111}.

12. *True* or *False* Quartiles have the same width.

13. *True* or *False* If two distributions have the same mean and standard deviation, the distributions must look exactly alike.

14. *True* or *False* The standard deviation for a data set is always less than the mean.

15. *True* or *False* On a test covering encyclopedias, Student A scored at the 66th percentile while Student B scored at the 33rd percentile. This means that Student A's test score is twice that of Student B's test score.

Answers

1. *True* Measures of dispersion tell the statistics consumer how far data are from the measure of central tendency.

2. *True*   When a distribution contains open intervals, no range can be calculated because X_H or X_L are not known.

3. *True*   In a symmetrical distribution, the average value equals the middle value.

4. *False*   Range is the difference between the largest value and the smallest value of the data set. Hence $R = 26 - 3$, or 23.

5. *False*   Percentiles $(P_1, P_2, \ldots, P_{99})$ divide a distribution into 100 equal parts.

6. *True*   The standard deviation tells the investigator how far the typical or average data point strays from the mean.

7. *False*   The midpoint of the interval cannot be determined for use in the calculation.

8. *True*

$$ s = \sqrt{\frac{\sum_{i=1}^{n} (X_i - \bar{X})^2}{n - 1}} $$

9. *True*   The interquartile range focuses on the center 50 percent of the data.

10. *False*   The standard deviation of both sets is the same.

11. *False*   The deviations from the mean are less for the first data set than for the second.

12. *False*   The proportion of data in each quartile must be 25%, but the width may not be the same for each.

13. *False*   The two distributions could be skewed differently.

14. *False*   Consider, for example, a data set such as {0, 100} where the mean is 50 and the standard deviation is 70.7.

15. *False*   All that can be said about Student A's test score is that it is higher than Student B's score and that both students should study harder.

DISCUSSION QUESTIONS AND PROBLEMS

1. Contrast the advantages and disadvantages of the range with the interquartile range as measures of dispersion. Illustrate examples of numerical distributions where each is a superior measure of variability.

2. The library's trustees are concerned about complaints regarding parking space availability. To study the issue, the librarian has a clerk tally the length of time (in hours) that cars are parked in the library's parking lot.

Hours parked:	1	2	3	4	5	6	7	8	9	10
Number of cars:	3	9	15	25	15	11	9	6	5	2

   a. Find the mode, median, and mean.
   b. Find the range.
   c. Find Q_1, Q_2, and Q_3.
   d. Find the standard deviation.

3. The cataloger reviewed the work of five clerks. The errors for each were {2, 0, 0, 1, 2}. Determine and interpret the standard deviation.

4. What is the effect of the following on the range, standard deviation, and variance?
   a. Increase each score by 10 points.
   b. Increase each score by 10%.
   c. Decrease each score by 10 points.
   d. Decrease each score by 10%.

5. The number of sick days reported for a library's staff over a two-year period were as follows:

Year 1 ($n = 26$)

3	4	10	2	7	3	1	10	0	11	11	2	7
6	5	3	10	3	7	6	8	6	5	4	3	6

Year 2 ($n = 31$)

5	2	7	5	4	0	4	4	5	3	4	7	4	3	3	1
2	7	4	2	5	0	4	5	3	7	3	0	7	6	1	

   a. Determine the mean, standard deviation, and coefficient of variation for Year 1 and Year 2 data. What does the coefficient of variation reveal about the two distributions?
   b. In Year 2, the library's trustees instituted a policy about paid sick days. Is there any evidence of its effect?

6. During one month, the staff at a state library association returned 120 telephone calls to members:

Length of reference call (minutes)	Number of calls
0 and under 2	49
2 and under 4	39
4 and under 6	15
6 and under 8	5
8 and under 10	4
10 and under 12	4
12 and under 14	2
14 and under 16	0
16 and under 18	1
18 and under 20	1

   a. Examine the distribution and comment on its shape.
   b. Determine the mean, the median, and the skew. Does the mean or the median better characterize the distribution's average?
   c. Determine the standard deviation and the variance. Identify the units for the standard deviation and for the variance.
   d. Determine the interquartile range.
   e. Using Chebyshev's theorem, at least how many values should lie between one and one-half standard deviations of the mean? If the distribution is approximately normal, how many values should lie in this interval? Identify the points ($\overline{X} - 1.5s$) and ($\overline{X} + 1.5s$). What percent of observations lies within this interval?

f. Based on your calculations in (c) through (e), is the interquartile range or the standard deviation a better measure of the dispersion of this data set? Explain.

7. A library consortium recently surveyed its 50 member libraries to determine the days of downtime of each library's computer system during the previous 90 days. Member responses were as follows:

Days of downtime	Frequency
0	6
1	7
2	10
3	14
4	7
5	3
6	2
7	1

a. Compute the mean and standard deviation. Are these good measures of central tendency and dispersion? Explain.

b. Your out-of-state librarian colleague told you that 12 members in his or her library's consortium reported downtimes between 0 and 12 days for a similar 90-day period. Estimate this standard deviation and discuss the variation between the two distributions.

8. For some time you have wondered whether your library's 21-day loan period is ideal. You and a colleague, a librarian at a similar-size library with a 14-day circulation period, decide to examine 75 recently circulated items. The frequency distribution is as follows:

Days	21-day circulation	14-day circulation
0–2	2	3
3–5	3	5
6–8	4	8
9–11	5	16
12–14	7	19
15–17	9	12
18–20	18	7
21–23	16	2
24–26	8	2
27–29	2	1
30–32	1	0

a. For each distribution, determine the mean, median, and standard deviation. For each distribution, do you expect the mean or the median to be a better measure of central tendency? Explain.

b. Calculate and explain each distribution coefficient of variation.

c. Which distribution is more desirable in terms of maximizing each library's collection turnover rate? Why?

   d. What is the effect on the library's inventory if books circulate for too long?

   e. Discuss the effect on the library's inventory of limiting the number of items that may be checked out to a borrower on a single visit.

9. A state library association is interested in studying the hours of service for all public libraries in the state ($n = 401$). It surveyed all institutions and then developed the following frequency distribution that summarizes library hours of service per week:

Hours open per week	Frequency
1–5	3
6–10	25
11–15	31
16–20	56
21–25	64
26–30	58
31–35	33
36–40	39
41–45	21
46–50	29
51–55	17
56–60	17
61–65	8

   a. Find the mean, median, range, and standard deviation.

   b. Find and interpret the 80th percentile, P_{80}.

   c. Determine the percentile, compared with other public libraries, for the institution that is open 50 hours per week.

10. A corporate library recently installed a new telephone system. Among its many features is software that monitors variables for each telephone such as the number dialed and the duration of each outgoing call. Wishing to analyze telephone use, the librarian collected data on the telephone activity of each of the 28 staff members for the first four months that the new system was in operation. The 112 observations were grouped, and the data are as follows:

Phone minutes per month	Number of employees
0	20
60	37
120	23
180	16
240	10
300	3
360	2
420	0
480	1

The data range from one staff member who placed a 1-minute outgoing call during a single month to a staff member who placed calls totaling 510 minutes for a single month. The distribution's mean is 110.4 and its standard deviation is 92.73.

a. Identify the modal class and, without calculation, estimate the distribution's median.
b. Identify any extreme values.
c. Identify the distribution's skew as positive or negative.
d. Identify the number of staff whose duration of calls is greater than two standard deviations above the mean.
e. If this library's reference services are provided principally to clientele who telephone the library, comment on the total number of hours of staff time that may be lost in "personal" telephone calls.

11. A librarian collected the following data points {3, 5, 6, 6, 8, 9} and determined the median, mean, and standard deviation. In checking over several notes, the librarian notices that the data point 9 should have been recorded as 10. Explain the effect that the data correction will have on the following statistics:
a. median
b. mean
c. range
d. standard deviation

seven

LINEAR REGRESSION AND CORRELATION ANALYSIS

After reading this chapter, you will be able to do the following:

1. Interpret the meaning of a linear relationship between two variables.

2. Calculate and interpret the slope of a line.

3. Apply the least squares method to calculate the equation for the regression line that shows the relationship between a dependent and an independent variable.

4. Calculate and apply the correlation coefficient to measure the strength of a linear relationship.

5. Calculate and interpret the Pearson correlation coefficient and the coefficient of determination.

6. Calculate and interpret the Spearman rank order correlation coefficient and illustrate the ways in which it differs from the Pearson correlation coefficient.

The two previous chapters discussed measures widely used in descriptive statistics to describe central tendency and data variation within a distribution. The measures of central tendency are mode, median, and mean. The measures of variation are range, percentile, interquartile range, and standard deviation.

This chapter presents several important statistical measures that can be used effectively to reveal information about how two variables are related. The techniques and measures that are presented are limited to those that describe a linear relationship between two variables.

A *linear relationship* exists between two variables if an increase in one of the variables results in an exactly proportional increase in the other. That is, if one of the variables doubles, the other variable doubles. If one of the variables is reduced by one-half, the other variable is reduced by one-half. Linear relationships are "straight-line." Not all relationships between variables are linear, however. Some may initially be linear, but then become nonlinear. The focus of this chapter is exclusively on techniques that can be applied to solve problems with data from variables that are linearly related.

For an example of a linear relationship between two variables, consider the connection between the hours that a library clerk works and the clerk's wages. The wages that a clerk earns each pay period depend upon the number of hours that the clerk works during the pay period. If the employee, who normally works 15 hours per week, doubles the number of hours worked, the amount of gross wages (before-tax wages) will double. The amount of wages moves in exact proportion to the number of hours worked. In this example, the clerk has control over the number of hours that he or she works. Hence, the variable "hours" is known as the *independent variable* or the *input variable*. The other variable, which is "wage" in this example, is called the *dependent variable,* or *output variable.*

In another example, if the price of a particular item in the library's gift shop is kept fixed, the library's revenue R is linearly related to the number of items sold. In this example, the independent variable is the number of items sold. The dependent variable is the revenue that the library derives from selling the items.

LINEAR REGRESSION ANALYSIS

Imagine a circuit-rider librarian who, as part of a grant, travels from community to community each day of the week to provide library service. For record-keeping purposes, the librarian records the number of miles driven each day and also records the amount of gasoline consumed. For the past six trips, the data show the following:

Trip	1	2	3	4	5	6
Miles driven	21	19	41	108	80	106
Gallons of gas consumed	1	1	2	5	4	5

The number of miles that the librarian drives is the input variable. The amount of gasoline consumed for the day is the dependent variable. In examining the data, the miles driven and gasoline consumed are linearly related. Of course, the relationship between the miles driven and gasoline consumed is not exact. The reason for this is that the librarian's car sometimes gets 21 miles per gallon of gasoline and other times only 19 miles per gallon. What the data show is that the librarian's car consumes twice as many gallons of gasoline to travel 40 miles as it does to travel 20 miles, or twice as many gallons to travel 80 miles as it does to travel 40 miles. Since the proportions between distance driven and gasoline consumption are so close, it can be concluded that the two variables are linearly related.

FIGURE 7-1  Circuit Rider Librarian

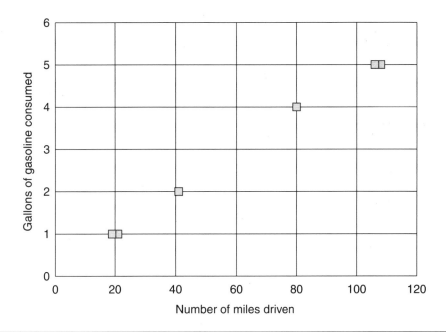

Using the data labeling methods described in Chapter 2, the librarian assigns the label X to the number of miles driven. Label X will be assigned to the miles driven. Hence, the librarian associates {21, 19, 41, 108, 80, 106} with the labels x_1, x_2, x_3, x_4, x_5, and x_6, respectively. Similarly, the gallons of gasoline consumed {1, 1, 2, 5, 4, 5} are labeled y_1, y_2, y_3, y_4, y_5, and y_6, respectively. These can be matched as ordered pairs, (x_i, y_i). The interpretation of this labeling is that the first observation for variable X, which is "miles driven," is 22 miles. The first observation for variable Y, which is "gallons of gasoline consumed," that is associated with the $x = 22$ is $y = 1$ gallon, or (22, 1). For the six trips, the ordered pairs are (21, 1), (19, 1), (41, 2), (108, 5), (80, 4), and (106, 5).

Trip	1	2	3	4	5	6
(miles, gallons)	(21, 1)	(19, 1)	(41, 2)	(108, 5)	(80, 4)	(106, 5)

The graph of the ordered points is called a *scatter diagram,* which is illustrated in Figure 7-1. The purpose of a scatter diagram is to show how the variables X (miles) and Y (gas consumed) are related. In the driving and gasoline example, the number of miles was a variable that is under the librarian's control. For this reason, "miles driven" is the independent or input variable, and the amount of gasoline consumed is the dependent or output variable.

REGRESSION ANALYSIS

To determine the relationship between any two sets of variables, librarians use *regression analysis.* This type of analysis allows the ordered pairs of two data sets to be plotted to obtain an equation for a line that passes through the plotted points.

It is not always obvious nor easy to decide which variable is the independent variable and which one is the dependent variable. A general rule of thumb is that the independent variable is the variable that is under control. Unfortunately, this generalization sometimes fails, particularly if the variable is time, distance, atmospheric pressure, or outdoor temperature. But, while such variables cannot be controlled, they can be measured.

When performing a regression analysis, one of the librarian's first tasks is to decide in advance which data set comprises the *y*s (dependent variable) and which set comprises the *x*s (independent variable). It is not unusual to perform two regression analyses with the variables. First, one of the variables is regressed on the other and then the situation is reversed. Since this happens often, one should not hesitate to ask about the basis for selecting variables as dependent or independent. Further, it is appropriate to ask if reversing the variables produces a more useful regression analysis.

When reading a report that applies the techniques of regression analysis, one may encounter suggestions that changes in the independent variable *cause* changes in the dependent variable. For example, in an analysis about the conservation of documents, a librarian may read that pollution causes document loss. This is an appealing idea, and many people generally believe it. In fact, many people may even interpret the statistical results to support this conclusion. However, strictly speaking, cause is a metaphysical rather than a statistical notion. Regression analysis shows only that two variables are related. Without additional evidence, causality cannot be inferred.

Linear Regression Analysis and the Linear Regression Line

Linear regression analysis is a statistical technique used to predict one variable (the dependent or output variable) from another (the independent or input variable). The methods of linear regression analysis are to describe the relationship between two variables by identifying an equation.

The result of linear regression analysis is a *regression line,* a straight line that passes through the points that form the scatter diagram. The regression line is the basis for the equation that summarizes the relationship between the variables. The regression line also is used for describing the location of the values of the dependent variable.

Derivation of a regression line requires reference to the basic rules of algebra and properties of straight lines. This is seen in Formula 7-1 and is illustrated in Figure 7-2. The equation for a straight line is calculated by Formula 7-1:

Formula 7-1

$$Y = mX + b$$

In Formula 7-1, b is the *Y-axis intercept.* That is, b is that point on the Y-axis where the straight line intercepts (crosses) the Y-axis. Or, it is the point on the Y-axis where the line would cross the vertical if it were extended.

In Formula 7-1, m is the regression line's *slope.* The slope of a line has to do with its steepness of incline or descent. Every nonvertical line has a slope. The slope measures the amount of a line's vertical change compared with the amount of its horizontal change. In other words, the slope of a line between two points (x_1, y_1) and (x_2, y_2) is the ratio of the

FIGURE 7-2 ▌ Determination of the Slope of a Straight Line

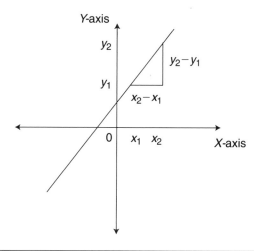

change in the values of *y* to the change in the values of *x*. Written as an equation, the result is Formula 7-2:

Formula 7-2

$$m = \frac{(y_2 - y_1)}{(x_2 - x_1)}$$

Figure 7-2 is helpful in understanding Formula 7-2, where the slope may be expressed as the ratio of the change in vertical distance $(y_2 - y_1)$ to the change in horizontal distance $(x_2 - x_1)$.

The sign of the slope, *m,* which is either positive or negative, identifies whether the line is ascending or descending. If the slope *m* is positive ($m > 0$), as in the left graph in Figure 7-3, the line is ascending from left to right. If *m* is negative ($m < 0$), as in the center graph of Figure 7-3, the line is descending from left to right. The absolute value of the slope, *m,* corresponds to the steepness of the line. The slope of $m = 1$ is less steep than the slope *m* $= 2$, which in turn is less steep than $m = 5$. Likewise, the slope of $m = -1$ is less steep than the slope $m = -2$, which in turn is less steep than $m = -5$. A line with slope $m = 0$ is horizontal, as in the right-hand graph in Figure 7-3.

A regression line's slope shows whether the variables have a *positive* or *negative relationship.* If the regression line's slope is positive, $m > 0$, the relationship between the two variables is *positive* or *direct.* When the relationship between two variables is positive, increases in the independent variable result in proportional increases in the dependent variable. For example, in a library, a positive relationship usually exists between library hours (an independent variable) and the number of items circulated (a dependent variable). If the library is open longer, more materials generally will be circulated. Similarly, the larger the collection, the greater the circulation.

If a regression line's slope is negative, $m < 0$, the relationship between the variables is

FIGURE 7-3 ▓ Positive Slope ($m > 0$), Negative Slope ($m < 0$), and
Zero Slope ($m = 0$)

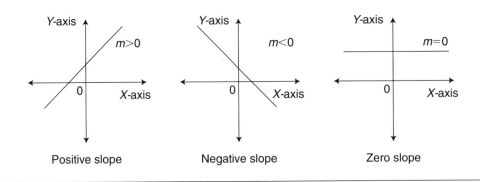

Positive slope   Negative slope   Zero slope

described as inverse. An *inverse relationship* means that increases in the independent variable are associated with proportional decreases in the dependent variable. In a library, for example, a negative relationship usually exits between the backfile age of a periodical (an independent variable) and the periodical's use (a dependent variable). That is, as the periodical's age increases, its use decreases.

A slope of $m = 0$ tells librarians that there is no statistical relationship between the two variables. The regression line is horizontal. In other words, the amount, degree, or frequency of the dependent variable is unaffected by increases or decreases in the independent variable. In a library, for example, there is probably no relationship between library hours (an independent variable) and collection size (a dependent variable). As library hours increase, the size of the collection will neither increase nor decrease.

Think of a regression line as the straight line that best passes through the middle of the data points on a scatter diagram. A regression line is determined by Formula 7-3, which portrays three relationships:

Formula 7-3

$$\hat{Y} = aX + b$$

$$\text{where } b = \overline{Y} - a\overline{X}$$

$$\text{and } a = \frac{n\left(\sum XY\right) - \left(\sum X\right)\left(\sum Y\right)}{n\left(\sum X^2\right) - \left(\sum X\right)^2}$$

and n = the number of data points (number of ordered pairs)

Figure 7-4 provides summation expressions for each of the expressions in Formula 7-3. In performing calculations, it may be convenient to add columns to the tables. The extension to the tables also helps to clarify the calculations that are based on the data found in the tables.

Attention is drawn to the "hat" symbol over the $\hat{Y}$, read "Y-hat." This is used in the general equation for the linear regression line, Formula 7-3. This symbol differentiates the

FIGURE 7-4 ▌ Summations Used in Regression Calculations

Sum of the independent variables	$\sum X = (X_1 + X_2 + \cdots + X_n)$
Sum of the dependent variables	
Sum of the squares of the independent variables	$\sum Y = (Y_1 + Y_2 + \cdots + Y_n)$
	$\sum X^2 = (X_1^2 + X_2^2 + \cdots + X_n^2)$
Square of the sum of the independent variables	$(\sum X)^2 = (X_1 + X_2 + \cdots + X_n)^2$
Sum of the product of independent and dependent variables	$\sum XY = (X_1Y_1 + X_2Y_2 + \cdots + X_nY_n)$
Product of the sums of the independent and dependent variables	$\sum X \sum Y = (X_1 + X_2 + \cdots + X_n)$
	$\times (Y_1 + Y_2 + \cdots + Y_n)$

regression equation from that of a straight line through a locus of points, and it signals that the equation is an estimation. Formula 7-3 often is called the *least squares method*.

The least squares method is like balancing a seesaw. If two people of equal weight sit equal distances from the center, the seesaw will balance; however, if one person moves farther away from the center, his or her end of the seesaw will lower and the opposite end of the seesaw will rise. The distance the ends of the seesaw move is related to the *square* of the distance that the person sits from the center of the seesaw.

Thinking of the regression line in a similar way, the position of the regression line also is affected by the square of the distance of data points from the regression line. The regression line is balanced when the sum of these squared distances is minimized.

Thus, the regression line balances data pairs. In this respect, the regression line is like the mean that balances a distribution's data points. The regression line reveals the central tendency of two data sets, just as the mean reveals the central tendency of a single data set.

The following example illustrates the use of Formula 7-3 to determine the equation of a regression line. Using the library's maintenance log, a librarian determines the monthly repair costs for six photocopy machines. The age of each machine is provided in Table 7-1. Substituting in Formula 7-3 to find coefficient *a* yields the following:

$$a = \frac{n(\sum XY) - (\sum X)(\sum Y)}{n(\sum X^2) - (\sum X)^2}$$

$$= \frac{6(218) - (15)(81)}{6(43) - (15)(15)}$$

$$= \frac{1308 - 1215}{258 - 225}$$

$$= \frac{93}{33} \text{ which is } 2.8182.$$

The value of the coefficient is then substituted in the next part of Formula 7-3 to find coefficient *b*, with the following result:

TABLE 7-1 ▌ Copy Machine Maintenance Log

Copy machine (n = 6)	Age (years) X	Maintenance cost ($ per month) Y	X²	XY	Y²
1	3	15	9	45	225
2	2	10	4	20	100
3	1	11	1	11	121
4	3	12	9	36	144
5	4	20	16	80	400
6	2	13	4	26	169
Totals	15	81	43	218	1159

$$b = \frac{86}{6} - (2.8182)\frac{15}{6}$$

$$= 13.5 - (2.8182)(2.5)$$

$$= 13.5 - 7.0455 \text{ which is } 6.4545.$$

Now substitute values for coefficients a and b in the last part of Formula 7-3 to obtain the regression equation:

$$\hat{Y} = 2.8182X + 6.4545.$$

The common practice is to carry the calculations for the regression equation to 4 decimal places.

This equation can now be used by the librarian to describe the central tendency of monthly repair costs for machines of varying ages. For example, to determine the monthly maintenance cost that will be required for a four-year-old photocopy machine, the following calculations are performed:

$$\hat{Y} = 2.8182(4) + 6.4545$$

$$= 11.2728 + 6.4545 \text{ which is } \$17.73 \text{ per month.}$$

In other words, the repair costs for machines that are 4 years old will average $17.73 per month. The librarian who performs the analysis could say that the central tendency of maintenance costs (y) is $17.73 per month, when the age is 4 (x = 4).

The librarian also could use this regression equation to predict the monthly repair cost of a five-year-old machine:

$$\hat{Y} = 2.8128 (5) + 6.4545$$

$$= 14.0640 + 6.4545 \text{ which is } \$20.52 \text{ per month.}$$

Notice that one gets a different mean for the repair cost if a mean value is calculated for the y values. To verify this, with $n = 6$, the calculations yield the following:

$$\hat{Y} = \frac{\sum\limits_{i=1}^{n} Y_i}{n}$$

$$= \frac{\$15 + \$10 + \$11 + \$12 + \$20 + \$13}{6}$$

$$= \frac{\$81}{6} \text{ which is } \$13.50 \text{ per month.}$$

Figure 7-5 illustrates a scatter diagram of the age and monthly repair costs for the six photocopy machines described in Table 7-1. The figure also shows the descriptive power of regression analysis by illustrating the regression line that is a "best fit" for the data. The regression line shows that the central tendency of repair costs depends upon the age of the machines. This demonstrates what the librarian suspects—that if the machines are new, the mean maintenance costs are low. Similarly, if the machines are old, the average maintenance costs are high.

The regression equation is $\hat{Y} = 2.8182X + 6.4545$. The librarian can interpret this equation in the following way: for any specific age of a photocopy machine (X), the predicted monthly maintenance cost is 2.8182 times the age of the machine plus 6.4545. Hence, the monthly cost for maintaining a 4-year-old machine is $17.73, since $\hat{Y} = 2.8182(4) + 6.4545$.

A regression equation provides good information about the distribution of the dependent variable. For this reason, the regression equation can be used to predict a mean value for an

FIGURE 7-5 ▌ Copy Machine Maintenance Log

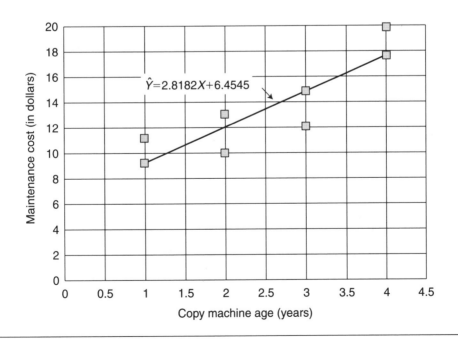

outcome variable that is associated with the independent variable. The requirement for predicting dependent values based on the independent variable is that the independent variable's values for X and Y must lie within the range of the sample data.

In Table 7-1 data, this means that the librarian can forecast the monthly maintenance cost for any equipment that is between one and four years old. However, the librarian steps on thin ice when forecasting monthly repair costs for equipment that is more than four years old.

In summary, regression analysis is a quantitative method. Its products are a scatter diagram and a regression equation for the best-fit line that passes through data points that make up the scatter diagram. Advanced techniques, not discussed in this book, allow hypotheses to be formed and tested about relationships between two sets of data.

Example 7-1

Interpreting a Linear Regression Equation

A librarian conducts research that yields the following coordinate pairs:

$(1, 3,), (2, 3), (4, 4), (5, 5), (6, 5)$.

1. Draw a scatter diagram for the points.

2. Prepare an extended table for the ordered pairs.

3. Verify that the best fit regression line is given by the regression equation $\hat{Y} = 0.4651X + 2.2356$.

4. Predict the dependent variable if $x = 3$, $x = 4$, $x = 5$, and $x = 6$. Interpret each forecast.

5. Predict the dependent variable if $x = 6.5$. Interpret.

Analysis

1. Figure 7-6 is a scatterplot.

2. The x-coordinates represent the independent variable. The y-coordinates represent the dependent or output variable. Data are summarized in Table 7-2, which features several extended columns.

3. To find the regression equation, where $n = 5$, the calculations are as follows:

$$a = \frac{n \left(\sum XY\right) - \left(\sum X\right)\left(\sum Y\right)}{n\left(\sum X^2\right) - \left(\sum X\right)^2}$$

$$= \frac{5(80) - (18)(20)}{5(82) - (18)*18}$$

$$= \frac{400 - 360}{410 - 324}$$

$$= \frac{40}{86} \text{ which is } 0.4651.$$

Figure 7-6   Librarian Research Project

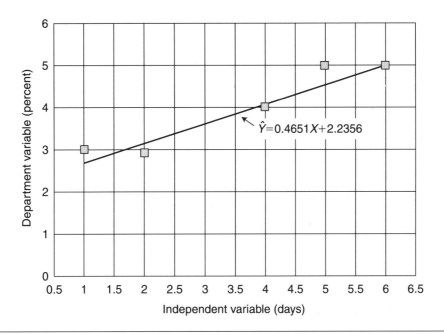

Table 7-2   Data for Forecasting Using Regression Analysis

Observation (n = 5)	Independent variable (x)	Dependent variable (y)	X^2	XY	Y^2
1	1	3	1	3	9
2	2	3	4	6	9
3	4	4	16	16	16
4	5	5	25	25	25
5	6	5	36	30	25
Totals	18	20	82	80	84

Now, calculate the *b* value, which is the *y*-intercept:

$$b = \frac{(20)}{5} - (0.4651)\frac{(18)}{5}$$

$$= 4 - \frac{8.3718}{5}$$

$$= 4 - 1.6744 \text{ which is } 2.3256.$$

This means that the best-fit regression line is given by the equation, $\hat{Y} = 0.4651X + 2.2356$.

4. The regression equation is $\hat{Y} = 0.4651X + 2.2356$. This is the "best-fit" line for the data. Think of the regression line as a model that describes the data. The purpose of the model is to predict Y for some specific value of X. For best results, the X value must be within the range of the data. For this example, the range is 1 to 6 for the independent variable. Hence,

if $x = 3$, $\hat{Y} = 0.4651(3) + 2.2356$

$$= 1.3953 + 2.2356 \text{ which is } 3.6309.$$

if $x = 4$, $\hat{Y} = 0.4651(4) + 2.2356$

$$= 1.8604 + 2.2356 \text{ which is } 4.0960.$$

if $x = 5$, $\hat{Y} = 0.4651(5) + 2.2356$

$$= 2.3255 + 2.2356 \text{ which is } 4.5611.$$

if $x = 6$, $\hat{Y} = 0.4651(6) + 2.2356$

$$= 2.7906 + 2.2356 \text{ which is } 5.0262.$$

5. To forecast the dependent value, use the regression equation keeping in mind that the independent value ($x = 6.5$) is outside the range of the data for the independent variable on which the regression equation is based. This means that the calculation is an educated guess. The model may not be accurate. If $x = 6.5$, then the equation becomes $\hat{Y} = 0.4651(6.5) + 2.2356$ so that $\hat{Y} = 5.2588$.

CORRELATION

Regression analysis can be used to determine the equation of the line that passes through a collection of ordered points that form a scatter diagram. The technique also can be applied to determine whether two sets of data are positively or negatively related.

The next logical step is to try to quantify how strong the linear relationship is between the two variables. To accomplish this, the *correlation,* a method for determining what proportion of the variability in one set of scores can be predicted by the variability in another set of scores, is used. For example, the librarian from a previous example may wish to determine what proportion of the variability in machine maintenance costs can be predicted or explained by differences in machine age.

This section explores *simple correlation analysis,* a technique that analyzes the linear relationship between a dependent variable and a single independent variable. In more advanced treatments, *multiple correlation analysis* can be explored, which examines the relationship between a dependent variable and several independent variables. Further, *partial correlation analysis* examines the relationship between one of the variables in a multiple correlation and the dependent variable. This book does not discuss either multiple or partial correlation analysis, however.

Coefficient of Correlation

The strength of the evidence of a linear relationship between two variables is described by the *coefficient of correlation,* the symbol for which is r. This measure has no units such as degrees, dollars, inches, or minutes. The coefficient of correlation always assumes a value between -1.00 and $+1.00$. While there are several methods to calculate this coefficient, the usual practice is to round the result to the nearest hundredth.

Perfect correlation is evidenced by a value of $r = -1.00$ or $r = +1.00$. This tells that a single regression line can be drawn through all the paired data points in the scatter diagram. It also means that all of the points lie on this line.

Examples of variables that show positive correlation include education and income of library clientele; the price of a book and its length in pages; and library attendance and library hours. Examples of variables that show negative correlation are the age of documents and their frequency of use; the years of play and average score for golfers; and the age of a car and its price.

A correlation coefficient of $r = -1.00$ is equally strong as is $r = +1.00$. The sign of the value of r identifies whether the correlation between the variables is positive or negative. That is, the sign establishes whether the relationship is direct (positive correlation) or inverse (negative correlation). The left-hand section of Figure 7-7 shows positive correlation and the center section shows negative correlation.

A positive correlation between variables tells that respondents who achieve high scores on the independent variable also tend to achieve high scores on the dependent variable. Similarly, respondents who obtain low scores on the independent variable also tend to obtain low scores on the dependent variable.

A negative correlation tells that respondents who achieve high scores on the independent variable tend to obtain low scores on the dependent variable. Similarly, respondents who achieve low scores on the independent variable tend to obtain high scores on the dependent variable. This kind of relationship is called an *inverse relationship*.

A result of $r = +0.70$ is the same strength of correlation as $r = -0.70$. As the value of r approaches zero from either direction on the number line, the evidence of correlation decreases. A value of $r = 0$ means that there is no statistically measurable linear relationship between the variables under study.

While a relationship exists between the coefficient of correlation and the size of the data set, the following approximations are helpful in interpreting the strength of either positive or negative correlation:

Value of r	Interpretation
0.00–0.25	little or no relationship
0.30–0.45	fair relationship
0.50–0.75	moderate to good relationship
0.80–1.00	strong relationship to perfect correlation

The correlation coefficient moves from $+1$ or -1 toward zero when paired data points become more dispersed around the regression line. That is, the strength of the correlation between the independent and dependent variables approaches $+1$ or -1 as the points in a scatter diagram more closely form an imaginary straight line through the points that make up the scatter diagram. Figure 7-7 illustrates a scatter diagram and the dispersion of points away from an imaginary line through the center. The reader who is new to correlation analysis can profitably spend several minutes examining the three panels that comprise Figure 7-7.

In the left-hand panel of Figure 7-7, the correlation between the two variables is moderate to strong. The reason is the dispersion of the data points around an imaginary regression line

FIGURE 7-7 ▧ Scatterplots with Positive, Negative, and No Correlation

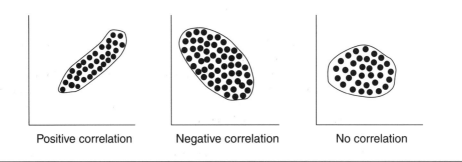

| Positive correlation | Negative correlation | No correlation |

drawn through the center of the distribution is low. In other words, the points cluster around, or are confined near, the best-fit regression line.

In the center panel, the correlation between the two variables is fair to moderate. The reason is the data are more scattered or dispersed from an imaginary "best-fit" regression line that a librarian might draw through the data points.

In the third panel, there is no correlation between the two variables. The reason is that the points that make up the scatter diagram are very widely dispersed.

METHODS OF DETERMINING CORRELATION

There are several ways to calculate the coefficient of correlation. The algorithms fall into two categories. The first category, *parametric methods,* requires data—sometimes called parametric data—that are expressed in interval or ratio scale measurement.

Parametric data come from populations about which some important assumptions are made. One of these is that the population elements are normally distributed, or that the elements that are under study are drawn from populations with the same spread of scores. This assumption is important because it allows the use of the mean and standard deviation to describe the data.

Parametric methods are statistical techniques that use parametric data. These techniques are powerful statistical tools that can be used to determine the strength of the relationship between two variables. These methods also may be used to predict the value of a dependent variable based on the value of the independent variable.

In contrast, *nonparametric methods* use nonparametric data, or data that are expressed in nominal or ordinal scale measurement. Nonparametric methods are well suited to library studies in which the librarian frequently works with data that rank or classify observations descriptively rather than quantitatively. Nonparametric methods are particularly useful when dealing with data obtained from subjective evaluation, as in assessing attitudes, perceptions, or client satisfaction.

Parametric measures provide valuable and accurate information, and thus are regarded as "hard data." In contrast, nonparametric data often are (incorrectly) regarded as "soft data." Generally, people perceive nonparametric measures as providing less powerful results than parametric measures. Even so, the use of nonparametric methods is often more realistic because of the sometimes difficult requirement of collecting parametric data. Nonparametric methods allow the study of variables for which less "hard" information is available.

Nonparametric methods work best when the data sets are continuous, linearly related, and roughly symmetrical. When data are discontinuous, nonlinear, or irregularly shaped, strive to use parametric methods, if possible. In this way, accurate results will be obtained.

The Pearson Correlation Coefficient

The *Pearson product-moment correlation coefficient* was developed by the English mathematician Karl Pearson. Pearson's *r*, expressed by Formula 7-4, is a parametric method that uses interval- or ratio-scale, linearly related variables. The name of the algorithm is somewhat overwhelming, and thus is a good beginning point for developing an understanding of the method.

Product refers to multiplication results, and *moment* is a statistical term for deviate scores. Hence, this technique, also called *Pearson's r*, involves multiplying certain scores. (Already, the measure sounds less threatening to manage and use.)

Those applying the algorithm will appreciate the value of computer software for the computations. Some of the more common statistical programs that are widely available in personal computer versions are Minitab, SAS, and SPSS. When the Pearson correlation coefficient technique is performed manually, a calculator that features at least 10 digits may be required. Thus, readers not using a computer should use the table extension method that is demonstrated in examples throughout the book.

Formula 7-4 yields the following calculations:

Formula 7-4

$$r = \frac{n \sum XY - \sum X \sum Y}{\sqrt{\{[n\sum X^2 - (\sum X)^2] [n \sum Y^2 - (\sum Y)^2]\}}}$$

Refer to Figure 7-4 (p. 207) for help on the meaning of the summations in the formula.

To demonstrate applying Pearson's *r*, suppose the data illustrated in Table 7-3 have been collected about ten rural libraries and the communities they serve. Applying Formula 7-4 yields the following:

$$r = \frac{10(219.83) - 15.7(128.8)}{\sqrt{\{[10(27.29) - (15.7)^2] [10(1829.46) - (128.8)^2]\}}}$$

$$= \frac{2198.3 - 2022.16}{\sqrt{\{[272.9 - 246.49] [18,294.6 - 16,589.44]\}}}$$

$$= \frac{176.14}{\sqrt{(26.41) (1705.16)}}$$

$$= \frac{176.14}{\sqrt{45,033.28}}$$

$$= \frac{176.14}{212.21} \text{ which is } 0.83.$$

TABLE 7-3 | Expenditures for Selected Rural Community Libraries

Library	Population (1000s) X	Expenditures ($1000s) y	X^2	XY	y^2
1	2.3	14.9	5.29	34.27	222.01
2	2.4	17.2	5.76	41.28	295.84
3	1.6	14.9	2.56	23.84	222.01
4	1.1	6.7	1.21	7.37	44.89
5	1.1	13.5	1.21	14.85	182.25
6	1.0	7.4	1.00	7.40	54.76
7	1.0	8.4	1.00	8.40	70.56
8	1.7	15.5	2.89	26.35	240.25
9	2.1	19.5	4.41	40.95	380.25
10	1.4	10.8	1.96	15.12	116.64
Sum	15.7	128.8	27.29	219.83	1829.46

In Table 7-3, the columns have been expanded to include calculations for determining the regression line equation through the ten data points. The interested reader can verify that the regression line for Table 7-3 data is $\hat{Y} = 6.6694X + 2.4090$.

The correlation coefficient (Pearson's r) is 0.83. Figure 7-8 provides a scatter diagram for the ten scores, and the regression line is drawn through the scores. The interpretation of the Pearson r is that a strong correlation exists between the variables of community size and operating expenditures. The information's usefulness for an administrator is that library costs for one community can be compared with those of another similar-size community to determine whether cost differentials exist.

Coefficient of Determination

In addition to the Pearson's r, parametric data can be used to calculate another important coefficient, the *coefficient of determination*. Using this coefficient, one can determine the proportion of variation in the dependent variable that can be explained by variation in the independent variable.

Because the determination coefficient expresses the relationship between variables in terms of percent of accountable change, it provides a different perspective on variable relationships than does correlation.

The numerical value of the coefficient of determination varies from 0 to 1, inclusive. A value of 0, for example, means that none of the change in the dependent variable is due to change in the independent variable. On the other hand, a value of 1 means that 100% of the change in the dependent variable is explainable by change in the independent variable.

The coefficient of determination is calculated by squaring the Pearson r correlation coefficient, that is, it is r^2. As an example, using Table 7-3 data about selected rural community library expenditures, the Pearson $r = 0.83$. This coefficient was interpreted to mean that there is a strong relationship between the variables of community size and library operating expenditures. The coefficient of determination is r^2, which equals 69% [$.6889 = (0.83)^2$]. The

FIGURE 7-8 ▓ Selected Rural Community Library Expenditures

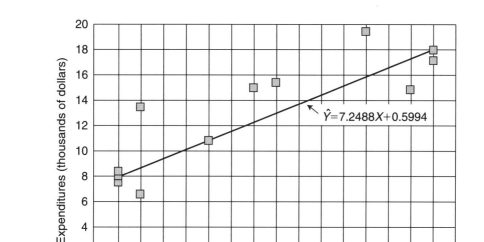

interpretation of this measure is that 69% of the changes in operating expenditures can be explained by changes in community size.

Given that the coefficient of determination for Table 7-3 data explains 69% of the variation, what about the remaining 31% $[0.31 = 1 - 0.69]$ that it does not explain? The unexplained variation is called the *coefficient of nondetermination,* or the *coefficient of alienation.* Its value is $1 - r^2$.

For Table 7-3 data, the coefficient of nondetermination is 31% $[0.31 = 1.00 - 0.69]$. This figure is large and suggests that there may be other important considerations that could explain differences in expenditures. These may be random factors, error, or other unrelated changes in the independent variable.

When reading or preparing a report that uses a correlation coefficient (Pearson r) or the coefficient of determination (r^2), it is important to avoid the assumption that either coefficient suggests causation. It is not unusual to read or hear someone incorrectly state that the coefficient of determination, $r^2 = 0.90$, means that 90 percent of the change in the dependent variable is *caused* by change in the independent variable. Such a statement is inaccurate and misleading, however, because the coefficient of determination does not measure causation. Rather, it provides statistical *evidence* for a relationship between the variables. Understood in this way, the determination coefficient can be used to measure how well one variable describes changes, or "moves along" with another.

Similar comments can be made about the Pearson r coefficient. Again, the correlation coefficient does not measure causation but provides evidence of a relationship. It often happens that a presenter will confuse the two coefficients. A sign that this has happened is when

FIGURE 7-9 ⬛ Interpretation of Various Parametric Coefficients

1. *Pearson* r. Shows perfect positive ($+1.0$) or no association (zero value) or perfect negative inverse (-1.0) evidence of a relationship between two variables. The Pearson *r* reveals how well the regression line describes or fits the points in a scatter diagram.

2. *Coefficient of determination, r^2.* Shows the proportion of total variance in the dependent variable, (*Y*), that is explained by variation in the independent variable, (*X*).

3. *Coefficient of nondetermination, $1 - r^2$.* Shows the percent of change in the dependent variable that is due to random factors or error or that is otherwise unrelated to changes in the independent variable.

---

the correlation coefficient is (inaccurately) reported as a percent. For example, for $r = 0.60$, one might hear or read the following: "Sixty percent of the change in the dependent variable is explainable by change in the independent variable." This statement is inaccurate, however, because the determination coefficient is the measure that is necessary for making this type of assertion.

In summary, a correlation coefficient places the relationship between two variables on a scale of -1.0 to $+1.0$. The interpretation of a correlation coefficient such as $r = 0.60$ is that it shows moderate to good correlation between the two variables. The determination coefficient is r^2, which is 36% [36% = $(0.60)^2$]. The interpretation of this measure is that 36% of the change in the dependent variable is explained by change in the independent variable. The coefficient of nondetermination, $1 - r^2$, shows that 64% [.64 = $1 - .36$] of the change in the dependent variable is not accounted for by change in the independent variable. This suggests the presence of other influences of perhaps greater importance. Figure 7-9 offers guidelines for the interpretation of these parametric coefficients.

The Spearman Rank Order Correlation Coefficient

Charles Edward Spearman (1863–1945) was a psychologist who, late in the nineteenth and early twentieth centuries, wrestled with problems of applying correlation analysis in the measurement of general intelligence. In 1906, he proposed the Spearman rank order correlation coefficient. Among his many other contributions is a statistical methodology called factor analysis.

The *Spearman rank order correlation coefficient, r_s,* is a nonparametric correlation measure. It is applicable where parametric data are not available or where parametric data have been rank-ordered. The measure is very useful for the librarian because ordinal data are fairly common and often are easier to obtain than interval or ratio data.

The Spearman coefficient is represented by a lowercase *r* with subscript *s*, r_s. The algorithm uses ordinal scale data, and it assumes *n* ranked data pairs $\{(X_1, Y_1), (X_2, Y_2), \ldots, (X_N, Y_N)\}$. The Spearman correlation coefficient is calculated by Formula 7-5:

Formula 7-5

$$r_s = 1 - \frac{6 \sum\limits_{i=1}^{n} D_i^2}{n \, (n^2 - 1)}$$

$$= 1 - \frac{6(D_1^2 + D_2^2 + D_3^2 + \ldots - D_n^2)}{n^2 \, (n^2 - 1)}$$

where D = rank A − rank B for each data pair, and

n = number of data pairs

The Spearman coefficient tells the strength of the relationship between two variables that are measured on ordinal scales. If only one of the two variables is ordinal scale, the Spearman coefficient still can be determined by converting the other variable to rank.

The Spearman coefficient shows the strength and type (positive or negative) of linear correlation between two variables. Like the Pearson coefficient, its value ranges from − 1.0 (perfect inverse agreement) to zero (no association) to + 1.0 (perfect agreement). The interpretation of the numerical value of both coefficients is the same. When properly computed, the value of the Pearson r and Spearman r_s are the same for the data. The Spearman coefficient, however, *cannot* be used to find the correlation of determination.

An advantage of the Spearman coefficient is that it is not affected by extreme values because it is based on rankings. Extreme values in a rank correlation do not produce a large rank difference.

The Spearman coefficient can be illustrated in an example involving the training of library clerks. Seven newly hired library clerks are trained in journal shelving and retrieval procedures, then tested on each procedure. The test results are illustrated in Table 7-4, the columns of which have been extended to facilitate calculations. Figure 7-10 is a data scatter plot.

In this example, the reader should notice that the data will be converted to ordinal scale. In assigning each score a rank, the librarian separately ranks the X scores and then the Y scores. Substituting in Formula 7-5, where $n = 7$, yields the following:

$$r_s = 1 - \frac{6 \sum\limits_{i=1}^{n} D_i^2}{n \, (n^2 - 1)}$$

$$= 1 - \frac{6(D_1^2 + D_2^2 + D_3^2 + \cdots + D_n^2)}{n \, (n^2 - 1)}$$

$$= 1 - \frac{6[(7 - 6)^2 + (4 - 5)^2 + (5 - 4)^2 + (2 - 2)^2 + (6 - 7)^2 + (1 - 1)^2 + (3 - 3)^2]}{7 \, [(7) \, 2 - 1]}$$

$$= 1 - \frac{6[(1)^2 + (-1)^2 + (1)^2 + (0)^2 + (-1)^2 + (0)^2 + (0)^2]}{7 \, [49 - 1]}$$

$$= 1 - \frac{6[1 + 1 + 1 + 0 + 1 + 0 + 0]}{7 \, (48)}$$

$$= 1 - \frac{6(4)}{7 \, (48)}$$

$$= 1 - \frac{24}{376}$$

$$= 1 - .07 \text{ which is } 0.93.$$

TABLE 7-4 ▎ Test Results and Rankings of Library Trainees

Clerk	Score Test 1	Score Test 2	Rank Test 1	Rank Test 2	Rank difference	D^2
1	90	94	7	6	7 − 6 = 1	1
2	77	88	4	5	4 − 5 = −1	1
3	80	84	5	4	5 − 4 = 1	1
4	62	77	2	2	2 − 2 = 0	0
5	84	96	6	7	6 − 7 = −1	1
6	60	72	1	1	1 − 1 = 0	0
7	72	82	3	3	3 − 3 = 0	0
Totals					0	4

The interpretation of r_s is that a high correlation exists between performance on the first test and performance on the second test. This may tell librarians that there is no need to conduct a second test—a decision that would conserve staff time without affecting training efficiency.

In ranking the observations, 60 is the lowest shelving test score for Test 1. It is assigned rank 1. The next lowest score, 62, is assigned rank 2, and so on, until score 90, which is assigned rank 7. The same procedure is applied to Test 2 scores for journal retrieval.

FIGURE 7-10 ▎ Scatterplot Showing Test Scores

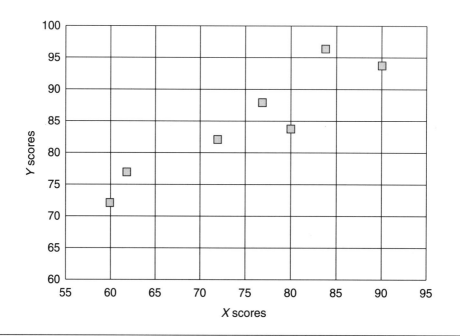

If a score appeared more than once in the distribution, the rank that the librarian assigns to the duplicating scores is the mean value of their ranks. For example, the scores {30, 32, 32, 32, 34, 35} produce the ranking 1, 3, 3, 3, 5, and 6. This ranking is because the score 32 occupies second, third, and fourth places in the distribution. The mean rank for the second, third, and fourth places is 3 [3 = (2 + 3 + 4)/3].

Rank difference is determined by subtracting one set of ranks from the other. It is important to verify at this stage that the differences between the ranks sum to zero. If the sum is not zero, an arithmetic error has been made. The differences are then squared. The result, always positive, is recorded in column D^2, as shown in Table 7-5.

To further illustrate the Spearman coefficient, assume that six of the seven clerks still are employed by the library ten weeks later. The two managers who supervise them rank the skills of each clerk from 1 = highest to 6 = lowest. An assumption is that different supervisors will rank performance by using varying mixtures of subjective and objective criteria. To learn whether there is any correlation between the rankings, the Spearman coefficient algorithm is applied; the results are shown in Table 7-5. Substituting in Formula 7-5, where $n = 6$,

$$r_s = 1 - \frac{6 \sum\limits_{i=1}^{n} D_i^2}{n\,(n^2 - 1)}$$

$$= 1 - \frac{6(D_1^2 + D_2^2 + D_3^2 + \cdots + D_n^2)}{n\,(n^2 - 1)}$$

$$= 1 - \frac{6[(-1)^2 + (0)^2 + (-0.5)^2 + (0)^2 + (1.5)^2 + (0)^2]}{6[36 - 1]}$$

$$= 1 - \frac{6[1 + 0 + 0.25 + 0 + 2.25 + 0]}{6[35]}$$

$$= 1 - \frac{6(3.5)}{6(35)}$$

$$= 1 - \frac{21}{210}$$

$$= 1 - 0.10 \text{ which is } 0.90.$$

TABLE 7-5   Ranking of Skills of New Library Employees

Clerk	Director A ranking	Director B ranking	Rank difference	D^2
1	4	5	4 − 5 = −1	1.00
2	2	2	2 − 2 = 0	0.00
3	3	3.5	3 − 3.5 = −0.5	0.25
4	1	1	1 − 1 = 0	0.00
5	5	3.5	5 − 3.5 = 1.5	2.25
6	6	6	6 − 6 = 0	0.00
Total			0	3.50

Despite the possibility of subjective influences in each manager's evaluation, it appears from $r_s = 0.90$ that they are measuring the same qualities or dimensions in the clerks. This may suggest that there is a duplication of effort in asking both managers to review each clerk. A new procedure, such as alternating reviewers, or splitting the reviews between the managers, may be more efficient.

When scores are converted into ranks to apply the Spearman rank order correlation coefficient, it may happen that two or more of the scores are identical. If scores have the same value, they should have the same rank. The following procedure is helpful for assigning the proper rank to the scores:

1. Arrange all of the scores in ascending order (smallest to largest), including the scores that are identical.

2. Assign ranks, beginning with the first, second, third, fourth, and such, to each score in the listing.

3. If two or more scores are tied, they are assigned an average rank. That is, if the second and third scores are tied, they are assigned the rank of 2.5 [$2.5 = (2 + 3)/2$], which is the average of the rankings. Further, if three scores are tied for fourth, fifth, and sixth place, they should be assigned the average rank of 5 [$5 = (4 + 5 + 6)/3$].

Notice in Director B's rankings that clerks 3 and 5 were tied. This means that the ranking that is assigned will be a mean of the third and fourth rankings. This value is 3.5 [$3.5 = (3 + 4)/2$].

When applying the Spearman correlation coefficient, keep in mind that the Spearman coefficient is not a measure of how well a straight line fits the points in a scatter diagram. Rather, it is a measure of how well Y increases when X increases (positive correlation) or how well Y decreases when X increases (inverse correlation). When variables are related in this way, they are called *monotonic*. Of course, if a relationship is linear, it is monotonic. However, if a relationship is monotonic, it is not necessarily linear.

Thus, the Spearman r_s measures the degree to which two variables are monotonic. The Pearson r measures how well the points that make up the data set cluster about the best-fit line that passes through the data. A low Pearson r means that there is no best-fit line through the scatterplot of points.

In summary, the Spearman method offers many conveniences for determining the degree of association between sets of ranked data. This is true even if the sources of these rankings are subjective or are obtained from different people. Also, the arithmetic associated with the Spearman method is easier than that required for other correlation techniques, such as Pearson's r. The Spearman method is indeed an excellent tool for analyzing complex data that have been arranged into rank order.

SUMMARY OF CRITICAL CONCEPTS

1. *Correlation analysis* is a statistical technique for establishing the degree of relationship between variables or among groups of variables. *Simple correlation analysis* concerns the relationship or association between two variables. A *multiple correlation analysis* concerns the degree of relationship of a dependent variable to two or more independent variables.

2. Variables can be *dependent* or *independent.* Changes in the dependent variable (*Y*-axis) are said to be related to changes in the independent variable, (*X*-axis).

3. Relationships between and among variables are classified as *linear,* or *straight line,* and *nonlinear.* This chapter explores only linear relationships within the context of simple correlation techniques.

4. The relationship between two variables is shown by a scatter diagram. The independent variable is scaled on the horizontal axis (*X*-axis) and the dependent variable is scaled on the vertical axis (*Y*-axis). The points on the diagram are paired historical observations for the two variables.

5. The *regression line* is the "best fit" straight line drawn through the paired points on the scatter diagram. This line is determined by the *least squares method.* It expresses a mean relationship between the variables, based on the paired data points. A regression line describes the central tendency of the dependent variable, given the independent variable.

6. A *correlation coefficient* shows two things: positive or negative association between the independent and dependent variables and the strength of their linear relationship, if any. *Positive association* evidences a positive or direct relationship between the variables. This means that an increase in the independent variable is accompanied by a proportionate increase in the dependent variable. *Negative association* evidences an *inverse relationship* between the variables. That is, an increase in the independent variable is accompanied by a decrease in the dependent variable, and vice versa. The absolute value of the correlation coefficient is an index of the strength of association between the variables. In perfect correlation—either $r = -1.00$ or $r = +1.00$—the paired points fall directly on the regression line. As the points become scattered about the regression line, the correlation coefficient approaches zero. A value of $r = 0$ means that there is no linear correlation. Correlation coefficients are expressed to the nearest hundredths.

7. The coefficient's sign describes only the nature of the relationship. That is, it identifies the relationship as direct (positive) or inverse (negative). A correlation of $r = -1.00$ is just as strong as $r = +1.00$. A coefficient of $r = -0.65$ shows the same strength or degree of association between the variables as $r = +0.65$.

8. The *coefficient of determination* (r^2) is the ratio of explained variance to total variance. This measure shows the proportion of the total variance in the dependent variable that is explained by variation in the independent variable. The *coefficient of nondetermination* is $1 - r^2$. The coefficient of nondetermination reveals the percent of change in the dependent variable that is due to random factors, or error, or that is otherwise unrelated to changes in the independent variable.

9. Correlation techniques are of two types, parametric and nonparametric. *Parametric methods* require parametric data—that is, data expressed in interval or ratio scale measure. *Nonparametric methods* use nonparametric data, or data that are expressed in nominal scale or ordinal scale measure.

10. The *Pearson product-moment correlation coefficient r* is a parametric measure. The coefficient of determination (r^2), is calculated from the Pearson coefficient. The *Spearman rank order correlation coefficient* r_s is a nonparametric measure. Only rank-ordered data can be used in this technique, even if higher-order data are available. The coefficient of determination is meaningless if computed from the Spearman coefficient.

11. The *Pearson r* measures the degree of linear relationship between two variables. This is equivalent to saying that the Pearson *r* measures how well the data cluster about a best-fit straight line that is passed through them on a scatter diagram. In contrast, the *Spearman rank order correlation coefficient* r_s describes the degree of monotonic relationship between two variables. One might think of the Spearman method as measuring the general consistency of relationship between the two variables. That is, if the variables are consistently related, their ranks will be consistently related. It is possible for the Spearman rank order correlation coefficient to reveal a perfect correlation ($+1.0$ for perfect agreement or -1.0 for perfect inverse agreement) for a set of data, but for the Pearson coefficient to equal zero. Also, a Spearman correlation coefficient can be calculated on nonlinear data. Note, however, that the Spearman correlation coefficient cannot be used to calculate the coefficient of determination. Only the Pearson *r* value can be used for this purpose.

KEY TERMS

Least squares method.   A technique for passing or "best fitting" a straight line through the approximate middle of a set of paired data points. This is done in such a way that the sum of the squared vertical distances between the line and the paired points is minimized.

Nonparametric methods.   Methods, techniques, or algorithms that use nonparametric data. Such data must be in ordinal (rank) scale and usually are drawn from a study of attitudes or subjective assessments. An example of a nonparametric method is the Spearman rank order correlation coefficient.

Regression analysis.   A method of predicting from historical data the value of a dependent variable from one or more independent variables, X_i. *Linear regression techniques* determine how much the dependent variable changes for a specific change in the independent variable. They also determine the equation of the regression line that connects the variables. Further, they estimate the accuracy with which the dependent variable can be predicted from historical values.

Scatter diagram, scattergram, or **scatterplot.**   A graph of paired data points on the rectangular coordinate plane. The *independent variable* is plotted on the *X*-axis and the *dependent variable* is plotted on the *Y*-axis. A scatter diagram is an effective portrayal of the relationship between two variables.

SELF-ASSESSMENT QUIZ

1. *True* or *False*   If (x, y) are the coordinates of a point P in the *xy*-plane, then *x* refers to the *x*-coordinate of P and *y* refers to the *y*-coordinate of P.

2. *True* or *False*   The slope of a horizontal line is zero.

3. *True* or *False*   The correlation coefficient yields the equation of the line that is the best fit for two variables.

4. *True* or *False*   The correlation coefficient has the same sign as the slope of the regression line through the scatterplot.

5. *True* or *False*   If the relationship between data points for two variables can be described by a straight line, the variables are linearly related.

6. *True* or *False*   If coordinate pairs were plotted on a scatter diagram and the points outlined a circle, the correlation coefficient would be perfect, or $r = 1$.

7. *True* or *False*   A determination coefficient of $r^2 = 0.90$ means that 90% of the dependent variable's variation is caused by changes in the independent variable.

8. *True* or *False*   Nonparametric statistical methods are required for dealing with data that are shaped by consumer attitudes or subjective management decisions.

9. *True* or *False*   A rank correlation method is less sensitive to extreme observations than is a parametric method.

10. *True* or *False*   The stronger the Pearson correlation between two variables, the closer r^2 is to 1. Conversely, the weaker the relationship, the closer r^2 is to 0.

Answers

1. *True*   The coordinates (x, y) provide the location or address of a point P on the XY-axes. The first coordinate, (x), is the point's location on the X-axis. The second coordinate, (y), is the location on the Y-axis.

2. *True*   The slope of a horizontal line is zero because there is zero change in the y-coordinates and zero divided by any number is zero. Refer to Figure 7-3 and Formula 7-2.

3. *False*   The correlation coefficient tells the degree of relationship between two variables. It also describes how well the regression line passes through the points on a scatterplot. Hence, the regression equation is the line that is the best fit for the data.

4. *True*   The slope of the regression equation (m value) and the correlation coefficient will always have the same sign. This is because the correlation coefficient measures how well the regression line describes or fits the points. The regression line is the "best-fit" line through the points. Negative slope means the regression line descends from left to right; positive slope means the regression line ascends from left to right.

5. *True*   In a linear relationship, data move together. That is, Y increases when X increases (positive association) or Y decreases as X increases (inverse association). When the two variables move together in the exact same proportion, they are linearly related.

6. *False*   Only relationships that can be described by a straight line are linear. If the scatter diagram looks like a circle, no linear relationship exists. In this case, $r = 0$.

7. *False*   The interpretation of the coefficient of determination, r^2, is not that one variable causes an effect on another. Correlation is not about causation. Rather, the coefficient of determination describes the proportion of variation in the dependent variable that is explained by variation in the independent variable.

8. *True*   Subjective or attitudinal data are necessarily measured on an ordinal scale. Ordinal scale data can be analyzed only with nonparametric methods, such as the Spearman rank order correlation coefficient.

9. *True*   No matter how extreme a score is, its rank will be limited by the number of observations in the data set.

10. *True* The coefficient of determination, r^2, is the measure of the percent of variation in the dependent variable that is explained by variation in the independent variable.

DISCUSSION QUESTIONS AND PROBLEMS

1. Explain what is meant by the positive linear and negative linear relationship of two variables. Illustrate with a library example.

2. Suppose each of the following pairs of variables is linearly related. For each pair, identify the independent and dependent variable and list reasons for your choice. For each pair, would you expect that there is a positive or negative correlation coefficient between the variables?
    a. college entrance examination and high school grade point average
    b. college entrance examination and college grade point average
    c. electricity usage and current outdoor temperature
    d. amount of food consumed and body weight
    e. supervisor's skill and employee output
    f. ticket prices and passengers per 100 miles
    g. noise level of environment and employee morale
    h. rate of library circulation and publication date of book.

3. Distinguish between a regression line's slope and the correlation between two variables. What overlapping information does each provide? What unique information, if any, does each provide?

4. Plot the following 10 pairs of data points on a scatter diagram: (1,2), (1,4), (2,2), (2,4), (2,5), (3,2), (3,4), (3,3), (4,4), and (6,14).
    a. Verify that the coefficient of correlation for these points is $r = 0.7616$ and that the coefficient of determination is 0.58. Interpret each measure.
    b. Verify that the regression line is given by the equation $\hat{Y} = 1.8010X - 0.4627$. Graph this equation on the scatterplot.
    c. Exclude the coordinate pair (6,14). Using the remaining 9 data pairs, verify that the correlation coefficient is $r = 0.1118$, the determination coefficient $r^2 = 0.0125$, and that the regression equation is $\hat{Y} = 0.125X + 3.0417$. Interpret each measure. Explain the effect of excluding the extreme data point (6,14).
    d. Use the regression equation from (b) for the ten data points to calculate a predicted value for $x = 1$, $x = 2$, $x = 3$, $x = 4$, $x = 5$, and $x = 6$. Interpret each.
    e. Using the regression equation from (b), find a predicted value for $x = 7$. What concerns, if any, are there with this prediction?

5. Explain why the value of the correlation coefficient is not affected if the dependent and independent variables are interchanged.

6. Data on the operating expenditures for ten rural libraries are provided in the text, Table 7-3. Regress operating expense on population. Verify that the regression equation is *expense* = 6.6694(*population*) + 2.40903. Reverse the variables. Regress population on operating expense. Verify that the regression equation is *population* = 0.1033(*expense*) + 0.2395. Show that the correlation coefficient, *r*, is the same, regardless of which variable is independent and which is dependent.

7. A variety of material formats is available in the library. In a recent study, one library ranked its formats in order of use as follows:

	Rank order of use (1st survey)	Rank order of use (2nd survey)
Books	2	1
Computer printouts	8	12
Films (pictorial)	13	13
Government publications	4	6.5
Manuscripts	1	3
Maps	9	10
Microcopies	10	5
Newspapers	6.5	4
Other pictorials/Photos	11	9
Periodicals	3	2
Research reports	5	8
Tape/Sound recordings	12	11
Theses/Dissertations	6.5	6.5
Videotapes	14	14

a. Calculate the Spearman's coefficient of correlation.

b. Does it appear that the two surveys are comparing the various physical formats on the same bases of use? Explain.

8. A media center technician maintains a record of repair costs for each piece of equipment in the center. A sample of similar machines shows repair costs as follows:

Repair cost	Repaired unit's age
$ 57	1
70	2
90	3
177	7
199	1
49	1
76	3
60	2
114	5
133	6

a. Determine the best-fit regression equation and plot it through the scatter diagram. Interpret.

b. Determine the correlation coefficient. Interpret.

c. Calculate predicted values for each age of equipment from $x = 1$ through $x = 7$.

d. Provide a meaningful estimate of the cost to repair equipment that is 8 years old. Explain.

9. At the end of fiscal Year 2, the library trustees asked the librarian to report on the relationship between moneys allocated for buying new books and the circulation of books by subject category. Unfortunately, there are no expenditure data for fiscal Year 1. The issue arose because some new board members believe that acquisitions ought to be driven strictly by demand, as shown by circulation. The librarian developed the table below to

begin analyzing data for the library, which serves a community of 30,000 residents. The data exclude expenditures for reference material purchases. The acquisitions budget for the materials identified is $325,000.

Do the data support the librarian's views that there is close agreement between the staff's buying decisions and the public's wants? Explain your answer. Apply appropriate statistical analyses.

Dewey class	Circulation			Acquisitions	
	Year 1	Year 2	Year 3	Year 2	Year 3
000–099	2,205	2,732	3,564	$ 6,785	$ 7,785
100–199	5,297	5,245	5,222	7,680	11,400
200–299	2,375	2,754	2,704	4,030	4,320
300–399	14,083	14,677	16,917	27,160	36,940
400–499	1,063	962	1,061	1,400	2,320
500–599	4,324	4,214	4,362	6,980	9,525
600–699	13,733	10,550	9,314	62,335	20,335
700–799	17,331	18,379	16,655	33,560	36,365
800–899	6,861	7,359	7,473	12,470	16,320
900–999	14,975	16,859	18,289	39,075	39,000
Biography	4,364	4,682	6,263	7,725	9,675
Fiction	48,549	47,805	47,741	82,525	100,000
Mystery	13,613	12,926	14,006	26,250	30,565
Science Fiction	2,096	1,791	1,978	7,025	4,500

SAMPLING STRATEGIES AND TALLYING A SURVEY

After reading this chapter, you will be able to do the following:

1. List advantages for using a sample to learn about a population.

2. Identify a sampling plan and differentiate between a probability sample and a nonprobability sample.

3. Identify and list the key tasks for a data project manager and a data collection specialist.

4. Identify and list seven key considerations for gathering data.

5. Describe the survey method as a data collection technique.

6. Describe the advantages and disadvantages of personal interviewing and telephone interviewing.

7. Describe focus groups and how they function.

8. Demonstrate using a random number table to identify a sample.

9. Differentiate between a sample that has been selected by use of a random number of table and a systematic sample.

10. Construct a data tally of a survey instrument.

11. Identify the advantages of conducting a pilot study before launching a survey.

Data are at the core of measuring and improving library services. Data are the foundation for shaping policy and setting goals to establish performance objectives. On the strength of data, short- and long-range goals that are part of the library's strategic planning process are developed. Data also serve to justify the need for existing or new services.

For the librarian interested in constructing and tabulating a local study, this chapter presents some useful design and sampling techniques for gathering data. It also suggests ways to illustrate tabulated data. Note, however, that the issues involved with control or experimental groups are not explored here, nor does this chapter venture into inferential statistics.

SAMPLING: DESIGN AND TECHNIQUE

Sampling is the process whereby items are selected from a population. The items are then analyzed in order to generalize the findings to the population from which the sample was drawn. Using a sample is an effective and efficient technique to learn about a population. Ideally, samples are *representative* of the population from which they are drawn.

Getting a good sample is the aim of all data study. Logically, a sample is good if it yields results that are very close to those that would be obtained from examining the whole population. There are two major considerations for obtaining a good, or representative, sample. The first is that the sample be representative of the population from which it is drawn. Logically, this means that the relevant characteristics of the population need to occur in the sample at the same frequency that they occur in the total population. The second consideration in obtaining a sample is that the size of the sample be sufficient to reflect the whole population. If either of these considerations is not met, a flawed sample may result. At best, analyzing a nonrepresentative sample can only uncover information about the elements that make up the sample. The danger in studying a poor sample is in drawing conclusions and making decisions that are inappropriate for the target population. Even though the information obtained from studying an unrepresentative sample may have some value, generally it is too narrow for conveying a more complete "picture" of the population that is under study.

A well-known example of an inaccurate conclusion coming from a nonrepresentative sample occurred in the 1948 presidential election. Writing in the *Chicago Tribune* and other newspapers, journalists prematurely reported the election victory of Republican candidate Thomas E. Dewey over Harry S. Truman. The journalists had relied incorrectly on opinion poll comments from persons who were not representative of the majority of voters who supported Mr. Truman.

Sampling offers many advantages for studying a population. For example, studying a sample is less time consuming and costly than studying an entire population. Some populations are very large, such as the population of children between the ages of four and nine who have a library card. Other populations are partially inaccessible, such as seniors who are residents of nursing homes and extended care facilities and who enjoy reading popular fiction. A second advantage is that sampling allows an evaluation of the population after the sample itself is rendered unusable. Specifically, a population might be evaluated after sampling in testing adhesives and book repair tape. Example 8-1 discusses other applications of sampling in the library environment.

Example 8-1

Uses of Daily Sampling in the Library Environment

---

1. Monitoring the length of time required for clientele to complete various transactions at the circulation desk to evaluate staffing levels and convenience for clients.

2. Checking stacks to determine whether library materials are shelved correctly so that clientele can successfully find items.

3. Checking the heating or air-conditioning levels throughout the library building to make sure that the library's physical environment is comfortable and inviting for clientele use.

4. Taking advantage of a company's trial period to test equipment or to try a service or product in the library environment.

The plan for selecting sample elements from a population is called the *sample design* or *sampling plan.* Generally, sample designs fall into two categories: *nonprobability samples* and *probability samples.*

Nonprobability sampling is popularly used because of cost considerations and the non-availability of subjects through a probability sample. Among the types of nonprobability samples are convenience, haphazard, judgment, purposive, and quota.

The *convenience sample* is selected based on convenience or access. For example, a librarian may poll a dozen users who happen to be in the library. This is a convenience sample since the twelve users were selected because they were available and willing to participate. The volunteers are not necessarily representative of the population of library users from which they were drawn.

In a *haphazard sample,* the selection process is uneven in choosing participants. For example, the sample may consist of anyone from an "interesting looking" person who *seems* to be a student, to a short person or an Asian client.

For a *judgment sample,* persons or things would be selected for inclusion in the sample based on one's familiarity with the relevant characteristics of the population. Hence, the quality (validity) of a judgment sample is dependent on the sampler's experience, wisdom, and intuition in choosing subjects that are representative of the population that is under study.

A *purposive sample* is intended to meet a specific definition. For example, a librarian might survey the deans from six leading institutions that have a large program of library science instruction. Rather than interview deans from both large and small programs, including leading and average programs, the librarian defines a specific subset of deans in the belief that their opinions will reflect and mirror those of all deans who oversee library science instruction programs.

Finally, a *quota sample* is a selection based on possession of certain given characteristics. Drawing from a heterogeneous population, one might wish to have a sample of persons by age, ethnicity, race, or sex, for example.

In contrast, in selecting *probability sample,* each population member or element has an equal chance of being selected for inclusion in the sample. That is, there is no convenience or judgment involved in selecting a probability sample.

A population usually is very large. Its size is denoted statistically by the uppercase letter *N.* A listing of the persons or items in the population from which a sample (subset) is chosen is called the *sampling frame.* The purpose and value of the sampling frame is to identify all of the elements that potentially may be included in a sample. An example of a small sampling frame that is easy and inexpensive to produce is the names of all paid and volunteer personnel in a local library. Since such a listing most likely contains the names of the target population, it is called an *exhaustive sampling frame.* In contrast, the sampling frame that consists of the names of all persons in California who have a library card is less easy and more costly to prepare. No actual listing may occur, but such a listing could theoretically be produced.

Once a sampling frame has been identified, the next task is to select elements that are representative of the population for inclusion in the sample. The number of elements in the sample usually is denoted by a lowercase letter, n. Of course, when $n = N$, the sample consists of the whole population and the analysis is a *census*. More information will be presented about probability samples and the use of a random number table later in this chapter.

DATA COLLECTION PROJECTS

For data to illuminate an issue, the decision maker has to understand clearly the question that the data were collected to answer. This means that one has to be certain that the data are both reliable (replicable, consistent, dependable, predictable, stable) and valid (pertinent for answering the question, so there is a clear relationship between the evidence and the argument). For example, data collected concerning librarian's salaries would not be considered valid data if the project's purpose is to try to increase Sunday afternoon visits to a public library. Data from other local or area libraries about their Sunday hours and their collection holdings would prove more useful in developing a rationale for an expanded Sunday program.

Some data collection projects are large and require more than one person for the project's success. Typically, at least two persons are part of a large project—the data project manager and the data collection specialist. The data project manager's job description includes the following types of tasks:

- Conducting briefings and hearings
- Designing the data-collection instrument
- Developing a data-collection calendar
- Developing and monitoring the project's budget
- Interpreting data and explaining its significance
- Planning, organizing, and directing project activities
- Providing liaison with other library units
- Providing progress reports and authoring the final report
- Providing training to project personnel
- Scheduling and monitoring time-on-task progress.

The data collection specialist's job description includes the following types of tasks, among others:

- Assisting the project manager in all tasks and activities
- Identifying misinformation
- Preparing summary data reports
- Scheduling appointments and gathering data from data contributors
- Scrutinizing data patterns, anomalies, and missing information
- Summarizing and analyzing data
- Presenting findings.

Gathering data requires a planning strategy that is characterized by seven key considerations, summarized in Figure 8-1. Each of these is worthy of careful attention. The first five

FIGURE 8-1 ▍ Seven Key Considerations for Gathering Data

1. *Why* (to answer what specific question or problem) are the data being collected?

2. *From whom* will the data be collected?

3. *What* data will be collected?

4. *Where* will the data be collected?

5. *When* will the data be collected?

6. *How* will the data be collected?

7. *Political context,* since ongoing and new activities have stakeholders whose interests and concerns may affect aspects of the data collection process.

are the five familiar *W*-words *who, what, where, when,* and *why.* The two remaining considerations are *how* and *political context.*

The type of activity that occurs in a data collection project does not vary significantly according to the size of the project. However, in a smaller project, the tasks of the project manager and the data specialist may be combined. In a larger library project, it is not unusual for the librarian, the project manager, or the researcher (all three positions may be filled by the same person) to work with an advisory team. The importance of the advisory group is to make certain that all aspects of each key concern identified in Figure 8-1 are explored to ensure optimal results. For example, clearly stating the problem to be explored is not an obvious or easy task. A reaction group can bring a synergy in identifying nuances and subtleties that might escape someone working alone on the statement.

DATA COLLECTION METHODS

There are many excellent data sources available. For the librarian, examples of primary source data available in the library's administrative offices are business and financial files, collection records, library reports, and transaction activity records. Some of these sources are listed in the first chapter, in Figure 1-1. Librarians also can obtain data by conducting a survey, collating data that appear in published sources, conducting an observational study, and designing and conducting an experiment.

When seeking information from people, a number of techniques may be used to elicit responses. Some include the following: written questionnaires; interviews by telephone or in person, or through electronic mail or teleconferencing; focus groups; and direct observation.

The method that is chosen often depends on budget, familiarity with the technique, and the time available to complete the study. For example, it usually takes more time to schedule and conduct interviews in person than to interview persons over the telephone.

Surveys

A *survey*, sometimes called an environmental scan, is a data collection technique that is employed to gather data from people by means of an interview or questionnaire.

The survey questionnaire is an instrument for gathering data about services, practices, and the "seven Ls" of library building operation—leaks, lights, lawns, locks, ledgers, liabilities, and lawsuits. Parking, too, can be added to the list. Evidence of the popularity of surveys is seen in the number of them that librarians receive weekly. Typically, the requestor wants to do one of the following: begin a new service; eliminate, reduce, or broaden an existing service; emphasize a continuing service; evaluate an activity in a meaningful context with other libraries; allocate scarce human or financial resources more efficiently or equitably; or change a library policy.

The librarian's mailbox includes the electronic mailbox, called *e-mail*. Today, electronic mail brings surveys from around the world into the librarian's office. Increasingly, a librarian who is seeking input will electronically reach out to the library community by using one of the Internet's many electronic journals, called *listservs*. This can be done by posting a question or elaborating about a library situation to an electronic journal. A librarian reluctant to respond to a paper survey may be more inclined to e-mail an answer to an electronic survey.

After a question is posed on a listserv, it is not unusual for the requestor to read hundreds of electronic e-mail replies from librarians and library technicians around the world. In this regard, the process works well, since the requestor is seeking comments and receives many. Example 8-2 illustrates some examples of library survey questions.

Example 8-2   **Topics of Library Survey Questions**

- Weekend and evening hours. A librarian is considering expanding or changing public service hours and wants to know the hours of operation of other libraries of similar size, type, or location.

- Use of portable scanners or laptop computers in the library. Do other libraries allow clients to bring electronic devices such as these into the library? Do some libraries provide these devices as a service to their clients?

- Parking. How are other libraries providing parking for clientele and staff?

- Saturday morning programming for children. The requesting librarian seeks advice on developing a monthly Saturday Morning Children's Theater featuring programs such as puppet shows and storytelling.

- Providing government-related services such as tax forms and voter registration. Do other libraries offer such services? How much staff time, monetary expense, and floor space are required?

- Public Internet service access. Do other libraries offer Internet access, provide training for users, and offer public services via a Library World Wide Web homepage?

- Periodical retention period. How long do other libraries keep periodicals on the shelf (two years, five years, ten years)? Do other libraries acquire titles in microform? If so, how is the hard copy managed after the microform is received?

Librarians who have Internet access to the World Wide Web can obtain a listing of available listserv names by visiting http://tile.net/listserv/ on the Web. This service continually scans the Internet for newly formed listservs.

A librarian can be a member of several listservs at the same time. It is easy to subscribe, and the breadth of discussion on each can be considerable. One soon learns, however, not to limit membership to two or three groups because of the volume of mail that each can generate. The members of an active listserv can easily produce over one hundred postings each day, so that one's electronic mailbox is continually full.

Written Self-Reports

Written self-reports are a popular survey data collection device. Generally, the respondent is asked to provide short narrative answers or to place check marks against a series of predetermined responses to questions.

To encourage a survey recipient to complete a written survey and return it, a questionnaire often is accompanied by a self-addressed, postage-paid envelope. In addition, it is not unusual for the responder to be offered an inducement—some small token for completing the survey. This may consist of a cash inducement such as a one-dollar bill, or the survey sponsor may offer to make a cash contribution to the charity that the respondent selects from a menu of choices. Figure 8-2 lists advantages and disadvantages of written self-reports.

Interviewing

An interview can be conducted in person, over the telephone, electronically or through computer teleconferencing, or in a small group setting. In an interview, both the interviewer and the respondent react to what they hear and how they perceive something that is said. For this reason, interviewing requires good language and listening skills for collecting data on attitudes, events, feelings, intentions, meanings, motivations, opinions, or recollections. Figure 8-3 lists advantages and disadvantages of personal interviewing.

Figure 8-2 ▒ Advantages and Disadvantages of Written Self-Reports

Advantages

1. Relatively inexpensive way for reaching people nationally or internationally
2. Can be completed anonymously
3. Discomfort at answering difficult or stressful questions is reduced or eliminated in an anonymous setting
4. Likely to be completed by the most knowledgeable person available

Disadvantages

1. Requires that responder have good reading and language skills; persons with visual or motor skill challenges may be limited in ability to participate in providing responses
2. Length may reduce participation, particularly if detailed responses are required
3. Must be returned, and many require a follow-up mailing, including second copy of the survey
4. May not accurately describe the respondent's situation or address the problem under study

FIGURE 8-3 ▌ Advantages and Disadvantages of Personal Interviewing

Advantages

1. Produces a lot of information in a short period
2. Effective for establishing personal relationships

Disadvantages

1. Generally expensive and time consuming
2. Scheduling difficulties may limit who can be interviewed
3. Language differences between interviewer and respondent can limit the interview
4. Listening and interpretive skills are critical

Telephone Interviews

Telephone interviews allow national or international contact within seconds at an economical cost. While the interviewer's physical appearance is not an issue in this situation, an interviewer's appropriate telephone voice becomes critical, since voice and intonation convey an impression. Similarly, the interviewer must have very good listening skills to hear and interpret responses.

The success of a telephone interview depends on the respondent understanding the interviewer's question and formulating an answer that the interviewer must successfully hear and interpret. Thus, interview questions need to be simple and direct, and the interviewer has to clearly understand the question to successfully comprehend the range of answers. In telephone interviewing, the caller generally uses a written list of specific questions arranged in a logical sequence.

A sample of persons in a telephone survey usually constitutes a convenience sample. One of the problems with telephone interviews is nonresponse. Also, some people have unlisted numbers and others screen their calls with answering machines. Figure 8-4 lists advantages and disadvantages of a telephone interview.

Focus Groups

Focus groups are sometimes called *advisory panels, briefing groups,* and *consensus groups.* The purpose of a focus group is for a researcher to develop a preliminary understanding of attitudes about a complex topic in a very short time, perhaps within 24 hours. Focus groups are used frequently in advertising, market research, and political campaigning applications. Professional library associations also make wide use of focus groups to understand membership issues.

A focus group consists of eight to twelve persons, often seated together around a table. They are asked to respond through structured and semistructured discussion to the concerns and interests of the sponsor. The participants are selected because they share one or more specific characteristics of interest to the researcher. These characteristics may be factors such as age, economic status, library usage, marital status, sex, or type of employment, among others.

FIGURE 8-4 ▓ Advantages and Disadvantages of Telephone Interviewing

Advantages

1. Easy to plan and administer
2. Economical, and can be conducted at almost any time
3. Almost anyone can be contacted

Disadvantages

1. "Cold-calling" is time consuming and frustrating
2. Difficult to get calls returned
3. High nonresponse rate, since responders do not want to spend a lot of time on the telephone answering questions
4. Respondents may experience distractions or interruptions during call

---

After the first group of eight to twelve persons has provided its views and comments during a session that may last up to two hours, additional panels of persons are similarly interviewed. Typically, focus-group research uses the results of one to six separate groups. Associations and companies that use focus groups may sponsor a series of sessions across the country to explore geographic variation in attitude among the panel members.

When a focus group is conducted, the session may be audio-recorded or videotaped through a one-way mirror. Videotaping the session(s) allows researchers to study the body language of focus group members and to hear their thoughts and concerns expressed in a context. In most cases, focus group members are paid an honorarium for their participation.

For example, if a librarian is exploring community feeling about the library's programming for children, four groups of up to 48 adults from the community might be invited to spend ninety minutes on a specific evening to discuss their views. The participants might consist of adult community residents who have library cards and who visit the library at least once a month with a child who borrows library books. The focus-group sessions might be conducted each evening until all sessions are completed, or there might be multiple sessions each evening. Generally, the same group facilitator conducts all sessions. Once a session is completed, the group members are thanked for their participation and may receive an honorarium.

A librarian studying the library's programming for children might choose to form several focus groups consisting of children, since the research objective is to improve programming for children. For example, the librarian might question a group of eight-year-olds, a group of eleven-year-olds, and a group of fourteen-year-olds.

In general, children under the age of six are not included in a focus group, since the child's parent or guardian cannot also attend the session. For a focus-group session including children to be successful, the participants must be old enough to feel comfortable without their parents or guardians. The children who are selected for the study might be drawn from library-card holders who visit the library at least once each month and who attend representative schools in the community. The library trustees might also want to include children who are not library visitors to learn why that is so. Like an adult participant, a child participant should receive an honorarium.

Focus groups work well. The participants hear one another's comments and feel secure expressing their thoughts. People build on and react to each other's remarks, resulting in discussion that is creative and insightful. The group's facilitator, who may or may not be the librarian in a library focus group, maintains the topic focus and paces the discussion. Figure 8-5 lists advantages and disadvantages of focus groups.

Example 8-3 illustrates using focus groups to research public opinion.

Example 8-3

Using a Focus Group for Researching Public Opinion

The library trustees are contemplating a bond issue to expand the library. On the advice of a consultant, the trustees authorize $25,000 to hire a marketing firm to conduct four focus-group sessions. The research will gauge community feelings and identify attitudes and possible barriers among voters to a library bond issue. At present, about 60% of the jurisdictional population have library cards. To conduct its analysis, the marketing firm may begin by identifying 48 persons in the community, of whom 30 (62% of the 48 persons) have library cards and 18 do not. The participants must live in representative areas of the community and must have voted in both of the previous elections. Each session, lasting approximately 75 minutes, will be videotaped, and the marketing firm will prepare a comprehensive report for the trustees. Each participant will receive an honorarium for his or her time.

FIGURE 8-5   Advantages and Disadvantages of Focus Groups

Advantages

1. Results available at the end of the session; a preliminary report usually available within 24 hours

2. Viewers observing sessions through one-way mirrors receive instant feedback

3. Questions can be adjusted for subsequent groups, if found to be ineffective or ambiguous

4. Facilitator can receive communications from observer outside the conference room directing a change in topic or a request for clarification

5. A respondent's comment may trigger the imagination of the client

Disadvantages

1. Discussion can break down if one or more of the group members is too dominant

2. Poorly prepared facilitator can reduce a focus group meeting to a question-and-answer session, rather than a dynamic discussion among participants

3. A respondent's comment may be misunderstood or misinterpreted by the client

Direct Observation

Direct observation is a data collection technique in which an observer collects information passively while viewing or listening to activities in the research setting. Direct observation may be used when, for example, librarians want to observe some dynamic such as children's reactions during puppet shows or storytelling.

In observation research, the observer sometimes is visible. This can result in bias, however, since an observed subject may alter his or her usual behavior. To reduce this possibility, the observer usually is concealed from the respondent by means of a one-way mirror or hidden camera. To minimize interference and maximize benefits, an observer strives to be unobtrusive and an effective listener.

Data that have been collected by direct observation usually are highly regarded. In court, for example, such data are called *evidence*. In research, the observer must make judgments about what he or she is seeing. In order to evaluate behavior, the observer must first define the behavior to be observed. To help with this task, the observer may develop a checklist of behaviors. Definition of behavior is important since it can be used to answer questions about validity.

In large studies, training sessions may be held to allow evaluators to practice. In smaller studies, an evaluator can gain valuable practice by observing pilot-study participants. The issue of reliability can be addressed by having a second recorder. The two evaluators can then compare the extent to which they agree in their observations.

PROBABILITY SAMPLES

Although there are no guarantees for getting a good sample, two considerations improve the odds. The first is that the sample must be the right size and the second is that it must be random.

Sample Size

Sample size is important, because a sample has to include a sufficient number of elements to reflect the population as a whole. If a sample is small, a few extreme values exert an undue influence. In general, the larger the sample's size, the greater the potential that the sample will accurately reflect the target population.

There are specialty tables that may be used to determine appropriate sample size; however, their discussion is beyond the scope of this book. But as a general rule, if a librarian's sample includes 100 elements, the survey findings usually will yield reasonable results about the target population.

Random Sample

A *random sample* is a collection of objects, each of which has an equal chance for inclusion in the data set. If some people or elements in the sampling frame are more likely to be selected than others, the sample is not random.

To randomly select three people from among ten, for example, the procedure might be accomplished by writing each person's name on a slip of paper and placing all the slips in a bowl. By vigorously mixing the papers and blindly drawing three names out of the bowl, three persons could be randomly selected. The process is random since each name in the bowl has an equal chance of being selected from among the pool of names.

Of course, when manipulating a large number of data elements, it is neither efficient nor practical to draw names from a bowl. Instead, numbers are selected from a random numbers table such as Table 8-1. This table lists columns of random numbers that were generated by Lotus spreadsheet software, Release 4.01 for Windows PC. The numbers are presented in blocks of three digits. Tables may list random numbers in digit blocks of two, four, five, or more.

The feature that characterizes random numbers is that they have no pattern or order. By using random numbers, an unbiased sample can be constructed similar to that which could be produced by drawing names from a bowl.

Using a Random Numbers Table

Suppose a librarian has a listing of 975 special libraries ($N = 975$) and plans a random survey of 100 librarians ($n = 100$). The librarian begins by assigning a unique number to each of the 975 institutions, such as 001 for the first and 975 for the last, since $N = 975$.

The next step is to identify the 100 random numbers from the table that match to the institutions. Although the librarian could begin anywhere in Table 8-1, for purposes of this example suppose that the librarian begins at the top left-hand column of the section shown below. That three-digit number is 147. The first few rows and columns of numbers that the librarian sees are as follows:

147	670	695	284	848	034	260	446	016	857	085	720	845	396	894	682
810	485	319	617	444	544	532	055	428	831	717	181	900	728	096	602
746	811	255	380	854	468	895	146	825	946	529	732	202	797	609	706
399	026	245	575	888	499	461	590	572	403	029	944	581	957	455	955
520	212	599	233	196	402	211	944	467	477	272	026	463	381	006	058

Since the librarian is using a three-digit table, only the numbers 001 through 975 are within the acceptable range ($N = 975$). Viewing numbers across the top of the table, beginning with 147, all of the numbers in the first row are acceptable {147, 670, 695, 284, 848, 034, 260, 446, 016, 857, 085, 720, 845, 396, 894, 682}. The librarian continues to select numbers that are within the range of 001 through 975 from the next rows until 100 numbers have been identified ($n = 100$). Of course, no duplicate numbers are allowed. Finally, to complete the identification of the random sample, the numbers are matched to the institutions. This procedure is summarized in Figure 8-6 (p. 243).

Example 8-4 illustrates the procedure for selecting a random sample by using a random numbers table.

TABLE 8-1 ▌ Random Numbers Table

147	670	695	284	848	034	260	446	016	857	085	720	845	396	894	682
810	485	319	617	444	544	532	055	428	831	717	181	900	728	096	602
746	811	255	380	854	468	895	146	825	946	529	732	202	797	609	706
399	026	245	575	888	499	461	590	572	403	029	944	581	957	455	955
520	212	599	233	196	402	211	944	467	477	272	026	463	381	006	058
695	636	823	335	969	576	746	898	541	615	668	842	954	463	282	071
461	745	569	375	903	886	489	981	045	664	861	927	391	139	158	009
549	246	673	358	647	672	536	882	901	223	611	908	206	044	265	164
974	085	497	815	462	503	306	555	258	806	307	048	306	505	671	367
090	075	568	443	788	274	618	601	167	933	860	419	331	715	382	272
528	374	228	955	081	621	779	822	386	199	252	325	014	007	960	131
908	907	131	790	330	247	970	862	438	828	851	001	924	950	279	016
881	770	174	927	914	454	811	684	752	628	834	163	144	244	585	755
959	701	768	006	168	422	899	819	895	749	331	673	526	841	183	878
467	855	248	719	823	129	518	568	675	225	304	872	772	337	417	364
703	316	400	289	176	612	525	289	881	488	638	796	210	108	439	139
111	043	935	849	617	191	481	027	725	797	563	671	372	909	873	591
155	162	081	812	686	125	220	368	289	354	985	095	703	322	069	677
524	978	403	869	540	041	630	927	332	480	189	341	514	073	309	979
044	874	525	331	416	994	607	291	581	744	450	457	918	351	715	858
959	193	488	303	820	410	043	027	060	114	930	346	289	665	169	549
883	353	316	512	098	702	932	544	412	943	570	041	310	067	938	828
198	511	130	677	545	148	134	822	460	812	969	427	944	468	307	180
034	219	255	200	963	598	641	697	983	958	057	051	249	044	904	327
640	210	769	208	712	878	553	617	740	627	730	819	474	112	740	630
527	732	976	790	489	924	156	117	692	030	542	619	413	019	409	992
554	076	501	371	418	321	830	347	451	217	593	533	817	892	847	227
126	924	780	268	504	238	333	634	420	551	175	832	131	585	708	289
062	498	114	234	654	220	038	598	576	413	291	799	792	520	617	531
047	929	860	813	093	909	316	837	548	589	235	524	215	686	766	102
086	328	889	370	091	220	508	057	724	047	575	261	948	994	202	999
921	404	165	830	577	791	549	403	816	621	663	140	273	728	732	386
371	196	062	485	518	741	386	280	625	550	583	961	086	687	336	801
553	875	032	160	655	288	773	467	128	428	812	915	056	247	816	338
492	161	213	381	996	982	353	310	637	190	092	523	555	628	331	303
730	683	659	350	866	578	036	680	805	536	723	022	361	156	657	955
478	283	218	607	628	352	346	324	131	966	207	636	433	257	601	021
288	759	659	160	733	701	632	931	431	939	637	506	069	061	333	012
360	149	490	977	122	619	166	738	540	681	834	450	925	990	492	676
744	311	467	565	345	266	783	166	241	030	917	617	448	100	112	653
452	666	366	686	786	782	181	610	740	808	245	450	337	717	489	956
802	485	489	996	394	126	408	384	642	607	230	258	486	250	299	753
949	348	910	042	489	707	348	874	755	325	545	614	832	926	323	103
751	122	769	368	864	462	322	319	617	795	929	784	627	957	784	275
816	165	255	603	076	116	801	485	862	883	541	716	138	872	384	520
543	961	535	553	128	319	936	249	952	977	809	920	959	049	083	799
360	732	927	082	097	264	084	924	312	768	830	777	352	502	943	277
665	485	611	167	110	442	030	404	901	838	889	448	558	769	221	660
335	688	040	984	256	120	389	937	356	159	027	081	831	825	834	123
891	132	195	320	736	494	873	657	151	037	241	812	595	013	492	354

(*Continued*)

TABLE 8-1 ▌ Random Numbers Table (*continued*)

641	934	184	360	454	315	161	214	268	592	365	738	662	288	638	748
019	667	343	744	666	399	425	017	808	852	720	524	636	351	109	652
981	229	483	835	098	576	201	168	710	570	755	742	285	056	667	397
920	072	300	874	970	434	424	903	507	546	702	039	111	490	994	436
365	574	985	623	890	266	719	985	243	706	265	430	489	448	526	371
687	618	814	355	395	514	066	365	291	774	653	522	662	972	019	268
152	958	724	625	854	467	370	553	070	994	840	016	243	380	525	114
421	192	893	630	082	782	118	055	622	932	528	581	466	368	190	459
958	726	101	451	013	663	906	971	234	676	847	025	087	471	970	082
224	797	616	128	532	570	110	032	036	736	307	262	221	346	849	756
463	842	930	784	170	672	354	187	002	243	709	135	737	836	868	865
418	825	140	509	745	959	346	334	606	166	539	378	054	739	520	118
356	276	681	463	051	268	621	040	611	293	292	633	016	970	392	546
978	220	400	542	262	220	822	309	603	920	605	633	448	823	945	520
052	929	971	281	506	251	349	593	967	771	539	188	666	265	200	701
072	152	813	063	462	453	284	933	398	296	961	245	187	559	710	491
756	950	672	857	595	321	812	714	005	886	390	222	603	555	135	992
775	773	251	785	505	652	673	978	185	399	133	830	308	997	366	964
881	793	492	963	334	856	026	136	684	670	445	461	970	168	462	080
253	760	471	029	841	474	205	420	283	798	256	373	663	391	136	637
837	994	727	872	806	109	409	551	233	355	052	110	333	587	761	938
292	710	709	671	545	540	187	638	423	659	262	134	928	843	858	923
477	758	841	577	055	372	630	105	442	025	549	850	456	477	581	363
541	769	413	909	374	706	638	526	252	144	558	507	721	622	226	858
019	469	979	906	638	812	263	375	259	188	095	383	045	079	553	884
131	999	047	588	793	428	445	753	507	745	609	655	886	605	858	051
665	524	468	042	159	624	138	072	394	860	736	681	612	272	616	198
800	376	366	213	239	329	065	838	910	333	923	899	270	559	920	431
406	509	411	427	644	859	366	664	795	547	766	158	584	300	985	115
360	292	003	225	396	568	749	624	507	115	955	585	969	097	168	261
328	158	820	788	790	415	046	138	475	273	162	216	590	759	029	270
893	702	239	851	132	339	285	800	557	016	915	446	069	437	190	872
812	461	354	167	974	072	012	621	186	058	017	635	556	761	810	972
433	780	853	519	806	498	496	308	769	946	402	710	721	775	522	961
083	701	711	590	587	573	645	096	833	337	137	549	693	278	819	868
709	977	296	547	633	679	952	712	496	681	985	775	411	499	707	149
463	589	719	232	273	589	887	074	267	375	898	462	867	840	402	073
605	594	493	489	535	903	904	743	748	558	625	249	917	058	587	052
255	983	932	520	053	877	635	765	110	560	566	542	309	469	095	387
228	886	796	739	318	314	890	435	942	633	718	216	529	656	525	399
383	479	370	938	167	424	748	348	621	549	630	021	502	489	423	208
186	799	679	498	713	655	424	992	764	397	044	972	081	716	384	984
793	777	794	790	141	771	414	786	222	167	076	547	247	802	025	100
911	129	774	971	064	244	831	306	499	831	910	268	769	381	697	458
591	587	927	068	091	224	283	703	006	516	765	909	295	983	808	191
701	455	777	990	500	204	505	518	215	621	768	488	088	840	579	484
324	971	292	854	706	655	107	016	413	991	063	495	433	081	599	634
534	102	280	951	882	297	516	924	078	945	908	080	924	642	431	715
503	761	185	616	090	943	051	655	148	652	808	420	943	841	042	427
689	815	806	434	279	449	666	978	977	655	890	022	047	890	706	220

FIGURE 8-6 ▌ Procedure for Using a Random Numbers Table

1. Assign each population member a number from 1 to N. For example, if the population consists of 1000 elements, then $N = 1000$. If there are 250 population items, then $N = 250$.

2. Decide how large the sample will be. This number is represented by n. For example, if the sample is to consist of 25 members, then $n = 25$.

3. Decide the beginning point in the random numbers table. Some people do this simply by looking away and blindly pointing at any starting number. Any starting point is acceptable since the numbers are random.

4. Generally, use only as many digits of the random numbers table as there are in N. For example, if $N = 100$, look for numbers in the table that range between 001 and 100. If $N = 1000$, look for numbers that range between 0001 and 1000. If the table shows only three digits, then the first digit of the next column is used, or the last digit of the preceding column is used. All numbers from the table that are outside of the range are discarded. Numbers are used only once.

5. Select random numbers by moving up or down the table's columns or from left to right. If the end of the table is reached before sufficient numbers are selected, begin fresh from another starting point.

Example 8-4 ▌ **Selecting a Random Sample Using a Random Numbers Table**

A librarian develops a survey to be sent to the deans of twelve ALA-accredited library schools that offer a master's degree in library and information studies. The survey participants will be selected by random sample.

Analysis

The librarian proceeds as follows:

a. The librarian identifies the ALA-accredited institutions that offer a master's degree in library and information studies. This is the population from which the librarian will obtain a sample. The (exhaustive) sampling frame of $N = 50$ institutions in the United States and Puerto Rico is shown in Table 8-2. Currently, the table is organized by state. Hence, the first university program is located in Alabama (AL) and the last entry is in Wisconsin (WI).

b. The librarian assigns a unique two-digit number to each element in the sampling frame (also shown in Table 8-2). If there had been more than 99 elements, the librarian would have assigned a unique three-digit number to each entry.

c. The librarian uses Table 8-1 to identify twelve random numbers ($n = 12$) that are between 01 and 50. When the random numbers are selected, each will be matched with the unique two-digit numbers assigned to the master's programs. Hence, the number 00, numbers that are greater than 50, and any repeat numbers will be ignored.

d. Using Table 8-1, the librarian arbitrarily begins at the far right-hand column, the first number of which is 682. Using the last two digits and ignoring the digit in the hundreds place, the twelve random numbers that meet the criteria are {02, 06, 09, 31, 16, 39, 49, 28, 27, 30, 01, and 03}. In identifying these numbers by moving vertically down the column, some table numbers were ignored because they exceeded 50 or they duplicated a number that was already selected, such as 02, 27, and 31.

e. Arranged in ascending order, the random numbers are the following: {01, 02, 03, 06, 09, 16, 27, 28, 30, 31, 39, 49}. These numbers match to the following institutions:

01	AL Tuscaloosa	02	AZ Tucson	03	CA San Jose
06	CT New Haven	09	FL Tampa	16	KS Emporia
27	NY Brooklyn	28	NY Flushing	30	NY Syracuse
31	NY Albany	39	PA Philadelphia	49	WI Milwaukee

TABLE 8-2   U.S. American Library Association Accredited Master's Programs in Library and Information Studies, 1994

The following listing provides location information (two-digit state code and city) for U.S. universities that offer an ALA-accredited master's degree in library and information studied.

01	AL Tuscaloosa	02	AZ Tucson	03	CA San Jose
04	CA Berkeley	05	CA Los Angeles	06	CT New Haven
07	DC Washington, DC	08	FL Tallahassee	09	FL Tampa
10	GA Atlanta	11	HI Honolulu	12	IL River Forest
13	IL Champaign	14	IN Bloomington	15	IA Iowa City
16	KS Emporia	17	KY Lexington	18	LA Baton Rouge
19	MD College Park	20	MA Boston	21	MI Ann Arbor
22	MI Detroit	23	MS Hattiesburg	24	MO Columbia
25	NJ New Brunswick	26	NY Brookville	27	NY Brooklyn
28	NY Flushing	29	NY Jamaica	30	NY Syracuse
31	NY Albany	32	NY Buffalo	33	NC Durham
34	NC Chapel Hill	35	NC Greensboro	36	OH Kent
37	OK Norman	38	PA Clarion	39	PA Philadelphia
40	PA Pittsburgh	41	PR San Juan	42	RI Kingston
43	SC Columbia	44	TN Knoxville	45	TX TWU-Denton
46	TX UNT-Denton	47	TX Austin	48	WA Seattle
49	WI Milwaukee	50	WI Madison		

Nonrandom Samples That Sound Random

A *systematic sample* is a type of sample that sounds like it is based on probability, but it is not. The technique is popular and effective and is used frequently by librarians. In systematic sampling, every k-th item is selected until the desired sample size is obtained. That is, every 7th item is selected, or every 15th item is selected until the desired sample size is achieved. In this way, the librarian selects items from the sampling frame using a predetermined, regular interval. A requirement is that the sample frame be exhaustive.

For example, if a librarian has a sampling frame in which $N = 500$, to obtain a sample of 50 items, $n = 50$, every 10th item is selected [10 = 500/50]. The selection interval is 10. That is, from any beginning point in the population, every tenth item is selected until 50 items are identified. These 50 items form the systematic sample. If selection is begun toward the

FIGURE 8-7 ▌ Procedure for Selecting a Systematic Sample

1. Begin with an exhaustive sample frame from which the sample elements will be drawn.

2. Determine the proportion of the population to include in the sample. For example, if $N = 200$ and $n = 20$, then the sample proportion is 10% [0.10 = 20/200].

3. The sampling interval is determined by the ratio of N/n. For example, if the sampling frame contains 100 elements, $N = 100$, and if the sample is to contain 20 elements, $n = 20$, then the sampling interval (k) is 5 [5 = 100/20]. The sample proportion is 20% [0.20 = 20/100].

4. Beginning from any place in the sampling frame, select every k-th item. That is, elements are identified by systematically proceeding down the list and selecting elements at the predetermined, regular interval of k. For example, if $N = 100$ and $n = 15$, then the interval $k = 6$ [6.66 = 100/15]. (Round down.) Hence, from some beginning point, every sixth element is selected until a sample of size 15 is identified. If $N = 100$ and $n = 15$, the sampling proportion is 15% [0.15 = 15/100].

bottom of the population and the bottom is reached before the sample is complete, then selection continues from the top of the sample and goes on until all sample items are identified. The proportion of the population that is to be included in the sample is called the *sampling fraction*. Figure 8-7 outlines the procedure for selecting a systematic sample.

Example 8-5 illustrates constructing a sample using systematic sampling.

Example 8-5 ▌

Constructing a Sample Using Systematic Sampling

A librarian develops a curriculum survey to send to the deans of twelve ALA-accredited library schools that offer a master's degree program in library and information studies. The survey participants will be selected via systematic sampling.

Analysis

The librarian proceeds as follows:

1. The librarian identifies the ALA-accredited institutions that offer a master's degree in library and information studies. The sampling frame is shown in Table 8-2.

2. There are 50 programs, $N = 50$, and the librarian wishes to survey 12 deans, $n = 12$. Hence, the librarian can construct a sample of 12 programs by selecting every fourth program [4.2 = 50/12] from the sample frame. This means that the sampling interval, k, is 4. The sample proportion is 24% [0.24 = 12/50].

3. The librarian can select the first program for the sample from any point in the sampling frame. Suppose the librarian begins with the 12th program in Table 8-2 and then selects each fourth program after that. These are programs with the numbers {12, 16, 20, 24, 28, 32, 36, 40, 44, 48, 02, and 06}. Notice that the librarian counted the last two items at the bottom of the listing before moving to the top of the listing to continue counting.

4. The librarian selects the following programs:

12	IL River Forest	16	KS Emporia	20	MA Boston
24	MO Columbia	28	NY Flushing	32	NY Buffalo
36	OH Kent	40	PA Pittsburgh	44	TN Knoxville
48	WA Seattle	02	AZ Tucson	06	CT New Haven

The Survey Instrument

A discussion about writing survey questions is beyond the scope of this book. Indeed, anyone who has written and tabulated a survey knows that the task is not easy. The key point to remember, however, is that there are almost always surprises when the survey is ready to be tallied. To be better prepared to manage these surprises, researchers should conduct pilot studies and tabulate the results before launching the full study.

The pilot study has the following purposes: to test the survey questions for clarity among the respondents; to give researchers a preview of the type and variety of survey responses to anticipate; and to provide researchers with experience in coding the survey responses for tally. There is no way to anticipate these aspects of the research except through a pilot study.

Further, in developing and testing a survey, expect to completely rewrite the survey instrument at least once. The pilot study is the researcher's alpha (α) and beta (β) test period. And finally, a rule of thumb about time estimates is to multiply all preliminary estimates by a factor of three for the project to barely finish on time!

Tallying the Survey Instrument

Tallying of survey results can be accomplished manually with paper and pencil, performed manually with computer assistance, or automated completely. The automated option is appealing, of course, and excellent personal computer statistical software such as Minitab, SAS, and SPSS is available for the task.

Using a computer to analyze a survey allows the storage, manipulation, and retrieval of large amounts of data. Also, when using a computer to analyze data, one can be certain that calculations are performed accurately and that the printouts are uniform. However, the drawback to using a computer is that the researcher must invest considerable time to learn how to accurately code the data before they can be processed by means of statistical software. In addition, even if the researcher plans to use computer software, the surveys from the test studies will be tallied manually, though a spreadsheet program may be used to calculate counts and percents. Example 8-6 shows a method for tallying survey items.

Example 8-6

Tallying Survey Items

Using systematic sampling, a librarian surveys $n = 50$ librarians by using the survey shown below in Figure 8-8. Figure 8-9 expresses the frequency tabulation in percents. For the first survey item, 38 people responded Yes, 10 responded No, and 2 responded

Not sure. Since there are 50 responses [50 = 38 + 10 + 2], the percent for each is calculated with 50 as the base. Hence, for Yes, the distribution is found to be 76% [0.76 = 38/50]. For No, the distribution is 20% [0.20 = 10/50], and for Not sure, it is 4% [0.04 = 2/50]. The base for these five items always is 50 because a blank response is tabulated and counted as a blank.

FIGURE 8-8 Frequency of Responses to Survey Questions

Question	Responses ($n = 50$)			
	Yes	No	Not sure	Blank
1. Does a collaborative relationship between library director and librarians exist at your college?	38	10	2	0
2. Does the director at your library encourage librarians to participate in decisions?	36	8	2	4
3. Have librarian decisions in your library resulted in innovation?	30	10	8	2
4. Do librarians at your institution actively participate in collection development?	38	8	2	2
5. Does the director at your library seek librarian input on decisions related to library instruction?	38	9	2	1

FIGURE 8-9 Percent Distribution of Responses to Survey Questions

Question	Percent response			
	Yes	No	Not sure	Blank
1. Does a collaborative relationship between library director and librarians exist at your college?	76%	20%	4%	0%
2. Does the director at your library encourage librarians to participate in decisions?	72	16	4	8
3. Have librarian decisions in your library resulted in innovation?	60	20	16	4
4. Do librarians at your institution actively participate in collection development?	76	16	4	4
5. Does the director at your library seek librarian input on decisions related to library instruction?	76	18	4	2

Table 8-3 presents an interesting (hypothetical) yet more complex tabulation of the survey's first item. It reports together two pieces of information that are not included in Figures 8-8 or 8-9. The first is a frequency count, along with the percent that it represents. The second is a tabulation that reveals how people in various library jobs answered the item. This means that the researcher linked the responder's type of library job with the answers that the person in each job category provided. An extended version of Table 8-3 could include a tally by job type for all of the survey items.

Table 8-4 illustrates a hypothetical distribution, by location, of households in which there is at least one library user. The tally is useful because it provides a frequency count and percent distribution. Further, it is immediately apparent from the table that 80% of the households with no library user are located in the suburbs. This information might have been obscured in a simpler listing.

The librarian could augment Table 8-4 with a variety of charts that show the distribution of survey respondents by (1) age, (2) education level, and (3) attitude about the library. Of course, he or she would need to anticipate the charts to make sure that the questions needed to develop them are included on the survey. This preparation might come out of a pilot study.

TABLE 8-3   Frequencies and Percents of Response to Item 1

Item 1.   Does a collaborative relationship between library director and librarians exist at your college?

Job title	*n*	Yes		No		Not sure		Blank	
		Freq	**%**	**Freq**	**%**	**Freq**	**%**	**Freq**	**%**
Circulation	13	7	54%	5	38%	1	8%	0	0%
Reference	19	13	68	5	26	1	6	0	0
Serials	10	7	70	3	30	0	0	0	0
Systems	8	4	50	4	50	0	0	0	0
Totals	50	38	76%	10	20%	2	4%	0	0%

TABLE 8-4   Hypothetical Location of Residence Households of Users and Nonusers (*n* = 768) of the Iona County Public Library

	City		Suburb		Rural	
	n	*%*	*n*	*%*	*n*	*%*
Households with at least one library user, *n* = 553	151	27%	323	58%	79	14%
Households with no library user, *n* = 215	25	12	171	80	19	8

WORKING WITH REAL DATA

Let us assume that a librarian has gathered quantitative and qualitative data for 150 students on the variable listed below:

Variable A = current grade point average, GPA

Variable B = reported income level

Variable C = employment status

Variable D = sex

Variable E = year of birth

Variable F = class year status

Figures 8-10 through 8-12 indicate how the data for particular variables have been coded. Determining the coding schema usually follows one or more pilot studies; it normally requires considerable time to complete. A blank in the response column means that the particular data are missing, while an R in the column means that the student refused to provide the information, perhaps at an interview.

The data have been coded to facilitate tabulation. Figure 8-10 shows the coding for student income, Figure 8-11 shows the coding for employment status, and Figure 8-12 shows the coding for class year status. Example 8-7 illustrates how to tally a subset of a population.

FIGURE 8-10 ▌ Variable B: Income-Range Coding

Income	Income range
1	Less than $4,000
2	$4,000 to $7,999
3	$8,000 to $11,999
4	$12,000 to $15,999
5	$16,000 to $19,999
6	$20,000 to $23,999
7	$24,000 or more
R	Refused to respond
[Blank]	Missing

FIGURE 8-11 ▌ Variable C: Employment Status Coding

Employed	Employment status
1	Yes, 35 hours per week or more
2	Yes, fewer than 35 hours
3	No, but seeking employment
4	No
R	Refused to respond
[Blank]	Missing

FIGURE 8-12 ▌ Variable *F*: Class Year Status Coding

Class	Cumulative credit categories	Class standing	Division	Status
1	0–27.5	Freshman	Lower	Undergraduate
2	28–60.5	Sophomore	Lower	Undergraduate
3	61–93.5	Junior	Upper	Undergraduate
4	≥94	Senior	Upper	Undergraduate
5	0–36	Graduate	Graduate	Graduate
6	≥36.5	Graduate/ (Advanced)	Graduate	Graduate

Example 8-7 ▌

Tallying a Subset of a Population

Suppose we wish to determine characteristics about Freshman students in our population. To do so, we will determine a random sample of 20 students and tabulate the data that are available about them. The data are provided in Table 8-5 (pp. 253–56).

Analysis

Fifty-seven of the 150 students are identified as Freshman. That is, Variable *F* has a value equal to 1 for these individuals. Solving this example will be completed in a series of steps.

1. First, the persons for whom Variable $F = 1$ must be identified. Each will then be assigned a new unique identification number between 01 and 57. This new number can be assigned in any manner that the researcher chooses. Hence, using the abbreviation *ON* for Original Number and *NN* for New Number, the persons for whom Variable $F = 1$ are the following:

ON	NN	ON	NN	ON	NN	ON	NN	ON	NN
03	01	34	02	61	03	118	04	139	05
04	06	36	07	63	08	120	09	140	10
06	11	40	12	64	13	121	14	142	15
08	16	43	17	65	18	123	19	144	20
14	21	45	22	76	23	124	24	145	25
16	26	46	27	103	28	125	29	147	30
17	31	48	32	104	33	131	34	148	35
20	36	49	37	108	38	132	39	149	40
21	41	50	42	111	43	133	44	150	45
27	46	57	47	112	48	134	49		
28	50	58	51	116	52	136	53		
33	54	59	55	117	56	137	57		

2. Second, Table 8-1 is used to identify 20 random numbers that are between 01 and 57. Since the numbers in the table are random, the beginning point can be anywhere. We will begin in the first row at the top of the table with column seven, the first number of which is 260. The last digit will be ignored and only the first two will be used. That is, the number 260 will be read as 26. Moving down column seven, the acceptable random numbers are those that are between 01 and 57. These are {26, 53, 46, 21, 48, 30, 51, 52, 22, 04, 13, 55, 15, 33, 03, 31, 50, 54, 38, 35}. Listed in ascending order, these are the following: {03, 04, 13, 15, 21, 22, 26, 30, 31, 33, 35, 38, 46, 48, 50, 51, 52, 53, 54, 55}.

3. The numbers at the end of Step 2 are the new numbers (*NN*) that were assigned to the 57 items for which Variable *F* = 1. The new numbers need to be translated back to the original numbers (*ON*). They are students {61, 118, 64, 142, 14, 45, 16, 147, 17, 104, 148, 108, 27, 112, 28, 58, 116, 136, 33, 59} of the original group of 150.

4. The data for the 20 randomly selected students are the following:

	Variable					
Student	***A***	***B***	***C***	***D***	***E***	***F***
14	0			F	75	1
16	2.17	5	R	M	65	1
17	3.49			F	36	1
27	0	6	4	F	74	1
28	0			M	66	1
33	0			M	69	1
45	0			F	77	1
58	0.60			F	76	1
59	3.70			F	50	1
61	3.65			F	57	1
64	0			M	69	1
104	3.38	5	1	F	61	1
108	2.28			M	73	1
112	0			M	76	1
116	2.33			M	76	1
118	0			F	76	1
136	0	R	2	F	75	1
142	0			M	67	1
147	3.19	7	3	M	76	1
148	0.76	6	2	F	76	1

5. The responses of the random sample may now be tallied. First, consider some features of the overall tabulation. The first concerns Variable *A*. Scanning the column reveals that many students have a zero grade point average. There are two possible reasons for this. Some students may not have completed any classes yet and thus have no earned grades. Others may be transfer students who have received academic credit for courses completed at other institutions. However, the grades earned in those courses are not counted toward the student's GPA at the present college. Because the question about zero GPA was puzzling, an explanation should be included in the narrative. Also obvious at first glance is the large number of blanks for Variables *B* and *C*. They probably indicate that these students are not employed.

Tally

Variable *A:* Current Grade Point Average (GPA)

Grade point average	Frequency	Percent
0.0–0.99	12	60%
1.0–1.99	0	0
2.0–2.99	3	15
3.0–4.00	5	25
Refused to respond	0	0
Blank	0	0

Variable *B:* Reported Income Level

Reported income level	Frequency	Percent
1 Less than $4,000	0	0%
2 $4,000 to $7,999	0	0
3 $8,000 to $11,999	0	0
4 $12,000 to $15,999	0	0
5 $16,000 to $19,999	2	10
6 $20,000 to $23,999	2	10
7 $24,000 or more	1	5
R Refused to respond	1	5
Blank	14	70

Variable *C:* Employment Status

Employment status	Frequency	Percent
1 Yes, 35 hours per week or more	1	5%
2 Yes, fewer than 35 hours	2	10
3 No, but seeking employment	1	5
4 No	1	5
R Refused to respond	1	5
Blank	14	70

Variable *D:* Sex

	Frequency	Percent
M Male	9	45%
F Female	11	55
R Refused to respond	0	0
Blank	0	0

Variable *E:* Year of Birth

	Frequency	Percent
1930–1939	1	5%
1940–1949	0	0
1950–1959	2	10
1960–1969	6	30
1970–1979	11	55
Refused to respond	0	0
Blank	0	0

Table 8-5 shows the tally for the entire population ($N = 150$).

TABLE 8-5 ▌ Student Survey Population (N = 150)

Student	Variables					
	A	*B*	*C*	*D*	*E*	*F*
1	4.00			M	66	4
2	3.34	4	2	F	72	2
3	3.00	2	1	F	70	1
4	0			M	64	1
5	0	7	1	F	50	5
6	0	7	1	F	50	1
7	3.11	7	1	F	50	3
8	3.44	1	3	F	70	1
9	3.19	7	2	M	59	5
10	2.37	4	1	F	62	2
11	2.08	3	3	M	72	2
12	1.50			M	60	4
13	0			M	22	3
14	0			F	75	1
15	0			F	65	3
16	2.17	5	R	M	65	1
17	3.49			F	36	1
18	3.97	7	1	F	66	5
19	4.00			F	65	5
20	0			M	77	1
21	3.42	4	2	F	76	1
22	2.94	7	1	M	56	4
23	1.91			F	64	4
24	3.08	1	4	M	70	2
25	2.83	3	1	M	65	2
26	2.89			M	63	2
27	0	6	4	F	74	1
28	0			M	66	1
29	4.00	7	4	F	60	4
30	4.00	7	1	F	55	5
31	3.67	2	2	F	42	5

(*Continued*)

TABLE 8-5 █ Student Survey Population (*continued*)

Student	A	B	C	D	E	F
				Variables		
32	3.70	7	1	M	49	4
33	0			M	69	1
34	1.11	2	2	F	72	1
35	3.60	7	1	F	61	2
36	0	6	2	F	73	1
37	2.09	7	1	M	32	2
38	3.43	7	1	F	53	5
39	0	7	1	F	58	5
40	0	1	2	F	72	1
41	3.58	7	4	F	76	2
42	4.00			M	45	5
43	1.54			F	76	1
44	3.67	7	4	F	57	5
45	0			F	77	1
46	2.65			F	56	1
47	2.78	1	1	F	74	2
48	2.43	1	4	M	52	1
49	1.78	2	2	F	73	1
50	0	7	1	F	54	1
51	4.00			F	63	5
52	3.49	2	2	M	61	3
53	3.10	7	1	M	66	2
54	2.70	4	2	M	60	5
55	3.70			F	70	4
56	3.68			F	69	4
57	0			F	72	1
58	0.60			F	76	1
59	3.70	F			50	1
60	2.93			M	61	4
61	3.65			F	57	1
62	3.29	5	1	F	43	3
63	1.20	3	2	M	76	1
64	0			M	69	1
65	0			M	76	1
66	3.12	7	1	M	37	2
67	3.60	7	1	F	40	4
68	3.77	7	1	F	39	5
69	3.73	7	1	F	43	5
70	3.91	7	2	F	42	2
71	3.81	7	1	F	45	2
72	0	6	1	F	45	5
73	4.00			F	45	5
74	2.74	6	2	F	44	2
75	3.43	7	1	F	46	5
76	4.00	7	1	F	43	1
77	3.01	7	1	F	48	2
78	3.69	7	1	F	47	4

Student	Variables					
	A	*B*	*C*	*D*	*E*	*F*
79	4.00			F	46	5
80	4.00	7	3	F	43	5
81	3.76			M	46	2
82	3.37	7	1	F	47	3
83	0	7	1	F	47	5
84	3.50	7	2	F	62	2
85	2.22	7	1	M	35	2
86	3.26	7	1	F	54	4
87	3.54	1	4	F	50	2
88	2.59	5	4	F	51	3
89	3.81	1	4	M	59	5
90	3.71	7	4	F	57	3
91	3.78	7	1	F	54	5
92	3.64	7	1	F	50	2
93	3.24	2	4	F	55	3
94	3.93	7	4	F	54	4
95	0	7	1	M	52	5
96	3.70	7	1	F	54	5
97	3.58	7	4	F	53	2
98	3.77	7	2	F	54	2
99	0	7	1	M	55	5
100	4.00	7	3	M	55	5
101	2.80	2	2	F	59	2
102	2.69	7	1	M	66	4
103	3.85	7	1	F	60	1
104	3.38	5	1	F	61	1
105	3.33	7	2	F	74	2
106	4.00	7	1	M	62	4
107	2.00	7	2	F	74	2
108	2.28			M	73	1
109	2.52	7	1	M	66	2
110	3.78	7	1	M	68	4
111	0			F	62	1
112	0			M	76	1
113	2.84	2	2	F	66	2
114	3.71	6	4	F	73	3
115	1.89	4	4	F	74	2
116	2.33			M	76	1
117	3.00	7	2	F	75	1
118	0			F	76	1
119	2.75	4	4	F	76	
120	2.76	1	2	M	76	1
121	0	7	2	F	77	1
122	2.60	7	2	F	73	3
123	3.38			F	62	1
124	3.80	1	4	F	62	1

(Continued)

TABLE 8-5 ▊ Student Survey Population (*continued*)

Student	Variables					
	A	*B*	*C*	*D*	*E*	*F*
125	0	7	1	M	77	1
126	2.73	7	1	M	63	4
127	2.27	6	1	F	62	2
128	0	7	3	F	70	5
129	3.00			F	49	3
130	3.69	7	1	F	69	5
131	0	5	2	M	76	1
132	2.92	1	4	F	68	1
133	2.15	3	1	M	76	1
134	0	7	3	M	77	1
135	3.28	7	2	F	74	4
136	0	R	2	F	75	1
137	0	7	2	M	76	1
138	2.13	4	4	M	74	2
139	0.54	7	3	M	76	1
140	3.00			M	75	1
141	3.67	7	1	F	71	5
142	0			M	67	1
143	2.39	2	4	F	72	4
144	0			M	50	1
145	0			F	77	1
146	2.85	7	2	F	74	4
147	3.19	7	3	M	76	1
148	0.76	6	2	F	76	1
149	0			F	77	1
150	0			M	76	1

SUMMARY OF CRITICAL CONCEPTS

1. Data provide librarians with *quantitative information* that can be employed to shape policy, develop goals as part of the strategic planning process, and identify and quantify changing library needs and objectives.

2. Data collection methods include *surveys* that librarians receive or send through the postal mail and electronically through e-mail, *written self-reports, interviews* in person or over the telephone, and *direct observation.* The librarian's decision about which method to use depends on the budget, familiarity with the technique, and time.

3. *Data collection projects* may be large or small. The larger projects may have both a project manager and a data collection specialist. In a smaller project, one person may perform both jobs.

4. *Listservs* are electronic journals available over the Internet. They provide access to an international community of persons who have similar interests. These listservs may be used to pose questions and to read responses from listserv subscribers.

5. *Interviews* can be conducted in person, over the telephone, or in a small group setting. The technique produces a lot of information in a short period, but it may be expensive and time consuming.

6. *Focus groups* help librarians develop an understanding of attitudes about a complex topic in a short time, often within 24 hours. Focus groups consist of eight to twelve persons, each selected because of some quality in common with other group members. Focus groups also are known as advisory panels and consensus groups.

7. *Direct observation* involves directly viewing or listening to study participants and passively collecting information. The observer must be unobtrusive so that the respondent's behavior remains unaffected.

8. *Written self-reports* is a broad category that includes surveys, questionnaires, checklists, and rating scales. Often, narrative must be added to the instrument to expand or clarify a response.

9. A *population* consists of a collection of people or objects, called *elements,* all of which have at least one common characteristic. The number of elements in a population is identified by the uppercase letter *N*. A collection of population elements is called a *sample*. The size of a sample is denoted by the lowercase letter *n*. The *sampling frame* is a list of the items from which a sample is chosen.

10. *Sampling design* refers to the process of selecting elements for inclusion in a sample. The two categories of sampling design are *judgment samples* and *probability samples*. A judgment sample's validity depends upon the researcher's ability to select elements that are representative of the population from which they are drawn. A probability sample is one in which each element of the population has an equal chance of being selected for inclusion in the sample. There is no guarantee to selecting a good sample, but randomness and sample size are two factors critical to success.

11. A *random sample* is one in which each element has an equal chance of being selected. A random numbers table can be used to facilitate the process of selecting elements in a methodical "pattern" of randomness.

12. A *pilot study* is useful for testing questions for clarity, for identifying the scope of responses, and for developing ideas for coding the data when the instruments are returned.

13. *Tallying a survey* instrument can be done manually or by means of a personal computer using software such as Minitab, SAS, or SPSS. The advantage to using a computer is precision and accuracy after the data definitions and variables have been identified and programmed.

KEY TERMS

Convenience sample. A nonprobability sample in which sample members are selected mostly due to their availability. The selector believes that the sample members accurately represent the population that is under study.

Pilot study. A small-scale investigation that is designed to discover and identify problems, errors, or other barriers that might develop when a large-scale study is undertaken. Typically, a pilot study is conducted with a dozen or so participants.

Probability sample. A collection of elements selected for inclusion in a sample from a population in which each of the population elements had an equal chance of being selected.

Purposive sampling.   A process in which the selector uses his/her judgment about including persons in a sample based on whom the selector feels best represents the population that is under study. Purposive samples also are called *judgment samples.*

Random number.   A number whose digits are selected purely by chance.

Random sample.   A probability sample. Often the elements of a random sample are selected by use of *random numbers.* This procedure requires that each element in the population be assigned a number, and then a random number table is used to identify elements for inclusion in the sample from the population.

Systematic sample.   The process of selecting every *k*-th item from a population until a sample of desired size is obtained.

Survey.   A technique used to gather data from people by means of an interview or questionnaire. These data-collecting methods are directed toward a sample of people who are representative of a larger population.

SELF-ASSESSMENT QUIZ

1. *True* or *False*   A random sample is one in which each element drawn from the population has an equal chance of being selected.

2. *True* or *False*   A population census often is a quicker way than sampling to determine a population characteristic.

3. *True* or *False*   If a librarian were studying providing library services to homeless persons, a representative sample could be obtained by interviewing every third person who answered affirmatively to the librarian that he or she was homeless.

4. *True* or *False*   A town meeting is an acceptable forum where the librarian can collect data on issues.

5. *True* or *False*   A focus group consists of a random sample of persons who critique a librarian's research.

6. *True* or *False*   Each Sunday, a different member of the library board staffs a desk at a local mall to answer shoppers' questions about the library and to seek input about library issues. The sample of public opinion is random, since different shoppers provide their opinions.

7. *True* or *False*   Persons who volunteer to participate in a survey bias the survey.

8. *True* or *False*   A random sample reduces or eliminates bias in a sample.

9. *True* or *False*   A systematic sample is a random sample.

Answers

1. *True*   A sample in which each element has an equal chance of being selected from the population is a random sample.

2. *False*   A population is sampled when the researcher cannot perform a census of the population because it is too large or the process is too costly.

3. *False*   Most likely the sample is the best that the librarian could obtain, since a random sample of homeless persons would be very difficult to obtain. However, the librarian's sample is a nonprobability sample, also called a convenience sample.

4. *True*   The persons who attend a town meeting do not constitute a random sample. However, the attitudes expressed there about issues can provide valuable data to the librarian.

5. *False*   A focus group is a judgment sample of 8–12 persons who are brought together by a sponsor. The members share one or more characteristics. The group members are engaged in a structured and nonstructured interaction to reveal their opinions and attitudes to the sponsor.

6. *False*   Local mall shoppers constitute a convenience sample and not a probability sample. The reason is that the shoppers who respond are not necessarily representative of the population, assuming that the library board is interested in the entire community.

7. *True*   Persons who volunteer to participate in a survey (written or person-on-the-street) often have strong feelings about a given topic. Their views, regardless of whether they favor or oppose an issue, introduce bias.

8. *True*   Each element in a random sample has an equal chance for being selected. This reduces seasonal variation, volunteer bias, and other bias.

9. *False*   A systematic sample is one in which each third item or each seventh (or some other arbitrary interval) is selected. The systematic sample has a sense of probability to it, but it is not random, since each element in the sample does not have an equal chance for being selected. Even so, the method is very popular and is used often in studies.

DISCUSSION QUESTIONS AND PROBLEMS

1. Using Table 8-5, where $N = 150$, identify a random sample of 15 elements, $n = 15$. This sample will be Group I.

2. Identify a systematic sample of 15 elements, using Table 8-5. This sample will be called Group II.

3. Tally the data for Group I and Group II.

4. Using Variables A and F, construct a scatterplot for Group I data and a separate plot for Group II data.

5. Calculate the coefficients for r, r^2, and $1 - r^2$ for Variables A and F in Group I, and also determine the regression line equation where Variable A is the independent variable and Variable F is the dependent variable. Interpret.

6. A librarian wishing to study the impact of technology in the library environment plans to send a survey of about 25 questions to a systematic sample of 300 members ($n = 300$) of the state library association, ($N = 1850$). The survey is being developed in phases. The first five questions that the librarian sent out for pilot testing to four persons were the following:
   1. How has technology impacted your work?
   2. How quickly is your library implementing computer technology?
   3. Over the past five years, what have been the staffing implications of technology in your library?
   4. What is your educational preparation?
   5. How many years have you been a librarian?

After studying the replies, the librarian condensed and edited the results, which are presented below. Next, the librarian spoke with the director to obtain some advice and direction for continuing the study.

Question 1

- Lots of change
- Have learned new techniques
- I avoid computers
- Library has a computer person
- Made work easier

Question 2

- Began 3 years ago
- More staff training now than before
- Change is happening too fast
- No plan in place
- Need more staff training

Question 3

- Staff training
- Have hired a systems librarian
- Recruiting an Internet librarian
- Library uses a consultant

Question 4

- Taking an Internet course at a community college
- Attend seminars in database searching
- Completed master's in library science in 1997
- Have an M.L.S. and a master's degree in English

Question 5

- Have been librarian at this library for 4 years
- Librarian for 20 years
- Semiretired
- Part-time librarian
- Returned to library last year after a maternity leave

a. Speculate about the comprehensive conversation that the librarian had with the library director.
b. List some advantages to providing answer-choices rather than asking open-ended questions.
c. Develop answer-choices for each of the five questions that the librarian can test in a later survey study.
d. List the advantages of using a judgment sample rather than a systematic sample for the librarian's study.

7. A librarian is working with a higher-education specialist in a college admissions office. One of the librarian's first assignments is to examine and tabulate the data presented in Table 8-5. When tabulating the survey, group the data for Variable E into periods such as 1920–1929, 1930–1939, and so on.

8. Satisfaction forms are available on the desks and counters for persons to use to comment on the performance of individual librarians and the library in general. Each staff member wears a name tag to make it easier for members of the public to identify him or her. Questions are printed on the back of a business reply postcard. Some patrons mail the surveys, while others leave them at the circulation desk. The first four items ask the patron to respond to a statement, rating the librarian or the library on a scale from 1 to 5, where 1 is the least and 5 is the most. The respondent is then asked a few other questions. The questions are as follows:

1. The librarian was helpful.   Least   1   2   3   4   5   Most
2. The librarian was polite.   Least   1   2   3   4   5   Most
3. The librarian clearly explained the
   service in which I was interested.   Least   1   2   3   4   5   Most
4. The library's hours meet my needs.   Least   1   2   3   4   5   Most
5. How many times per week, on
   average, do you use the library?   0   1   2   3   4   5+
6. Are you male or female?   ___ Male   ___ Female

At the end of the week, the reference department director reviews the returns for a recently hired librarian. The results of the 17 replies are as follows:

Reply	Item #1	Item #2	Item #3	Item #4	Item #5	Item #6
1.	3	1	1	1	1	F
2.	5	2	4	2	2	F
3.	1	5	3	3	3	M
4.	2	1	5	3	4	M
5.	3	2	1	4	5	F
6.	3	2	5	2	4	M
7.	3	4	2	4	4	F
8.	5	1	3	2	3	F
9.	3	4	3	3	1	F
10.	4	2	2	1	2	M
11.	2	4	4	5	5	F
12.	1	3	4	2	3	F
13.	5	4	5	3	5	F
14.	4	1	4	5	5	F
15.	3	4	3	2	1	F
16.	3	4	5	3	3	M
17.	5	5	4	4	4	F

a. Tally the survey using a weighted average method, where the degree of agreement weights the item.
b. Tally the survey by showing the frequency and percent for each item's response.

ANSWERS TO CHAPTER DISCUSSION QUESTIONS AND PROBLEMS

Chapter 1

1. *Statistics* is an area of study within applied mathematics and refers to a body of techniques used to analyze information. Its techniques provide a methodology for collecting, organizing, and interpreting numerical data. Statistics has two general branches. *Descriptive statistics* techniques organize and analyze numerical data. The general purpose of descriptive statistics is to describe situations in quantitative terms. *Inferential statistics* techniques allow one to draw conclusions or make predictions on the basis of samples of data that reflect the population from which they are drawn.

2. A *variable* is a qualitative or quantitative characteristic of a sample or population on which the individual members differ. For example, among the many variables associated with a book are its author(s), color of binding, physical size, subject, call number, ISBN number, LC number, number of pages, copyright date, and cost. A *score,* or *value,* is the value of the variable. If the variable is hair color, the score for an individual may be blond, brown, black, red, or any other hair color. *Datum* is the singular for a score or value. *Data* (plural) refer to the values of a variable that have been collected from the individuals or items that belong to the sample or population.

3. In statistics, the term *population* refers to a collection of measurements regarding a particular variable of interest, such as the copyright date of all books in the Library of Congress or the reading level of all children aged 5 to 15 years who have a library card. A *sample* is a subset of a population. That is, a sample is any group of people or objects that are selected from a population. An example of a sample would be children aged 5 to 7 in a community who have a library card. The population is all the children in the community aged 5 to 7.

4. An example of a *variable* is the author of a book. A *data value* for the variable is Hafner, since Hafner is an author. Other values for the variable are the names of other authors. An example of a *parameter* is the average age of all children aged 3 to 15 years in the United States who have a library card. A *sample* is a group of ten children who visited a particular library today. A *statistic* is the average age of those ten children, or the average number of books they borrowed.

5. a. A rating system assigning varying numbers of stars identifies things as good-better-best. This is ordinal measurement.
   b. A value of male (M = 1) and female (F = 2) is a measure to identify and is qualitative. This is nominal scale measure.
   c. Standard and Poor's bond rating system is a ranking system, or ordinal scale measure.
   d. A measure that ranks a sports teams is ordinal measure.
   e. A survey question on state residence would result in a response such as IN for Indiana, MN for Minnesota, or NY for New York. This is nominal scale measure that produces an identification (qualitative) label.

6. a. The number of visitors to view a library exhibit by the minute, hour, day, week, month, year, or other time period is a discrete number since it is a whole number.
   b. Age is a continuous measure since it can be determined to any degree of accuracy.
   c. Humidity levels will be accurately measured by sensitive equipment, so humidity level is a continuous measure.

d. Light intensity will be accurately measured by sensitive equipment, so light intensity is a continuous measure.

7. a. Hair color is a nominal scale measure.

b. Whether a computer system is up or down is a "yes" or "no" answer, a nominal measure.

c. The number of parking spaces is a specific, whole number such as 25 spaces or 75 spaces. Thus it is a discrete measure.

d. The duration of a telephone call is a continuous measure since a more accurate clock will reveal a more accurate reading.

8. The population consists of all books that are on the shelf. The sample is the group of books that are selected. Whether the spine label is correctly affixed is nominal scale, or attribute data ("yes" or "no"). The initials of the technician, like the books' accession or classification numbers, are nominal scale measure, since they are identification numbers. Net cost, like the books' dimensions or weight, is continuous data.

9. The population consists of all students who are currently enrolled at the college. It is finite. The sample consists of the group of ten selected students. The number of courses is discrete data. The cost of supplies is a continuous measure. The method of payment is nominal scale measure (cash, charge, check).

10. In statistics, *reliability* concerns consistency and the extent to which data, or the results of a measurement, are replicable. That is, data are reliable if they are replicable, consistent, dependable, predictable, and stable. In other words, when the same or different people measure a variable using the same device, instrument, procedure, or rule, the person will consistently obtain the same result if the variable's measurement is reliable.

Chapter 2

1. a. Rounds to 8765.0 since the number to the right of the decimal point in the one-tenths place, 4, has a value less than 5.

b. Rounds to 8770 since the number in the ones place, 5, has a value of 5 or more.

c. Rounds to 8800 since the number in the tens place, 6, has a value of 5 or more.

d. Rounds to 9000 since the number in the hundreds place, 7, has a value of 5 or more.

e. Rounds to 8765.4 since the number in the hundredths place, 3, has a value less than 5.

f. Rounds to 8765.43 since the number in the thousandths place, 2, has a value less than 5.

g. Rounds to 8765.432 since the number in the ten-thousandths place, 1, has a value less than 5.

h. Rounds to 8765.4321 since the number in the hundred-thousandths place, which is understood to be zero, has a value less than 5.

2. The key to rounding to the nearest thousandth is to observe the number that is in the ten-thousandths place (fourth place to the right of the decimal point). If the number is 5 or more, round up. Otherwise, round down.

a. Rounds to 3.485 since the number in the ten-thousandths place is 2.

b. Rounds to 2.486 since the number in the ten-thousandths place is 7.

c. Rounds to 2.346 since the number in the ten-thousandths place is 6.

d. Rounds to 3.123 since the number in the ten-thousandths place is 4.

e. Rounds to 3.247 since the number in the ten-thousandths place is 8.

f. Rounds to 3.864 since the number in the ten-thousandths place is 2.

3. In these problems, let x represent the unknown number.

a. With $27\% = 0.27$, $x = 0.27$ (85), so $x = 22.95$ [$22.95 = 0.27$ (85)].

b. With $60\% = 0.60$, $x = 0.60(120)$, so $x = 72$ [$72 = 0.60$ (120)].

c. $x = 15/40$, so $x = 0.375$ [$0.375 = 15/40$].

d. $x = 80/160$, so $x = 0.5$ [$0.5 = 80/160$].

e. With $25\% = 0.25$, $0.25 x = 33$, so $x = 132$ [$132 = 33/0.25$].

f. With $11.9\% = .119$, $.119 x = 15$, so $x = 126.05$ [$126.05 = 15/.119$].

4. Let x represent the unknown quantity.
   a. With 7% = .07, x = .07 (225), so x = 15.75 [15.75 = 0.07 (225)].
   b. With 125% = 1.25, x = 1.25 (50), so x = 62.5 [62.5 = 1.25 (50)].
   c. 75 x = 15, so x = 15/75 or x = 0.20 [0.20 = 15/75].
   d. 100x = 105, so x = 105/100 or x = 1.05 which is 105% [1.05 = 105/100].
   e. 725x = 650, so x = 650/725 or x = 0.897 (rounded) which is 89.7% [0.897 = 650/725].
   f. With 120% = 1.20, x = 1.20 (80), so x = 96 [96 = 1.20 (80)].

5. Year 1. 10% of $10,000 is $1000 [$1000 = 0.10 ($10,000)].
   Year 2. 20% of $10,000 is $2000 [$2000 = 0.20 ($10,000)].

6. a. 1.066, expressed in percent and rounded, is 106.7%. Hence, the increase is 6.7%.
   b. The service now costs $130. Before, through the other vendor, the service cost $155 [$155 = $130 + $25]. The price change of $25 on a base of $155 is 0.161 or 16.1% [0.161 = 25/155]. In absolute dollars, annually the library will save $300.
   c. With 4% expressed as 0.04, the raise is $129.68 [$129.68 = 0.04 (3242)]. The new monthly salary is $3371.68 [$3371.68 = $3242 + $129.68].
   d. The equation is x − 0.30x = $8750, or 0.7$x$ = $8750 which means that x = $12,500 [12,500 = 8750/0.7].

7. a.

	First quarter	March	February	January
Biography	1771	637	562	572
Fiction	13,706	4825	4343	4538
Mystery	5293	1833	1626	1834
Science fiction	476	168	136	172
Totals	151,531	52,490	48,346	50,695

   b. The percent distribution for each month is shown in the following table:

	Percent 1st Quarter	Percent March	Percent February	Percent January
Biography	1%	1%	1%	1%
Fiction	9	9	9	9
Mystery	3	3	3	4
Science fiction	0	0	0	0

8. a–b. The exact circulation for the 31 categories is 514,572. When the categories are rounded to the nearest one hundred, the total is 514,600. The increase is 28 on over one-half million. This is 0.00005 or 0.005%. For all practical purposes, there is no percent difference caused by the rounding.

Categories in Descending Order of Circulation

	Exact count	Rounded count	Percent of total
J Picture Book	71,996	72,000	12
Fiction	57,066	57,100	10
Video	32,913	32,900	6
J Paperback	30,194	30,200	5
J Reader	24,233	24,200	4
J Fiction	23,306	23,300	4
Mystery	22,461	22,500	4

Categories in Descending Order of Circulation

	Exact count	Rounded count	Percent of total
Compact Disc	20,494	20,500	3%
Audio Book	20,403	20,400	3
J500	19,081	19,100	3
Paperback	18,934	18,900	3
910–919	16,217	16,200	3
J Video	12,335	12,300	2
J900	11,465	11,500	2
300s	10,696	10,700	2
Cap II Match	10,066	10,100	2
J300	10,069	10,100	2
700s	9,760	9,800	2
600s	9,475	9,500	2
J700	9,423	9,400	2
J600	8,777	8,800	1
Large Print	7,710	7,700	1
900s	7,618	7,600	1
610–619	7,392	7,400	1
J Board Book	7,282	7,300	1
YA PB	6,921	6,900	1
Biography	6,632	6,600	1
650–659	5,946	5,900	1
800s	5,531	5,500	1
Rental	5,159	5,200	1
100s	5,017	5,000	1
Total	514,572	514,600	87%
Total circulation	586,781	586,800	

c. The 31 categories explain 87% of the library's total circulation.

d. The categories identified with "J" (for Juvenile) represent a circulation of 228,200 items, which is 39% [0.39 = 228,200/586,800]. The circulation from other categories is 286,400 [286,400 = 514,600 − 228,200]. The percent of circulation from categories other than juvenile is 49% [0.49 = 286,400/586,800].

9. a. Library items published in the 17 languages have a combined circulation of 2897, which rounds to 2900. From Problem #8, the librarian knows that the library's total circulation for the year was 586,800. This means that the international language materials represent a circulation of 0.5% [0.0049 = 2900 / 586,800]. The annual percent by circulation is shown in the first column of the table that follows.

Language	Total	Fiction			Nonfiction		
		Adult	J	Subtotal	Adult	J	Subtotal
Chinese	207	138	1	139	60	8	68
Czech	11	8	0	8	3	0	3
Danish	4	4	0	4	0	0	0
French	34	13	18	31	3	0	3
German	36	27	4	31	5	0	5
Greek	4	4	0	4	0	0	0
Hebrew	15	4	9	13	1	1	2

Language	Total	Fiction			Nonfiction		
		Adult	J	Subtotal	Adult	J	Subtotal
Hindi	1	1	0	1	0	0	0
Italian	6	2	0	2	4	0	4
Japanese	41	24	4	28	10	3	13
Korean	1,686	1,170	1	1,171	510	5	515
Polish	353	305	0	305	48	0	48
Russian	341	226	3	229	112	0	112
Spanish	153	33	88	121	6	26	32
Urdu	2	2	0	2	0	0	0
Vietnamese	1	0	1	1	0	0	0
Swahili	2	0	2	2	0	0	0
Totals	2,897	1,961	131	2,092	762	43	805

b. The percent distribution is given in the table below.*

Language	Total	Fiction			Nonfiction		
		Adult	J	Subtotal	Adult	J	Subtotal
Chinese	7%	7%	1%	7%	8%	19%	8%
Czech	0	0	0	0	0	0	0
Danish	0	0	0	0	0	0	0
French	1	1	14	1	0	0	0
German	1	1	3	1	1	0	1
Greek	0	0	0	0	0	0	0
Hebrew	1	0	7	1	0	2	0
Hindi	0	0	0	0	0	0	0
Italian	0	0	0	0	1	0	0
Japanese	1	1	3	1	1	7	2
Korean	58	60	1	56	67	12	64
Polish	12	16	0	15	6	0	6
Russian	12	12	2	11	15	0	14
Spanish	5	2	67	6	1	60	4
Urdu	0	0	0	0	0	0	0
Vietnamese	0	0	1	0	0	0	0
Swahili	0	0	2	0	0	0	0

*Column total may not total to 100% due to rounding error.

c. The community has an international population of persons who borrow non-English-language materials from the library. These persons also have children who borrow juvenile items.

d. The librarian's plan may have two objectives. The first is to increase the circulation of the non-English-language titles among those persons who now use the library. The second objective is to reach out to persons who can read non-English-language materials but who do not know about the library's international language collection. The librarian might achieve immediate increased circulation by buying more items in Korean, Polish, Russian, and Chinese. Current users and nonusers might be informed of the availability of these materials through advertisements in ethnic stores and public service announcements during ethnic radio broadcasts.

10. a. $V_3 = 238$. The "V" means that the item is a videotape and the 3 refers to the third month. $D_5 = 40$. The "D" refers to disc and the 5 refers to the fifth month.

b.
$$\sum_{i=1}^{6} V_i = V_1 + V_2 + V_3 + V_4 + V_5 + V_6$$
$$= 240 + 252 + 238 + 244 + 255 + 225 \text{ which is } 1454.$$

c.
$$\sum_{i=1}^{6} D_i = D_1 + D_2 + D_3 + D_4 + D_5 + D_6$$
$$= 29 + 46 + 41 + 45 + 40 + 36 \text{ which is } 237.$$

d.
$$\frac{\sum_{i=1}^{6} V_i}{6} = \frac{V_1 + V_2 + V_3 + V_4 + V_5 + V_6}{6}$$
$$= \frac{240 + 252 + 238 + 244 + 255 + 225}{6}$$
$$= \frac{1454}{6} \text{ which is } 242.33.$$

e.
$$\frac{\sum_{i=1}^{6} D_i}{6} = \frac{D_1 + D_2 + D_3 + D_4 + D_5 + D_6}{6}$$
$$= \frac{29 + 46 + 41 + 45 + 40 + 36}{6}$$
$$= \frac{237}{6} \text{ which is } 39.5.$$

Chapter 3

1. a–b. Benefit-cost analysis and cost-effectiveness analysis are examples of summative evaluation. Both techniques examine efficiency of activities in terms of cost.

c. Feasibility assessment is formative evaluation. The assessment examines clientele reaction and measures success opportunity for a concept or the delivery of an activity or service before significant resources are committed.

d. Impact evaluation is summative evaluation. The evaluation examines the library's program and its ripple effects as a whole.

e. Implementation evaluation is formative evaluation. It measures what is planned (tasks, tactics, strategies) and compares it with what actually happens.

f. Needs assessment is formative evaluation. It identifies the clientele who need the proposed activity and measures the extent of their need. It also analyzes what specific activity might meet clientele needs.

g. Output evaluation is summative evaluation. It analyzes the demonstrable effects on specific library outcomes.

h. Process evaluation is formative evaluation. It analyzes the process or mechanism for delivery of the library's program. It may explore both primary and alternative delivery mechanisms. This analysis often focuses on technology as the delivery medium.

2. The table, when completed, looks as follows:

	Personnel	Nonper-sonnel	Total	Percent of college budget Personnel	Nonper-sonnel
Administration	$9,360	$4,204	*$13,564*	*69.0%*	*31.0%*
Instruction	*330*	504	*834*	*39.6*	60.4
Library services	1,215	*435*	1,650	*74.0*	26.0
Student services	*3,562*	246	*3,808*	*93.0*	6.5
Total	$41,207	$5,393	$46,600	88.4%	11.6%

The Total's total is $46,600, a value stated in the problem. Administration: The total is the sum of personnel and nonpersonnel costs, which is $13,564 [13,564 = 9360 + 4204]. Instruction: 60.4% of the category is $504 in nonpersonnel costs. This means that $.604x = 504$, so $x = 504/.604$, which is $834. This means that the personnel cost for Instruction is $330 [330 = 834 − 504].

Library services: Nonpersonnel is $435 [435 = 1650 − 1215]. Percent personnel is 74% [0.74 = 1215/1650]. Percent nonpersonnel is 26% [0.26 = 435/1650].

Student services: Nonpersonnel costs are 6.5% of the category, so $0.065x = 246$ or $x = $3562 [3562 = 246/.065].

3. a–b. The data expressed in percents is shown in the table. It appears that the library suffers from expenditure stagnation.

	Year 4	Year 3	Year 2	Year 1
Book	8.0%	7.0%	10.0%	10.5%
Serials	4.0	5.0	5.0	9.0
Journals	79.0	80.0	77.0	76.0
Audiovisual	0.2	0.4	0.1	0.4
CD-ROM services	7.0	6.0	6.0	3.5
Other	1.8	1.6	1.9	0.6
Total	100.0%	100.0%	100.0%	100.0%

4. a. **Orders Placed through Vendors**

	Adult	Reference	Young adult	Juvenile	Total
January	$ 1,142	$ 245	$ 104	$ 870	$ 2,361
February	2,415	1,017	128	1,275	4,835
March	3,403	758	49	800	5,010
April	2,618	239	340	1,177	4,374
May	2,954	139	694	800	4,587
June	1,343	192	349	194	2,078
July	2,607	586	447	317	3,957
August	2,288	119	327	2,309	5,043
September	2,122	277	362	31	2,792
October	2,311	674	152	804	3,941
November					
December					
Running total	$23,203	$4,246	$2,952	$8,577	$38,978

Orders Placed with Publishers

	Adult	Reference	Young adult	Juvenile	Total
January	$ 0	$ 587	$ 0	$ 0	$ 587
February	504	78	0	12	594
March	65	1,586	1,819	94	3,564
April	37	1,951	0	157	2,145
May	12	226	0	763	1,001
June	66	624	0	34	724
July	0	200	0	46	246
August	169	1,144	0	306	1,619
September	23	66	0	550	639
October	52	1,716	175	34	1,977
November					
December					
Running total	$928	$8,178	$1,994	$1,996	$13,096

b. **Combined Direct and Vendor-Placed Expenditures**

	Adult	Reference	Young adult	Juvenile	Total
January	$ 1,142	$ 832	$ 104	$ 870	$ 2,948
February	2,919	1,095	128	1,287	5,429
March	3,468	2,344	1,868	894	8,574
April	2,655	2,190	340	1,334	6,519
May	2,966	365	694	1,563	5,588
June	1,409	816	349	228	2,802
July	2,607	786	447	363	4,203
August	2,457	1,263	327	2,615	6,662
September	2,145	343	362	581	3,431
October	2,363	2,390	327	838	5,918
November					
December					
Running total	$24,131	$12,424	$4,946	$10,573	$52,074

Percent by Category of Combined Direct and Vendor-Placed Monthly Expenditures

	Adult	Reference	Young adult	Juvenile	Total
January	38.7%	28.2%	3.5%	29.5%	100.0%
February	53.8	20.2	2.4	23.7	100.0
March	40.4	27.3	21.8	10.4	100.0
April	40.7	33.6	5.2	20.5	100.0
May	53.1	6.5	12.4	28.0	100.0

	Adult	Reference	Young adult	Juvenile	Total
June	50.3	29.1	12.5	8.1	100.0
July	62.0	18.7	10.6	8.6	100.0
August	36.9	19.0	4.9	39.3	100.0
September	62.5	10.0	10.6	16.9	100.0
October	39.9	40.4	5.5	14.2	100.0
November					
December					
Running total:	46.3%	23.9%	9.5%	20.3%	100.0%

c. The library has spent approximately $39,000 through vendors. The average discount rate is 27 percent, so that the library pays 73 percent of an item's list price. So, $0.73x = \$39,000$ which is \$53,425 [$\$53,425 = \$39,000/0.73$].

5. There are many ways to approach this problem. Although there is no single best solution, the following points may provide some approaches:

a. The librarian's salary for the current year is \$28,000. Fringe benefits are 28%, which is \$7840 [$\$7840 = \$28,000 \times 0.28$]. Rounded to the nearest \$25, this is \$7850.

The librarian's projected salary is \$28,980 [$\$28,980 = \$28,000 \times 0.035$]. Rounded off, this is \$29,000. The fringe benefit is \$8114 [$\$8114 = \$28,980 \times 0.28$]. Rounded off, this is \$8125.

b. The assistant is part-time, working 16 hours per week. On an annual basis, the person works 832 hours [$832 = 16 \times 52$]. The assistant's hourly wage of \$6.50 translates to \$5408 [$\$5408 = 832 \times \$6.50$]. Rounded, this is \$5400. There are no fringe benefits since the assistant works fewer than 17 hours each week.

The assistant's projected hourly wage also assumes a projected 3.5% annual cost-of-living increase, which is \$0.2275, or an hourly rate of \$6.7275 [$\$6.7275 = \$6.50 + 0.2275$]. Note that money amounts usually are computed to four decimal places and then rounded. The projected annual wage for the next year is \$5597.28 [$\$5597.28 = 832 \times \$6.7275$]. Rounded, this is \$5600. Again, no fringe benefits are anticipated.

c. Supplies for the current year are \$1500 [$\$1500 = \$125 \times 12$]. Since the problem anticipates an increase of 4% for the next year, the projected annual cost for the next year is an additional \$60 [$\$60 = 0.04 \times \$1500$]. This is \$1560 [$\$1560 = \$1500 + \$60$] which rounds to \$1575.

d. Equipment costing over \$500 is considered "inventorial" (that is, it is recorded on the institution's inventory logs). The librarian plans to purchase a plain-paper fax machine. This must be included in the budget. In addition, the librarian needs to ask whether there is a special procedure for requesting capital equipment. The machine will require an outside telephone line. Its use may reduce the need for certain journal subscriptions which are available thorough interlibrary loan or document delivery.

e. The CD-ROM subscription is recorded in category 259, which does not make sense since it is a journal subscription that is in a CD-ROM format. Even so, the accounting office may require it to be reported in this way because it sounds like a data processing item. The current annual cost is \$1450. The projected cost of subscriptions for the next fiscal year includes a 10% increase of \$145 [$\$145 = \$1450 \times .10$]. Hence, the expected cost is \$1595 [$\$1595 = \$1450 + \$145$]. Rounded, this is \$1600.

f. Book costs are being squeezed in the current year because no additional money was allocated for the 10% price increase. Rather, the price increase was absorbed by a reduction in the book budget. Since journals increased by $1750 [$1750 = $17,500 × .10], the current year book budget was decreased by $1750. Hence, the current year book budget is $3250 [3250 = $5000 − $1750].

Book expenditures for the coming year will be further reduced by the inflation increase in periodicals. Since periodicals are expected to increase by $1925, the book budget must be further reduced by $1925. Hence, the projected book budget would be $1325 [$1325 = $3250 − $1925]. This category points out a crisis in the book budget. Journal expenses are now $21,175. When they increase by at least 6.26%, which is $1326 [$1326 = $21,175 × 0.0626], the book budget will be exhausted. Many librarians have seen increasing journal costs erode the book budget, since journals are often prized over books.

The current year's journal costs are $1925. Journal costs for the coming fiscal year are projected to increase again by 10%, which is an increase of $1925 [$1925 = 19,250 × 0.10]. Hence, the projected cost is $21,175 [$21,175 = $19,250 + $1925].

g. Current year telephone costs include an inside and outside line. This is a monthly cost of $45 [$45 = $30 + $15] for an annual cost of $540 [$540 = 12 × $45]. Rounded, this is $550. Projected telephone costs are higher since the librarian plans to have a fax machine that will require a dedicated outside line. The monthly cost is $75 [$75 = $60 + $15], which is an annual cost of $900 [$900 = 12 × $75].

6. The librarian should consult with the assistant administrator about how to budget for books and journals. Two possible strategies are: 1. for the institution to allocate additional moneys, or 2. for the librarian to consult with appropriate user groups in the hospital to restructure the library's journal collection, not renewing certain titles. If the second option is pursued, the librarian and the assistant administrator should allocate the book/journal budget, specifying the percent for each. Using last year's numbers of $5000 for books and $17,500 for journals, books command 22% [0.22 = $5000/$22,500] of the budget and journals command the remaining 78%. In the current budget, the distribution is 14% books and 86% journals. Without intervention, next fiscal year the allocation is projected to be 6% books and 94% journals. A decision to maintain the proportion 22%/78% would require the librarian to limit the number of periodicals unless additional funds were allocated.

7. Contingency plans of 5% and 10% budget reductions are painful to develop. Since this librarian is new to the position, it is not easy to identify budget items for which reductions would be least disruptive. Yet, the librarian must identify a 5%/10% plan based on the proposed budget of $74,350, which excludes the space allocation amount, since that item is not subject to retrenchment. A 5% reduction is $3717.50 [$3717.50 = $74,350 × 0.05], which rounds to $3725.

5% Reduction Contingency Plan ($3725)

- Reduce the assistant's time from 16 hours each week to 12 hours. This is a reduction of 208 hours [208 = 4 × 52] and is a cost reduction of $1399.32 [$1399.32 = 208 × $6.7275], which, when rounded, is $1400.
- Reduce the journal budget by $2325. This is slightly more than the 10% journal increase.

10% Reduction Contingency Plan ($7450)

- Reduce the assistant's time from 16 hours each week to 8 hours. This is a reduction of 416 hours and is a cost reduction of $2800.
- Reduce the journal budget by $4650. This leaves a journal allocation of $16,525, which still is 93% of the combined book and journal allocation of $17,850 [$17,850 = $16,525 + $1325].

8. There are 4000 bound journal volumes and 500 books. These volumes are shelved on stacks that contain 125 volumes. Hence, there are 36 sections [36 = 4000/125] in the library.

9. Since the stacks are at capacity, the most realistic option is to keep fewer backfiles. Another

option is to move older volumes into storage, if storage is available. There are about two volumes per year per title [1.86 = 325/175] based on the current binding of 325 volumes that are to be sent out. Since there are 4000 volumes in backfiles, there must be about 23 volumes for each title [22.86 = 4000/175]. Hence, there are about 10 to 12 years in back files for each title [11.5 = 23/2]. This is a strong collection, if the journal titles are key titles in their field.

10. There are 75 titles on open display. Since each shelf displays 24 titles, the library most likely has three sections of display shelving. [3.1 = 75/24].

Chapter 4

1. a. There are $N = 62$ institutions. From Table 4-4, a distribution with 62 scores should be organized into seven class intervals.

   b. To determine the class width, the librarian would apply Formula 4-1:

   $$\text{class width} = \frac{\text{largest score} - \text{smallest score}}{\text{number of classes}}$$

   $$= \frac{\$1{,}260{,}798 - \$315{,}729}{7}$$

   $$= \frac{\$945{,}069}{7} \text{ which is } \$135{,}009.85, \text{ or } \$135{,}010.$$

   An ideal class interval should possess two qualities. The first is that it should be a multiple of five. This helps to easily determine the class interval midpoint. The second quality is that it should be wide enough to cover all of the observations. The librarian could begin the class interval at $315,729, but the chart looks better if the librarian begins with a number such as $315,725.

   c. To find the class midpoint, the librarian applies Formula 4-2. For the first interval:

   $$\text{class midpoint} = \frac{\text{lower class limit} + \text{upper class limit}}{2}$$

   $$= \frac{\$315{,}725 + \$450{,}735}{2}$$

   $$= \frac{\$766{,}460}{2} \text{ which is } \$383{,}230.$$

   The librarian performs similar calculations to determine the other class interval midpoints. The class intervals and class midpoints are as follows:

Class interval	Class midpoint
$ 315,725–450,735	$ 383,230
450,736–585,746	518,241
585,747–720,757	653,252
720,758–855,768	788,263
855,769–990,779	923,274
990,780–1,125,790	1,058,285
1,125,791–1,260,801	1,193,296

2. a.

Ungrouped frequency distribution		Grouped frequency distribution	
Score (x)	Frequency (f)	Interval (x)	Frequency (f)
0	6	0–2	23
1	7	3–5	24
2	10	6–8	3
3	14		50
4	7		
5	3		
6	2		
7	1		
	50		

b. Figures 4-A and 4-B are bar graphs that illustrate the ungrouped and grouped data, respectively.

3. See Figure 4-C.

4. a. Begin by building a grouped frequency distribution to easily identify the largest and smallest scores. The data array is {52, 56, 57, 59, 59, 60, 60, 61, 61, 63, 63, 64, 65, 66, 67, 68, 69, 74, 74, 77}. From Table 4-4, since there are 20 observations, there should be six class intervals. Using Formula 4-1 to calculate the class width:

FIGURE 4-A

Consortium Members' Computer Down Time (Ungrouped Data)

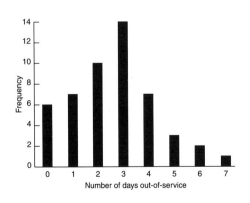

FIGURE 4-B

Consortium Members' Computer Down Time (Grouped Data)

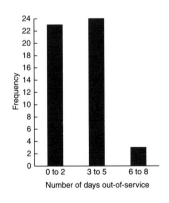

FIGURE 4-C

Operating Budget of Public Libraries

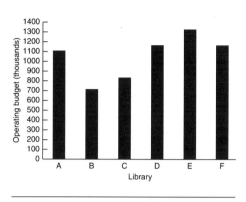

$$\text{class width} = \frac{\text{largest score} - \text{smallest score}}{\text{number of classes}}$$

$$= \frac{77 - 52}{6}$$

$$= \frac{25}{6} \text{ or 4.2, which is rounded down to 4.}$$

The class midpoint is calculated from Formula 4-2. For example, the first class midpoint is 54 [54 = (52 + 56)/2].

Class interval (x)	Frequency (f)	Class midpoint	Relative frequency	Cumulative frequency
52–56	2	54	10%	10%
57–61	7	59	35	45
62–66	5	64	25	70
67–71	3	69	15	85
72–76	2	74	10	95
77–81	1	79	5	100
	20		100%	

b. See Figure 4-D.

c. The relative frequency for each class interval is included in (a) above. The librarian computes the relative frequency of each class interval by dividing the class interval's frequency by the total frequency. Hence, for the first category, the relative frequency is 0.1 or 10% [10% or 0.1 = 2/20]. For the second class interval, the relative frequency is 35% or 0.35 [0.35 = 7/20].

d. The cumulative frequency is determined by adding the relative frequency for each interval, beginning with the first interval. Hence, the first interval's cumulative frequency is 10%. The second interval's cumulative frequency is 45% [45% = 10% + 35%] since it is the first class plus that of the second class.

FIGURE 4-D ▐ Hours of Public Service at College Libraries

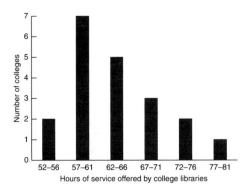

FIGURE 4-E ▐

"Less than" and "More than" Frequency Distribution

FIGURE 4-F ▐

Videocassettes Owned by the Library (January–July)

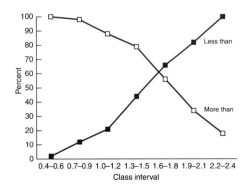

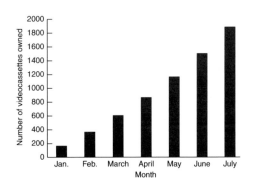

5. a. The frequency distribution is as follows:

Class interval (x)	Frequency (f)	Cumulative "less than"	Cumulative "more than"
0.4–0.6	2	2	100
0.7–0.9	10	12	98
1.0–1.2	9	21	88
1.3–1.5	23	44	79
1.6–1.8	22	66	56
1.9–2.1	16	82	34
2.2–2.4	18	100	18
	100		

b–c. See Figure 4-E.

FIGURE 4-G

Library Videocassette Circulation
(January–July)

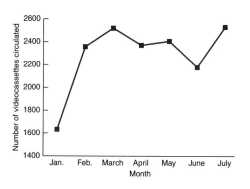

FIGURE 4-H

Microcomputer Applications among
Member Institutions

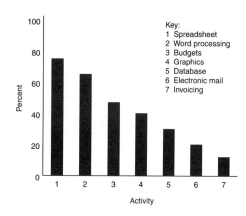

6. a. See Figure 4-F
    b. See Figure 4-G.
7. See Figure 4-H.
8. a–b. See Figure 4-I.
9. a. The table, when extended, shows the following columns:

	Number of titles	Total number of circulations	Circulations per title	Percent of collection
Fiction				
Adventure	105	1,869	17.8	8.7%
Mystery	66	1,958	29.7	5.5
Romance	135	5,154	38.2	11.2
Science Fiction/				
Fantasy	132	6,220	47.1	11.0
Western	91	2,021	22.2	7.6
Other	138	2,315	16.8	11.5
Total	667	19,537	29.3	55.5%
Nonfiction				
Biography	134	1,392	10.4	11.2%
History/Travel	255	2,699	10.6	21.2
Humor	37	748	20.2	3.1
Literature	52	1,247	24.0	4.3
Local interest	6	15	2.5	0.5
Self-help	35	627	17.9	2.9
Other	16	64	4.0	1.3
Total	535	6,792	12.7	44.5%
Grand total	1,202	26,329	21.9	100.0%

FIGURE 4-I
Job Activities Categorized by People, Things, Ideas

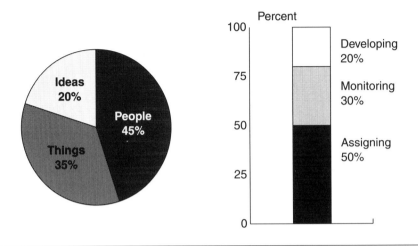

b. Graph: See Figure 4-J. In the chart, the "Local interest" category is included in "Other."

c. In this collection, the emphasis is on circulation per title. The data show that the most popular fiction categories are science fiction and fantasy, romance, and mystery. The least popular categories are the fiction books that do not fit the other categories, along with adventure and westerns.

   Using circulation per title as the measure, the data show that the most popular nonfiction categories are literature, humor, and self-help books. The least popular categories are books of local interest and titles that do not fall into the other categories.

FIGURE 4-J   Fiction and Nonfiction Circulation

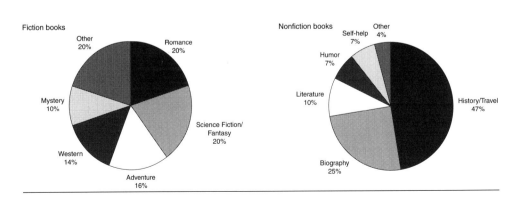

10.

	Usually		Occasionally		Rarely	
	Number	%	Number	%	Number	%
Abstracting journals	62	69%	21	23%	7	8%
Bibliographies/book footnotes	46	51	35	39	9	10
Bibliographies/journal footnotes	15	17	34	38	41	46
Colleagues	11	12	34	38	45	50
Librarians/library staff	13	14	50	56	27	30
Subject bibliographies	13	14	17	19	60	67
Other	2	2	12	13	76	84

11. Toward the last six weeks, the incremental change between points increases at an increasing rate. That is, the difference between 60 and 75 is +15; between 75 and 100, +25; between 100 and 150, +50, and so on.

For the first six weeks, the incremental change between points increases at a decreasing rate. That is, the difference between 300 and 330 is +30; between 330 and 350, +20; between 350 and 360, +10, and so on.

12. See Figure 4-K.

13. a. See Figure 4-L.

b. A total of 100 students participated [100 = 36 + 28 + 14 + 4 + 6 + 12].

c. See Figure 4-M.

14. a. There are many possible good names for the graph. One such title is Library Exit Counts for Six Weeks ($n = 8200$). See Figure 4-N.

FIGURE 4-K

Time Periods for Receiving Orders by Vendor

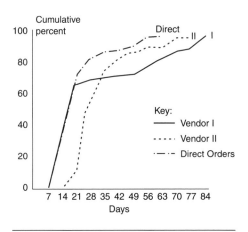

FIGURE 4-L

Student Attitude on Library Survey ($n = 100$)

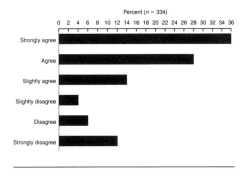

FIGURE 4-M ▨

Student Attitude by Percent
(*n* = 100)

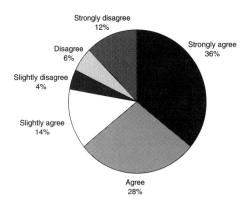

FIGURE 4-N ▨

Library Exit Counts for Six Weeks
(*n* = 8200)

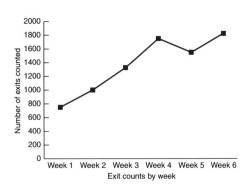

b. The *X*-axis (independent variable) records the Exit counts by week, that is, Week 1, Week 2, . . . , Week 6. The *Y*-axis (dependent variable) is the frequency or actual exit count.

c. Attendance was at its highest during Week 6 when it was 1825 persons.

d. From first to second week, 250 [250 = 1000 − 750]; from the second to the third week, 325 [325 = 1325 − 1000]; from week three to week four, 425 [425 = 1750 − 1325]; from week four to week five, −200 [−200 = 1550 − 1750]; from week five to week six, 275 [275 = 1825 − 1550].

e. Between the first week and the last week there was an attendance change of 1075 [1075 = 1825 − 750].

Chapter 5

1. The midpoint for the class intervals is as follows:

Age (*x*)	Frequency (*f*)	Midpoint (*M*)	Product (*f*ᵢ*M*ᵢ)
1 and under 10	15	5	75
10 and under 20	20	15	300
20 and under 30	26	25	650
30 and under 40	18	35	630
40 and under 50	15	45	675
50 and under 60	3	55	165
60 and under 70	2	65	130
70 and under 80	1	75	75
Total	100		2700

Formula 5-3 is used for calculating the mean:

$$\overline{X} = \frac{15(5) + 20(15) + 26(25) + 18(35) + 15(45) + 3(55) + 2(65) + 1(75)}{100}$$

$$= \frac{75 + 300 + 650 + 630 + 675 + 165 + 130 + 75}{100}$$

$$= \frac{2700}{100} \text{ which is } 27.$$

The median is calculated from Formula 5-1:

$$\tilde{X} = L + \frac{w}{f}\left(\frac{n}{2} - F\right)$$

$$= 20 + \frac{10}{26}\left(\frac{100}{2} - 35\right)$$

$$= 20 + \frac{10}{26}(50 - 35)$$

$$= 20 + \frac{10}{26}(15)$$

$$= 20 + 5.77 \text{ which is } 25.77.$$

2.

Arithmetic function applied to each X_i	Effect on mean	Effect on median	Effect on mode
Add 5 to each score	$+5$	$+5$	$+5$
Subtract 5 from each score	-5	-5	-5
Increase each score by 5%	$+5\%$	$+5\%$	$+5\%$

The distribution's mean is increased by 5 if 5 is added to each data point in the distribution. It is decreased by 5 if each data point is decreased by 5, and so on. It is worthwhile to check several numbers to be convinced that this is true.

3. a. Figure 5-A illustrates the frequency distribution for the 18 books.

Number of circulations (X)	Number of titles (f)
1	1
2	1
3	1
4	2
5	3
6	4
7	3
8	2
9	1
	18

Figure 5-A   ▌   Circulation of Popular Novels

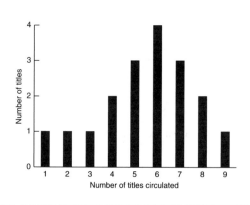

b. The modal class for the distribution is 6, since more novels were circulated six times more often than any other number of times.

4. a. The mean number of titles per inch of shelflist is calculated by using Formula 5-2 as follows:

$$\text{Mean} = \frac{94 + 106 + 99 + 96 + 102 + 103 + 97 + 104 + 98 + 101}{10}$$

$$= \frac{1000}{10} \text{ which is } 100.$$

Since there are 500 inches of cards in the shelflist, the best estimate for collection size is 500 inches × 100 titles per inch, which is 50,000 titles.

b. The mean number of titles from counting books on the shelf is determined by Formula 5-2 as follows:

$$\text{Mean} = \frac{180 + 195 + 185 + 193 + 164 + 156 + 170 + 169 + 160 + 178}{10}$$

$$= \frac{1750}{10} \text{ which is } 175.$$

Since only 75% of the available shelving is filled, the best estimate for collection size is as follows:

$$\text{Collection size} = 75\% \times 376 \text{ sections} \times 175 \text{ titles/section}$$
$$= .75 \times 376 \times 175 \text{ which is } 49,350 \text{ titles.}$$

c. The percent difference between the estimates is calculated as follows:

$$\frac{(50,000 - 49,350)}{50,000} (100\%) = \frac{650}{50,000} \text{ which is } 0.013, \text{ or } 1.3\%.$$

　　d. The unoccupied shelves account for 25% of the shelving. Since there are 376 sections and since each section can accommodate 175 volumes, the capacity is determined as follows:

$$\text{Capacity} = 25\% \times 376 \times 175$$
$$= .25 \times 376 \times 175 \text{ which is } 16,450 \text{ titles.}$$

5.　a. See the columns below, labeled Percent change Adult and Percent change Juvenile.
　　b. The mean adult percent change is 7.6%. The mean juvenile percent change is 66.8%.
　　c. See columns labeled "Juvenile: Adult" for Year 1 and Year 2, below.
　　d. The mean Juvenile: Adult ratio in Year 1 was 0.35; in Year 2, it was 0.55.
　　e. The ratios for the 400–499 Dewey classification range differ widely from their means in both Year 1 and Year 2. The values from which these ratios are calculated are small. This may result in the calculated ratios not accurately reflecting the data.

	Percent change Adult	Percent change Juvenile	Year 2 Juvenile: Adult	Year 1 Juvenile: Adult
000–099	17.8	−48.3	0.28	0.64
100–199	−11.4	7.1	0.38	0.32
200–299	−31.7	−81.8	0.05	0.18
300–399	32.6	11.8	0.17	0.20
400–499	−50.0	600.0	2.33	0.17
500–599	16.7	44.2	1.19	0.96
600–699	24.3	−26.9	0.10	0.18
700–799	17.1	14.9	0.16	0.16
800–899	49.6	31.0	0.22	0.26
900–999	10.7	67.4	0.27	0.18
Fiction	9.9	153.1	0.56	0.24
Biography	5.9	29.5	0.88	0.72

6.　a. Percents for the table are as follows:

Number of days (X)	Class midpoint (M)	Days before ordering	Days for vendor to fill order	Days to process item
1–7	4	16.4%	0.2%	8.0%
8–14	11	28.4	0.2	9.8
15–21	18	28.9	0.2	12.5
22–28	25	16.1	18.6	29.5
29–35	32	8.9	19.1	16.1
36–42	39	1.1	2.3	11.4
43–49	46	0.2	5.0	6.6
50–56	53	0.0	3.9	2.0
57–63	60	0.0	3.4	1.6
64–70	67	0.0	1.1	1.1
71–77	74	0.0	0.5	0.9
78–84	81	0.0	0.0	0.5
		100.0%	52.5%	100.0%

　　b. See Figure 5-B.

FIGURE 5-B ▌ Acquisitions

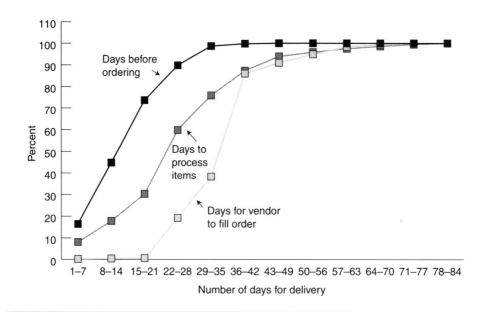

c. Mean number of days before ordering:

$$\overline{X}_w = \frac{4(72) + 11(125) + 18(127) + 25(71) + 32(39) + 39(52) + 46(1)}{440}$$

$$= \frac{288 + 1375 + 2286 + 1775 + 1248 + 2028 + 46}{440}$$

$$= \frac{9046}{440} \text{ which is 20.56 days.}$$

Mean number of days for vendor to fill order:

$$\overline{X}_w = \frac{\begin{array}{c}4(1) + 11(1) + 18(1) + 25(82) + 32(84) + 39(10) + 46(22) + 53(17) \\ + 60(15) + 67(5) + 74(2)\end{array}}{440}$$

$$= \frac{4 + 11 + 18 + 2050 + 2688 + 390 + 1012 + 901 + 900 + 335 + 148}{440}$$

$$= \frac{8,457}{440} \text{ which is 19.2 days.}$$

Mean number of days to process items:

$$\overline{X}_w = \frac{\begin{array}{c}4(35) + 11(43) + 18(55) + 25(130) + 32(71) + 39(50) + 46(29) + 53(9) \\ + 60(7) + 67(5) + 74(4) + 81(2)\end{array}}{440}$$

$$= \frac{\begin{array}{c}140 + 473 + 990 + 3250 + 2272 + 1950 + 1334 \\ + 477 + 420 + 335 + 296 + 162\end{array}}{440}$$

$$= \frac{12,099}{440} \text{ which is 27.5 days.}$$

7. a.

Library	Acquisitions/Collection size (%)
1	5.1%
2	13.5
3	5.0
4	6.2
5	0.6
6	7.7
7	5.9
8	6.5
9	6.5
10	6.7

b.

$$\text{Mean} = \frac{5.1 + 13.5 + 5.0 + 6.2 + 0.6 + 7.7 + 5.9 + 6.5 + 6.5 + 6.7}{10}$$

$$= \frac{63.7}{10} \text{ which is } 6.37.$$

c. Libraries that have only recently begun operation might be expected to have a higher than average level of acquisitions compared to collection size. Since the collection is being developed and is growing rapidly, the number of acquisitions will be high while the total collection size still is small. Hence, the ratio of acquisitions to collection size will be high.

d. The low ratio suggests that the collection is becoming increasingly obsolete, old, and dated because of a reduced level of new acquisitions. It may also be because of a failure to weed the collection regularly, which has resulted in a large collection size, so that the denominator of the ratio overwhelms the numerator.

8. The distribution seems to be skewed since the mean and median would have to be more nearly equal for the distribution to be symmetrical. Since the mean is pulled or displaced toward the distribution's tail and since its value is less than the median, the distribution is more likely negatively skewed.

9. The number of scores is an even number. This is because the scores are discrete and hence whole numbers. If there were an odd number of scores, the value would be a whole number. Since the median is a mixed number (whole number plus a decimal part), it must be the simple average of two integers, most likely 15 and 16 to produce 15.5.

10. a. Data set A has 10 scores; and data set B has 15 scores.

b. For data set A: mode is 4, median is 4, and the mean is 4.8.
[4.8 = (3 + 4 + 4 + 4 + 4 + 4 + 6 + 6 + 6 + 7)/10 or 48/10].
For data set B: mode is 4, median is 4, and the mean is 4.8
[4.8 = 1 + 1 + 1 + 1 + 2 + 4 + 4 + 4 + 4 + 4 + 6 + 7 + 10 + 10 + 13)/15].

c. The scores in data set A cluster closer together than do the scores in data set B. Data set B has an outlier, 13. Both data sets are skewed since the mean and median of each are not equal.

11.

	Association A	Association B	
Mode	8 and 9	4 and 5	(both distributions are bimodal)
Median	7.5	5.0	
Mean	6.9	4.7	
Sum	138.0	93.0	

Association A offers 48% more interesting sessions than does Association B.

Chapter 6

1. The interquartile range is superior to the range if the data are wide-tailed or if the distribution has open ends. The range, however, is easier to calculate and is superior to the interquartile range if the data are narrow-tailed.

2.

Hours parked in library lot	Frequency (f)	$(X \cdot f)$	$(X - \bar{X})$	$(X - \bar{X})^2$
1	3	3	-3.83	14.7
2	9	18	-2.83	8.0
3	15	45	-1.83	3.3
4	25	100	-0.83	0.7
5	15	75	0.17	0.0
6	11	66	1.17	1.4
7	9	63	2.17	4.7
8	6	48	3.17	10.0
9	5	45	4.17	17.4
10	2	20	5.17	26.7
	100	483	6.7	86.9

$$s = \sqrt{\frac{86.9}{100}} \text{ which is 0.93.}$$

a. The mode is 4 since it is the score that occurs most often. The median is between the 50th and 51st values. This value is 4. The mean is 4.83 [4.83 = 483/100].
b. The range is 9 [9 = 10 − 1].
c. Since there are 100 values, the quartiles are easy to calculate since Q_1 is the 25th value, Q_2 is the 50th value, and Q_3 is the 75th value. To determine these values, count the frequencies. $Q_1 = 3$, $Q_2 = 4$, $Q_3 = 6$.
d. Extended columns to the table above help to produce the standard deviation result, which is 0.93.

3. By inspection, one can see that the standard deviation will be small since there is not much variation in the data. To calculate the standard deviation, construct a table:

Errors in library work	Frequency (f)	$(X \cdot f)$	$(X - \bar{X})$	$(X - \bar{X})^2$
0	2	0	-1	1
1	1	1	0	0
2	2	4	1	1
	5	5		2

$$s = \sqrt{\frac{2}{4}} \text{ which is 0.71.}$$

4. The following table is helpful:

	Range	**Standard deviation**	**Variance**
a.	No change	No change	No change
b.	Increases by 10%	Increases by 10%	Increases by 10%
c.	No change	No change	No change
d.	Decreases by 10%	Decreases by 10%	Decreases by 10%

5. a. The mean, standard deviation, and coefficient of variation for Year 1 sick days, where $N = 26$:

$$\overline{X} = \frac{\sum\limits_{i=1}^{N} X_i}{N}$$

$$= \frac{143}{26} \text{ which is 5.5 days.}$$

$$s = \sqrt{\frac{\sum\limits_{i=1}^{n} (X_i - \overline{X})^2}{n - 1}}$$

$$= \sqrt{\frac{246.25}{25}}$$

$$= \sqrt{9.85} \text{ which is 3.14 days.}$$

$$V = \frac{3.14}{5.50}(100\%) \text{ which is 57.1\%.}$$

The mean, standard deviation, and coefficient of variation for Year 2 is $\overline{X} = 3.77$ days, $s = 2.12$ days, and $V = 56.2\%$. The coefficients of variation for Year 1 and Year 2 data sets are nearly equal. This suggests that the two distributions have the same variability, and therefore that the difference between means is a good measure of the average difference between the two distributions.

  b. The new policy appears to have had two effects. First, the average number of sick days per employee has declined by almost two days from 3.77 to 2.12 days. Second, the number of employees taking sick leave has increased from 26 to 31. Nonetheless, the total number of sick days has declined from 143 days to 117 days.

6. a–b. The data are heavily skewed to the right. This suggests that the median may be a better measure of central tendency than the mean since it is not influenced by the skew of the distribution.

$$\tilde{X} = L + \frac{w}{f}\left(\frac{n}{2} - F\right)$$

$$= 2 + \frac{2}{39}\left(\frac{120}{2} - 49\right)$$

$$= 2 + \frac{2}{39}(11) \text{ which is 2.56 minutes.}$$

Using Formula 5-3,

$$\bar{X} = \frac{\begin{array}{c} 1(49) + 3(39) + 5(15) + 7(5) + 9(4) + 11(4) \\ + 13(2) + 15(0) + 17(1) + 19(1) \end{array}}{(49 + 39 + 15 + 5 + 4 + 4 + 2 + 0 + 1 + 1)}$$

$$= \frac{49 + 117 + 75 + 35 + 36 + 44 + 26 + 0 + 17 + 19}{120}$$

$$= \frac{418}{120} \text{ which is 3.48 minutes.}$$

c. Using Formula 6-6,

$$s = \sqrt{\frac{[(1 - 3.48)^2]49 + [(3 - 3.48)^2]39 + \ldots + [(19 - 3.48)^2]1}{(49 + 39 + 15 + 5 + 4 + 4 + 2 + 0 + 1 + 1) - 1}}$$

$$= \sqrt{\frac{[(-2.48)^2]49 + [(-0.48)^2]39 + \ldots + [(15.52)^2]1}{120 - 1}}$$

$$= \sqrt{\frac{301.3696 + 8.9856 + \ldots + 240.8704}{119}}$$

$$= \sqrt{\frac{1359.968}{119}} \text{ which is 3.38 minutes.}$$

The variance is the square of the deviation, which is 11.42 minutes $[11.42 = (3.38)(3.38)]$.

d.

$$Q_3 - Q_1 = \left[L + \frac{w}{f}\left(\frac{75n}{100} - F\right) \right] - \left[L + \frac{w}{f}\left(\frac{25n}{100} - F\right) \right]$$

$$= \left[4 + \frac{2}{15}(90 - 88) \right] - \left[0 + \frac{2}{49}(30 - 0) \right]$$

$$= 4.267 - 1.224$$

$$= 3.043.$$

e. Chebyshev's theorem predicts that 55.6% of the data will fall in the range of $[\bar{X} \pm 1.5s]$. This is within $[3.48 \pm 1.5 (3.38)]$ which is the interval $[3.48 \pm 5.07]$. The left endpoint of the interval is -1.59 $[-1.59 = 3.48 - 5.07]$ and the right endpoint is 8.55 $[8.55 = 3.48 + 5.07]$. All the data points in the classes 0 and under 2, 2 and under 4, 4 and under 6, and 6 and under 8, are greater than -1.59 and less than 8.55. This is a total of 108 data points. In addition, there are some data points in the class 8 and under 10 that are also less than 8.55. If we spread the four data points in this range evenly over the width of the range, they would fall $X_{109} = 8$, $X_{110} = 8.5$, $X_{111} = 9.0$, and $X_{112} = 9.9$. Thus, X_{109} and X_{110} are also less than 8.55. A total of 110 data points falls within the range $\bar{X} \pm 1.5s$. In percent terms, this is equal to 92% $[0.9166 = 110/120]$. Thus the percent of data contained in the range far exceeds the percent estimated by Chebyshev's theorem.

f. As shown above, the standard deviation overestimates the dispersion of these data. The interquartile range is the preferred measure of deviation because it accurately shows that 50% of the data are contained in the range (1.2, 4.3).

7. a. The distribution has a slight negative skew, $N = 50$.

$$\overline{X} = \frac{\sum X_i}{N}$$

$$= \frac{0 + 7 + 20 + 42 + 28 + 15 + 12 + 7}{50}$$

$$= \frac{131}{50} \text{ which is 2.62 days.}$$

$$s = \sqrt{\frac{137.78}{49}} \text{ which is 1.677 days.}$$

b. The standard deviation can be estimated from the equation $4s = $ range. Since the range is 7 [7 = 7 − 0] then $4s = 7$ or $s = 1.75$. This is a good approximation of the calculated standard deviation of 1.677. The same equation ($4s = $ range) can be used to estimate the standard deviation of the out-of-state data. So, $4s = 12$ (range is 12 − 0) and, thus, $s = 3$. The estimated standard deviation for the out-of-state values is larger than the standard deviation for the in-state values. However, the largest-out-of-state value, 12, is larger than the largest in-state value, 7. This implies that the mean for the out-of-state values probably is higher than the mean for the in-state values. The result is that the coefficients of variation for the two data sets will be roughly equal.

8. a. The distribution for the library with the 14-day policy is more symmetrical and has a smaller mean than the distribution for the library with the 21-day policy.

21-day policy

$$\overline{X} = \frac{1308}{75} \text{ which is 17.44 days.}$$

$$\tilde{X} = 18 + 2\left(\frac{8}{18}\right)$$

$$= 18 + 0.889 \text{ which is 18.89 days.}$$

$$s = \sqrt{\frac{3192.48}{74}} \text{ which is 6.57 days.}$$

14-day policy

$$\overline{X} = \frac{933}{75} \text{ which is 12.44 days.}$$

$$\tilde{X} = 12 + 2\left(\frac{6}{19}\right)$$

$$= 12 + 0.632 \text{ which is 12.63 days.}$$

$$s = \sqrt{\frac{2280.48}{74}} \text{ which is 5.55 days.}$$

The mean and median for the 21-day policy differ by over one day, while the mean and median for the 14-day period are nearly the same. This confirms that the 21-day distribution is skewed left and the 14-day distribution is nearly symmetrical. In a skewed distribution, the median is a better measure of central tendency; in a symmetrical distribution, the mean is preferred.

b. **21-day policy**

$$V = \frac{100s}{\overline{X}}$$

$$= \frac{657}{17.44} \text{ which is } 37.67\%.$$

14-day policy

$$V = \frac{555}{12.44} \text{ which is } 44.61\%.$$

The 14-day distribution has a slightly higher variance than the 21-day distribution.

c. Under the 14-day policy, books are returned, on average, 5 days earlier [$5 = \overline{X}_{21} - \overline{X}_{14} = 17.44 - 12.44$]. The 14-day policy maximizes turnover rate.

d. The effect of a too long circulation period is that the library's inventory (collection) is not available for circulation. This reduces the opportunity for greater circulation turnover.

e. The effect of limiting the number of items each client can borrow is to keep more inventory (collection) in the library to be available for others to borrow or use in the library. Clients who complain that the library "never has what I want when I want it" will become discouraged and not use the library. Having collections available for client use is a librarian's major challenge.

9. a.

$$\overline{X} = \frac{\begin{array}{c} 3(3) + 8(25) + 13(31) + 18(56) + 23(64) + 28(58) + 33(33) \\ + 38(39) + 43(21) + 48(29) + 53(17) + 58(17) + 63(8) \end{array}}{401}$$

$$= \frac{11,973}{401} \text{ which is } 29.86 \text{ hours.}$$

$$\tilde{X} = L + \frac{w}{f}\left(\frac{n}{2} - F\right)$$

$$= 26 + \frac{4}{58}(200.5 - 179)$$

$$= 26 + 0.069(21.5)$$

$$= 26 + 1.484 \text{ which is } 27.48 \text{ hours.}$$

Range $= 65 - 1$ which is 64 hours.

$$s = \sqrt{\frac{81,440.90}{400}} \text{ which is } 14.27 \text{ hours.}$$

b. $P_{80} = L + \dfrac{w}{f}\left(\dfrac{80n}{100} - F\right)$

         $= 41 + \dfrac{4}{21}(320.8 - 309)$

         $= 41 + 0.19(11.8)$ which is 43.25 hours.

     The interpretation of P_{80} is that 80% of all libraries in the survey are open 43.25, or fewer, hours per week.

   c. There is a group of libraries that are open 50 hours per week. They occur at the upper limit of the class 46–50. Because the cumulative frequency at class 46–50 is 359, there are 359 observations that are less than or equal to 50 hours per week. Thus, a library that is open 50 hours per week is open as many or more hours than 0.9 [0.9 = 359/401] or 90% of the other libraries. $P_{90} = 50$ hours.

10. a. The modal class, with a frequency of 37, is centered at 60 minutes per month and ranges from 30 to 90 minutes per month. A good approximation for the median is 90 minutes per month. In a skewed distribution, the median lies between the mode and the mean but is closer to the mean.

   b. The three observations centered at 300 minutes per month, the two observations centered at 360 minutes per month, and the single observation centered at 480 minutes per month all are extreme values.

   c. The distribution is positively skewed since the scores are concentrated at the low end of the scale.

   d. Call durations per month of 295.9 [295.9 = 110.4 + 2(92.73)] are greater than two standard deviations above the mean. Thus, the six extreme values cited lie outside and above the first two standard deviations of the mean.

   e. The hours of work lost per employee per month may be estimated from the mean number of minutes of phone usage on outgoing calls. The value of 110.4 minutes per employee per month is equivalent to 1.84 hours of staff time lost per employee per month on personal calls.

11. a. The median value is unchanged since the correction occurs at the end of the distribution. The median would be affected only by a change in the value of the middle values.

   b. Changing the 9 to a 10 will increase the value of the mean. The reason is the way that the mean is calculated. It requires that all score values be added and then the sum be divided by the number of scores that were added. Thus, the value of 10 would increase the sum.

   c. The range increases, since the range is the largest value minus the smallest value. For this problem, with the value of 10 replacing the 9, the range is 7 [7 = 10 − 3].

   d. The standard deviation increases since it is a measure of data dispersion. The value of 10 means that the data are more dispersed than they were when the value was incorrectly reported as 9.

Chapter 7

1. In a positive linear relationship, an increase in the independent variable is accompanied by an equally proportional increase in the dependent variable. In a negative association between two variables, an increase in the independent variable is accompanied by an equally proportional decrease in the dependent variable. An example of positive association is the hours that the library is open and the number of clients served. An example of negative association is the number of years since a book was published and its circulation.

2.

Independent variable	Dependent variable	Association
a. high school G.P.A.	college entrance exam	positive
b. college entrance exam	college G.P.A.	positive
c. outdoor temperature	electricity usage	positive
d. food consumed	body weight	positive
e. supervisor's skill	employee output	positive
f. ticket prices	passengers/100 miles	positive
g. noise level	employee morale	negative
h. publication date	library circulation	negative

3. The regression line's slope shows the average amount of change in y for a specific change in x. Correlation shows how strong this relationship is. Both the slope and the correlation show whether the relationship evidences a positive association, no association, or a negative (inverse) association.

4. a. Begin by creating a table for the ten data points:

n	X	Y	X^2	XY	Y^2
1	1	2	1	2	4
2	1	4	1	4	16
3	2	2	4	4	4
4	2	4	4	8	16
5	2	5	4	10	25
6	3	2	9	6	4
7	3	4	9	12	16
8	3	3	9	9	9
9	4	4	16	16	16
10	6	14	36	84	196
	27	44	93	155	306

$$r = \frac{n \sum XY - \sum X \sum Y}{\sqrt{\{[n \sum X^2 - (\sum X)^2][n \sum Y^2 - (\sum Y)^2]\}}}$$

$$= \frac{10(155) - (27)(44)}{\sqrt{\{[10(93) - (27)^2][10(306) - (44)^2]\}}}$$

$$= \frac{362}{475.31} \text{ which is } 0.7616.$$

The coefficient of correlation, 0.7616, tells that the X and Y variables are moderately well correlated. The coefficient of determination is 0.58 [$0.5800 = (0.7616)(0.7616)$]. This coefficient means that 58% of the total variance in the dependent variable is explained by variance in the independent variable.

b. $\hat{Y} = aX + b$. Begin by first calculating the a value:

$$a = \frac{n\left(\sum XY\right) - \left(\sum X\right)\left(\sum Y\right)}{n\left(\sum X^2\right) - \left(\sum X\right)^2}$$

$$= \frac{10(155) - (27)(44)}{10(93) - (27)(27)}$$

$$= \frac{1550 - 1188}{930 - 729}$$

$$= \frac{362}{201} \text{ which yields } 1.8010.$$

Now, calculate the b value, which is the y-intercept:

$$b = \frac{(44)}{10} - (1.801)\left(\frac{27}{10}\right)$$

$$= 4.4 - 4.8627 \text{ which is } -0.4627.$$

This means that the best-fit regression line is given by the equation, $\hat{Y} = 1.801X - 0.4627$. See Figure 7-A.

FIGURE 7-A   Scatterplot Showing Test Ranks

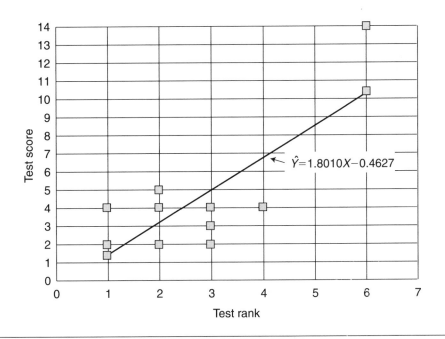

c. Create a table that reflects the data points:

n	ΣX	ΣY	ΣX^2	ΣXY	ΣY^2
9	21	30	57	71	110

$$r = \frac{9(71) - (21)(30)}{\sqrt{\{[9(57) - (21)^2][9(110) - (30)^2]\}}}$$

$$= \frac{639 - 630}{\sqrt{\{[513 - 441][990 - 900]\}}}$$

$$= \frac{9}{\sqrt{\{[72][90]\}}} \text{ which yields } 0.1118.$$

This yields a coefficient of determination of 0.0125 [0.0125 = (0.1118)(0.1118)]. Hence, excluding the extreme data point (6,14) decreases correlation from 0.7616 (moderate) to $-.1118$ (poor). This is because the remaining data form an oval pattern. The extreme point is a *point of high influence* since it increases correlation.

d–e. The best-fit equation from (b) is $\hat{Y} = 1.8010X - 0.4627$. Hence,

if $x = 1$, $\hat{Y} = 1.8010(1) - 0.4627$, which is 1.3
if $x = 2$, $\hat{Y} = 1.8010(2) - 0.4627$, which is 3.1
if $x = 3$, $\hat{Y} = 1.8010(3) - 0.4627$, which is 4.9
if $x = 4$, $\hat{Y} = 1.8010(4) - 0.4627$, which is 6.7
if $x = 5$, $\hat{Y} = 1.8010(5) - 0.4627$, which is 8.5
if $x = 6$, $\hat{Y} = 1.8010(6) - 0.4627$, which is 10.3
if $x = 7$, $\hat{Y} = 1.8010(7) - 0.4627$, which is 12.1

The independent value $x = 7$ lies outside the range of the data that was used to build the regression equation in (b). This means that the dependent value $y = 12.1$ is an educated guess. Its accuracy depends upon the quality of the model. Using a value that is too far beyond the range of the data that was used to build the regression equation introduces error and reduces the value of the prediction for planning purposes.

5. Correlation is a measure of the degree of relatedness between two variables. Each variable has the same degree of relatedness to the other, regardless of which is considered independent and which is considered dependent. Formula 6-5 for the Pearson r confirms this since both variables are treated equally. Regardless of which variable is the independent or dependent variable, the value for the coefficient will be the same. While this is true in correlation analysis, it is not true in regression analysis, for which the choice of independent and dependent variable makes a difference.

6. Using Table 7-3 data, and regressing the operating expenses (Y) on population (X):

ΣX	ΣY	ΣX^2	ΣXY	ΣY^2
15.7	128.8	27.29	219.83	1829.46

$$\hat{Y} = aX + b.$$

Begin by first calculating the *a* value:

$$a = \frac{n\left(\sum XY\right) - \left(\sum X\right)\left(\sum Y\right)}{n\left(\sum X^2\right) - \left(\sum X\right)^2}$$

$$= \frac{10(219.83) - (15.7)(128.8)}{10(27.29) - (15.7)(15.7)}$$

$$= \frac{2198.30 - 2022.16}{272.90 - 246.49}$$

$$= \frac{176.14}{26.41} \text{ which yields } 6.669.$$

Now, calculate the *b* value, which is the *y*-intercept:

$$b = \frac{(128.8)}{10} - (6.669)\left(\frac{15.7}{10}\right)$$

$$= 12.88 - 10.47 \text{ which is } 2.41.$$

This means that the best-fit regression line is given by the equation $\hat{Y} = 6.669X + 2.41$. Hence, if the independent variable *X* is *population*, then *expense* = 6.669(population) + 2.41.

Regression of population (*Y*) on operating expense (*X*) from Table 7-3:

$\sum X$	$\sum Y$	$\sum X^2$	$\sum XY$	$\sum Y^2$
128.8	15.7	1829.46	219.83	27.29

$$\hat{Y} = aX + b.$$

Begin by first calculating the *a* value:

$$a = \frac{n\left(\sum XY\right) - \left(\sum X\right)\left(\sum Y\right)}{n\left(\sum X^2\right) - \left(\sum X\right)^2}$$

$$= \frac{10(219.83) - (15.7)(128.8)}{10(1829.46) - (128.8)(128.8)}$$

$$= \frac{2198.30 - 2022.16}{18,294.6 - 16,589.44}$$

$$= \frac{176.14}{1705.16} \text{ which is } 0.1033.$$

Now, calculate the *b* value, which is the *y*-intercept:

$$b = \frac{(15.7)}{10} - (0.1033)\left(\frac{128.8}{10}\right)$$

$$= 1.57 - 1.331 \text{ which is } 0.239.$$

Hence, the best-fit regression line is given as follows:

$$\hat{Y} = 0.1033X + 0.239.$$

So, if the independent variable X is *expense, population* $= 0.1033$ *(expense)* $+ 0.239$.

7. a. Begin by creating a table for the data as follows:

Format	1st rank	2nd rank	D	D^2
Books	2.0	1.0	-1.0	1.0
Computer printouts	8.0	12.0	4.0	16.0
Films (pictorial)	13.0	13.0	0.0	0.0
Government publications	4.0	6.5	2.5	6.25
Manuscripts	1.0	3.0	2.0	4.0
Maps	9.0	10.0	1.0	1.0
Microcopies	10.0	5.0	-5.0	25.0
Newspapers	6.5	4.0	-2.5	6.25
Other pictorials (photos)	11.0	9.0	-2.0	4.0
Periodicals	3.0	2.0	-1.0	1.0
Research reports	5.0	8.0	3.0	9.0
Tape/Sound recordings	12.0	11.0	-1.0	1.0
Theses/Dissertations	6.5	6.5	0.0	0.0
Videotapes	14.0	14.0	0.0	0.0
				74.5

Substituting in Formula 7-5, where $n = 14$, yields the following:

$$r_s = 1 - \frac{6 \sum_{i=1}^{n} D_i^2}{n(n^2 - 1)}$$

$$= 1 - \frac{6(D_1^2 + D_2^2 + D_3^2 + \cdots + D_n^2)}{n(n^2 - 1)}$$

$$= 1 - \frac{6(74.5)}{14(196 - 1)}$$

$$= 1 - \frac{447}{2730}$$

$$= 1 - 0.164 \text{ which is } 0.836, \text{ or } 0.84.$$

b. The two surveys appear to be comparing the physical formats on the same bases of use. A correlation coefficient of 0.84 shows a strong linear relationship between the two variable sets.

8. A media center librarian's experience is that repair costs increase as equipment ages. This tells that the independent variable is age and the dependent variable is cost.

a. The scattergram is shown in Figure 7-B. It includes the best-fit regression equation, which is $\hat{Y} = 11.4802X + 66.9114$, as shown in the table opposite.

FIGURE 7-B ▍ Equipment Age and Repair Cost

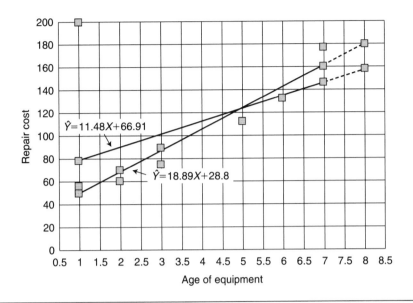

b–d. The first step for determining the best-fit regression is to prepare a table:

X	Y	X^2	XY	Y^2
1	57	1	57	3,249
2	70	4	140	4,900
3	90	9	270	8,100
7	177	49	1,239	31,329
1	199	1	199	39,601
1	49	1	49	2,401
3	76	9	228	5,776
2	60	4	120	3,600
5	114	25	570	12,996
6	133	36	798	17,689
31	1,025	139	3,670	129,641

To calculate the Pearson r, use Formula 7-4:

$$r = \frac{n \sum XY - \sum X \sum Y}{\sqrt{\{[n \sum X^2 - (\sum X)^2][n \sum Y^2 - (\sum Y)^2]\}}}$$

$$= \frac{10(3670) - (31)(1025)}{\sqrt{[(10)(139) - (31)^2][10(129,641) - (1025)^2]}}$$

$$= \frac{36,700 - 31,775}{\sqrt{[1390 - 961][1,296,410 - 1,050,625]}}$$

$$= \frac{4925}{\sqrt{[429][245,785]}}$$

$$= \frac{4925}{\sqrt{105,441,765}}$$

$$= \frac{4925}{10,268.48} \text{ which is } 0.4796.$$

Since $r = 0.4796$, $r^2 = 0.230$, and $1 - r^2 = 0.770$.

The coefficient of correlation, 0.48, indicates a positive linear relationship (moderate to good). The coefficient of determination, 0.23 [0.23 = (.4796)(.4796)], indicates that 23% of the changes in repair cost can be explained by changes in equipment age. The coefficient of nondetermination, 0.770 [0.770 = 1 − 0.23], is a large value and suggests that there may be other important considerations that explain repair costs.

To calculate the regression equation:

$$a = \frac{n(\sum XY) - (\sum X)(\sum Y)}{n(\sum X^2) - (\sum X)^2}$$

$$= \frac{10(3670) - (31)(1025)}{10(139) - (31)(31)}$$

$$= \frac{36,700 - 31,775}{1390 - 961}$$

$$= \frac{4925}{429} \text{ which is } 11.480.$$

Now, calculate the b value, which is the y-intercept:

$$b = \overline{Y} - a\overline{X}$$

$$= \frac{(1025)}{10} - (11.480)\left(\frac{31}{10}\right)$$

$$= 102.5 - (11.480)(3.1)$$

$$= 102.5 - 35.588 \text{ which is } 66.912.$$

This means that the best-fit regression line is given by the equation, $\hat{Y} = 11.48X + 66.91$.

Thus, the best-fit regression line passes through the coordinate pairs (1, 78.39) and (7, 147.27). Using the equation $\hat{Y} = 11.48X + 66.91$, these values were obtained as follows:

substituting $X = 1$, $\hat{Y} = 11.48(1) + 66.91$, or $\hat{Y} = 78.39$

substituting $X = 7$, $\hat{Y} = 11.48(7) + 66.91$, or $\hat{Y} = 147.27$.

Using this method and rounding the values to the nearest one-tenth, the coordinate pairs for $x = 1$ through $x = 7$ are the following: (1, 78.4), (2, 89.9), (3, 101.4), (4, 112.8), (5, 124.3), (6, 135.8), and (7, 147.3).

Estimating repair cost of equipment that is eight years old by using the regression line is not very reliable since the correlation coefficient is $r = 0.48$—hardly a blockbuster. Even so, an estimated guess for the cost from the data for the eighth year is $158.75. A reasonable cost estimate is $175. If the extreme value (1, 199) is eliminated, the result is that $r = 0.976$ and $r^2 = 0.95$ so that $1 - r^2 = 0.05$. The regression line becomes $\hat{Y} = 18.89X + 28.8$. This means that the forecasted repair cost for eight-year-old equipment is $179.91.

9. The librarian begins by developing a table that shows percentages for Year 2 Circulation and for Year 2 Expenditures.

	Circulation		Expenditure	
Category	**Year 2**	**Percent %**	**Year 2**	**Percent %**
General	2,732	1.8%	$ 6,785	2.1%
Philosophy	5,245	3.5	7,680	2.4
Religion	2,754	1.8	4,030	1.2
Social Science	14,677	9.7	27,160	8.4
Language	962	0.6	1,400	0.4
Pure Science	4,214	2.8	6,980	2.1
Technology	10,550	7.0	62,335	19.2
The Arts	18,379	12.2	33,560	10.3
Literature	7,359	4.9	12,470	3.8
Geography & History	16,859	11.1	39,075	12.0
Biography	4,682	3.1	7,725	2.4
Fiction	47,805	31.7	82,525	25.4
Mystery	12,926	8.6	26,250	8.1
Science Fiction	1,791	1.2	7,025	2.2
Total	150,935	100.0%	$325,000	100.0%

The percent column for Year 2 Circulation shows the percent of total circulation that the category provides. Hence, books classified as General (Dewey class 000–099) account for 1.8% of the total circulation, and titles classified as Philosophy (Dewey class 100–199) account for 3.5% of all circulation. Similarly, the percent column for expenditures identifies the total percent of moneys spent for each category of items. Titles that were classified under Religion (Dewey class 300–399) received 1.2% of the moneys, and titles classified as Fiction received 25.4% of the moneys.

From examining the percentages, the librarian can see that expenditures for each category closely follow the category's contribution to total circulation. For example, the table shows that almost each category's percent of circulation and percent of expenditure are very close for eight categories (General, Religion, Language, Pure Science, Geography and History, Biography, Mystery, and Science Fiction). Eleven categories are within 1.3 percent of each other. The two categories that are an exception are Technology and Fiction. Technology titles account for 7% of circulation but receive 19.2% of the money. In contrast, Fiction accounts for 31.7% of the circulation but receives only 25.4% of the money.

To determine the correlation between Year 2 Circulation and Year 2 Expenditures, the librarian can calculate the Pearson r. It turns out, however, that the numbers are too large and exceed the capacity of most handheld calculators. If the librarian uses a spreadsheet program, such as Excel or Lotus 123, the Pearson correlation coefficient is $r = 0.8753$, which indicates a strong positive relationship.

When the numbers are too large, an effective technique is to determine the Spearman Rank Order correlation coefficient. To use this method, the first step is to build the familiar table that facilitates the calculations:

	Circulation Year 2 X	Expenditure Year 2 Y	Rank X	Rank Y	Rank Diff	(Diff)²
General	2,732	6,785	12	12	0	0
Philosophy	5,245	7,680	8	9	−1	1
Religion	2,754	4,030	11	13	−2	4
Social Science	14,677	27,160	4	5	−1	1
Language	962	1,400	14	14	0	0
Pure Science	4,214	6,980	10	11	−1	1
Technology	10,550	62,335	6	2	4	16
The Arts	18,379	33,560	2	4	−2	4
Literature	7,359	12,470	7	7	0	0
Geography & History	16,859	39,075	3	3	0	0
Biography	4,682	7,725	9	8	1	1
Fiction	47,805	82,525	1	1	0	0
Mystery	12,926	26,250	5	6	−1	1
Science Fiction	1,791	7,025	13	10	3	9
Total	150,935	325,000			0	38

Applying Formula 7-5 with $n = 14$ and $D = \text{rank } X - \text{rank } Y$,

$$r_s = 1 - \frac{6 \sum\limits_{i=1}^{n} D_i^2}{n(n^2 - 1)}$$

$$= 1 - \frac{6(D_1^2 + D_2^2 + (D_3^2 + \cdots + D_n^2)}{n(n^2 - 1)}$$

$$= 1 - \frac{6(38)}{14(196 - 1)}$$

$$= 1 - \frac{228}{2730} \text{ which is } 1 - 0.0835, \text{ or } 0.9165.$$

The Spearman coefficient indicates a strong relationship between circulation and expenditure. The advantage of calculating the Spearman is that it can be done in a few minutes, the numbers are manageable, and the result is substantially the same as for the Pearson.

The interested reader can verify that the Pearson correlation coefficient for circulation between Year 1 and Year 2 is 0.995 and that the Spearman coefficient is 0.996. Both indicate near perfect positive correlation. The percentages and the correlation show that expenditures closely follow circulation.

Chapter 8

1. The student numbers identify each element of the population. The Random Numbers Table, Table 8-1, is used to identify fifteen random numbers that are between 001 and 150 in the table. Since all numbers are random, any beginning point in the table is acceptable. Table 8-1 shows three-digit numbers. Scan down a column to identify numbers that have a form beginning with 001 through 150. If the table consisted of four-digit numbers, the researcher would search for numbers 0001 through 0150. Because the digits are random, any approach can be used if it is systematically applied so that no number is favored over another.

   The approach used in this problem solution is to search for fifteen numbers in Table 8-1 that have the form 001 through 150, beginning with the first number at the top of the second column, which is 670. Numbers will be selected by moving to the right horizontally across the row. Hence, the numbers are {034, 016, 085, 055, 096, 146, 026, 029, 006, 058, 071, 045, 139, 009, 044}. Notice that any number not in the range of 001 thorough 150 was excluded.

   Arranged in ascending order, the random numbers are {006, 009, 016, 026, 029, 034, 044, 045, 055, 058, 071, 085, 096, 139, 146}. These match to the following students in the population:

Group I

Student	Variables					
	A	*B*	*C*	*D*	*E*	*F*
6	0	7	1	F	50	1
9	3.19	7	2	M	59	5
16	2.17	5	R	M	65	1
26	2.89			M	63	2
29	4.00	7	4	F	60	4
34	1.11	2	2	F	72	1
44	3.67	7	4	F	57	5
45	0			F	77	1
55	3.70			F	70	4
58	0.60			F	76	1
71	3.81	7	1	F	45	2
85	2.22	7	1	M	35	2
96	3.70	7	1	F	54	5
139	0.54	7	3	M	76	1
146	2.85	7	2	F	74	4

2. Since there are 150 student entries, the choice is to select every 10th one [10 = 150/15] for inclusion in the sample. Begin anywhere among the 150 students and then count out each ten. For no special reason, begin with the third student and then select each tenth survey after the third one. The student numbers selected are the following: {3, 13, 23, 33, 43, 53, 63, 73, 83, 93, 103, 113, 123, 133, 143}. Notice that some of the elements have no score for certain variables; for example, Student 13 has no score reported for Variables *B* or *C*. For this reason, the entry is left blank. The blanks are counted in the final tally. The systematic sample of student surveys for Group II are the following:

	Variables					
Student	**A**	**B**	**C**	**D**	**E**	**F**
3	3.00	2	1	F	70	1
13	0			M	22	3
23	1.91			F	64	4
33	0			M	69	1
43	1.54			F	76	1
53	3.10	7	1	M	66	2
63	1.20	3	2	M	76	1
73	4.00			F	45	5
83	0	7	1	F	47	5
93	3.24	2	4	F	55	3
103	3.85	7	1	F	60	1
113	2.84	2	2	F	66	2
123	3.38			F	62	1
133	2.15	3	1	M	76	1
143	2.39	2	4	F	72	4

3.

Variable A* **Grade point average**	**Group I (Random)** **Frequency/Percent**	**Group II (Systematic)** **Frequency/Percent**
0.0–0.99	4/27%	3/20%
1.0–1.99	1/7	3/20
2.0–2.99	4/27	3/20
3.0–4.00	6/40	6/40
Refused	0/0	0/0
Blank	0/0	0/0

Variable B* **Reported income level**	**Frequency/** **Percent**	**Frequency/** **Percent**
1 Less than $4,000	0/0%	0/0%
2 $4,000 to $7,999	1/7	4/27
3 $8,000 to $11,999	0/0	2/13
4 $12,000 to $15,999	0/0	0/0
5 $16,000 to $19,999	1/7	0/0
6 $20,000 to $23,999	0/0	3/20
7 $24,000 or more	9/60	0/0
R Refused to respond	0/0	0/0
Blank	4/27	6/40

Variable C* **Employment status**	**Frequency/** **Percent**	**Frequency/** **Percent**
1. Yes, 35 hours per week or more	4/27%	5/33%
2. Yes, fewer than 35 hours per week	3/20	2/13

*May not sum to 100% because of rounding

Variable C* (*continued*) Employment status	Frequency/ Percent	Frequency/ Percent
3. No, but seeking employment	1/7	0/0
4. No	2/13	2/13
R Refused to respond	1/7	0/0
Blank	4/27	6/40

Variable D* Sex	Frequency/ Percent	Frequency/ Percent
M Male	5/33%	5/33%
F Female	10/67	10/67
R Refused to respond	0/0	0/0
Blank	0/0	0/0

Variable E* Year of birth	Frequency/ Percent	Frequency/ Percent
1920–1929	0/0%	1/7%
1930–1939	1/7	0/0
1940–1949	1/7	2/13
1950–1959	4/27	1/7
1960–1969	3/20	6/40
1970–1979	6/40	5/33
Refused to respond	0/0	0/0
Blank	0/0	0/0

Variable F* Class year Status	Frequency/ Percent	Frequency/ Percent
1 0–27.5	6/40%	7/47%
2 28–60.5	3/20	2/13
3 61–93.5	0/0	2/13
4 ≥94	3/20	2/13
5 0–36	3/20	2/13
6 ≥36.5	0/0	0/0
Refused to respond	0/0	0/0
Blank	0/0	0/0

*May not sum to 100% because of rounding

4. See Figures 8-A and 8-B.

FIGURE 8-A   ▮   Student Grade Point and Class Standing, Random Sample
($N = 150$, $n = 15$)

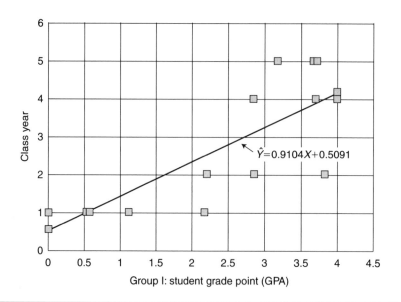

Group I: student grade point (GPA)

$\hat{Y}=0.9104X+0.5091$

FIGURE 8-B   ▮   Student Grade Point and Class Standing, Systematic Sample
($N = 150$, $n = 15$)

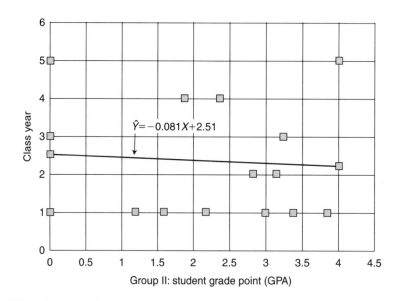

Group II: student grade point (GPA)

$\hat{Y}=-0.081X+2.51$

5. First, create a table that shows columns for X^2, XY, and Y^2, including the sums since this will facilitate the calculations. The table for Group I is illustrated as follows:

X	Y	X^2	XY	Y^2
0	1	0	0	1
3.19	5	10.1761	15.95	25
2.17	1	4.7089	2.17	1
2.89	2	8.3521	5.78	4
4.00	4	16.0000	16.00	16
1.11	1	1.2321	1.11	1
3.67	5	13.4689	18.35	25
0	1	0	0	1
3.70	4	13.6900	14.80	16
0.60	1	0.3600	0.60	1
3.81	2	14.5161	7.62	4
2.22	2	4.9284	4.44	4
3.70	5	13.6900	18.50	25
0.54	1	0.2916	0.54	1
2.85	4	8.1225	11.40	16
34.45	39	109.5367	117.26	141

To calculate the Pearson r, use Formula 7-4:

$$r = \frac{n \sum XY - \sum X \sum Y}{\sqrt{\{[n \sum X^2 - (\sum X)^2][n \sum Y^2 - (\sum Y)^2]\}}}$$

$$= \frac{15(117.26) - (34.45)(39)}{\sqrt{[(15)(109.5367) - (34.45)^2][15(141) - (39)^2]}}$$

$$= \frac{1758.9 - 1343.55}{\sqrt{[1643.0505 - 1186.8025][2115 - 1521]}}$$

$$= \frac{415.35}{\sqrt{[456.248][594]}}$$

$$= \frac{415.35}{\sqrt{271,011.31}}$$

$$= \frac{415.35}{520.587} \text{ which is } 0.798.$$

Since $r = 0.798$, $r^2 = 0.637$, and $1 - r^2 = 0.363$.

The Pearson r is 0.798, which indicates high positive linear correlation between grade point and year class standing.

The coefficient of determination, $r^2 = 0.637$, indicates that 63.7% of the changes in class standing can be explained by changes in grade point.

The coefficient of nondetermination, $1 - r^2 = 0.363$. It is a large value and suggests that there may be other important considerations that explain class standing.

To calculate the regression equation, apply Formula 7-3:

$$a = \frac{n(\sum XY) - (\sum X)(\sum Y)}{n(\sum X^2) - (\sum X)^2}$$

$$= \frac{15(117.26) - (34.45)(39)}{15(109.5367) - (34.45)*(34.45)}$$

$$= \frac{1758.9 - 1343.55}{1643.0505 - 1186.8025}$$

$$= \frac{415.35}{456.248}$$

$$= 0.9104.$$

Now, calculate the b value, which is the y-intercept:

$$b = \frac{(39)}{15} - (0.9104)\left(\frac{34.45}{15}\right)$$

$$= 2.6 - (0.9104)(2.297)$$

$$= 2.6 - 2.0909 \text{ which is } 0.5091.$$

This means that the best-fit regression line is given by the equation, $\hat{Y} = 0.9104X + 0.5091$.

This means that the best-fit regression line passes through the coordinate pairs (0, 0.51) and (4, 2.54), shown in Figure 8-A. The interested reader can verify for Group II that $r = -0.072$, indicating no correlation, which is illustrated in Figure 8-B. This is in sharp contrast to Group I findings. That is not to say or suggest that random sampling is superior, or that it will give better results over systematic sampling. The regression equation for Group II is $\hat{Y} = -0.081X + 2.51$. The best-fit regression line passes through the coordinate pairs (0, 2.5) and (4, 2.1).

6. a. The director confirmed the librarian's view that the topic is timely, interesting, and important. In general, the director has reservations about the questions and their potential for eliciting the data that the librarian wishes to study.

b. Along with the librarian, the director also sees that the answers to the pilot study are widely spread. This difficulty can be solved by the librarian providing answer-choices that will help the responders narrow their answers. Answer-choices will also simplify the librarian's task of coding the responses when they are returned as part of the full survey.

c. Following the pilot study, the librarian has an opportunity to redesign each survey question to change its format from open-ended, where each responder can write a few words or a paragraph, to answer choices, with a predetermined menu of responses. Question 1 revision: The question asks, How has technology impacted your work? The librarian might phrase this question differently. For example, the responder might be asked to complete the following question: Technology has made my work . . . (a) easier; (b) harder; (c) no impact. Question 2 revision: The question asks, How quickly is your library implementing computer technology? This is very subjective. Staff who are not informed concerning the library's short-term and long-range planning will answer with responses such as "too fast," "too slow," or "just about right." If these are the kinds of responses that the librarian seeks, however, the question is appropriate. Question 3 revision: The question asks, Over the past five years, what have been the staffing implications of automation in your library? This question is not easy to answer. Several staff will not have been employed at the library for at least five years. Further, some responders will wonder whether the question is asking about hiring nonlibrarians to perform technical jobs in the library environment or about computers displacing library staff. If the question is about library automation displacing staff, it is unlikely that nonsupervisory personnel would have an informed opinion about it, and even less likely that informed personnel would discuss it because of possible legal implications. Question 4 revision: The question asks, What is your educational preparation? People in the pilot study did not understand the item. The question should be rephrased, What is your educational level? Answer choices will help to provide uniformity, such as: (a) B.A. or B.S. only; (b) one master's degree; (c) two master's degrees; (d) Ed.D. or Ph.D.; (e) other training (describe). Question 5 revision: The question asks, How many years have you been a librarian? The pilot study showed confusion on the question. The librarian should rephrase the question to ask, How many years have you worked as a part-time or full-time librarian? or How many years have you worked where you are now employed? Possible answer-choices for these questions are (a) 0–2; (b) 3–5; (c) 6–10; (d) more than 10.

   d. The librarian is considering a systematic sample of 300 members who represent about 16% [0.16 = 300/1850] of the state library association. The library director suggests that the librarian consider a judgment sample. In a judgment sample, the librarian selects persons who have special knowledge, experience, or skills to participate in the survey. The potential for obtaining quality answers for the librarian's research would greatly increase.

7. Tabulation of Table 8-5, $N = 150$, $n = 150$

Variable A* Grade point average	Frequency/ Percent
0.0–0.99	40/27%
1.0–1.99	7/5
2.0–2.99	32/21
3.0–3.99	59/39
4.0–4.99	12/8
Refused	0/0
Blank	0/0

Variable B* Reported income level	Frequency/ Percent
1 Less than $4,000	10/7%
2 $4,000 to 7,999	9/6
3 $8,000 to $11,999	4/3
4 $12,000 to $15,999	7/5
5 $16,000 to $19,999	5/3
6 $20,000 to $23,999	7/5
7 $24,000 or more	64/43
R Refused to respond	43/29
Blank	1/1

Variable C* Employment status	Frequency/ Percent
1 Yes, 35 hours per week or more	49/33%
2 Yes, fewer than 35 hours per week	29/19
3 No, but seeking employment	8/5
4 No	20/13
R Refused to respond	1/1
Blank	43/29

Variable D* Sex	Frequency/ Percent
M Male	53/35%
F Female	97/65
R Refused to respond	0/0
Blank	0/0

Variable *E* Person's year of birth	Frequency/ Percent	Variable *F* Class year status	Frequency/ Percent
1920–1929	1/1%	1 0–27.5	57/38%
1930–1939	5/3	2 28–60.5	32/21
1940–1949	21/14	3 61–93.5	12/8
1950–1959	31/21	4 ≥ 94	20/13
1960–1969	38/25	5 0–36	29/19
1970–1979	54/36	6 ≥ 36.5	0/0
Refused to respond	0/0	Refused to respond	0/0
Blank	0/0	Blank	0/0

*May not sum to 100% because of rounding.

The scattergram for Variables *A* and *F* is illustrated in Figure 8-C. The correlation coefficient is $r = 0.40$, which suggests a fair relationship. The regression line equation is $\hat{Y} = 0.4181X + 1.5732$, and it passes through the coordinates (0, 1.6) and (4, 3.2).

FIGURE 8-C ▍ Student Grade Point Class Year Status (*n* = 150)

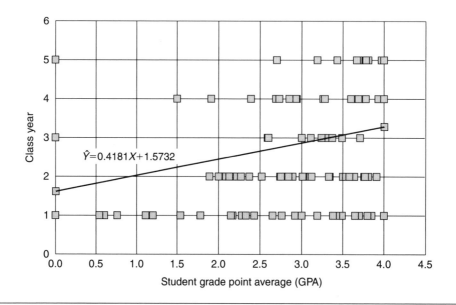

8. a. Tallying the survey using a weighted average.

Least	1	2	3	4	5	Most	Weighted average
Item #1	2	2	7	2	4		3.24
Item #2	4	4	1	6	2		2.88
Item #3	2	2	4	5	4		3.41
Item #4	2	5	5	3	2		2.88
Item #5	3	2	4	4	4		3.24
Item #6	5 Male;	12 Female					

In calculating the weighted average, each response that is 1 is given the weight of 1. Each response that is 2, is given the weight of 2. In this way, the weighted average of the item is calculated as follows:

Item #1

$$Sum = (2)(1) + (2)(2) + (7)(3) + (2)(4) + (4)(5)$$
$$= 2 + 4 + 21 + 8 + 20 \text{ which is } 55.$$

The sum is divided by the number of responders, which is 17. Hence, the weighted average is 3.24 [3.24 = 55/17].

Item #2

$$Sum = (4)(1) + (4)(2) + (1)(3) + (6)(4) + (2)(5)$$
$$= 4 + 8 + 3 + 24 + 10 \text{ which is } 49.$$

The sum is divided by the number of responders, which is 17. Hence, the weighted average is 2.88 [2.88 = 49/17].

The weighted average is frequently encountered when reading survey results. The caution is that the number is an average, but a score of 2 is not twice as good as a score of 1, nor is it half as good as a score of 4.

b. Tallying the survey by showing frequency and percent.

Item number	Frequency/Percent
1. The librarian was helpful.	
1 Least agreement	2/12%
2	2/12
3	7/41
4	2/12
5 Most agreement	4/24
2. The librarian was polite.	
1 Least agreement	4/24%
2	4/24
3	1/6
4	6/35
5 Most agreement	2/12

Item number	Frequency/Percent
3. The librarian clearly explained the service in which I was interested.	
1 Least agreement	2/12%
2	2/12
3	4/24
4	5/29
5 Most agreement	4/24
4. The library's hours meet my needs.	
1 Least agreement	2/12%
2	5/29
3	5/29
4	3/18
5 Most agreement	2/12
5. How many times per week, on average, do you use the library?	
0	0/0 %
1	3/18
2	2/12
3	4/24
4	4/24
5	4/24
6. Are you Male or Female?	
Male	5/29%
Female	12/71

Bibliography

Anschutz, Eric E. *TQM America: How America's Most Successful Companies Profit from Total Quality Management.* Bradenton, Fla.: McGuinn & McGuire, 1995.

Baker, Sharon L. *The Measurement and Evaluation of Library Services.* 2d ed. Arlington, Va.: Information Resources Press, 1991.

Camp, Robert C. *Business Process Benchmarking: Finding and Implementing Best Practices.* Milwaukee, Wis.: ASQC Quality, 1995.

Graham, Alan. *Statistics.* Chicago: NTC Publishing Group, 1994.

Hernon, Peter. *Statistics: A Component of the Research Process.* Revised edition. Norwood, N.J.: Ablex Publishing Corporation, 1994.

Hernon, Peter, and John V. Richardson. *Microcomputer Software for Performing Statistical Analysis: A Handbook Supporting Library Decision Making.* Norwood, N.J.: Ablex Publishing Company, 1988.

Miller, Irwin, and Marylees Miller. *Statistical Methods for Quality: With Applications to Engineering and Management.* Englewood Cliffs, N.J.: Prentice Hall, 1995.

Stamatis, D. H. *Total Quality Service: Principles, Practice, and Implementation.* Delray Beach, Fla.: St. Lucie Press, 1995.

Swisher, Robert, and Charles R. McClure. *Research for Decision Making: Methods for Librarians.* Chicago: American Library Association, 1984.

Van House, Nancy A. et. al. *Output Measures for Public Libraries: A Manual of Standardized Procedures.* 2d ed. Chicago: American Library Association, 1987.

Zelazny, Gene. *Say It with Charts: The Executive's Guide to Successful Presentations.* 2d ed. Homewood, Ill.: Business One Irwin, 1991.

Zweizig, Douglas, and Eleanor Jo Rodger. *Output Measures for Public Libraries: A Manual of Standardized Procedures.* Chicago: American Library Association, 1982.

INDEX

About the Author

ARTHUR W. HAFNER is dean of university libraries at Seton Hall University (South Orange, New Jersey). Previously, he has served as professor and chief librarian at the City University of New York (CUNY), College of Staten Island; director of the Division of Library and Information Management at the American Medical Association (Chicago); director of library services and associate professor of library science at the Chicago College of Osteopathic Medicine (now Midwestern University); and director of the health sciences library at the Duluth Campus of the University of Minnesota.

Dr. Hafner received his Ph.D. in library science (1974) and his M.S. in mathematics (1969) from the University of Minnesota. In his work as a librarian and educator, Dr. Hafner has conducted numerous workshops and seminars for librarians on the topic of descriptive statistical techniques.